D1236646

# Harambee City

# Harambee City

### The Congress of Racial Equality in Cleveland and the Rise of Black Power Populism

*Nishani Frazier*

The University of Arkansas Press

Fayetteville

2017

*For the Cleveland CORE members who are no longer here,*
*but whose spirits I carry with me always:*
*My mother, Pauline Warfield Frazier*
*My uncles, Antoine Perot, Nate Smith, and Jay Arki*
*For my spirit uncles Bruce Klunder, Alex and Cyril Weathers, and Chuck Burton*
*And finally, for the many more unnamed. You are missed.*

# Contents

# *Preface*

## The Wiz behind the Curtain

"Nishani, isn't there something you want to say?" Mere seconds passed before I said, "Unh, no."[1]

I sat on a panel session with other contributors to *The Business of Black Power* in Richmond, Virginia, at the Association for the Study of Afro-American Life and History. The book's coeditor, Laura Hill, had asked that question. Initially, I was befuddled. Well, I suppose more like petulant. What had I not covered about my article on Cleveland and economic development that I should say now?

Consternation crossed Laura's face and she further prompted me, "Nishani! You know about Frank Anderson." Lightning struck. I could feel my eyes beginning to roll. She meant for me to "out" myself as it were. You see, Frank Anderson is my uncle, and he features prominently in my article on community development in Cleveland, Ohio. Laura was not the first person to encourage me to tell on myself or rather revealing my relationship to the people who figure heavily in my work on CORE, Cleveland, and black power. Historian Sundiata Cha Jua reviewed earlier drafts of this book, and chastised me for not clearly outlining my use of oral history, explaining my relationship to the interviewees, or asserting myself more fully as the historical authority. My Miami University colleague at the time, Bill Meier, also noted his disappointment with the absence of an oral history analysis. All pushed me to further detail and critique this background as part of my history on CORE. I, however, was still petulant. Oral history was not the story I intended to tell. My family strongly influenced my work but hardly dictated my critical approach or its outcome. Family in an analytical history was still history, and I was no less *the* historian in the process. Yet with all the insistence that I explain my personal relations, I began to wonder had I somehow violated some unsaid historians' code of ethics? Was it even possible to write what some might consider, though I did not, a family history while retaining professionalism or at least its appearance?

In part, my use and thinking about oral history provided some cover to this question. However, the presumption that oral history "needed explanation" also implied that it occupied some other space than what real historians do—particularly in handling "better," read less subjective, sources. This, in spite of the fact that I could write a soliloquy on why newspapers and FBI papers were problematic sources for writing about the black freedom movement. Histories with family members had to be explained. Oral histories had to be explained. Accordingly, I was told often to address this in the introduction to my book. Possibly, my hardheaded refusal to engage these issues as concerning to the story underlay the occasional exasperated urgings and/or criticisms. However, it particularly bothered me that some verbose academic-eez might hamstring my introduction. The book was about the rise of black power and its ideological variants in CORE. As far as I was concerned, the introduction should reflect the book project.

Secondly, implicitly or explicitly, these conversations floated dangerously into questions of objectivity. Not that they suggested that I was a liar or overbearingly bias. It was that the presence of oral history and family somehow weighted my text more toward these questions than other historical sources or books. It was an idea repeated by history scholar Raymond Arsenault in his *New York Times* review of Beryl Satter's *Family Properties: Race, Real Estate, and the Exploitation of Black Urban America*. Historians, he noted, "who write about close friends or relatives do so at their peril. Personal engagement, so essential to the memoir, can confound historical judgment and scholarly detachment, especially when family honor hangs in the balance."[2] Sociologist Patricia Hill Collins noted a similar conundrum in her book, *Black Feminist Thought: Knowledge, Consciousness and the Politics of Empowerment*. According to Collins, by identifying herself as a "participant . . . observer of black women's community" she ran the risk of being labeled too "subjective and hence less scholarly."[3]

These questions forced me to confront underlying and lingering beliefs that "science-based" history necessitated a distant viewpoint in writing history. But despite such warnings, part of me wished to stand stalwartly against this paradigm. After all, were not all historians likely to fall far from the obligatory goal of "objectivity?" Since, and even previous to, the publication of Peter Novick's *That Noble Dream: The "Objectivity Question,"* the field questioned the idealistic expectation of texts unfettered by author frailty.[4] Alternately, historical truth was attainable if scholars embraced impersonality, neutrality, dispassion, and nonpartisanship. Perhaps too lengthy a requirement list, academics reimagined these defining elements of history research and writing as "scholarly detachment." The presumption then followed that scholarly detachment enabled impartial judgment, balance, and even-handedness.

As orderly as the idea sounded, it still made my eye twitch. It seemed to me, like a proverbial Wizard of Oz, historians used the curtain of "scholarly detachment" to cover and hide exercises of identity and power not at all "detached." We operate within chronological, political, and cultural contexts and so did/do our sources.[5] If our interpretations came through a filter of first ourselves and secondly, our sources, then the more important goal was "to construct our interpretations responsibly, with care, and with a degree of self-consciousness about our disabilities and the disabilities of our sources."[6] I would add as well our identities and the identities of our sources. The Self asserted its way into history creation in subtle and obvious ways.

I was not neutral, not dispassionate, not nonpartisan, and certainly not detached. However, I had to reflect on who I was and what I brought to the subject to ensure I produced a critical, observant, considerate, analytical, verifiable, documented, honest, and accurate work.[7]

I had not purposefully intended to deny that personal and professional circumstances greatly affected my choice of subject, relationship to the subject, and approach in framing the subject. I saw this information as important but not in a way that obligated me to question this narrative or my historical voice. As a historian, I was trained to construct a reasoned, evidenced-based book. Even if my identity was construed as baggage, I certainly was not the only one. A good many historians came with the same baggage—though mine perhaps weighed more.

I had within me many personas. I am the child of civil rights activists, a sixties black freedom movement scholar, and a public historian and archivist. Eventually, it occurred to me that Laura, Sundiata, and Brian had a point though perhaps not in the way they intended. These identities had found their way into this book, informed by my particular thought process despite my insistence that author identity echoed in all histories. Nevertheless, the key question was how had it entered the text. For me, this translated as epistemology and power, not scholarly detachment or oral history theory.

It was true that my parents' experiences greatly directed my intellectual development. I am the "child" of activists. But, this statement did not fully incorporate the number of people or persons who entered my life and affected how I saw the world, past and present, especially with regard to the freedom movement. Many of them appear in the book and are considered relatives. Not all related by blood, they constitute part of the African American tradition of extended family. These persons include, in alphabetical order, Frank Anderson, Jay Arki, Herb Callendar (aka Makaza Kumanyika), Gordon Carey, Don Bean, Art Evans, Pauline Frazier, John Frazier, Tony Perot, Nate Smith, and Ruth Turner (Perot). These persons shared their lives and CORE background with me during my lifetime and formally in interviews, but not all agreed with the study's analysis, and none contributed to how I formulated a theoretical model for interpreting those experiences. I also maintained my proclivity not to interrupt the introduction with an explanation about them, as that section centers on why we've failed to see black power or the distinctive approaches to it within CORE.

Still, I recognized that epistemology was at work. So, references to family interviewees can be found in the preface, acknowledgments, introduction, footnotes, as well as the online website (http://uqr.to /harambee-city or via the QR code).[8] Acknowledging this information in multiple locations shifts the balance of power from myself, the author, to the reader at the earliest possible moment and in multiple ways so that he or she can comprehensively, reflectively engage this text. Family

interviews also act as a source for archival research, audience critique, and testimony. In this way, I lay bare before readers the personal connections that influenced
my intellectual sensibilities.

Some historians might actually scoff at the "inevitable" pitfalls of familial
sources. Yet at the start of the 1970s, feminist scholars countered notions that "distant" history writing was relevant to or synonymous with good history writing.[9]
The editors of *The Challenge of Feminist Biography*, for example, argued that "biographers can reveal their attachments and detachments even while maintaining a
critical, scholarly stance."[10] Two of its contributors, Dee Garrison and Jacqueline
Dowd Hall, biographers of Mary Heaton Vorse and Jessie Daniel Ames, respectively,
struggled with how proximity to subject shaped storyline, what they included, or
excluded. They contended that scholarly distance was no hindrance to the historian's presence in the narrative. The author's hand was visible in document use,
narrative focus, anecdotal emphasis, and quote selection. Authors handpick among
various choices according to their affinity to the subject. As such, claims of distance
and detachment hardly hid author power.[11]

These affinities encompass more than ephemera choice. Undeniably attachments occur between activists and academics as well. Conferences, anniversaries/
reunions, phone calls, activist networks, listservs (e.g., SNCC list-serv), Facebook
pages (e.g., New Corelator), and websites have become pivotal spaces of engagement related or unrelated to text creation. And some, like myself, need no electronic
grid to lay claim to such associations. Matthew Countryman's *Up South: Civil Rights
and Black Power in Philadelphia* incorporated both interviews and/or experiences
from his grandparents, Virginia and William Canady, and parents, Joan and Peter
Countryman. However, no discernible discussion or statement appeared regarding
the use of familial resources or appearance of blood/extended family relations in the
text. The reader either caught the information in the acknowledgments or deduced
from the text the obvious correlation in last name.

Although women's history scholars struggled to find a language to explain the
relationship of the author to the subject, such was not the case for writers of the
black freedom movement. The resulting process has been one in which historical
production has swung left and right on whether to say or not say the nature of the
relationship. While Countryman chose not to outright explain the obvious (after
all, how many Philadelphia Countrymans can there be?), Beryl Satter, much like my
own approach, ran headlong into revelation. Her book, *Family Properties: Race, Real
Estate, and the Exploitation of Black Urban America*, simply began as "Introduction:
The Story of My Father." Intriguingly, the death of her father, Mark Satter, in her
early childhood influenced how she came to explore the subject, and to explain the
subsequent fact-finding mission to divulge a long-buried family past.[12]

Disruption or disjointedness in family history partially repressed the appearance of subjectivity, and the act of retrieval implied some degree of scholarly distance. Matthew Countryman had no such shield consciously explained to the reader and thus his introduction simply started like any other historical text—a statement of why Philadelphia was understood as Up South. I, however, have no family discontinuity, and I do not choose a conventional start. Instead, I declare that I can and should critically account for a CORE my mother and relatives knew, because their experiences have historical and academic validity for its own sake as well as the larger history of CORE. In fact, without it, our understanding of CORE is not just stilted; it's just plain wrong. More important, I emphatically dispute that because I eschew these techniques I improperly write history—or, its oppositional, that authors who follow "the rules" of detachment do it better.

Of course, even if I excluded relatives from making a text guest appearance, "scholarly detachment" problems would still emerge. My work resides within a sphere of highly politicized scholarship. Black and freedom movement studies arose from the tumultuous protests and conflicts of 1960s and 1970s street activism. The field aimed to give intellectual and academic credence to black lives, and in so doing unearth black silences. The process inevitably dragged many scholars into contentious debates in and out of the academy, as these social histories became inherently political, by nature or necessity. Undeniably, these books inhabit a philosophical and political reality that still remain part of the 1960s democracy wars. Resultantly, scholars found themselves drafted, intentionally or not. Jacqueline Dowd Hall, for example, partially argued that public perception and revision of civil rights narrative perverted the freedom movement into a flat, uncomplicated reflection of American values. The movement was made "easy" and thus less threatening to the nation's democratic identity. Jeanne Theoharis, Komozi Woodard, Peniel Joseph, and others explained the materialization of recent black power and freedom studies as an effort to upend civil rights historiography despite efforts to hold to a politically potent image of golden age black/white alliance and the ever-present triumph of American democracy.[13]

Jennifer Denetdale, an indigenous scholar, who wrote *Reclaiming Diné History: The Legacies of Navajo Chief Manuelito and Juanita*, found herself within a similar political context. Most Navajo studies mirrored perspectives based in "systems of power and authority that privileged certain kinds of knowledge" over others.[14] These scholars brought epistemology and politics into scholarship that contradicted what the Diné thought was important about themselves and their history, particularly the role of women. Instead, these histories silenced Diné women's presence and supplanted it with an elite male-centered account. Denetdale bluntly and unequivocally argued that her book existed as a corrective for her community's history. In this case, non-Diné identity based scholarship stirred the personal, the personal (how this outside epistemology warped the inner self) comprehended it as political, and the political (community as definer) became Diné identity-based scholarship. This politically reflective and scholarly based book arguably inched too close to Arsenault's warning about "family" honor. Yet, Denetdale's text was not a failure of detachment. It was a rescue from oblivion. She intended for historians to recognize that multiple epistemologies were at work against, in relation, or parallel to one another. Or rather, as Patricia Hill Collins suggested, it determined "which questions merit investigation, which interpretive framework will be used . . . and to what use any ensuing knowledge will be put."[15] Most importantly, dominant/mainstream epistemology weighted by its own political concerns and identities could undermine and impact more vulnerable communities if not challenged by a counter knowledge base.

Diné women's historical obscurity was partially an aspect of non-Diné method, but another crucial concern existed. Silences painfully found their way into the very making and collection of sources on or about the Diné. The sources then swayed what Ralph Trouillot in *Silencing the Past* called historical production.[16] This silence also plagued a great deal of document recovery and preservation on the black freedom movement. Typical authoritative evidence (government materials, newspapers, etc.) acted in past and present to subjugate, subvert, or subdue the voices of our subjects. Activist conflict with the state and local media led to protests over misrepresentation, false or misinformation, police brutality, subversion and surveillance, and even assassinations. Thus, the matter was both political and an academic quagmire for historians who used those documents.

Archives weren't exactly an uncomplicated alternative. Quite a few did not begin collecting materials on the civil rights movement until the 1980s. Additionally, contact by an archive or awareness of archival importance determined who kept or donated papers. No one asked my mother, a lowly CORE member, for her papers. Cleveland-based archives, Western Reserve Historical Society, did ask my father for his organizational materials given his position as minister of the Euclid Street Unitarian Church. Yet, my mother, a native Clevelander, knew more people and had greater involvement in the city's freedom movement than my father. The collection process was hierarchal, subjective, and in various ways plain haphazard.[17]

Black freedom movement historians needed an alternative source to equalize dubious documents and capricious collection. Oral history became an undeniably essential method by which to balance source distortion and silence, but it also heavily depended on how historians collected and understood the significance of these sources. Well-known historians August Meier and Eliot Rudwick, for example, heavily depend on oral histories. An important contribution, I used many of their transcripts. However, a number of them were not verbatim, but constituted notes that interrupted the voice. Additionally, these reports ascribed value to certain information over others, a decision partly influenced by *their* associations within CORE, particularly Meier, who was formerly an active member of Essex CORE. By extension, it also made it unclear who was "talking," the interviewee or the interviewer. Additionally, Meier and Rudwick's oral history collection occurred in the midst of CORE's movement activities. Thus, the subjects' awareness of being "watched" had implications for who shared information and under what circumstances, especially during increased racial tensions. Their very presence in the moment of history making undermined the distance either supposedly had as historians.[18]

In fact, that lack of distance showed in their writing. Meier and Rudwick had a tendency to question the interviews of black nationalists in contrasting ways to others. Terminology in their notes, e.g., "admitted," "further questioning," etc., reflected an unspoken interrogation about their versions of events. Most intriguing is that Meier and Rudwick (likely Meier) assessed some people, including James Farmer, based on personal observations without explaining either the context or the presumptions at work.[19]

Despite Meier and Rudwick's dependence on hundreds of oral histories to tell the history of CORE, I still could not find my mother's version in their book. It was a problem of invisibility. A basic reading of their text somewhat explains the reason for that absence. Their historical interpretation of CORE posits that the organization was founded on interracial goodwill direct action, and subsequent events pushed it away from its original lofty moorings. White and some black members who held to the "real" CORE's interracial vision and rules of conduct figured prominently in the making and success of CORE, while mostly black and some white members took a backseat because they purportedly heralded CORE's philosophical transformation, and eventual demise via black power's rise.[20]

When I read Rudwick and Meier's book, *CORE*, I read it as my mother's child and a black scholar. I comprehended it through these two perspectives. From these identities, I came to know CORE in a particular way, not to the exclusion of others—to the contrary, but as part of a myriad of views that played out locally and nationally in the organization's complicated development toward black power. Who I was heightened my view of the kind of silences found in the book. My exposure to their experiences was a benefit, not a disadvantage to my historical production. This is not to say that it was valid because I was my mother's child or invalid because I was my mother's child. Simply, their experience fit within a larger background and fluid tension of black power in CORE. My mother, aunts, and uncles were, in fact, authoritative sources of historical knowledge (not just facts) about CORE's black power period. Why should I not tell "their" story? How could I not tell their story given their influence in CORE's black power era?

Therein lay the difference between how I understood oral history's import versus other historians including Meier and Rudwick. For me, oral history interviews were more than a compilation of facts, data, and proof. I'd seen how the philosophical transformation of CORE to black power worked its way into my mother and family's personal, professional, and political lives—long after the organization's demise. Black power was not a failure. Its lessons lived with them and in them long after their CORE died. To understand their experience, you had to do more than speak to them. You had to hear. You had to know. And through it, I came to appreciate a different CORE.

That was the power of oral history. More than an evidential source, it was a living testimony of the voice's power. The echo of "I" and "we" being, these interviews did not just detail what happened, but who I am, who we are, and how I/we became.[21] It was a creation story, how a past became building blocks in a person's life. Meier and Rudwick ignored, overlooked, and/or rather neglected my mother's creation story, partly because they believed that my mother's CORE had no value for the story they wished to tell. They missed something in how my mother became and that something was inextricably tied to CORE and black power. Oral history theory gave me insight into the failure of "scholarly detachment" to account for flagrant exercises of authority and exclusion. While some might worry over my scholarly detachment as my mother's child, oral theorists concerned themselves with my use of power. That question held greater weight for me. It framed how I understood and read Meier and Rudwick's silence. More importantly, it structured how I grappled with my *own* use of power even as I held on to my identities (civil rights child and black studies scholar).

Consequently, oral history was important to the storytelling in this text in two ways—aurality and author reflection. Aurality and its dissemination through this text first established the person's existence. [22] The interviews functioned to illustrate symbolically the power of voice in storytelling and to undergird theoretical belief in the voice's right to tell its own story. This approach also corresponded with my archival training, the foundation of which was to ensure dissemination of primary materials for ready research by any persons with an interest in African Americans in Cleveland, CORE, and black power. As such, readers will see a great deal of oral history use in the text as well as the online digital archive Harambee City.

Secondly, oral history here reflected a combination of collective memory and the testimonio tradition. While collective memory unveils the personal within a broader historical experience and group identity, testimonio boldly embodies a political act in which the voice becomes an instrument and expression of the collective's past. This theory proved particularly effective for persons involved in social activism. Interviewees spoke as part of a group, referenced other community members, and viewed their actions within a larger context of philosophical and tactical struggle within CORE and the wider black freedom movement. Effectively, testimonio/collective memory resembled historian Walter Ong's theory that shared knowledge through oral language served to enhance community unity and connectedness. Testimonio thus provided insight into both individuals and groups within CORE. However, such communal thinking also made it difficult to flesh out internal conflicts. [23]

Oral histories also became a complex interplay between the interviewee and the interviewer, where voice, memory, rhetorical style, positionality, identity, and narrative creation became a delicate and not so delicate balance of control. And unlike historians, who pretended identity somehow dissipated into the ether, oral history theory required constant critical awareness of my relationship to the subject even as it legitimated, perhaps even celebrated, my attachments and bonds. Thus, oral history's ability to reveal the deeper aspects of interviewee voice and identity was hardly a one-way street. It obligated the interviewer to recognize power in the exchange between sharer and receiver. It assumed naturally the implications of interviewer perspective. Was I an outsider or an insider, had generation or gender made a difference? How did my identity impact the information I received? Could I balance these considerations?

An internal process took place between the source creation and myself before and after the voice appeared in the narrative. Different methods helped to counteract my "insider" position. It included, for example, asking relatives both during and after the interview difficult questions about personality conflicts, gender, ideology, and power. I avoided as much as possible leading questions. Through feminist and life story approach, I focused on larger lived experiences before venturing into fact-based information. I also had them read controversial sections of the text and requested feedback. It resulted in a historical production that was partially a shared experience, or what Michael Frisch called *shared authority*. I wanted to achieve balance between the narrator's authoritative voice and the right of the voice to speak for itself. Feminist and Third World oral history theorists lent support to this consideration in that they challenged the interviewer status as expert knowledge producer and eliminated the social distance between the interviewer and interviewee to restrict potentially exploitive situations.[24]

That being said, the historian and the oral theorist did occasionally run counter to each other, particularly in the case of my aunt, Ruth Turner Perot.[25] My initial reaction was to accept the subject's own assessment of *herself* as not very powerful within CORE because oral history insisted that the voice speak for itself not that I narrate over it. But in reality, other oral history interviewees and secondary sources saw the subject as more powerful than she saw herself. Thus, the question of who had power in the National Advisory Council of CORE had less to do with policy creation than with actual perception, which could be equally influential.

Ultimately, I included the subject's argument that she was not powerful, while still making it clear that both historical events and perception by others reflected the opposite notion.

To be sure, my aunt and uncle were not totally happy with the historian's interpretation of events. They disputed my construction of Cleveland CORE history as "Gladys Knight and the Pips." In other words, my aunt and uncles figured too prominently in the text for their taste. This proved particularly an issue because both saw their interview as part of a collective. Their oral histories were meant to be freedom movement testimonio. Some persons had not been included in the narrative (I was constantly reminded to include blind CORE activist Chuck Burton), and the history, perhaps rightly so, was seen as flawed because of it. The essence of CORE and the movement was one of people not leadership hierarchy. It was the people who made CORE. It was the people who made black power.

To a certain extent, they were right in their assessment. I used a storytelling trope that focused on individuals as the lens to tell a larger story. Yet, as the historian, I had to choose some interpretative framework and certain realities lent themselves to the focus of my aunt and uncle in the story. Namely, they served on the national advisory board of CORE, held positions in the national office, ran the first black power project in Baltimore, wrote the proposal for CORE's second black power project, and selected Cleveland as its site. As such, whether they liked it or not, Gladys and her Pips popped up in powerful positions throughout CORE's black power period.

Nonetheless, the oral history theorist in me insisted that their concerns and that of others be considered. Consequently, I shared the dissertation with many interviewees, though not all of them. A few gave feedback. Some, due to illness, could not read it. Others simply sent no response, or I never heard from them again. Conversely, interviewees who reviewed my dissertation could turn an encounter into a very harrowing process, particularly when a power struggle ensued between the interviewee and myself. For example, one member was not pleased with my assertion that James Farmer started CORE through the Brotherhood Mobilization Plan. Partly, the conflict revolved around definition—founder versus starter. Mostly, the origin of CORE was still hotly contested, beginning with the publication of Farmer's autobiography *Lay Bare the Heart*. Taking Farmer's "side" irritated old conflicts and actually led to a shut down in communication due to my refusal to be "open" to the other side. Though I followed the chronology and documents to this conclusion, truthfully, what I wrote firmly placed me in the Farmer camp. That made me persona non grata for a couple of people. In this case, we both asserted our power—theirs not to grant an interview and mine to insist on my own authoritative voice.

In any case, oral history at least required a grappling with the question of who had power—especially when it came to the narrative. Frankly speaking, my name on the book cover effectively bequeathed to me final power. In fact, all historians had the final say, which was why scholarly detachment was an illusory process. It hid the author's identities from the reader and required no exercise of self-examination or open explanation—a reality that partially informed my petulant resistance to why I should explain that I indeed had a technique or process.

Ultimately, the oral historian in me spoke loudest in its challenge that I openly reveal power. As such, I freely acknowledge and admit that it was I who gave credence to the source's origin, selected the source for use, wrote the narrative, and altered/defended it when challenged. What I did was by no means a clean and ordered process. And certainly, my identity's presence in this product might also reflect silences. Key for me and for the reader, however, is that I do not claim to be the Wiz feigning scholarly detachment. In fact, I am an oral historian, black freedom scholar, and my mother's child. I aspire here to openly, analytically, critically illuminate for readers the history of CORE and the genuine, legitimate collaboration between activists and historians, which helped me to tell it. I hope to temper the power that resides with me, and I do so by telling you no tales of being the all-knowing Great Historical Wiz. Rather, in this space, right at the *front*, I give you the truth of it. I am the girl with the ruby red slippers.

# Acknowledgments

There are numerous supporters whom I count among my family and friends who helped to get me through this very long and daunting process—all of whom did it with love, patience, humor, housing, and money! First and foremost, I thank my father and godmother, John Frazier and Czerny Brasuell, without whom this task would have been impossible. Your love and care has sustained me through this process and made me stronger. This paltry acknowledgment does not begin to explain your importance to my life and this book. I also thank my grandmother, Mary Brasuell—for all those prayers!

There are scores of friends who put up with my disappearing acts during various periods of this book's development. They were the foundations of my life and I cherish them still. These persons include John Frazier, Jonathan Brasuell, Tonya Taylor, Alicia and Lamont Redrick, Cynthia P. Lewis and the Lewis Clan (Adrienne, Lillianne, Brianna, and Lonzy), Zaheer Ali, Elaine Hall, Katie and Fedelma Dixon, Sabya Frazier, Susie Anderson, Alexandra Fair, and last, but certainly not least, my godbrother, Amadou Cisse, whose example pushed me through the last stages.

Of course, this book would not be possible without the willingness of my extended CORE family who shared their memories. I spent many moments in their presence and each transformed me and parts of this book as they told their stories, revealed their pain, and sometimes made me laugh. To say that I received encouragement from Ruth Turner Perot and Antoine Perot would understate their significance. Not only was it their unassuming suggestion that "maybe I could do something on Cleveland CORE," they also gave me the first small grant to do research. Several uncles gave me access to their memories and warmly welcomed me as if they'd only seen me yesterday as opposed to years. Nate Smith, Art Evans, Don Bean, Stuart Wechsler, Danny Gant, and Franklin Anderson were all wonderful and kind to me, and each one narrated CORE with verve and humor. I relived their CORE in each syllable and outburst of laughter. Stanley Tolliver, Bonnie Gordon, Bruce Melville, Joanne Hardy, George Houser, Juanita Morrow Nelson, Wilfred (Will) Ussery, and Alice Huffman, whom I met along the road of doing research, greatly contributed and I am grateful. I particularly wish to remember Juanita Nelson, who died months before the publication of this book. She and her husband, Wally Nelson, were stalwart members of CORE and fiery advocates of freedom. I someday hope to see more about their work in the movement than what I've written. National CORE members joined this community sharing: Gordon Carey, Alan Gartner, David Dennis, Val Coleman, Sheila Michaels, Roy Innis, and

Norman and Velma Hill. For those I interviewed, I tried to do justice to your memories and experiences. And I want to thank Gordon Carey, in particular, who reminded me to incorporate a broader national narrative about CORE. In the process, he became another of my CORE uncles along the way.

While living in Cleveland and doing research, there were many people who proved beneficial to my life, career, and research. First among them are the members of Quad A of Western Reserve Historical Society (WRHS)—especially Regennia Williams, Sherlynn Allen-Harris, and Margaret Barron, whose support gave me the energy to keep going! I will always be grateful for the previous curators of the African American Archives: Olivia Martin and Sam Black. I followed in your footsteps as an archivist and benefited from your work as a scholar. Archivists Margaret Burzynski-Bays, Ben Blake, Pat Stahley, and Regina Costello kept me smiling while I worked and researched at WRHS! During my time in Cleveland, there were a number of black community folks who were very encouraging, helpful, and informative including Dick Peery (an encyclopedia on black Cleveland), Joan Washington, Harllel Jones, and the ladies of the Black Women's Political Action Committee were all key to expanding my knowledge base of Cleveland.

There were a number of readers and advisers who gave indispensable insights and suggestions. First, I am thankful for the encouragement of Dr. John Hope Franklin, who represents a shining beacon and example of a true scholar, historian, activist, and gentleman. I miss him dearly. At Bates College, the comments and advice of Professor John McClendon, Professor Balthasar Fra-Molinero, and Professor Charles Nero regarding the dissertation proved important for its transition into a book. Additionally, under their tutelage both the dissertation and I matured. Several historians read this manuscript and did not laugh. They urged me to advance my thinking on concepts and improve clarity. I always listened, even though I did not always follow their advice. Still, they were patient. Thanks to Curtis Austin, Sundiata Cha Jua, Laura Hill, Raymond Arsenault, Jeanne Theoharris, John Bracey, and James Marshall. My colleagues Mary Frederickson, Mary Cayton, and Allan Winkler kept me on task and all made great observations about the manuscript. I am eternally grateful for their occasional meddling, critical analysis, and genuine mentorship. The trio were a breath of fresh air. I especially wish to remember Andrew Cayton, who told a colleague in passing that I should write with my own voice. Those words set my path from dissertation to book.

Other Miami members sustained me and my work with words of encouragement: Jacky Johnson, Mary Jane Berman, Cheryl Johnson, Charlotte Goldy, and Rodney Coates were powerful career models. But more importantly, they always made me feel like a person first and an academic second. For that, you all will always have my gratitude. The broader Miami University community also offered crucial backing and insights that helped me fully contour CORE's history. Kelly

Quinn and Alison Lefkowitz, who through their research interests guided me to the work of Beryl Satter, always gave me great feedback. Benjamin Kern and Dan Cobb helpfully referenced historian Jennifer Denetdale's work. I most assuredly appreciate the efforts of Markus Wust with Digital Library Initiatives at North Carolina State University and Elias Tzoc with Interactive Media Services (IMS) at Miami University. IMS provided space for the archival documents now found on the Harambee City website and North Carolina State University helped me build the site bit by bit. Markus I will owe you lunch in perpetuity. While at Miami University, one collective in particular saved this book and my academic life: the writing group—Adrian Adisa Price, Carlia Francis, and Levar Smith. They bestowed me with motivation, inspiration, coercion, and free psychiatric service.

Scholar sisters heard me whine and babied me just a little before they let me analytically have it. To the Y's ladies—Emilye Crosby, Robyn Spencer, and Wesley Hogan—I owe you too much to account here. You are all extraordinary women who make me better. Brother historians listened to me and pushed me forward despite myself: Clarence Lang, Lionel Kimble, Dwight Watson, Derrick Aldridge, and Maurice Hobson, I cherish you for who you are as scholars and human beings.

No scholar writes a text without grants to help traverse from one archive to the next. Two fellowships took me from dissertation to manuscript, the Bates College Mellon Resident Teaching Fellowship and the Heanon Wilkins Fellowship at Miami University. The Department of History Junior Faculty grants were instrumental and vastly essential for the manuscript's completion. The Publication, Reprint, Exhibition, and Performance Program wonderfully provided funds for photo permissions. Institutions who had the forethought to preserve the history of a movement have my utmost appreciation. Thanks to the Brisco Center for American History at the University of Texas, Wisconsin Historical Society, Howard University Moorland Spingarn, Schomburg Center for Research in Black Culture, Robert Schmidt and Miami University Archives, Swathmore College Peace Collection, Southern Historical Collection, and of course, Western Reserve Historical Society, Cleveland Public Library, and Cleveland State University. These entities enabled this book's existence from manuscript to photographs. Vern Morrison, William Barrow, and Lynn Bycko were beyond helpful. Nick Durda and especially Adam Jaenke steadfastly searched for photos.

I know fully well this is not a complete list of all those I should thank or that I tremendously owe. I beg the forgiveness of those who should be here but are not. I suppose I foolishly thought I might not make it here and did a poor job of keeping a full account. Please know that in my mind and my heart, you reside as part of the legion who got me from graduate school all the way to this first book. You are all a part of my Harambee nation.

# Introduction

## Things like That Happen in History

"There ain't no doggone CORE. Fool!" My mama was standing with hands on hips yelling at the television. Well, she wasn't yelling at the television so much as screaming at the screen version of Roy Innis. Again. It was something Pauline Warfield Frazier was apt to do anytime her eyes set upon his features. Roy Innis aggravated my mama to no end, and any mention of the man was likely to elicit a figurative steam billow from her Afro. Her opinionated outrage inevitably led to a litany of charges and emphatic declarations. "CORE gone!" or "CORE dead!" followed by bulleted insults about Innis that included "stole," "fool," "spy," "sold," and "get on my nerves."

Which programs elicited these outbursts, I cannot recall specifically. Though truth be told, there were a few reasons why former activists from the Congress of Racial Equality (CORE) might cringe when it came to Roy Innis. On the *Geraldo* talk show in 1988, Innis choked white supremacist John Metzger, and touched off a media storm that led to a spate of Metzger-Innis public bouts that resembled boxing matches rather than debates. There was also the Morton Downey Jr. appearance where Innis turned gangster in front of the national audience. He jumped up and pushed Reverend Al Sharpton, another black leader, to the ground. There were so many of those moments. The changes seemed not only antithetical to CORE, but just downright embarrassing. Each incident elicited in Pauline Warfield Frazier, and many others, a feeling of outrage, perhaps shame, that Roy Innis should be the last representation of CORE. And so, they disappeared CORE—as in made it nonexistent. That death-like state began shortly after Innis's capture of the organization in 1968. Under his leadership, CORE phased through various stages of black power ideology eventually settling with a staunch ultraconservatism so extreme few comprehended it. In fact, Roy Innis reshaped CORE so massively during the 1970s, it was unrecognizable by the 1980s and 1990s. The "real" CORE was dead. But, Innis was dragging its carcass from show to show, and his antics made mockery of the CORE my mother knew. The CORE my mother loved. That CORE shaped her worldview. From school desegregation to black economic development, her activism in the Cleveland, Ohio, chapter of the Congress of Racial Equality brought her face to face with the structural inequalities and institutionalized racism that ushered black power into being. Through Cleveland CORE, she became immersed in a river of people, events, places, and ideas that flowed into her social and political life—all of it determining the woman she became.

From early childhood, whether by stories or rants, I came to understand that CORE had a greater, deeper history than its present incarnation implied. As I grew to become a black freedom movement scholar, I also learned that the histories, which purported to tell the organization's story, didn't quite capture my mother's CORE either. Somehow, it was the way that each failed to take into account how black power worked its way into the fabric of CORE's philosophy, transforming its membership and the communities they served. It was apparent that they concealed something essential about this aspect of CORE. Or rather, it was an obvious deduction to me, because this philosophical leftover appeared rather insistently in many aspects of my mother's life beginning immediately after her departure from Cleveland.

My parents, John Frazier (former NAACP Mississippi civil rights activist) and Pauline Warfield Frazier, moved from Cleveland, Ohio, to North Carolina in 1974.[1] CORE life in Cleveland dissipated, but a new movement percolated in the eastern part of North Carolina. Floyd McKissick, former executive director of CORE, favored black capitalism and economic development as the avenue to freedom, security, and independence. He left CORE with this vision of black power, and created in rural North Carolina an emblem of black economic independence and community building—Soul City.[2] Soul City called out to many black activists looking to reach the next level of black power. My parents, among them, joined as pioneers in this experimental, but eventually failed venture.

Despite the demise of Soul City, the CORE way persisted within my mother. She wrote in 1975 for a list of former CORE members in North Carolina.[3] It also represented itself through the constant visits of Uncle Nate (Smith), Aunt Ruth (Perot) and Uncle Tony (Perot), the eventual North Carolina residence of former CORE colleagues Uncle Frank (Anderson) and Uncle Makaza (Kumanyika aka Herb Callendar), or the occasional brief sightings of Uncle Don (Bean) and Uncle Jay (Arki) during holiday travels to Cleveland. In the early years, these small efforts simply kept my mother connected with people who knew and understood the movement, who knew and understood CORE. But perhaps the most obvious expression of the CORE way materialized in the work my mother did after leaving Ohio. In Cleveland, my mother dedicated her life to community activism, organizing, and economic development. Her time in North Carolina was no different. Through the 1970s and 1980s, Pauline Frazier worked for nonprofit social organizations, which included Offender Aid and Restoration (OAR), Opportunities Industrialization Center (OIC), and the Young Women's Christian Association (YWCA). However, the most evident incarnation of CORE notably emerged in the early 1990s, when one area of her activism surged forth—economic development.

Pauline Frazier became second director of Southeast Raleigh Community Development Corporation (SRCDC) in 1990. Initially a one-woman staff person, she cultivated SRCDC's growth in the midst of a rapid increase of North Carolina

CDCs during the 1980s and 1990s—an expansion that signaled a renewed movement for black economic power.[4] The organization's budget included a million-dollar federal grant for its Youthbuild program, a project that paid young adults on the job while they attained a GED degree. Programing and economic development incorporated participation in freedom schools, creative financing for low-income housing, planning for a Martin Luther King Jr. shopping center, consultation to other neighborhood CDCs, and negotiations for a business partnership with the Burundi government. It was a feat reminiscent of CORE, and it similarly compelled SRCDC to both challenge white financial institutions and, in some cases, accept monies from them. But in the end, step by step, Southeast Raleigh neighborhood became "an economic force to be recognized."[5]

As executive director, my mother reclaimed the tradition of community building. SRCDC's activist and aggressive economic development style directly derived from her history in Cleveland as a member of CORE, and also as a staff person of Hough Area Development Corporation (HADC), a 1960s Cleveland-based community development group that included former CORE members. Both CORE and HADC, nationally and locally, formulated a plan for individual and communal economic growth that seized political control, provided job training, advocated community stock ownership, sponsored global commercial outreach, and made provisions for low-income housing. In fact, SRCDC's proposed Martin Luther King Jr. Center came directly from HADC's similarly titled shopping center project.

Within five years SRCDC ranked among the top CDCs in North Carolina and that status resulted from the reapplied and updated version of CORE's (and to some extent HADC) black power and nation building. From neighborhood organizing to global networking, SRCDC benefited from the early skills my mother learned during the black power movement. Pauline Frazier's CORE gave her the tools to transform Raleigh's black community and made SRCDC the soul offspring of CORE. This historical link was the lynchpin of why Pauline Frazier shouted down Roy Innis's screen image. My mother's CORE was powerful. *Her* CORE was community focused. *Her* CORE was transformative. *Her* CORE was uplifting. *Her* CORE was BLACK POWER!

The ownership she felt for *that* CORE, however, differentiated from any number of other visions. Roy Innis radically drifted from that CORE. But then, *her* CORE wildly departed from the original pacifist moorings of the early 1940s—at least it seemed. Though Pauline's CORE formally took shape after 1964, it met numerous challenges from many fractured visions of CORE. In many ways, most people remain unaware of this diversity or conflict of ownership. Indeed, what most people know, historians and laypersons alike, runs the gambit from blank stares of pure ignorance to general catch phrases of James Farmer, Freedom Rides, 1942 pacifist and student founders, and maybe some recognition that CORE embraced black power. CORE, to a certain extent, became among historians the freedom movement's proverbial stepchild. There was no "Martin Luther King" of stature leading the organization. CORE was not the NAACP with its one-hundred-year history and *Brown vs. Board of Education* moment. There was no fiery Stokley Carmichael to push out whites or declare parental dominion over radical offspring like the Black Panther Party. Piled over by a plethora of images that centered the story of the movement around SCLC and King, the NAACP, and SNCC, CORE mostly became a historical version of "Where's Waldo"—always in the picture, though you had to look to find it.[6]

There was and is only one historical synthesis of CORE. Leading scholars August Meier and Elliot Rudwick's tome, simply titled *CORE*, dominated the field—what little there was—and defined how we understood the organization's origins, ideological underpinnings, development, membership, rise, and decline. My mother's CORE made a short appearance (several references were made to Cleveland CORE and its members' role in the group's acceptance of black power), but only in what appeared to be a small hiccup in an inevitable downward spiral away from goodwill, pacifist-inclined, interracial CORE into doom-and-gloom black power.[7]

So pervasive was the telling of CORE's interracial, pacifist identity, that this particular perspective/proprietorship congealed into how we saw the organization's history and contribution, as well as who was included or not.[8] The early account of faithful devotion to racial brotherhood and goodwill direct action submerged the muddier, more difficult problems of chapter deviation, membership composition, black nationalism, self-defense, and ideological conflict over direct action. The organization's life history transitioned from utopic interracial idealism through the heroic 1961 Freedom Rides.[9]

Some CORE founders and members perpetuated a customized telling of this nonviolent lineage. George Houser's 1951 *Erasing the Color Line* enhanced the idea of an integrated brotherhood of freedom fighters. Denouncing previous methods of legal action by groups like the NAACP, and the ill-fated violent upheaval of the Denmark Vessey rebellion—only interracial, nonviolent, goodwill direct action's application could end discrimination and segregation. While Houser extolled the early virtues of 1940s CORE, CORE in the 1950s underwent little makeover in the next decade with its second history by James (Jim) Peck, *Cracking the Color Line*. CORE was still an integrated brotherhood of goodwill nonviolent advocates, except for the additional caveat of an active southern presence and increasingly successful demonstrations.[10]

Little more than five years later, however, the history and tone regarding CORE took a turn when the organization's national director, James Farmer, wrote a short book that reflected the mood of the day for freedom now! *Freedom, When?* characterized the high wire act CORE walked between its old purported self and the rising call for black power, reassessment of integrationist goals, and ambivalent reaction to white membership. To some, Farmer's effort to resituate CORE in this new era while still propagating the early framing of an integrated brotherhood equated to holding back the sea with one hand.[11]

Sometime after 1966 and the declaration of black power, CORE drastically changed its image. Those transformations raised uncomfortable questions about its relationship to black power and ran afoul of the organization's construction of its origin history. And yet, it proved a pivotal period for CORE as it navigated the changes in the freedom movement, attempting to innovate and transform the political and economic lives of the black community.

By the mid-1970s, however, a number of factors lent itself to nostalgia for the "old CORE" irrespective of its achievements in the latter 1960s. In 1973, August Meier and Elliot Rudwick published *CORE*, which effectively ended CORE's history in 1968, with a final epilogue regarding the ascendency of Harlem chapter leader Roy Innis to the rank of national director. Secondly, James Farmer and Floyd McKissick filed suit against Roy Innis amid questions of fund misappropriation, dubious retention of the national directorship, and totalitarian rule of "their" CORE. CORE's romanticized historiography gave credence to the belief by some members, many of whom were white activists, that black power was the death knell for the CORE they knew. The organization appeared to be an aberrant reflection of Roy Innis's uncontrolled mismanagement, and an unmitigated disaster in black power experimentation. What followed was a spiral into conservatism, support for right-wing politicians like Ronald Reagan, and on-television brawls that defined Innis's CORE up until the writing of this book, though now including appearances by his heir-apparent and son, Niger Innis, on conservative media outlets like Fox News.[12]

It was no wonder that both former members and the general public yearned for and harkened back to CORE before the rise of black power. And so the history went, the best of CORE came before 1966, and the worst after it. Defined by its interracial character and quest for nonviolent brotherhood, the old construction of CORE's history returned, and the image lasted. Years later, civil rights activists joked about CORE's ardent belief in "real-real integration"—a tongue in cheek allusion to the philosophical embrace of racial brotherhood along with the many interracial marriages among its members—personalized goodwill integration. That was CORE.[13]

Cofounder James Farmer, of course, epitomized CORE's "real-real" integration with his interracial marriage to CORE leader Lula Peterson Farmer. However, the former national director was still displeased by the cultivation of this perspective in CORE histories and studies. Where it appeared in history books, the pacifist and static organizational representation of CORE held. The organization originated from integrated, idyllic Christian idealists and nonviolent followers more interested in loving admonishment and direct action militancy, no dissension—ideological or otherwise. It ended in a quagmire of black power ineptitude and philosophical corruption, no dissension—ideological or otherwise.[14] In between, CORE weaved in and out of local histories, but none of these spoke to the scope of contact between local struggles and national CORE.[15] Nor, did they contextualize how local movements changed national CORE, or how national CORE impacted the broader black freedom struggle beyond the Freedom Rides. These local studies expanded our knowledge of the movement's complexities, but not our overarching sense of CORE, and particularly its members. Excluding the Freedom Rides and to some extent Freedom Summer, it seemed as if only certain people or aspects received consideration. There were few, if any, exceptions to this rule until Brian Purnell's *Fighting Jim Crow in the County of Kings: The Congress of Racial Equality in Brooklyn.*[16]

Of the many COREs, scholars rendered least important, even excluded, James Farmer's contributions. In 1991, he wrote, "I was particularly stressed that they botched up the origins of CORE," and that CORE "desperately needed" a history of its chapters in the north during the fifties and sixties.[17] Historians August Meier and Elliot Rudwick, authors of the first major work on CORE, constituted the "they" of Farmer's letter. Two issues were attached to Farmer's complaint. First, the origin omitted the degree to which black participation (specifically his own) or the pursuit for black participation directed CORE's trajectory. Second, northern CORE chapters played the equivalent role of the bugaboo by ushering in more dramatic tactics that heightened militancy and the rise of black nationalism that led to Innis's takeover.

Meier responded to Farmer's concerns by telling him not to "worry about it Jim, things like that happen all the time in history," and offered to revise the organization's origin history in the second edition, though he had no plans anytime soon for a second edition.[18] For Farmer, the wait to correct CORE's history lasted more than a decade. In answer to Meier and Rudwick's seminal text *CORE,* Farmer wrote his own organizational/autobiographical history on the CORE he knew, entitled *Lay Bare the Heart.* James Farmer reinserted black influence within CORE and complicated the racial and political dynamics that shaped the organization's relationship to black nationalism. CORE intended to lead an integrated mass movement. But mass participation, especially from the black community, also engendered a natural division in which two kinds of members emerged—the "means-oriented" and the "ends-oriented." The means-oriented, philosophically supported nonviolence and sought to transform not just the law or the policy but the heart and mind of the segregationist. For them, the segregationists' transformation ranked equally, if not over, the necessity to change the behavior or policy itself.[19]

The second group, the ends-oriented, comprised what Farmer called the "masses of Negroes."[20] Ends-oriented required no ideological allegiance to nonviolence or pacifism, and likely employed the strategy until it held no tactical use for breaking down racial inequality. Though early CORE members recognized that an influx of ends-oriented brought with it a potential break down in nonviolent discipline, mass black participation was an essential component to becoming a freedom organization of any significance. Thus, according to Farmer, it led to "a kind of dual parentage for CORE"—the pacifists and the ends-inclined coalition.[21]

Farmer hoped that the two types could coexist, though disagreement abound as to which group formed the center of CORE's identity. Resultantly, it was precisely this dual parentage, the merger of ends-oriented and means-oriented membership groups, that eventually precipitated internal strife. This particularly occurred when either membership encountered and numerically overwhelmed the other, turning the organization into "their" CORE. In the early 1940s, the ends-oriented held no influence and therefore no control. CORE was small and consisted of mostly well-educated white members, many of whom were pacifists.[22] Although other types of members far exceeded the pacifists' numerical strength, their presence defined the structure, guidelines, and actions. Pacifist possession of CORE so impacted the organization that white CORE founder Bernice Fisher in 1944 expressed concern over an influx of participants inclined toward "converting the exploiter [rather] than in ending the exploitation."[23] Yet, she too still operated under the belief that a "creative balance" could be found between the two sides and that both groups could still own CORE.

Nonetheless, the hard truth was that no such "creative balance" ever existed. Indeed, Cleveland's unique connection to the ends-oriented CORE obliterated any such theories as far back as the mid-1940s when it exposed inconsistencies between the two membership types. Goodwill, direct action, and self-defense all came into question—not just through events in Cleveland, but in other anomalous behaviors and ideas by CORE members and chapters. But, the atypical CORE member seemed irrelevant given their small numbers.

Essentially, the conflicting sides vied and attempted to make CORE into its own image from creation in the spring of 1942 until the final takeover by black power separatists under Roy Innis in the 1970s. Through the mid-1960s, James Farmer also held out hope that CORE might achieve an equilibrium, although he was well aware that ends-oriented members had taken over CORE by the time he published *Freedom, When?* in 1965. The following year, the cry "Black Power!" entered the American lexicon. It was the full fruition of the ends-oriented rise across the nation. Farmer had no other choice but to step aside, as ends-oriented, now black power activists, attained dominance and made CORE theirs.

Farmer's description of the ends-oriented collective, however, was imprecise and failed to reflect the growing divide and perspective on black power, particularly among new militant members. Black power supporters appeared singular, static, and unsophisticated. In fact, the broad typology constricted ends-oriented members to one monolithic group calling for black power in a single declaration. Other early CORE members also saw black power uniformly. Bayard Rustin, 1940s CORE member and organizer of the 1963 March on Washington, demonized black power in a 1966 *New York Times* op-ed. Although the article never mentioned CORE specifically, most saw it as a refutation, couching the ideology as reactionary and a betrayal of the core principles of the civil rights movement. Rustin believed black power had no coherent philosophy or program, and worse, was killing the movement. That included CORE.[24]

Scholars, too, pigeonholed black nationalism in CORE, and generally characterized it by Roy Innis's separatist faction, as if he were the only reflection of black power within CORE. The abandonment of the nonviolent, integrationist philosophy purportedly resulted in funding loss and member desertion. According to others, the organization became permeated by a reformist vision of black power, which looked more like ethnic pluralism combined with an economic plan of laissez-faire capitalism, painted black.[25]

The historical record on CORE's black power activities, however, proved incongruent to these assumptions. CORE was far more diverse in its ideological subtleties, local and national intricacies, and tactical complexities. The ends-oriented membership within CORE constituted multiple black power voices in the latter 1960s. Black nationalism among CORE's members took shape and developed differently from South to North, chapter to chapter. CORE's community organizing and black power programming emerged out of complex processes and recognition of the economic and political factors hindering black development in these locales. Thus, many voices for black power or multiple owners—as it were—influenced it.

This unique character of CORE, in part, lies at the heart of how we understand CORE during black power. Its cell-like structure of local community groups formed and then applied for membership to the national office. As a result, each local chapter of CORE came out of the interests of the individual communities that birthed it. Although these local groups followed the rules and regulations laid out by CORE, by its very nature, local circumstances just as heavily influenced chapter character as national events. Such a structure also facilitated a higher degree of autonomy, which also meant that local groups were as likely to be in line with the national office as not. In effect, each chapter was its own CORE.

The sheer number of variables in a case like this created great difficulties in cultivating a work that captured the totality of CORE. Or, it has the deleterious effect of lifting one aspect (or owner) of CORE over the other. A condensed version of CORE's history therefore misses the various elements that impact the national office. But far more relevant, the structure defied all attempts to make CORE a representation of any one idea when it was, in reality, a compilation of the many.

What actually appeared in CORE was a hodge-podge of black power ideologies. However, Cleveland CORE and a few other chapters failed to fit within these categories.[26] Although much of their work emulated a pluralist perspective (political participation and ethnic power accumulation), their economic standpoint was anything but pluralist. This faction acknowledged capitalism's failure to build wealth in the black community, but deemed the system too omnipresent to overturn. Thus left with one remaining possibility, they attempted to tweak the system to give the masses access to capitalism. What these CORE members created became a fourth stream of black nationalism within CORE that I argue is black power populism.[27] Black power populism encapsulated socialist elements of wealth sharing that forced the American economic system to open its doors to more citizens. From 1966 to 1969, a few CORE leaders fashioned and pushed through an economic project, which sought to broaden capitalism and turn one black community into an economic force. They chose the city of Cleveland, Ohio, as the site of this experiment, and named the project *Harambee*, a Swahili word meaning pull together and connoting the idea of self-help. *Harambee*'s placement in Cleveland was a direct outgrowth of the rise of local CORE members into the national office whose critique of capitalism and advocacy of community control paved the way for *Harambee*'s existence. More than any site, Cleveland represented the best of black power populist efforts to reshape and empower the black community, and the ways in which it did so form the structure of my mother's CORE.

This book is divided into two sections and it is chronologically and thematically based. As such there are areas of overlap, especially between 1963 to 1968. Part 1 highlights early variances in CORE philosophy before it reached a full expression of black power in the mid-1960s. Chapter 1 examines CORE's beginnings from 1942 to 1945. It narrates a new origin history and inserts philosophical nuances that become the basis for how black power later comes to exist within CORE. It also explains how clashes with CORE's parent organization, the Fellowship of Reconciliation (FOR), determined the high degree of pacifist influence in its early period. In chapter 2, I introduce readers to Cleveland CORE from 1946 to 1953. Most significantly, I track the contradictory behavior of Cleveland CORE and other chapters and/or members that deviate from CORE rules. These members exposed fault-line fractures in organizational philosophy in areas related to self-defense, black nationalist philosophy, and contention over protest etiquette.[28] Chapters 1 and 2 reset CORE's birth and pave the way for understanding why 1960s Cleveland CORE actually reflected a longer history of militancy within the organization as a whole.

In chapter 3, I summarize events that led to the national office's revival and Cleveland chapter's 1962–1964 reincarnation. As national CORE seeks to expand black participation, philosophical inclinations toward black leadership determine Cleveland CORE's leadership makeup. Chapter 4 expands discussion on Cleveland chapter's locally based experiences with particular attention given to its 1964 school desegregation fight. The school desegregation movement engulfed the city in a civil rights blitz of rallies and demonstrations that solidifies Cleveland CORE's position as a major player in the freedom movement, and the most militant civil rights organization in Cleveland. Taken together, chapters 3 and 4 demonstrate how local people and regional circumstances can influence chapter development and push it beyond the boundaries set by national office.

Part 2, CORE's black power era, follows the philosophy's sporadic appearance in early 1960s Cleveland, Ohio. This section traces its movement to the national office, and then returns to Cleveland when the city becomes a programmatic site for CORE national's black power policy. For chapter 5, I double back over Cleveland's formative years from 1962 to 1965 to explain how local and regional dynamics inspired and foreshadowed a growing disposition toward black power. Five then moves the conversation from local to national when CORE headquarters decrees a "New Direction," a community-organizing stratagem devised to reflect changing circumstances on the ground. Conflict over this new tactic effects social and political ties in both Cleveland and the national office. Chapter 5 represents the fluid dynamics among local, regional, and national events that move all of CORE ever closer to black power.

We learn in chapter 6 that not every CORE member willingly accepts these changes. Circa 1965–1966, Cleveland chapter leader Ruth Turner becomes a symbolic target of black power fears. These confrontations end with the departure of key white officers, and national officially announces its support for black power. Meanwhile, CORE's new arsenals for freedom—the Target City Projects—combine community organizing around the ballot and the people's use of the bullet to erupt forth a new city when Cleveland's Carl Stokes becomes the first black mayor of a major urban city in 1967.

Chapters 7 and 8 transition from black political power to an innovative economic agenda that sought to develop a massive wealth share program. CORE Enterprises Corporation (CORENCO) and local CORE participation in groups like Hough Area Development Corporation and Operation Black Unity (OBU), a black power umbrella group based in Cleveland (chapter 8), constitute national and local efforts in Cleveland to modify capitalism. The Community Self Determination Bill (chapter 9) extends CORE efforts to make a more responsive economic system for black working and poor classes via the creation of a federally backed community development corporation. The bulk of chapters 7 through 9 are given over to the national office's activities in and related to the Cleveland Target City Project. They introduce a new aspect to CORE's black power period and expand the conversation on CORE's activities to 1970.

This black power populist approach receded after 1971 due to the exit of key leaders, funding loss, Roy Innis's refusal to abdicate his directorship, and the philosophical transition to black separatism. Although minor efforts were made to revamp Cleveland CORE, the chapter entered a state of permanent decline, becoming one of the last branches to fold. The intent of this book is plainly outlined in three goals. Rescue CORE from historical oblivion. Draw on Cleveland's unique fellowship with CORE to explore CORE's black power development. Give historians another way to look at black economic power outside the constraints of capitalism.

Harambee City fits within the changing historiography of the black freedom movement and capitalist studies. Outside the South, rethinking old constructs of a good/bad binary within the movement, this text uniquely argues for the Midwest's equally impactful role in black power. It seeks to move the discussion beyond guns and dashikis to articulate a complex interplay between the local and national, grassroots activism and federal politics. The last chapters, in particular, readjust capitalist studies' tendency to focus on how the system impacts the people versus how the people act to change capitalism. Even more important, it joins other scholarly efforts to reinsert women back into the freedom movement narrative. Leadership title, as most historical studies now recognize, said little about women's power within a given organization. This proved particularly the case for CORE where power was direct (chapter leader, national office, national action council) and indirect (secretaries, literature writers, organizers).

Finally, it is important to note that this is not a local study. It is a conversation between forces on the ground and the national arena. Incorporating municipalities and the federal government, local chapters and the national office, local/regional community organizing and private funding, this narrative is about how the Congress of Racial Equality navigates within, from, and related to Cleveland, Ohio. The lens changes with each perspective. Thus, it is not about the city alone. Black power in Cleveland signifies something much larger at stake for both CORE and black liberation. Hence, I specifically chose for the subtitle the preposition *in*—Congress of Racial Equality *in* Cleveland.

What this account should tells us is that there is so much more to the Congress of Racial Equality than a tale of Freedom Riders and second-tier arrivals to black power. CORE was dynamic. A complex organization in origin and "death," it used black power to transform itself and the communities in which it worked. CORE activists genuinely fought to creatively retune the American political and economic systems to change and lift up black people's lives. Through this effort, they became steeped in the spirit of black power. This is the story of my mother's CORE. It is the history of the many other members whose lives were forever shaped by the events of the 1960s and who, though proud of CORE's wins and disappointed with its losses, took with them all the days of their lives the ideals of activism and the guiding principles to fight for equality and build a nation.

HARAMBEE!

I

# 1

# How CORE Began

JAMES LEONARD FARMER JR. could not stand the sight of blood. Between youth and young adulthood, Farmer's discovery of this one unassailable fact led him on a new life path and career. As a seventeen year-old junior at Wiley College, he discarded his premed college major and professional aspirations to become a Negro doctor, and instead pursued an education in his true passion—the application of Christian gospel to the race question in America. In 1937, he obtained much of that education through his service as captain of Wiley's debate team, but also through civic-minded political and religious organizations. Farmer tested the waters of social action and attended two national conferences—the National Methodist Youth Conference and the Southern Negro Youth Conference in Richmond, Virginia.[1]

Of the two, the Christian conference was the most compelling in its long-term intellectual impact. The National Methodist Youth Fellowship gave Farmer an intellectual and organizational grounding in small group activism, "Christian" economics/ethical capitalism, and interracial brotherhood. Beyond that, the conference introduced him to a bevy of religious scholars, ministers, and leaders, particularly Harold E. Fey, the executive director of Fellowship of Reconciliation from 1935 to 1940. At various times and in various ways, the Methodist youth group invited FOR affiliates and incorporated emerging literature on the power of nonviolent protest. Though a small presence among the conference invitees, the Methodists' association along with the small Christian pacifist FOR helped to introduce Farmer to an organization and idea that came to dominate his life for the next decade.

Though it was unclear whether Farmer actually grasped at the time the implications of this early initiation to nonviolent direct action, inevitably his exposure after Wiley College reinforced these lessons. In 1938, he received an intensive crash course in nonviolent civil disobedience during his postgraduate years at Howard University in the Department of Religion, headed by Dean Benjamin E. Mays. Dr. Mays, the soon to be Morehouse College president, had recently returned from a world tour that included a visit with the revered leader of the Indian independence movement, Mohandas (Mahatma) Gandhi.[2] Refreshed from his sabbatical, Mays resumed his position as dean of the School of Religion at Howard University in the fall of 1937, and settled into the more mundane aspects of university life. One of those duties included the hire of a new professor for the upcoming academic year. He chose a most respected and well-known theologian of the period, James Leonard Farmer Sr., perhaps smoothing the way for Junior's entrance into Howard University's master program in religion. Of course, as a child prodigy who enrolled in Wiley College at fourteen, it hardly stood to reason that Howard University would not have admitted the precocious young Farmer.

By the fall of 1938, the eighteen-year-old Farmer entered the intellectually dynamic environs of Howard University, a predominantly black institution in Washington, DC. Farmer, an incoming master's student in religion, inhabited a world that boasted a veritable crème de la crème of black intelligentsia. To Farmer, Howard University was the "black Athens."[3] He roamed a campus filled with scholars of the black experience, among them historians Rayford Logan and Carter G. Woodson; founder of Black History Month, psychologist, and future famed Doll Test creator, Kenneth Clark; sociologist E. Franklin Frazier; philosopher Alain Locke; political scientist, and later the first African American Nobel Peace Prize winner, Ralph Bunche; and famed writer Sterling Stuckey.[4] But among them, one man ranked highest in Farmer's estimation and contributed the most to his intellectual and career trajectory. This man was philosopher and theologian Howard Thurman. Thurman, also just returned from India, turned his courses into intellectual incubators on Gandhi and the mass application of nonviolence. These discussions became the foundation for many of his lectures and chapel sermons.[5] Farmer avidly attended Thurman's classes, and to Thurman he credited his introduction to Mahatma Gandhi. Farmer developed a hungry fascination for the "little brown man in India," which he satiated with hours of readings on the spiritual leader's life and work.[6] What simply generated as idea during his Wiley years, became intent under Thurman. Through Thurman, Farmer found validation for his desire to utilize Christian social gospel and Gandhian nonviolence to tackle race inequality in America.[7]

Farmer also owed one more thing to Howard Thurman. While still a graduate student at Howard University, he recommended Farmer to John Swomley, noted minister and Methodist pastor, for a post as a part-time student secretary with the Fellowship of Reconciliation in Washington, DC. Farmer's arrival at FOR marked a turning point in his life and career. Among the youth members in FOR, he discovered a cadre of black and white pacifists primed to act on the race question and examining with close interest the progress of nonviolent direct action in India.

FOR, in fact, was the perfect ground to feed Farmer's ambitions. The Fellowship of Reconciliation formed in 1914 at the initiation of European Christians and opened its United States headquarters in New York a year later. By the 1930s, FOR began to advance an agenda of societal transformation through pacifism, moral persuasion, and nonviolent resolution. This transition to a social justice focus became complete in 1940, the year before Farmer graduated from Howard University, when Abraham Johannes (better known as A. J.) Muste followed Harold Fey as executive secretary of FOR. Muste moved FOR toward an acceptance of Gandhian nonviolent philosophy as an instrument for activism. Muste sought to redefine and broaden FOR's antiwar philosophy to include a larger social agenda against all forms of violence—poverty, racial discrimination, and other social inequalities. The Gandhi nonviolent ideology was key to FOR's legitimacy as a frontline vanguard. Though the FOR Nashville branch, and others like it, condemned Gandhian nonviolence as coercive and fomenting violent reaction, the national office pushed forward with its new agenda to explore the feasibility of this new protest method.[8]

In 1941, FOR expanded its commitment to racial justice when it encouraged its newest staff member, Bayard Rustin, to assist the March on Washington Movement (MOWM). A. Philip Randolph, famed unionist and socialist, birthed MOWM into existence January 25, 1941, with a national call for a march against racial inequality in defense hiring and the armed forces in Washington, DC. MOWM challenged America's claim that it defended democracy and freedom from Nazi Germany's racial superiority propaganda and military conquests.[9] As president of the Brotherhood of Sleeping Car Porters, a black labor organization, Randolph ensured MOWM's success with a ready base of followers from among Brotherhood union members. Randolph's confrontation with American hypocrisy inspired many in the black community to join MOWM's ranks, and chapters spread like wildfire across the United States. President Franklin D. Roosevelt's fear of an all-black summer march on the grounds of the nation's capital urged the administration into action. The president issued Executive Order 8802, which barred any businesses receiving government contracts from discriminating in hiring on the basis of race. It also established the Fair Employment Practices Commission (FEPC), a government body authorized to enforce Executive Order 8802. Randolph and leaders of MOWM considered the Roosevelt edict a win for black equality, and called off the demonstration, much to the dismay of many, particularly Bayard Rustin.[10] Randolph, however, maintained MOWM chapters and continued smaller protests throughout 1941 and 1942, readying for its next potential mass protest.

Meanwhile, FOR/Muste eagerly awaited MOWM's development of a mass nonviolent strategy. They hoped the organization could serve as an incubator for Gandhian protest methods by the black community.[11] Bayard Rustin hurried to advance MOWM's adoption of nonviolent direct action strategy. Pauli Murray, FOR member and Harvard University law student, also swayed MOWM's transition to mass civil disobedience.[12] An avid reader of Gandhian texts, Murray often speculated about its applicability within the United States. As a member of FOR, she was fully aware of its shift in this direction, and she added her voice to that of Rustin. Additionally, she convinced Randolph to acknowledge the parallel struggles between black Americans and India's plight.[13] Murray's foray into nonviolence also extended to Howard University students Juanita Morrow (Nelson) and Ruth Powell, who employed Gandhian protest methods in a series of sit-ins during the early 1940s in Washington, DC.[14]

While FOR staff and membership assertively engaged in activities that reflected a new nonviolent thrust, the organization's intellectual space also characterized a greater receptiveness to this approach. FOR board adviser J. Holmes Smith spent several years with Gandhi. He returned to America and built an interracial house cooperative in New York, also known as the Harlem Ashram, where various members of FOR and later CORE stayed. Richard Gregg, another FOR National Council associate, published *Power of Nonviolence* in 1935. Gregg's book stemmed from his experience living abroad with Gandhi as well. Gregg argued that peaceful direct action was a method to uplift both the victim and victimizer. It became a popular text among 1940s Christian youth and antisegregation activists.[15]

In 1939, Krishnalal Shridharani's *War without Violence* followed. Shridharani drastically strayed from Gregg's thinking by arguing that *satyagraha*, "spirit force" or the spiritual notion behind Gandhian nonviolence, was not inextricably linked to moral persuasion, but a militant tool of activism. Shridharani contended that nonviolence was "a weapon to be wielded by masses of men for earthly, tangible, and collective aims and to be discarded if it does not work."[16] Surprisingly, Shridharani had far greater import for future CORE. Having read and reread Krishnalal Shridharani's book, many FOR members and associates, including James Farmer and Pauli Murray, embraced its sectarian, pragmatic definition as the stepping-stones to freedom.[17] In fact, Shridharani often visited and debated the merits of Gandhian-style protest at the FOR New York office, located mere blocks from where he attended Columbia University.

Thus, intellectually and by deed, FOR's philosophical atmosphere proved a ripe atmosphere for Farmer's goal of a national confrontation against racial inequality. FOR transformed his social gospel into a career trajectory when, what began as a student internship, turned into a permanent part-time position after graduation. Farmer had hoped to join FOR headquarters in New York, but the organization rerouted him to a large Midwest town in Illinois. In the windy city of Chicago, he spent his early months braving the cold, falling in love for the first time, traveling on behalf of FOR, lecturing, keenly watching MOWM's new direction, and crafting a document that would become the basis for a new nonviolent movement.[18]

At age twenty-one, James Farmer wrote the Brotherhood Mobilization Plan. Farmer constructed the proposal for mass protest over the 1941 Christmas holiday.

The manifesto argued that disciplined masses engaged in civil disobedience, economic boycott, and noncooperation can transform the American racial landscape within five to ten years. Farmer's idealized time frame aside, the Mobilization Plan had several compelling components, which formed the backbone of this new entity. First, it was semiautonomous from FOR, but a program under FOR's umbrella. Eventually, Brotherhood Mobilization aimed to become self-supporting and permanently separate. Its membership drew from pacifist and nonpacifist groups, with specific attention given to gathering participation from black churches, fraternal organizations, and schools.

Membership levels categorized participation as supportive, active, or financial. All persons opposed to racial discrimination and willing to advocate nonviolence formed the broadest level. The second group generated a financial base from a "cooperative community" employed in homespun products, farming, and housing, with a percentage of profit given to movement activities. Cooperative communities were particularly key in order to "free participants of the movement, as far as possible, from dependence upon the capitalist system."[19] The third portion drew the most militant faction from the former two sections, and comprised those trained and prepared to actively engage in nonviolent techniques. The Brotherhood Mobilization Plan intended to apply civil disobedience, depend on cooperative economics, set multiple donor categories, and include a sizable black membership. And yet, what it intended did not immediately materialize. Though the proposal became the basis for CORE's origin, its platforms fell by the side or emerged over time and under different circumstances than the actual growth pattern of early 1940s CORE.

The Brotherhood Mobilization Plan actually began to collapse almost from its first writing, mostly due to A. J. Muste, who played a key role in altering CORE's evolution away from Farmer's memorandum. January 8, 1942, Farmer forwarded his plan to Muste. Muste then requested feedback from various FOR members and colleagues on the substance of the proposal on February 19, 1942. He also suggested that Farmer further detail the action memo with a comprehensive plan for how he intended to create this nonviolent movement of civil disobedience. More important, Muste altered the nature of the plan by suggesting that James Farmer change the membership section from a mobilization of "all persons who want an end to racial discrimination" to "the movement must include many who are not pacifists, but that its nucleus and moving force must be composed of committed pacifists." Muste then noted that he thought his suggestion "thoroughly sound."[20]

Muste also expressed concern over Farmer's fund-raising ideas for CORE. The original memo included four alternatives: foundation grants, individual CORE donors, community institutions such as churches, social groups, Christian organizations, and subsidies from local economic cooperatives. According to Muste, foundation support was unlikely for a group like CORE. Instead, he insisted that

Farmer further flesh out the economic cooperative concept and outline specific dimensions to such a program. Ultimately, CORE had to cultivate its own support without utilizing the fund-raiser list built up by FOR.

Farmer buttressed the first memo with a second missive sent March 9, 1942. The second version extended cooperative fund-raising and created a national support system similar to FOR cells or its sister organization the American Friends Service Committee (AFSC), a Quaker institution open to persons of different religions committed to social justice. Muste forwarded the revised first memo and second comprehensive outline to FOR National Council in early March.[21] From that moment forward, there was nothing left for Farmer to do but wait.

Meanwhile, anxious Chicago-based Brotherhood advocates were unwilling to exercise patience. The proposal clearly illustrated the early influence of Christian-based organizations, and partially MOWM, on Farmer's thinking about such a crusade. Though both obviously gave creative impetus and validation to the Brotherhood Mobilization Plan, Farmer's most important inspiration came from a small band of pacifists in Chicago. White pacifists George Houser, James Robinson, Bernice Fisher, and other FOR members met in the fall of 1941 every Saturday to discuss the utility of nonviolence, Shridharani's *War without Violence*, and the race question in America.[22] The small committee further consisted of University of Chicago theologian students, Christian idealists, and community NAACP activists. Through workshop conversations they corroborated Farmer's ideas on nonviolent activism. While FOR National Council and executive director A. J. Muste contemplated "The Brotherhood Mobilization Plan" in the early months of 1942, this Chicago-based group served as a sounding board and source of intellectual exchange for Farmer.[23] In fact, Bernice Fisher, a FOR worker, divinity student at the University of Chicago, and a young white woman of particular conviction, proved especially important to pre-CORE/Brotherhood efforts. A close friend of Farmer, Fisher's membership in the University of Chicago study group bridged the idealists together. She also handed out copies of James Farmer's protest proposal, shoving it "under their noses as proof" that the group stood at the cusp of a burgeoning movement.[24]

Chicago FOR staffer George Houser was Farmer's colleague in Christian activism. Also a Methodist, Houser served as FOR youth director. Jimmy Robinson, a white master's graduate student in English at the University of Chicago and member of the anarchist, pacifist group, the Catholic Worker, challenged racial covenants and residential housing discrimination by setting up an interracial living residence in a white neighborhood. Later dubbed the Boys Fellowship House, its inhabitants eventually became founders and/or members of CORE. And Joe Guinn, a black youth NAACP activist "whose high forehead seemed about to burst with intelligence," also attended the Saturday assemblies. Together they became the plan's earliest advocates.[25]

Working in tandem with Farmer, select members of the Chicago study group moved in April 1942 from talk to action. In fact, according to James Farmer, it was Bernice Fisher who determined that a "group" should directly and aggressively begin work now. George Houser also noted in a letter to Muste that in interest of "seeing Brotherhood Mobilization get started . . . [we] started our own committee working along the lines which B.M. will be working."[26]

While FOR considered giving Brotherhood its wings, members pushed Chicago pre-CORE into the limelight with small local protests. The first selected site, White City Roller Rink, proved a short-lived effort. The direct action project failed to desegregate the de facto rink, forcing the group to turn toward a legal challenge.[27] As the White City Roller Rink case wound its way through the court system, A. J. Muste summoned Farmer before the April National Council meeting in Columbus, Ohio, to discuss the Brotherhood memo's request to start a FOR subdivision for nonviolent direct action. Bernice Fisher, George Houser, and Homer Jack, another Methodist minister and major advocate, joined the road trip to Ohio.[28]

During the conference, Farmer's memorandum became an object of dispute among FOR's National Council. Pacifists vigorously debated the merits of non-violent method, which some deemed coercive. The argument came as no surprise to Farmer, who wrote in the February 1942 *Fellowship Magazine* that "conscience should simply not only [be] refusal to participate in war, but also . . . [non]cooperation with all those social practices which wreak havoc with personality and despoil the human community."[29] But, not everyone's view of pacifism extended that far. Such assertive pacifism divided the FOR council and rendered Brotherhood an unacceptable choice as a new FOR project. Despite this division, the National Council reached a "compromise" in which FOR granted Brotherhood resources to develop itself but it would *not* grant it full program status within FOR. Thus, the nameless organization officially began on April 11, 1942, with backing from the Fellowship of Reconciliation's National Council.[30] Inevitably, this decision became an important part of CORE's development, and facilitated aid from FOR associates like Pauli Murray and Bayard Rustin, who tremendously promoted its growth and trained students in nonviolent protest strategy. FOR also permitted Farmer and other staff to recruit or work on Brotherhood's development. The National Council further authorized its administrators to help expand Brotherhood, which led the national office to establish an advisory board for the fledgling group.[31]

It was generally presumed that CORE's forefathers and mother included George Houser; Bernice Fisher; Jimmy Robinson; Joe Guinn; Homer Jack, a divinity student at the University of Chicago; Bob Chino, interracially Chinese and Caucasian university student; Hugo Victoreen, a cosmic ray scientist; Ken Cuthbertson, an American Friends Service Committee member; and, of course, James Farmer.[32] However, CORE's charter meeting in late April garnered a larger initiating meeting of fifty participants interested in CORE, especially after the group unofficially launched a desegregation effort against White City Roller Rink. White activists numbered in the majority during this meeting, a ratio balance that would continue to dominate much of CORE's early membership history.

Following the short White City demonstration, the Jack Spratt Coffee House protest became CORE's first official sit-in protest and second direct action challenge. The test case came unexpectedly to the new group on May 3, 1942, less than a month after its official start. Farmer and Jimmy Robinson had intended to discuss over coffee the potential negative reaction to the interracial house, now dubbed Boys Fellowship House, which Robinson founded in early 1942. Instead, the Jack Spratt manager refused to serve Farmer, and what they got with their coffee was an ideal occasion to put nonviolence to use. Farmer and Robinson decided to come back, this time with a larger interracial contingent that included Fisher and Guinn. Upon the second visit, May 5, the owners of Jack Spratt again chose to discriminate. Or rather, the manager threw the money at the exiting group and wrathfully commanded them to never come back. The group returned with twenty or more participants on May 15. After police refused to arrest protestors, Jack Spratt capitulated to the, as yet, no-name group, and the coffee house was successfully desegregated.[33]

The owner's treatment and the integration win only invigorated the small collective, but the group's initial excitement was hampered by one small problem. In the debriefings that followed the first miniature sit-in, one participant suggested that the group fill the coffee house with a large contingent of protestors, but Jimmy Robinson contradicted the idea and pointedly noted the obvious. There were not enough "Negroes with us" to make such an action viable.[34] Joe Guinn's tongue-in-cheek answer to larger numbers and black participation was to circulate a flyer that read Jack Spratt "serves Negroes free of charge."[35] Guinn's comedic comments and the Jack Spratt sit-in demonstration opened the door to one particularly noticeable fact about the formative years of CORE. Participation, so far, remained predominantly white. The Jack Spratt protests reflected this obvious absence. Sadly, Joe Guinn's girlfriend, Fleta Jones, and Farmer's reluctant first love, Winnie Christie, comprised half of the Jack Spratt black protestors in the first mini demonstration.[36] The second Jack Spratt sit-in reconfirmed this issue with its five black participants out of the twenty plus protestors.[37]

Early CORE members knew full well the difficulties of gaining a black membership if participation hinged on an ideological allegiance to Satyagraha. According to Farmer, at some point in this period, he, Robinson, and Fisher discussed the crux of their conundrum. "This could not be a white movement. I [Farmer] observed that Negroes who came in would be ends-oriented rather than means-oriented. They would join the movement because the program worked, produced results; not because of an ideological commitment to nonviolence."[38]

CORE members never quite hashed out the possible tensions that might come with large numbers of black ends-oriented or the possible failings of adherence to nonviolence. The focus, simply, was in more numbers to create an interracial membership. However, the numbers game wreaked havoc on CORE in other ways. FOR salivated over the potential power of an active youth movement under its organizational umbrella. After the Jack Spratt protests, the organization declared itself the Committee of Racial Equality (two years later, the organization retained the acronym but renamed itself Congress of Racial Equality) and began investigation of discrimination cases among downtown Chicago loop restaurants. Increased participation and public attention on Chicago CORE generated interest in FOR, and forced CORE founders to handle the growing problem of FOR's interference in CORE's structure and philosophical development.

CORE underwent a change that fundamentally (re)shaped its character in the 1940s. Despite George Houser's clear assertion that the pre-CORE entity was a Brotherhood experimental group, by September 1942 the organization had a dialectical history—with Houser claiming it had a nuclear beginning in a FOR race cell group and Farmer referring to Chicago CORE as the pre-Brotherhood Mobilization experiment. Actually, it was both, though obviously precipitated by the Brotherhood proposal.[39] The conflict in CORE origin, however, harbingered the first of many issues during this era—all of which vacillated around one central dispute. Who or what should represent CORE's philosophical center. The two origin stories symbolically reflected an underlying fight to define CORE's membership, and by extension its organizational belief system—pacifist led crusade (FOR race cell) or mass nonviolent movement (Brotherhood Mobilization).

Much of this argument became signified in tense debates regarding CORE's independence—or lack thereof. In September 1942, FOR firmly placed CORE under the directive of a designated advisory council. Or rather, it determined that the Brotherhood Mobilization Plan needed an advisory council. That advisory group, the Non-Violent Direct Action (NVDA) Committee, presumed that Chicago CORE, a Brotherhood experiment, naturally fell under its jurisdiction. The council further hinted that since the Brotherhood experiment was well underway in Chicago, James Farmer should be moved to New York to expand the experiment in conjunction with J. Holmes Smith, or other persons who could assist in filling the gaps in Farmer's "administrative weakness." FOR also charged the NVDA Committee with facilitating member interest and participation in CORE, or other nonviolent direct action projects.[40] Thus, the Brotherhood proposal clearly outlined the structure for any COREs that followed the Chicago branch. The NVDA sense of itself as CORE's council, however, was not in sync with what CORE leaders had in mind—particularly NVDA's tendency to try and dictate every aspect of CORE. Now that expansion plans for the Brotherhood Mobilization project were underway, committee members' first task was to change CORE's name. Purportedly, the question of title resulted from concerns that organizing might become difficult in some regions if "racial equality" partially made up the acronym name.[41]

It also didn't help that the committee was made up of FOR members who, in one way or the other, disliked CORE's presence or status within FOR. In most cases, despite the National Council's designation of CORE as independent, FOR administrators intended to benefit from an active, Gandhian-inspired youth group. Without CORE or successful nonviolent demonstrations, it was difficult to argue that FOR should be on the front wave of such a movement, a task made harder by the conservative pacifists within FOR. CORE either served FOR's larger mission, or sucked up resources while it operated separately—the latter being the least preferred. Worries over FOR's relationship to CORE led to various efforts by A. J. Muste and others, to stymy its independence. At every turn, Muste attempted to dictate CORE's goals, philosophy, and staff by directing and curbing the organization's growth. Other FOR staff raised questions about CORE activities appearing in FOR bulletins, staff and resource use, CORE's ill preparedness to be a mass organization, its insistence on distinguishing itself from FOR, and its refusal to accept FOR direction.[42] Farmer generally had an up-hill battle serving as the only CORE leader within the NVDA Committee, which included A. J. Muste and John Swomley, the associate secretary of FOR, who systematically argued for CORE to officially become a FOR program or go its own way.[43]

Luckily, over the course of CORE's early months, disputes with FOR amounted to only small skirmishes. Still small in size, it was not yet worth it to aggressively control CORE. Throughout 1942 and 1943, the Chicago-based group continually met, developed its configuration, and concentrated on small desegregation projects. Advised by A.M.E. minister Archibald Carey and Doctor Art Falls, the group initially housed its office in the black church of Reverend Carey.[44] CORE continued investigation into Chicago downtown restaurants, and negotiated with various managers of segregated diners. Stoner Restaurant became their next biggest project and its toughest opponent. Talks with the manager ended unsuccessfully, and CORE members were forced to move to direct action once again. The Stoner demonstration progressed into the next year, but eventually triumphed.[45]

The restaurant sit-ins gave CORE symbolic but genuine successes on which to build and gain additional race equality cells. In the first year of its life, Farmer along with FOR staffer and future organizer for the 1963 March on Washington, Bayard Rustin, established chapters in various cities they visited while on FOR speaking engagements. Farmer, along with other CORE founders, also crafted the organization's methodology and stages of protest. Utilizing *War without Violence*, CORE's "Action Discipline" reproduced Shridharani's step-by-step analysis of Gandhi's protest strategy: investigation, negotiation, and direct action. Annually, the organization made changes to its "Action Discipline," adding greater detail when necessary and crafting a set of rules and expectations for CORE members. Action Discipline eventually expanded to include eleven codes of conduct, including suffer the anger of your opponent, harbor no malice but remain humble and understanding, submit to assault without retaliation, no malicious slogans, noncooperation with segregated institutions, and no unauthorized actions on behalf of CORE or in direct contradiction to designated CORE leader.

By its first April anniversary, CORE had several chapters including Denver, Detroit, Syracuse, Columbus (OH), Baltimore, and, of course, Chicago. However, it still failed to gain a substantive number of black members to its participant roll. This barely changed, even with the addition of the Columbus Vanguard League. A fifteen-hundred-member strong off-shoot of the NAACP, the Vanguard League formed one year prior to the Committee of Racial Equality. Before joining CORE, the league practiced nonviolence protest, had an interracial base (though only a few whites), had standing in the black community, and reflected the 1930s traditions of Don't-Buy-Where-You-Can't-Work campaigns—economic boycotts of neighborhood businesses that refused to hire black residents.[46]

But despite the presence of the Vanguard League, few local COREs reflected an equal racial balance. Farmer chalked this up to the unpopularity of Gandhian thought. In his mind, "there was no shortage of whites with an awareness of Gandhi and interest in nonviolence, but were the blacks?"[47] Truthfully, Farmer must have known better. There were certainly African Americans leaders, theologians, and activists exploring nonviolence. Gandhi's appeal to the youthful and receptive Farmer was part of a growing interest by the black community in the Indian independence movement. For decades, Gandhi led a movement for freedom using Satyagraha. In laypersons' terms, he used nonviolent direct action and civil disobedience to protest British colonialist control of India. His use of nonviolence became a mass movement that, little by little, debilitated Britain's control over the Indian people. More than just a philosophy of Mohandas Gandhi, nonviolence proved to be a vital and effective tool for ousting the British Empire, a fact noted by colonized and oppressed peoples around the world.

The African American community was no less intrigued by the events of the Indian movement. As early as 1917, Hubert Harrison and later W. E. B. DuBois and Marcus Garvey referenced the Indian independence movement in speeches and writings.[48] By the time Benjamin Mays visited in 1936, a number of exchanges had taken place between black leaders and Gandhi and/or his acolytes. Howard Thurman, for example, first encountered Miriam Slade, an Englishwoman who left home to live with Gandhi. Through Slade, Thurman contacted Gandhi. Notably, the interest in the issue of inequality was not just one-sided. Thurman recalled being almost bombarded with questions by Gandhi about slavery, black religion, voting rights, lynching, public school education, and discrimination.[49] During his conversations with Gandhi, Thurman astutely noted the similarities in Negro spirituals and Gandhi's message of nonviolence and love force. Gandhi famously noted that if this were true, then it was "through the Afro-American that the unadulterated message of non-violence would be delivered to the world."[50]

Howard Thurman, Benjamin Mays, and others, many of whom attended or worked at Howard University, were major conduits for teaching and exploring the potential of Gandhi's Satyagraha for the African American freedom fight. Although it was unclear to what degree Thurman or Benjamin Mays actively advocated for civil disobedience, it was clear that they introduced their students to the idea. While it was Thurman who placed James Farmer on the path, Mays played the same role for Martin Luther King Jr. Mays acquainted the future 1960s civil rights leader with Gandhian work and philosophy during King's undergraduate years at Morehouse College.

The power of Gandhi's message hardly limited itself to a leader elite. Black newspapers discussed the utility of civil disobedience protest and helped to inculcate the idea in a broad fashion. Interest in nonviolent direct action reached such proportions that *Negro Digest* published a poll in 1943 asking participants to weigh the merits of its uses for black freedom. Approximately one-third agreed, an important signal that nonviolent action could gain traction in the black psyche.[51] Gandhi represented a strong symbol in the black imagination across class, which was also illustrated by black sociologist Horace Cayton's 1942 piece "Fighting for White Folks?" In it he claimed that even in the "poolrooms on South State Street in Chicago," India became the center of conversation. Of course, it hardly stood alone as a symbol of colored peoples rise around the world. The global upsurge of "dark people throughout the world" demonstrated a broader movement afoot for freedom and independence.[52] However, Gandhi's nonviolent strategy clearly and profoundly struck a chord among a broad African American audience.

But, before Negroes could deliver the message of nonviolence to the world, the idea first needed a receptive audience in the black community. Even then, not all Negroes would agree with the "message." Sue Bailey Thurman, for example, questioned Gandhi about its applicability in the face of lynching, and asked "how do you apply this [nonviolence] . . . where there are guns and lynching at the end of every trial, and there are no real trials anyway, and no courts to protect people?"[53]

It was a difficult question to answer even for Gandhi, and FOR executive secretary A. J. Muste hardly made the problem easier to solve with his insistence that CORE retain a pacifist character. This partly explained Farmer's worry that black Americans would not philosophically embrace Gandhian nonviolence. FOR added an extra layer of expectancy that black Americans should not only embrace CORE as a nonviolent direct action group, but as a *pacifist* nonviolent direct action group.

James Farmer, and Bernice Fisher especially, refused to accept the two as synonymous. Farmer's secular approach to nonviolence grated on Muste's nerves, but this perspective was not without precedent. Shridharani himself was the epitome of an atypical Gandhian acolyte. There was no robe, sandals, or prayerful poses for him. Shridharani was a portly, woman-chasing, chain-smoking, lavender silk shirt and ruby ring jewelry wearing philosopher who viewed many of Gandhi's ideas through a political light.[54]

And he was not the first person in Farmer's life to propagate this view of Gandhian philosophy. Farmer spent a great deal of his early graduate school days with George Goetz aka V. F. Calverton, a Marxist literary critic of the 1920s and 1930s infamously known for his writings on sex.[55] Farmer, himself, recalled his experiences with Calverton as being a period of university respites and "ribaldry" weekends. Given Calverton's hedonistic behaviors and general propensity for sexual promiscuity, one could only guess at the tawdry, perhaps bawdy, experiences of an impressionable young Farmer. However, Calverton was a keen intellect and his take on "the little brown man" steered Farmer toward a broader view of Gandhi as a powerful "strategist and tactician."[56]

CORE's challenge involved proving the strategic utility of nonviolent direct action for a wide-ranging base, black or white, but especially black. Pacifist philosophy or the spiritual focus on Gandhian nonviolence only muddied the water. This perspective gave additional force to founder decisions to keep CORE independent from FOR and broadly defined by the tactic and aim of nonviolent action for interracial equality.[57] It was also assumed by some founders that future CORE would include mass black participation, though the kind of participation was similarly at issue. Larger ends-oriented numbers potentially could hamper ideological adherence even to nonviolence as a strategy.

Conversely, not every CORE founder embraced such mass secular inclusion. James Robinson and to some extent George Houser leaned toward a smaller interracial cadre, because such extensive inclusion created a high degree of varied or ambiguous perspectives on nonviolence.[58] Thus, debate over CORE membership was not just a game of numerical figures. Philosophical consistency was at stake. Plus, it pointed to a major fracture in thought about CORE's role in and relationship to the black community.

A. J. Muste was quick to point out this "weakness" in CORE, implying that Farmer's refusal to accept a pacifist center within a mass-oriented CORE amounted to hiding his pacifism.[59] The accusation was repeated again by Bayard Rustin, who Farmer felt, in siding with Muste, attempted to undermine CORE's independence from FOR.[60] Farmer believed, and rightly so, that Muste's accusation was part of a larger effort to undercut an independent CORE. And so, conflict came again and again over CORE's position within FOR. No sooner than CORE's formation,

Muste expressed his concern that the organization was moving too quickly for its own good. Mostly, the issue was that CORE moved less with speed so much as without supervision from the Nonviolent Direct Action Committee. CORE continued to be a divisive issue between FOR and Farmer, so much so that he accused Muste of being both saint and Machiavelli when it came to CORE.[61]

Machiavellian Muste made a full appearance shortly before the first annual CORE conference in June 1943. That moment represented not only the fulfillment of the Brotherhood project, but also a blatant head to head between FOR and CORE. While CORE determined the role of its national office and chapter relations, FOR, or rather Muste, was busy arguing against the formation of an official national organization. Despite Muste and the NVDA Committee's suggestion, CORE went full speed ahead with its decision to hold its first annual conference. It resulted in a long letter by Muste, which George Houser and James Farmer received only days before the Chicago meeting. In it, Muste advised the two on the futility of creating a national organization and contended that this conference had only two possible outcomes. In the first, and "better option," Muste recommended that this conference serve as a clearinghouse for additional information about CORE, discussion of future organizational structure, and preliminary review of objectives, mission, and goals. Ultimately, no attempt would be made to set up a "rigid" national office. The second probability, not endorsed by Muste, included the formation of a national organization created without consideration to democratic principles, because it excluded other CORE chapters unable to send representatives. In Muste's language, this path also carelessly ignored the political problems inherent in CORE's relationship and interaction with the NAACP, Urban League, or MOWM, and forced the struggling small group to build a budget, office, and staff, which inevitably led to a fight over resources and funds.[62]

Muste was anything but supportive of a national CORE organization, to say the least. He also questioned, not surprisingly, the nature of FOR's relationship to such an organization. So far its patronage of CORE had been indirect, but Muste finally stated his obvious intention to have CORE frankly and openly sponsored by FOR, especially given the fact that FOR staff made up CORE's leadership. Muste maneuvered to situate FOR as a leading catalyst for a nonviolent direct action movement. Since CORE was a spinoff experiment of Brotherhood Mobilization, open support from FOR would make an independent CORE superfluous. By extension, according to Muste, "no one who has experience and a sense of responsibility will want to form new organizations if existing ones can do the job." In other words, the Fellowship of Reconciliation could do the job if CORE officially placed itself under the parent organization.[63]

The letter finally ended with Muste's musings about a potential position change for both Farmer and Houser which might expand their FOR work on nonviolent direct action. As Muste noted, he especially wished them to know this "now" because it indubitably would be a "factor in your thinking in connection with the CORE conference." He also admitted that "though this obviously suggests very large scale questions of strategy, etc.," they could meet, "to think and pray" on the meaning of these changing dynamics. Muste ended the letter with a request to see each of them in the fall, although one could hardly miss the obvious intention. Figuratively, the letter constituted three pages of stick and one page of carrot to rustle Houser, Farmer, CORE, or all three, into submission.[64]

David Schwartz, FOR National Council member, was particularly perturbed by the letter and quickly met with Swomley to express his outrage regarding Muste's political maneuvering. Schwartz also pointed out that the effort backfired, and that the letter had clearly passed among FOR members at the CORE conference, many of whom did not take well to the authoritarian nature of Muste's "recommendations." Scwartz also had little good to say about Farmer, Houser, or Fisher either. From his perspective, the trio were equally heavy handed in controlling the direction of the CORE conference—especially Farmer.[65]

CORE's decision to go rogue from FOR precipitated a series of back-and-forth memorandum between Swomley and Muste—all of which reflected a calculated attempt to bend CORE to the will of FOR. The Houser, Farmer, Fisher triumvirate became a factor that Swomley insisted should be taken into account when dealing with FOR's own direct action programming and Department of Race Relations. Swomley's take on the matter was that neither Houser nor Farmer would accept working on a FOR race relations program without it being tied to CORE, though he opposed the idea as a waste of FOR resources if CORE remained independent. Indeed, FOR would now have to back CORE, form its own group, or join with another.[66]

It also didn't help that Farmer dedicated his time to CORE activities at the expense of FOR's work with race relations and partnership plans with A. Philip Randolph's MOWM. Muste assigned Rustin, and later Farmer, to aid A. Philip Randolph and MOWM by pushing through a nonviolent direct action strategy. However, Farmer dismissively insisted that MOWM's civil disobedience strategy was just another stroke of Randolph's political pressure campaign, and it, like the originally planned march, would disappear. MOWM could be taught by CORE to "swim," but it would eventually do so alone. Should it be successful, CORE could still retain the mantel of vanguard group, but either way "CORE and Brotherhood Mobilization" were unrelated to MOWM's changing direction. According to Farmer, though CORE may not become a national movement, it should still prepare to "take the field."[67]

Despite acknowledging MOWM's potential, Farmer's flippant disregard led him to abandon MOWM's late June 1943 Chicago conference right at the moment

MOWM delegates were to decide whether to incorporate civil disobedience strategy. A Detroit riot only a month prior brought up questions about any mass campaign's ability to remain nonviolent.[68] Muste sent Rustin and Farmer to help usher in a positive verdict, but Farmer disappeared from the last sessions. Well, not quite disappeared. He was across town working on CORE-related activities. Rustin was so vexed by Farmer's abandonment that he argued that Farmer should be fired.[69] For Farmer's part, he'd clearly shed any pretense of doing FOR-related work, even though his absence from MOWM's 1943 conference peeked the annoyance and frustration of both Bayard Rustin and John Swomley.

Effectively, it marked the beginning of the end of Farmer's relationship with FOR. Following the first CORE conference, various FOR staff began to recount stories about Farmer's wishes to leave FOR and work for CORE full time. There were also other significant reasons why Farmer might have disappeared the last two days of the MOWM conference. The 1942 Report of the Committee on Program and Strategy had already successfully voted to accept nonviolent direct action techniques, thanks to the presence of MOWM committee member Pauli Murray. Although MOWM obviously accepted nonviolent direct action, the strategy had yet to deal with the key issue of civil disobedience, nonviolent direct action irrespective of legal prohibitions.

Secondly, the MOWM conference followed almost two weeks after the first CORE conference in mid-June 1943, when Muste sought to undermine CORE's independence from FOR and expansion as a national organization. Added to that, Farmer believed Randolph only intended to use Gandhian nonviolence and civil disobedience to give more life to a dying MOWM. As Farmer snidely noted, one could only "cry wolf" so often.[70] Then, of course, Muste also crafted various plans to connect with MOWM and make it FOR's conduit into the black community—which would crush the small, newly formed CORE. The combined implications lent itself to the stronger possibility that Farmer left the MOWM conference as an act of his own version of nonviolent noncooperation. Swomley, however, had a different take. He believed Farmer's behavior resulted in an upstaging of MOWM, failure to keep FOR commitments, an uptick in completing CORE reports and required documents, and a decline in timely submission of FOR-related materials. An irate Swomley wrote Muste, July 11, 1943, and proposed his own Machiavellian plans for Farmer and CORE.

1. Deny Farmer the Race Relations position or give it to him if he willingly made CORE an official FOR project.
2. Place Rustin in the position of Race Relations secretary over Farmer.
3. Locate Rustin somewhere *other than* Chicago, especially while George Houser was present or move Houser elsewhere.

4. Persuade George Houser to support CORE's permanent placement under FOR, and persuade Houser to influence Farmer in this
   direction.
5. Choose two paths for Farmer after his refusal to acquiesce. Fire
   Farmer. Or, "use him to the fullest in FOR work until he resigns."[71]

Swomley's memorandum contoured a step-by-step process to reward, regulate, or punish Farmer and Houser, and thus CORE. Meanwhile, Rustin's reward came with its own set of control mechanisms in place.

If Muste chose the final solution, Swomley planned to take Farmer to the West coast on a heavy speaking schedule. He also acknowledged that although "pacifist negroes with their [Rustin and Farmer] ability are hard to find," Rustin "intimated" to Swomley that a change in the Race Relations Department would need to occur if he were to continue with FOR. The decision was clear. Remove Farmer.[72] Muste also shared Rustin's belief that Farmer was a "problem" and that the now twenty-three-year-old was a "wreck when it comes to organization work"—an irony since their initial complaint was that all he did was CORE work.[73]

Yet again, buried within Swomley's staff "reorganization" plan, was the crux of the problem. Farmer battled FOR because CORE could not draw black participation if it insisted on being pacifist. Thus, Farmer rejected his original idea to associate with FOR and noted that he wrongly argued in his original memorandum for an umbrella relationship. FOR National Council effectively did CORE a favor, but Muste still viewed CORE as a pacifist instrument.[74] Farmer brazenly rebuked the idea of a FOR-directed CORE, and finally told Muste "the masses of Negroes will not become pacifists. Being Negro for them [was] tough enough without being pacifists, too."[75]

Muste was never satisfied with this answer. By fall 1943, FOR began to make a move against Farmer and Houser, as well as CORE. Muste transferred Farmer from Chicago to New York as part of a "promotion," which Farmer viewed more as a descent into the politically lethal world of pacifists "where deadly traps were to be set."[76] His assessment was the truth as George Houser also soon learned. Houser responded to Muste's pre-conference letter with wary interest in an expanded nonviolent direct action position, though he philosophically believed that CORE should retain its independence.[77] However, unlike Farmer, Houser claimed that he'd rather it not be a mass organization but a small disciplined group that could draw on larger participants in specific antidiscrimination projects. Realistically speaking, Houser could say little else. The handwriting was on the wall, FOR would not accept CORE as a national mass organization.[78]

Swomley reiterated his position that there was no need for CORE to work under FOR or receive financial aid and personnel, if members refused to accept guidance from a "responsible" Non-violent Direct Action Committee. Muste agreed with Swomley's stance, and argued that Houser could not have an independent CORE while FOR put its resources into it.[79] Of course, FOR hardly ranked among the largest or wealthiest of organizations. Funds were tight, although they were not impoverished, and thus it was not unreasonable to worry about the cost of supporting an independent organization, even if FOR originally set the terms.

Still, Houser countered with a suggestion for an alternate national organization of nonviolent direct actionists, originally based within FOR, but still operating independently. NDAs would either create nonviolent groups or work through other groups, unhampered by the conservative bent of FOR's National Council. Houser's idea amounted to a revamp of CORE but under FOR control and with the pacifist slant Muste so wanted.[80]

Nevertheless, Muste was unwilling to accept any independent groups or ideas separate from FOR as the designated nonviolent movement leader. He'd staked much of his writings and FOR tenure on a belief that nonviolent action by pacifists could generate a movement.[81] In fact, from his perspective, there could be no righteous freedom effort not tethered to Christian-based pacifism. Movements without this spiritual mooring potentially stood the danger of succumbing to violence, so he would not back any crusade without a pacifist center. To drive home the point, Muste made note that surely Houser could discern the difference between "devoting much time and energy to a non-pacifist agency such as CORE and on the other hand devoting time to another pacifist agency." As Muste told Houser, if he "could work along some such lines as I have indicated . . . I am myself strongly disposed to think that you are the person to undertake it."[82] In a nutshell, Muste intended to have his way—whether through CORE or a separate FOR program.

Houser was willing to accept the mission, though he still naively argued and believed CORE's independence from FOR could be maintained. By February 1944, Houser's new position with FOR was a done deal. Now a national staff member, he was given a salary, budget, office expenses, and a to-be-determined office location in Detroit, Pittsburgh, or Cleveland. The created position had no title, no list of duties, no budget, no city designation, and thus no office location. Houser selected his title and set the program parameters.[83] Despite the amorphous nature of the position, George Houser officially became Non-Violent Action Secretary. His duties included working with CORE and labor groups and stimulating nonviolent action projects for FOR.[84] The cross discussion between Houser and Muste begged the question of whether Muste found an entrée into controlling CORE through Houser. Letters between the two certainly inferred as much.

Though Houser likely carried some favor with Muste by agreeing to take the position, like Farmer, he too received a lesson from FOR. The proposal for George Houser's duties reinforced FOR's stance that CORE was not to become a large-scale national organization, and if he continued to spend any more time perpetuating that mission, he "ought to be on the CORE rather than the FOR pay-roll." Of course, Muste claimed to support CORE becoming a strong independent organization, but only if it could manage to do so on its own. Even if CORE should by some miracle become financially and structurally independent, Houser still had to decide between CORE and continuation with FOR.[85] FOR had now cut Houser and CORE off at the knees.

The stage was set to push the preeminence of pacifist-styled nonviolence over the more political utilitarian Shridharani. CORE had based its intellectual foundation on his advocacy of nonviolence as strategically secular versus spiritually motivated. Farmer's determination to govern CORE by this direct action style enabled maximum black participation, but FOR (and Houser, to some degree) insisted on Richard Gregg's vision from the *Power of Nonviolence*. Gregg's version took over CORE in the summer of 1944, when the second annual CORE conference elected Houser executive secretary of its new national office. Positioned as the only national CORE staff, Houser directed CORE under Muste's thumb, and thus, necessarily, reflected the goodwill, pacifist aspects of nonviolence. The intense emphasis by Houser and other CORE members on "goodwill," nonviolent direct action, tended to make challenging racial inequality a heavy-handed process of extended negotiation before moving along to direct action. George Houser's focus on acting with a "reconciling spirit" and "redemptive influence upon the wrongdoer" placed as much, perhaps more, interest in process as outcome.[86] Expectantly, the Gregg approach translated itself into the literature produced by CORE as outreach materials and in its first history, *CORE: A Brief History*, authored by Houser.[87] In effect, FOR/George Houser's viewpoint of CORE became the dominant perspective within and about the organization.

Cofounder Bernice Fisher, however, balked at the notion. She and others wished to avoid anything that smacked of FOR control or CORE as a FOR front. In fact, Fisher later accused Houser of wishing to "direct" CORE's development and feared that his allegiance to FOR and position as Non-Violent Action Secretary would lead Houser to blur organizational distinctions.[88] Fisher was especially insistent that there be a clear demarcation between the two. According to her unpublished account, "Confessions of an Ex-Liberal," CORE founders knew full well "even in the first months . . . that some of us believed in nonviolence as a principle and some of us believed in it as an effective technique." She went on to note that a "deep resentment" developed over CORE's origin among many CORE leaders and led some to unfailingly dissociate CORE from FOR.[89]

By extension, Fisher was also wary of the goodwill focus. Fisher expressed reticence over some members' attachment to nonviolence as a tool of education and conversion versus a serious confrontation against racism in America. In fact, she noted that many members were "woefully" unaware of black political and economic issues. Fischer felt that the lynchpin for CORE's successful 1944 Detroit conference hinged on attendee's recognition that CORE must begin to use "*real economic pressures*" to bring about change. This could become an ongoing development in which CORE might eventually "find it necessary to go beyond 'public places' if we're to attract the solid leadership we need."[90] Ironically, the tables turned on Fisher when a new Detroit CORE member challenged Fisher's insistence that the CIO be given time to unionize Sams Department Store before forcing the store to hire Negro clerks through a CORE demonstration. The new member defended direct action in lieu of unionizing and the attitude of "slow, educational tactics of 'some people.'"[91]

Of course, Fisher was not adverse to public accommodation desegregation as a reasonable start. However, CORE's separation from FOR allowed it to assert economic and political struggle over "witness" (a religious term for testimony, preach, or education) as an act of protest.[92] CORE could never sustain a mass movement if tethered to a belief that the masses of "Negroes" would concern themselves with the transformation of the perpetrator over a transformation of their material existence. For Fisher, that pacifist/goodwill would eventually hinder direct action's appeal. Accordingly, she contended that combining efforts with FOR "might well spell the end of dnva [direct nonviolent action] in the race struggle," altogether.[93]

Although Bernice Fisher hoped a balance could be found between the means/ends groups, she herself began to question the wisdom of absolute submission to nonviolent direct action.[94] She wrote to Houser that she found absolutes "demonic," and thus hesitated to argue for total adherence to nonviolence. According to Fisher, such dogma could be self-defeating in any struggle, and in the race question "it would be ineffective."[95] Plus, it made sense to her that there were occasions where violence might, in fact, be necessary. At minimum, this limited and suppressed other possibilities, strategies, and ideas. Her almost traitorous abandonment of both pacifism and nonviolence raised ire and concern from Swomley and Muste, who both promptly contacted George Houser. Fisher, however, was on her way out the proverbial pacifist door. She finally withdrew membership in FOR partly due to growing dissension over CORE.

Houser responded to Swomley and Muste's agitation by claiming that Fisher understood CORE's nonviolence depended on a pacifist nucleus. However, her backslide stemmed from a superficial fear that it was "a liability in one's politics to be known too much as a pacifist." The result was that she "bended over backwards" to ensure it was understood that FOR and CORE were separate entities. Houser assured the two that he intended to prevent any attempt by Fisher to scuttle plans to establish pacifist-inspired, nonviolent interracial groups. Assuaging Muste and Swomley's unease, Houser wrote, "I don't let her ideas along the lines of reacting against pacifists in CORE bother me one bit from pushing ahead pretty much in the program we agreed upon last September in my office in Chicago. I shall continue to work in that way. I expect to do as much as I can in my new work."[96]

Houser's disregard of Fisher's "contradictory self" soon became agitation when he learned from Swomley that Fisher actually questioned allegiance to nonviolence while lecturing on behalf of CORE in 1944. Houser knew Fisher had reservations regarding nonviolent strategy (especially given her transition into labor activism in St. Louis), still, it was unthinkable that she would raise the idea in any official capacity as a CORE representative or worse yet, as one of its founders. It was sacrilege. Houser told Swomley he would take the matter to CORE's newly formed executive committee.[97]

But, the problem hardly limited itself to the radicalized Fisher. Her jump ship to the ends-oriented side was only one complication in the FOR bid to determine the life of CORE. Outside and inside, the ends-oriented groups complicated CORE's membership selection, philosophical trajectory, tactical approach, and community relations; plus, it upset the equilibrium of the "goodwillers."

MOWM, for example, embodied the perfect counter model to nonviolence as goodwill, interracial mass action. Satyagraha in MOWM hands took unexpected turns in both organizational structure and social vision. Central to this distinction, Gandhian nonviolence necessitated no interracial membership, only its acceptance as a tool for freedom. MOWM was all black and fervently believed in a black-led movement, though Farmer criticized it, among many reasons, for not reflecting CORE's interracial spirit.[98] This was not to say Farmer totally disagreed with MOWM. He was quite enamored with Randolph, along with other members of CORE. Nonetheless, MOWM's black leadership sensibility troubled Farmer, who wrote that "in order to be effective in destroying racist tendencies the organizational instrument used must be consistent with the ends sought." "Racial chauvinism" had no place in a freedom struggle that depended upon all people to resist and practice noncooperation against segregation.[99]

A. J. Muste and Bayard Rustin also disliked MOWM's all-black character, though they lacked Farmer's convictions.[100] Additionally, MOWM's willingness to accept sister white groups potentially gave FOR the entrée into the black community it so badly wanted with the added bonus of a CORE withering on the vine. Jay Holmes-Smith, Harlem Ashram creator and Nonviolent Direct Action Committee member, particularly advocated the formation of such groups. He too argued that CORE was not adequately large enough to take on such a venture, and that a white nonviolent group or "Friends of the MOWM" should be formed to take over such a job.[101]

FOR member and CORE supporter Pauli Murray however actively sought for MOWM to retain its racial character. In fact, she served on MOWM's 1942 constitutional committee, which designed it that way. Although Farmer characterized it as "racial chauvinism," Murray had the opposite view. The committee re-codified MOWM's all-black identity and asserted that this decision was not a nod to black nationalism. In their words, MOWM did not promote the emigrationist impulse or the back-to-Africa movements. Hence, the committee distinguished black nationalism as distinct from black control, black financing, black leadership, black responsibility, and black solutions.[102]

According to MOWM, whites were welcome to work in friendly citizens' groups with MOWM, but their presence as members regrettably enabled financial and management dependence, or created internal confusion. The all-black composition helped to break down "slave psychology," nourished black independence and faith, and created room for black people to free themselves unfettered from external influence.[103] Murray was well read on Shridharani, a member of FOR, and had lived in J. Smith's Harlem Ashram after her time with MOWM. Despite her MOWM stance, she still considered herself an interracialist.

Ironically then, MOWM illustrated the logical extension of Farmer's belief that the mass movement must include black Americans who more likely tended to be ends-oriented. Inevitably, the issue of ends-oriented influence within any organization led to a broader question of who controlled the movement. If, at any point, the ends-oriented felt their stake larger in a freedom struggle, as in MOWM's case, the composition of leadership would fall under attack or potentially change to reflect a larger ends-oriented presence. For Murray and Randolph, then, their right to leadership characterized the ends-oriented, not the strategy they followed. And yet MOWM still considered itself an espouser of nonviolent direct action philosophy.

From 1942 to 1944, CORE was far from taken over by MOWM-minded black members, particularly given its large white membership and continued pacifist control. Although CORE chapters increased in these years, they were overwhelmingly white, youthful, highly educated, midwestern groups. Though FOR/Houser's pacifist proclivities clearly showed in CORE's national office, local chapters were also influenced by pacifist presence. These believers served as some of the strongest chairs of CORE chapters, and many were associated with FOR. Despite endeavors to hinder FOR influence, many CORE chapters tailored themselves to interracial, goodwill nonviolence.[104]

Conversely, pacifist control did not mean black membership or leadership was absent or that participation in CORE chapters hinged only on this belief. The ends-oriented sporadically appeared in CORE chapters and projects, despite their smaller numbers. As executive secretary, George Houser soon learned that navigating these contentious waters would not be easy, especially when left to carry the ball for national CORE. Houser defended CORE from FOR obstruction and sustained it through the highs and lows of its fledging creation.

Meanwhile, other CORE founders remained connected, but their presence became tangential to the organization's life. Farmer and Fisher, so crucial to CORE's origin, loosened their ties. Bernice Fisher left for St. Louis in the late 1940s, joined the labor movement, and started a local St. Louis CORE chapter. Joe Guinn, Bob Chino, and Hugo Victoreen floated away after CORE's first years of formation. Robison remained in Chicago and continued a relationship with Houser and CORE, but moved on to other projects after conflicts with Bernice Fisher.[105]

By summer 1945, Farmer left FOR altogether. Tensions finally came to a head, and the organization no longer saw any usefulness for a staff person with different priorities—especially CORE-related priorities. Although Muste initially hoped to keep Farmer around as head of the Race Relations Department, Swomley advocated his removal and by May 1945 Muste agreed. Farmer left under a face-saving "mutual" agreement in which he noted his lack of interest in administrative work and his wish to replace his current activities with freelance writing. Houser's take on the matter was that Farmer was not a "good organizational man."[106] Consumed with finding employment, divorce, and remarriage, Farmer floated in, around, and out of CORE.

Founders had dispersed, but CORE grew. After its first two years of expansion, notoriety, and avoidance of a FOR takeover, Houser was left to guide new chapters, produce literature, and respond to growing interest in nonviolent direct action—all while catering to a hyper-scrutinizing FOR. Still, the seeds of dissension were sown. The debate between Fisher and Houser, Farmer and Muste foreshadowed approaching schisms in CORE philosophical/tactical strategies and relations with the black community. Farmer's distinction between ends-oriented and means-oriented further highlighted these divisions, and unintentionally revealed two major questions. Namely, why should black activists presume that only nonviolent direct action could effectively change the condition of inequality? Second, why should black members adhere to the notion that interracial brotherhood intrinsically extended to leadership?

Farmer, Fisher, and Robinson had temporarily retreated, but Houser would soon confront these questions. As the guiding force for the organization, where Houser went, so did CORE. Once FOR decided the budget and duties of their new Nonviolent Direct Action officer, it selected the city headquarters. It had to be in the Midwest, and it needed local support. FOR received the most feedback from its members in Cleveland, Ohio, and thus chose it as Houser's next destination. It was an eventful decision. Cleveland unearthed and threw into the open all the issues that emanated from the FOR/CORE pacifist struggle, MOWM's all-black proclivities, and the ends/means divisions. In Cleveland, CORE met its earliest challenge to goodwill philosophy and nonviolent strategy, and in this city experienced the first of many breaks from the "CORE-way."

# 2

# Negroes Will Not Be Pacifists

GEORGE HOUSER likely rued the day he formed Cleveland's first CORE chapter. From its beginning to its end, the chapter portended dissident challenges to goodwill, nonviolent direct action and interracialist brotherhood. Houser's reaction to the Cleveland chapter also revealed deeper failures in CORE's ability to deal with behavioral aberrations. This ineffectual response created problems that reverberated not only among other locals, but also within CORE national.

From 1944 to 1946, George Houser devoted his time to national CORE (with FOR permission) and ran the small branch of nonviolent activists. CORE headquarters/Cleveland chapter had no separate or regular office space. Membership started small but eventually approximated forty to seventy persons during its most active period until its 1949 decline. The chapter's most dedicated participants numbered around twenty, so meetings were small enough to hold at the local community center, Phillis Wheatley Association, or at the home of Eula Morrow, a member of CORE and mother of the second chapter chairman Juanita Morrow. Cleveland CORE consisted of educated working and middle class participants, though a few battled periods of unemployment. The exact ratio of black and white members remains unclear, but a minimum approximation of black members stood around one-third the total membership, though one-half the most active associates.[1]

Cleveland CORE supporters included a who's who of black Cleveland. William Otis Walker (W. O. Walker), editor of the *Call and Post*, avidly advocated for the interracialists. After the *Cleveland Call* and *Cleveland Post* merged in 1931, Walker transformed the newspaper into the strongest forum in Ohio for political and social empowerment. His individual activism lasted well into the late 1970s.[2] Clayborne George, formally one of Cleveland's black councilmen, gained political clout for his shrewd maneuvers to end overt discrimination at City Hospital.[3] Lawrence O. Payne, also a black city councilman; Chester Gillespie, legal council for the 1940s NAACP and CORE's advocate through the 1960s; Perry Jackson, municipal judge; and Clarence Sharpe, lawyer and community activist also advised CORE.[4]

Clarence Sharpe's backing had special significance. Sharpe was a co-leader of the Future Outlook League, an Ohio 1930s—Don't Buy Where You Can't Work—organization. The Don't-Buy campaigns began in the early 1930s, and spread west from New York to other urban centers.[5] It eventually came to Cleveland via John O. Holly, a black southerner and founder of the Future Outlook League. Established in February 1935, the group promoted black business ownership. However, recalcitrant white financial institutions plus urgent employment needs brought on by the Great Depression forced the FOL to reconstitute its mission. Instead, it concentrated energies on finding wage work for black Clevelanders, defense of unfairly fired laborers, and advocacy for employees who faced punitive pay cuts.[6]

FOL boycotts were, as a rule, loud and combative. The original action plan for their demonstrations required participants to act nonviolently while on the picket line. This proved temporary when protestors faced brutal harassment by the Cleveland police. Even rumors of violent FOL demonstrations became enough to warrant a police presence, despite evidence that it was the police who precipitated the violence. Worse, early opposition against FOL by Cleveland's black conservative elite gave the organization few alternatives. Without allies, demonstrations warranted self-defense from FOL members' perspective. According to historian Kimberly Phillips, black Clevelanders raised "in the small towns and rural communities of the South, where such actions were quite common" due to southern state violence, saw no discontinuity in FOL's nonviolent ideology and self-defense stance.[7]

Despite its controversial tactics, FOL managed to gain the backing of W. O. Walker, who used the *Call and Post* as a recruitment tool and public platform. Increased membership and successful boycotts, however, paralleled a decline in FOL's militancy. Defense industry employment in the World War II expanded exponentially and thus, further reduced FOL's relevance. Ironically, its popularity skyrocketed as its mission became more obsolete. FOL subsequently diversified its objectives and targeted de facto discrimination in public accommodations and education. The organization also featured lectures related to black politics and culture. Finally, in 1946, it published its own history, entitled appropriately, *The Future Is Yours.*[8]

In the post-1946 period, Future Outlook League's reduced activities permitted groups like the NAACP to siphon members. Internal friction and increased union openness—though slight—hit the organization hard. Once Holly became a power-broker in the local and state Democratic Party, FOL lost its most prominent leader. Even though FOL's significance waned, the organization had distinguished itself as a major organizer and a fearsome defender of the black community.[9]

Interestingly, the extremely large and powerful FOL took a great deal of interest in the small Cleveland CORE. But, the feeling was not mutual. Akin to the

Columbus Ohio Vanguard League, association with FOL might have enhanced CORE's standing and numbers throughout the black community. In fact, CORE could have linked its chapters with FOL branches throughout Ohio. Houser, however, brushed off interest from John O. Holly. Unsure of his intentions, Houser viewed Holly suspiciously and as "something of a nationalist."[10]

Of course, Holly's viewpoint was indicative of many black Clevelanders. Houser chose to ignore or avoid this reality and walked a fine line with FOL, along with other cases he viewed as nationalist. Cleveland had a long history of MOWM-like black activism, precipitated by overcrowding, unemployment, poor housing, and other forms of racial discrimination. In the post–Civil War period, early Cleveland barely had 1,300 black dwellers, less than 1 percent of the whole population. By 1900, black population density increased, and two decades later, the city exploded with the first Great Migration. It rapidly went from 8,448 black residents in 1910 to 34,451 in 1920. Most arrived from the upper South—North Carolina, Virginia, and Kentucky—or from the Deep South states of Georgia and Alabama. Over 90 percent settled on the east side of the city along the Central Avenue corridor.[11]

A mass influx poured into Central Avenue again during the Great Depression through the post–World War II industrial years. From 1930 to 1950, Cleveland's black community mushroomed beyond its original boundaries and spread farther east into the former Jewish and ethnic neighborhoods of Glenville, Hough, and Mount Pleasant.[12] The Central Avenue community, which seemed to have sprung from nowhere in the 1920s doubled its size in 1930 with twice as many residents at 71,899. The Great Depression slowed the steady stream, but numbers slightly enlarged during the 1940s to 84,504. Coupled with white flight, black population expanded slowly but surely to become 10 percent of the overall population in Cleveland. And every aspect of black life felt the pressure of a community that literally bulged at the seams.[13]

Occupation represented the hardest hit area. In the 1930s, joblessness rose dramatically with one-third of the black community unemployed. Black businesses, which previously employed some residents, declined. In 1934, the city labeled 80 percent of its black population relief cases.[14] Four years later, 43 percent of the black population received some form of welfare or relief services and 59.6 percent managed to obtain emergency work through the New Deal programs.[15]

Poor and inadequate housing during the "roaring" 1920s, which became the basis of ghetto formation, worsened in the 1930s. Eighty percent of black housing remained tied to the Central Avenue area and most homes turned over as rental property well into the 1950s. Building deterioration resulted from un-enforced housing codes, and many homes were without indoor bathrooms or running water. In one census tract, 99 percent of the dwellings fell under the rubric of substandard.[16] Yet, the resulting economic boon of the war industry left a loophole for some to escape to more middle-class neighborhoods, including the Glenville, Hough, and Mount Pleasant areas. However, such "middle-class" living was short lived given the aging homes, most of which were built in the late nineteenth century.

Cleveland constructed low-income residencies, but this failed to relieve neighborhood population pressure. Housing projects like Outhwaite and Carver Park only partly replaced housing torn down for slum clearance. At the same time, unemployed southern-born black Clevelanders resided in the least desirable and most crowded living spaces in Central Avenue. The most extreme example was evidenced by families who lived in boxcars that the train company divided into three single-family spaces.[17]

Ultimately, black Clevelanders, like many Negro communities, depended heavily on a self-help ideology to confront some of its community ills. Black businesses cropped up to serve their community. Barbershops, funeral homes, salons, restaurants, and speak easies became a normative part of the black social and economic experience. Community folks prized products like Brown Girl Bread, with the logo "made by brown hands, delivered by brown boys, with the brown girl on every loaf." Such campaigns epitomized self-help, black business patronage, and racial pride.[18]

Institution building in Cleveland not only reflected a necessity, but also a burgeoning sensibility, identity, and political dignity. Political power expanded with the population. The black vote determined the winner of the mayoral race in 1933, 1935, and 1937. Beginning in 1927 with Clayborne George, Thomas Fleming, and Dr. Eugene Gregg's city councilmen appointments, the Central Avenue area kept a steady slate of three black council members until the 1950s.[19]

Black self-help also crept its way into Cleveland, expectantly, through groups like the Universal Negro Improvement Association (UNIA), and even the NAACP. Dr. Leroy Bundy, a dentist and later power player in the Republican Party, began his political career as the first leader for Cleveland's UNIA branch in 1921. Cleveland UNIA was among the most active American chapters, and Marcus Garvey himself visited the city three times. A great deal of UNIA's activities centered on political activism. However, as Garvey's organization declined in the city, the equally strong Cleveland NAACP pursued and insisted on greater inclusion of black workers. Its strong working-class bent challenged UNIA's uniqueness as the sole representative of militant activism. By 1946, the Cleveland NAACP had over 10,000 members, and ranked sixth among NAACP chapters nationally.[20]

Perhaps the greatest illustration of black self-help occurred with the Mercy Hospital fight. Cleveland's Mercy Hospital Association was part of a wider national movement to open black hospitals and counter discrimination against medical practitioners and patients. The northern movement for black hospitals, though partially a response to health inequality, also reflected the rising tide of independence and self-help. Cleveland's black city leaders and medical professionals, very much aware of their underserved community, attempted to establish hospitals in 1915 and 1921 with no success. In 1926 proponents for a black hospital made headway with the Mercy Hospital Association. But, a bitter showdown ensued and divided the black community between those who viewed it as Jim Crowism and those who believed segregation necessitated institution building. Organizations across the city took a side, and the NAACP was so overwhelmed with black southern self-help espousers, it simply remained "neutral" on the issue.[21]

Whether it was the Future Outlook League, UNIA, NAACP, Mercy Hospital, or the brown girl bread made with brown hands, CORE national was surrounded on all sides with reminders of blackness. Institutions, businesses, organizations, and citizenry incorporated, advocated, or skirted against what amounted to black nationalism. CORE stepped into Cleveland with an interracialist and activist zeal, but with little in the way to offer black Clevelanders fighting against systemic, institutionalized racism. Certainly, its small size was no help either. Although Houser eschewed close ties with Holly, the Future Outlook League had nearly 10,000 to 18,000 dues payers across Ohio, and even it had difficulty dealing with these issues.[22]

Not surprisingly, this predilection toward self-help philosophy inevitably pushed Cleveland CORE to operate in line with sister chapters versus partnership with black organizations. Cleveland CORE worked on small-scale direct action projects that stimulated some interest, and followed the usual CORE guidelines: research, negotiate, protest when necessary. Initial actions were rather innocuous events. The *Call and Post*, for example, highlighted CORE's investigations of segregated restaurants. The chapter found none.[23] Cleveland CORE also advertised an interracial party fund-raiser for a two-month summer training workshop in Chicago.[24] Indeed, most CORE meetings advertised via the *Call and Post* seemed to concentrate on guest lecturers and speakers.[25]

The group even gathered a religious assembly called the Church of All Peoples. The effort stemmed from CORE's belief that religious institutions represented one of the most segregated spaces in the city. The church organized "Christian people across all radical, cultural, and denominational lines . . . to give full expression to the application of the principles of Jesus to our racial, political and social life today."[26] The Church of All Peoples actually boasted participation by a number of prominent Cleveland black ministers including Dr. Charles Spivey of St. John, A.M.E. and Dr. Bernard C. Clausen of Euclid Avenue Baptist Church—both of whom greatly supported CORE. The Church of All Peoples oftentimes seemed to garner more attention than any other project. Approximately two hundred attended the first meeting on April 28, 1946. The second public meeting scheduled for May 19 also had a heavy turnout.[27]

Aside from the Church of All Peoples and public lectures, Cleveland CORE's direct action projects mostly centered on public accommodation and entertainment. Despite its previous assertion that there were no discriminatory eateries, the group spent little time on ending discrimination at a restaurant called the Forum; a short negotiation and protest resulted in an end to that policy. Houser attempted to lead a CORE attack against discrimination at Skateland almost as soon as the chapter formed. It was the group's first foray into joint protests with the NAACP, CIO, Church Federation, and other groups. Houser later noted that the protest was not too well thought out and spontaneous action led to failure.[28]

Although Cleveland CORE launched direct action demonstrations here and there, its impact was nominal. Houser's insistence on an interracial movement, via an interracial goodwill method for an interracial end, certainly garnered some support, but it also slowed CORE progress when it bumped against ideological currents like self-help. Houser was not unaware of how these differences affected CORE. As executive secretary, he ran afoul of A. Philip Randolph's all-black-organization perspective when the former MOWM leader refused to cosponsor a 1945 interracial project in Washington, DC, without "Negroes of Washington themselves" taking the lead. Houser refused, and the endeavor was grounded, leaving CORE without a DC project.[29]

Locally, Houser's stance played itself out in the same ambivalent reaction. For instance, Cleveland chapter avoided the Forest City Hospital debate. Seemingly a simple project, the rather nasty internal argument over its predecessor, Mercy Hospital, made Forest City a point of heated contention. Forest City reignited old debates in Cleveland over self-help versus Jim Crow facilities. On this occasion, the NAACP did not internally divide and took an aggressively antagonistic stance against Forest City as a Jim Crow facility. However, the black Progressive Business Alliance, and W. O. Walker in the pages of the *Call and Post* heavily supported Forest City Hospital and directly challenged the NAACP's position. Walker castigated NAACP leaders for spending too much time on Forest City Hospital and less on the job of integration.[30]

Although Cleveland CORE and Houser publicly chose no side, twice it invited discussion and speakers on the subject of Forest City Hospital. Charles Lucas, NAACP executive secretary, delivered a report that characterized it as detrimentally bolstering Jim Crow.[31] Although CORE clearly empathized with the NAACP, not much was done in the way of Forest City Hospital protests. CORE timidly situated itself on the periphery of this dispute and avoided conflict with either faction.

The chapter received more encouragement in 1945 for its case to end discrimination at the Young Men's Christian Association (YMCA). The Cedar branch YMCA had served the black community for several years, but lacked a few amenities. The YMCA downtown branch had the facilities that Cedar Avenue lacked, including overnight stays, a gym, and a swimming pool. However, the downtown YMCA prohibited access to black patrons.[32]

The YMCA responded to CORE's accusations of discrimination by claiming that it integrated its summer camp, but CORE challenged this argument on the basis that different branches used the summer camp at different times. The organization condemned the YMCA for its policy and gathered signatures from its allies—W. O. Walker, Clayborne George, Clarence Sharpe, Lawrence O. Payne, Chester Gillespie, and Perry Jackson.[33]

Houser and three other members of CORE, Herman Burrell, Don Wells, and George Morris, met with the YMCA trustee board to negotiate desegregation. The YMCA tried to dissuade CORE and promised to build a new Y with equivalent facilities in the Central Avenue area. Cleveland CORE contacted members of the Welfare Fund of Cleveland (a Y funding source) and threatened a boycott.[34] Further, Houser contended in an editorial for the *Call and Post* that the existence of the Cedar YMCA "sugar coated" segregation. Although he recognized that "distinctions should be made between the segregation aspect of the YMCA and the work which it does . . . [it was] hypocritical for Negroes to support Jim Crow practices when they say they are opposed to racial segregation."[35] Houser also argued for Cedar YMCA to maintain its activities, but disassociate from the YMCA until it changed its policy.[36]

Two black Clevelanders responded to Houser's open letter. Both insisted that Cedar YMCA served a central social function and this purpose outranked idyllic principles that ignored pragmatic realities. Cedar's Jim Crow status was irrelevant. As one editorialist suggested, "victims of this vicious practice" need not also "remain docilely and supinely idle" because of it. More importantly, the livelihoods of black youth could not be left to those who kept their "hand smugly clenched in . . . pocket, while our children run helter skelter about the doorsteps that lead into the ruinous house of crime."[37]

Notwithstanding Cleveland CORE's efforts, national YMCA's decision to integrate, excruciatingly slowly, led the Cleveland central YMCA to open its doors to black membership.[38] Two YMCA black board members, however, gave rather backhanded congratulations for this new direction. The Reverend Dr. Wade McKinney and Alexander Martin, authoritative allies of black self-help and militant civil rights activists, asserted that black members should continue to apply for membership at Cedar YMCA, "where they can demonstrate that Negroes possess all the finer sensibilities, aspirations, and abilities that make for Christian gentlemen."[39] Houser had little to say regarding Reverend McKinney's statement, and a good decision it was. McKinney was a powerful man, having served as pastor of the influential Antioch Baptist Church since 1928, and an instrumental supporter of Forest City Hospital.[40]

The fluidity of what constituted Jim Crowism versus black self-help changed from moment to moment, person to person. McKinney was not the only advocate of institutions built under Jim Crow conditions. Houser received help from W. O. Walker who avidly supported Forest City Hospital. Additionally, while Walker and Perry Jackson both helped CORE's efforts to desegregate the downtown YMCA, they also aided Cedar's membership drive. Ironically, Houser himself countered CORE noncooperation rules when he used Cedar meeting rooms for the CORE 1946 convention, thus illustrating the interwoven and conflictual relationship between interracial integration and pragmatic black self-help.[41]

Despite what appeared to be some interest in the YMCA struggle, Cleveland CORE still registered little in the black community's mind. That changed with the arrival of Juanita Morrow. Morrow's directorship represented a unique position among the CORE chapters, as the first branch led by a black woman. A Christian, pacifist, and race activist, she was also among the few women to write "serious" articles for the *Call and Post*. Morrow was born in Georgia, but migrated with her parents to Cleveland in the 1930s. Early in life, she recalled a low tolerance for racial inequality and segregation. In one instance, she became quite agitated when she and her mother accidentally boarded a segregated railroad car during a return trip from her grandparents' Georgia home. Morrow immediately demanded to change cars, but her mother feeling tired chose not to move. Morrow recollected that she "fumed and fussed" for some time before deciding to sit in every car in the train.[42]

This same Juanita Morrow, under the tutelage of Pauli Murray, led a sit-in protest against Washington, DC, five-and-dime stores. While enrolled at Howard University, Morrow ventured downtown during her sophomore year for lunch but instead confronted the city's stringent discrimination. Morrow purchased a hotdog at a dime store, but was told to stand and eat it. She left and came back with three friends to demonstrate. The manager reacted by overcharging the four protestors. The group insisted on paying the regular price, so the store supervisor called the police. Patrolmen arrested the four for refusal to pay. Incensed by their arrest and discrimination, the group asked for Pauli Murray's help and mentorship. Murray, then a law student at Howard University, had crafted an activist reputation through her associations with FOR, MOWM, and CORE. In the 1960s, she famously became a women's right advocate and a cofounder of the National Organization of Women. At Murray's suggestion, Morrow and her friends cocreated the Howard University Civil Rights Committee, an entity that Morrow claimed became the DC CORE chapter.[43] From that point onward, Morrow continued to protest discrimination in restaurants and five-and-dime stores in the capital until the abrupt end of her college career. Not long before her junior year, poor finances forced her to leave.

At age nineteen, Morrow returned to Cleveland and acquired a position as a staff writer for the *Call and Post*. "Church Notes," Morrow's regular column, reflected a thinly veiled platform for her philosophy of Christian spirituality as expressed through nonviolence and interracial cooperation. Morrow's articles included stories on black women and employment, racial bias in the war industries, gender inequality, fair employment, antiwar sentiment, CORE, the Euclid Beach Amusement Park demonstrations (of which she was actually a part), and the segregation of the Cleveland school system, just to name a few.

From 1944 to 1946, Morrow attended school, worked for the *Call and Post*, and volunteered for Cleveland CORE as its youngest member. Morrow's association with the chapter resulted from her previous experience in Washington, DC, interactions with George Houser via Cleveland activist networks, and knowledge about the Cleveland FOR office. She later recollected that most people thought she was "crazy" to work for CORE, and her time was better spent with the NAACP. Despite CORE's relatively nonexistent status in Cleveland's black and white communites, Morrow remained unmoved by such attitudes. As she noted, "[I] always wanted to do things directly, I liked the direct action of CORE. I did not like going through courts and taking time."[44]

Morrow's assertiveness and nonviolent training led CORE toward more hard-hitting segregation challenges. The largest of which, the Euclid Beach Amusement Park

(?) MacClennon, (?) Miller, Peter Wilkins, Ruth MacClennon,
Juanita Morrow, Margaret Abbott.
Photo: unknown photographer, circa 1940s.
From the Personal Papers of Juanita Morrow Nelson

*Front row unidentified;* George Houser, *standing; back row* Pauline (?) Coleman.
Photo: unknown photographer, circa 1940s.
From the Personal Papers of Juanita Morrow Nelson

protest, revealed the dangers of Farmer's ends-oriented manifestations. Soon after George Houser's departure for New York in mid-August 1946, Morrow led CORE into a confrontation with one of the most belligerent perpetrators of discrimination in the Cleveland area—the Euclid Beach Amusement Park.[45]

Euclid Beach Park had a long history of strident discrimination against black Clevelanders. Dating back to 1899, black organizations filed lawsuits declaring the park violated Ohio Civil Rights Law. In the 1930s, the NAACP challenged Euclid Beach Park's skate rink, dance hall, and beach segregation rules, and successfully compelled the Cleveland Board of Education to prohibit school picnics at the location.[46] In July 1946, the American Youth for Democracy (AYD) and the National Negro Congress staged their own interracial demonstration at Euclid Beach Park, but were quickly escorted out by park guards.[47] Not surprisingly then, Euclid Beach Park seemed an easy target and perfect showcase for CORE's nonviolent goodwill strategy.

August 23, 1946, twelve black and white CORE members entered Euclid Beach Amusement Park. Park policemen immediately informed them that "mixed couples were not tolerated on the premises." Demonstrators spent only fifteen minutes in the park before the Euclid Beach Park guards ejected them for "mixing." A few demonstrators, Pauline Coleman, Henry C. Crawford, Jessie Coleman, and Geneva Peters, later unsuccessfully sued on the basis of color discrimination and minor bruises incurred during the ouster.[48]

Not long after their departure, Albert Luster, a black member of CORE and FOL, arrived thirty minutes late for the demonstration. Park policemen, none too subtly, followed Luster around the park. Eventually, he called the homes of CORE associates to locate the other demonstrators. Purportedly, the last call explained their disappearance or rather updated him on their removal from the park. When Julius Vago, a Euclid Beach Park guard, started to linger near the phone booth, Luster ended his conversation. Luster exited the booth and planned to leave, but Vago immediately accused him of inciting fear among white women in the park. He also alleged that Luster's suspicious behaviors included loitering and hiding his hands in his pockets. According to Luster, he ignored Vago and sat down on a park bench. However, the guard suddenly attacked him. Vago swore that he only followed Luster to the bench, but that it was Luster who attacked first.[49]

Although there were two sides to how the altercation began, there was no confusion about the outcome. Contradictory to CORE rules, Luster defended himself during the fight with Vago, but little could be done when five or six other Euclid Beach Park officers joined in the beating. Afterward, the guards threw him out of the park and Cleveland city police took him to the hospital. Albert Luster's first major foray as a CORE member resulted in a fractured skull, a cut lip that required several stitches, and a number of lacerations and bruises about his legs, thighs, elbows, and feet.[50]

Albert Luster's membership in the Future Outlook League immediately placed him under its protection. The NAACP filed criminal and discrimination charges against Vago and Euclid Beach Park. The newly formed, mayor-appointed Amity Board on race relations advocated for an ordinance in city council that required all amusement parks to obtain a license of operation from the city of Cleveland. The new license prohibited any forms of discrimination in public amusements as outlined by the Ohio State Civil Rights Law. Simultaneously, the Amity Board devised a simpler solution for the Euclid Beach case. Revoke the amusement park's operation license. It was not long before more than fifty organizations joined to condemn the Euclid Beach incident and demand passage of the ordinance, including the Communist Party of Cleveland, the Jewish Community Council, the Cleveland chapter of the National Negro Congress, and even the Kimberly Avenue Block Club.[51]

To say that the NAACP and FOL shoved CORE aside constituted an understatement. Between the law cases handled by the NAACP, the new park ordinance before city council—pushed by the Amity Board—and the articles featuring Albert Luster as an FOL member, small wonder CORE received any credit for initiating the demonstration. Cleveland chapter clearly lacked the NAACP and the FOL's resources, political clout, and membership numbers. FOL called the first mass meeting on the Luster incident, a rally that attracted a large crowd of five hundred, and effectively designated it the clear leader in the confrontation with Euclid Beach Park. Of course, the NAACP annual activities brochure claimed itself as the head organization. Either way, CORE certainly lost its initial position, though it did sign its name among the other fifty groups in support of the ordinance. Ultimately, CORE's name became a backdrop to the story of Albert Luster's beating. Its position as the demonstration sponsor receded within a matter of weeks.[52]

Given the focus on Luster, the NAACP, FOL, and the Amity Board, it hardly shocked the imagination that CORE would again test the discriminatory policies of Euclid Beach Park. CORE chose to do so either to expand its campaign against Euclid Beach Park segregation or to reassert itself as the cutting edge of direct action protest. Whatever the reason, Saturday, September 21, CORE reentered Euclid Beach Park.[53]

The protest began with a walk through the park for forty-five minutes. Unmolested by guards, the group pushed their luck and entered the dance hall, a site guaranteed to elicit trouble. As soon as members began interracial dancing, Euclid Beach Park policemen intervened. Park officers outlined the policy against race mixing, but CORE protested by blocking the entrance to the dance hall. Once the guards grew tired of arguing the finer points of Ohio State Civil Rights Law, they shoved demonstrators outside the pavilion.[54]

From this point onward, newspaper stories claimed that two off-duty Cleveland city Negro policemen noticed a commotion. The Negro policemen then intervened to ensure public safety. Euclid Beach guards responded with the assertion that city policemen held no jurisdiction in the park. Then one of the guards grabbed the collar of Negro policeman Henry Mackey. Mackey slapped the guard's hand down. In retaliation, three other guards rushed Mackey, and one gave him a black eye.[55]

At the same time, Mackey's fellow Negro policeman, Lynn Coleman, entered the altercation and attempted to make an arrest on the grounds of assaulting an officer. In the ensuing melee, both Coleman and Mackey drew their revolvers to arrest the guards, though the two kept their weapons pointed downward. Newspaper articles later noted that they remained completely calm. Nevertheless, six park officers rushed the two men. During the struggle over the gun, Coleman's revolver accidentally went off. Coleman was shot. The bullet penetrated his left thigh barely above his knee. Instantly, a Euclid Beach guard snatched Coleman's gun while other park security men beat him with their fists and clubs.[56]

Suddenly, someone in the crowd yelled toward Coleman, "Kill him!" Mackey, who still had his gun drawn, tried to intervene. However, he backed down when Julius Vago of the Luster incident brandished a weapon and threatened to start shooting despite the presence of numerous onlookers. At the height of the brawl,

Juanita Morrow slipped away to call the city police but upon her return found a city policeman, Lieutenant John J. Smythe of the Race Relations Unit, trying to calm the situation. Smythe talked with Mackey while Coleman's wife, Pauline, who also happened to be present, gave her husband assistance. The incident ended when additional city police arrived and escorted Coleman and Mackey to the hospital.[57]

Historians called this incident the Euclid Beach Riot. It became a cause célèbre and roused major support for the Negro policemen's decision to defend themselves, their spouses, and the CORE protestors. *Call and Post* newspaper articles featured detailed accounts, with front-page features written by CORE chairman Juanita Morrow and the two Negro policemen.

This time, Euclid Beach guards faced charges. Community organizations gathered en masse and finally forced through the ordinance, though the process took weeks. The mayor required Euclid Beach Park to close one week early. Lawsuits from the Negro policemen and CORE members went on from fall 1946 into the following year.[58]

Seemingly a small but unimportant set of events in Cleveland's race relations history, these incidents marked a dramatic moment in the development of Cleveland CORE. The first incident, Luster's choice to defend himself, ran counter to CORE demonstration rules. Luster's membership with the Future Outlook League may or may not explain his decision to fight back. However, he clearly occupied a dual position in organizations with conflicting rules on self-defense and nonviolence, and it showed markedly in the altercation. Still, one could reasonably argue that the demonstration had ended, and Luster's aberrant actions were within bounds while he was alone. The second protest, though it degenerated to an all-out gun draw, absolutely ran counter to CORE regulations, but arguably ranked as an unfortunate accident. CORE members got caught in the middle of a fray between city police and Euclid Beach guards, except this possibility excluded one important but shocking detail. The two Negro policemen, who triggered the gun brawl at Euclid Beach Park, were not just bystanders. Coleman and Mackey were members of CORE, and so was Coleman's wife. In fact, officer Coleman's sister-in-law (Jessie Coleman) and wife (Pauline Coleman) both participated in the first demonstration against Euclid Beach Park.

Cleveland CORE had received its greatest media coverage ever. But Morrow, and especially George Houser (now appraised of the "riot"), hardly greeted this new prominence with quite the expected glee. Coleman's revolver going off at the demonstration created a high degree of anxiety and consternation among Cleveland CORE's leadership. Regulations clearly stated that all members of CORE could only participate as nonviolent activists in direct action protests. Mackey and Coleman's possession of firearms, even as a "requirement" for some off-duty policemen, created a difficult situation. Worse, Mackey and Coleman's "bystanders" pretense, contorted their relationship to CORE and manipulated its public relations face. The very night of the Euclid Beach "riot" Mackey and Pauline Coleman visited Morrow and swore their police testimony gave no hint they knew the demonstrators. Pauline Coleman also requested CORE grant aid to her husband, but Morrow refused her appeal and pointedly noted that the sworn testimony, "won't protect Lynn and Mackey since they shouldn't have been there under the circumstances without orders . . . Lynn knew the possibilities and should be willing to fight the thing out in the open."[59] Morrow went on to claim, much to Pauline Coleman's disappointment, that CORE could not openly support Coleman and Mackey.

Nevertheless, Morrow could not publicly distance herself or CORE from the two men either. She could join the public's fêted rush to make the policemen symbols of Cleveland's Jim Crow shame or she and CORE could retreat to the background. Publicly, of course, she chose the former. In actuality, Morrow had no choice in the matter. Already, newspapers told the story of Negro policemen as courageous onlookers. Interviews and articles characterized them as good officers accosted by the vagaries of segregation. Although no newspapers made mention of Henry Mackey and Lynn Coleman as CORE members, previous and subsequent articles confirmed their and Pauline Coleman's status as actively involved in the group. Indeed, a cursory glance at the 1946 CORE convention minutes listed Lynn Coleman as cochair of Cleveland CORE and the Friday night speaker for the open welcome to convention delegates.[60]

Mackey and Coleman's choice to bring firearms and refusal to openly acknowledge their membership in Cleveland CORE came much to the chagrin of George Houser, who received news of the Euclid Beach protest weeks after his arrival at FOR New York headquarters. Houser noted his displeasure in a letter to Juanita Morrow.

"I was afraid that something unfortunate might happen if Lynn was going along ready to use his gun. Just as unfortunate as the accidental shooting is the fact that he and his wife and McKay wanted to deny that they knew the group . . . It would take no amount of investigation at all for anyone to find out that Lynn was co-chairman last year . . . But on the grounds of principle I think the position you and the others took in refusing to be involved in the act which would really be a flagrant lie, was absolutely correct. . . . They should have thought this problem through before they went out there, for it certainly was mentioned at the meeting Rustin and I attended."[61]

Houser's letter to Morrow exposed two underlying issues within Cleveland CORE. First, discussion of the "problem" undoubtedly referred to the possibility of violent attack. Second, previous to the protest, Lynn Coleman clearly planned and prepared for a physical altercation. This might explain why Coleman and Mackey chose to publicly disavow any association with Cleveland CORE.

Although Houser characterized Morrow and the other CORE members as not participating in the "lie," it was more accurate to say that their participation was by silent omission. Still, Morrow had grave concerns and annoyance about the Euclid Beach incident. She wrote Houser back with the enigmatic and acerbic comment that she would "save discussion on Euclid Beach for personal talk. And there's plenty of it."[62] Morrow later recalled that she had no knowledge of Coleman's intention to bring a gun, and that it happened so fast, she didn't know what to think. She added that thinking back on it, "[maybe] the rest of us were pretty naïve."[63]

Coleman's claim in a subsequent interview, on the contrary, would imply that CORE members were not naïve at all. According to Coleman, whose questionable account twenty years later still denied association with CORE, a participant enlisted his presence at the event. This "friend of a member of CORE . . . anticipated difficulty with the guards."[64] Based on those circumstances Coleman and his wife went out as observers. Coleman revealed that it was Morrow who asked for his presence, although that seemed hardly correct given her propensity for pacifism. Whichever the veracity of either oral account, what remained clear was that Coleman as a CORE member or as a policeman friend of a CORE member represented a decided intention by CORE members to prepare for self-defense.[65]

On another note, decisions by the Negro policemen most likely came from the direction of black women. Jessie Coleman, Lynn Coleman's sister, more likely requested the "assistance" if Coleman's account was partially accurate. Though she was not present at this particular altercation, she was at the first. In addition, Coleman's repudiation of CORE membership led George Houser to have his own question of where the source of such a decision emanated. In a letter to Morrow, he asked, "Was Lynn involved in this too or was it his wife's idea?"[66]

In spite of Houser or Morrow's agitation, the Euclid Beach "riot" was Cleveland chapter's biggest demonstration to date. Basic common sense dictated that Cleveland CORE publicly remain or appear to remain cohesive about the Euclid Beach incident even if Mackey and Coleman's brazen actions implied dissent among the ranks. Additionally, not every member of Cleveland CORE believed Coleman's actions warranted condemnation. Thaddeus Tekla, a white socialist and CORE member, felt the need to weigh in on the situation in support of Coleman, writing that "fearless men like Lynn are going to beard the [Euclid Beach Park] lions in their den . . . [To] overlook this open and *shot* case is to commit a sin of omission; and invite a race riot."[67] Despite the inflammatory language, the letter also reflected the beliefs of many black Clevelanders, particularly as represented in the pages of *Call and Post*. Consequently, the prevailing mindsets pigeonholed Morrow into writing about Coleman and Mackey as the aggrieved policemen.

Crucially, the Euclid Beach incident also exposed a weakness in Farmer's ends-oriented premise. Neither Houser nor Morrow's nonviolence training affected the outcome of Coleman's action. Houser wrote Coleman to say that he was "sorry that the guns came into the incident . . . [and] terribly sorry that I wasn't in Cleveland for the whole incident."[68] Coleman's clipped response, however, made it clear that Houser's presence acted as no deterrent for violent action. After all, "I can well appreciate how tough it must be on you to be so vitally interested in the recent happening and yet to be so far away from the scene. However I am here, but the results are the same."[69]

As it were, the incident followed the path of the first Euclid Beach occurrence. It melded into the larger demonstration against Euclid Beach Park led by the NAACP, Amity Board, and FOL. Luster received some solace for his attack. An all-female mixed-race jury found Julius Vago guilty of beating Luster. Alternately, Mackey and Coleman were not so lucky. Deputy inspector E. J. Flanagan authorized the release of Mackey and Coleman's attackers after a call from Lieutenant John Smythe of the Race Relations Unit—a group that later investigated 1960s CORE members under the new designation Subversive Squad.[70]

Late fall 1946 through early winter, the city council debated passage of the ordinance. Finally, in February 1947, it decreed that the city must revoke amusement park licenses for any operators caught discriminating. Euclid Beach Park avoided the new edict by selling the skate rink and dance hall to "private owners" who determined membership by invitation. Discrimination remained a de facto presence in the park.[71]

Internally, Cleveland CORE had no further discussions, retraining, or repercussions related to the event. The chapter planned to conduct a third demonstration but failed to do so. Publicly, they appeared consumed with lawsuits against Euclid Beach Park. By spring 1947, Morrow sent Houser a letter noting that the last legal battle had ended. None was successful. Matters deteriorated when police caught Coleman with his personal gun, a snub-nosed .38 caliber revolver, in his hospital bed. He insisted he did so after Cleveland detectives attempted to intimidate him while hospitalized. The result was a job suspension for conduct unbecoming an officer. The policemen who Coleman claimed harassed him were officers Ungvary and Smythe of the Race Relations Unit. The article title in the *Call and Post* said it best, "A Frame-Up?"[72]

Coleman was not the only CORE member in the midst of a "set up." FOR transferred Houser to New York for a new job as co-secretary (along with Rustin) for the Racial Industrial Department. Houser was now in the belly of the beast, made immediately clear after FOR further decreased his CORE-related activities. Houser now geared much of his time to correspondence, executive meetings, and occasional literature dissemination. It was also "agreed" that Houser could not build a national CORE in New York unless it had a staff and budget.[73] Muste was even more frank in his August 1946 memorandum to Nevin Sayre, FOR assistant executive secretary. Reminiscent of previous memos, he wrote, "we also have a clear understanding that if it comes to anything more than this, George will have to shift his organizational connection as FOR is not going to put any more money and time into an effort to build a national CORE."[74] However, Muste did allow Houser to host a CORE yearly seminar on nonviolence, with the requirement that the central participation would come from FOR people.[75]

In the midst of the Cleveland debacle, Houser sustained national CORE under FOR watch. He cleverly linked national CORE to FOR events, making the organization appear active and viable while subtly retaining its national character despite Muste's objection. Simultaneously, the continual increase in chapter representation and spirited local action kept CORE in the position of vanguard direct action group. But sponsorship and training workshops were not enough. Houser needed to produce a vigorous direct action project not linked to locals or subsidized by FOR to such an extent that CORE appeared a sidekick. Right at the moment Cleveland CORE lost its last legal fight against Euclid, the national office launched its most important pre-1960s direct action project—the Journey of Reconciliation.[76]

George Houser and Bayard Rustin aspired to challenge Jim Crow laws in interstate travel, and thus invited locals to join the Journey of Reconciliation. Cleveland CORE contributed as a fund-raising chapter. Juanita Morrow wanted to join the ride. However, male organizers determined that the interracial nature of the project was provocative enough. The addition of women would only exacerbate the response. Morrow didn't agree, but she was excluded anyway.[77]

The Journey of Reconciliation was CORE's first national project. Houser and Rustin's idea for it came from the Irene Morgan Supreme Court case. Irene Morgan, an African American who had recently suffered a miscarriage, refused to relinquish her back seat to a white couple on a bus trip from Virginia to Maryland. After arrest and jailing, the NAACP won her case before the United States Supreme Court. The *Irene Morgan v. Virginia* ruling rendered segregation in interstate travel unconstitutional. However, southern states refused to follow the federal law.

Rustin and Houser received permission from Muste to move forward on a direct action test case of *Morgan v. Virginia*.[78] In April 1947, sixteen men left from Washington, DC, on a two-week trek to challenge segregation in interstate travel throughout the upper South. Eight black and eight white, the male participants included black riders Bayard Rustin; William Worthy, member of the NY Council for a Permanent FEPC; Chicago musician Dennis Banks; Attorney Conrad Lynn; and Greensboro A&T University affiliate Eugene Stanley. From Cincinnati CORE, social worker Nathan Wright, student Andrew Johnson, and CORE leader Wallace Nelson all joined the ride. White journeyist NY horticulturalist Igal Roodenko, Cincinnati biologist Worth Randle, Methodist ministers Louis Adams and Ernest Bromley, and Worker's Defense League activists Joe Felmet and James Peck boarded with CORE founders George Houser and Homer Jack.[79]

The trip took riders throughout the upper South to Louisville, Kentucky, and back to Washington, DC. Police arrested journeyists at many stops, but riders perceived their polite behavior as a positive sign that disciplined goodwill nonviolence worked. Most municipal courts dropped charges except Chapel Hill, North Carolina, where Rustin, Felmet, and Roodenko served out thirty-day terms of hard labor. In the report, among the various noted outcomes, Houser observed the role of women bystanders, whom riders found more open to discussion and willing to act as witnesses in their cases. Accordingly, this also resulted from the goodwill orientation of the trip. The Journey of Reconciliation was deemed an overall success.[80]

The Journey, however, was not exempt from the presence of Farmer's ends-oriented. Historians Meier and Rudwick noted, "true to CORE's founding, the organization's first major national project really depended on the initiative and idealism of a small group of pacifists." And though that may well be true, the ends-oriented were never far behind. A few journeyists gradually, sometimes starkly, departed from the CORE way and fluidly moved between interracialism and full-blown black nationalism. Journey of Reconciliation participants William Worthy, Nathan Wright, Conrad Lynn, and to a certain extent Wallace Nelson reflected the unrelenting presence of CORE's literal and figurative ends-oriented "dark-side." [81]

Nathan Wright two decades later coordinated the 1967 Newark Black Power Conference. CORE disavowed any support to William Worthy, an early progenitor of sixties black internationalism and global movement alliance, when he traveled to communist China and Cuba in violation of US State Department travel bans. Conrad Lynn, lawyer for militant civil rights activist Robert Williams, visited Williams in Cuba after he escaped conviction for armed self-defense against the Klan in Monroe, North Carolina.[82]

While black ends-oriented appeared in Cleveland and the Journey, white CORE activists in the vein of Bernice Fisher also lurked around CORE. The only violent episode during the Journey of Reconciliation took place in Chapel Hill, North Carolina, after blue-collar taxi drivers chased Reconciliation riders out of town. Charles Jones, local minister and FOR National Advisory Council member, was left with the inevitable violent fallout from his participation and aid to the demonstrators. A series of discussions and newspaper editorials followed, along with phone call and drive-by threats. Radical white students responded by guarding Reverend Jones's house. While CORE leaders "journeyed" on through North Carolina, white youth (some believe communists) occupied house grounds and sat atop the roof with shotguns. Fearing violence, Jones convinced the students to return home.[83]

While white student radicals crossed the nonviolent line in Chapel Hill, national CORE revealed no reaction to these events. That CORE was ill equipped to deal with the issue of violent resistance either internally or externally was not unique to Cleveland or the Journey of Reconciliation. The organization's inability to counteract the more virulent expressions of racism or the subsequent self-defense follow-up, generally represented itself in silence. National's avoidance of these conversations extended to other local chapters as well.

Chicago CORE chose not to follow constitutional rules after a spate of mob clashes occurred from 1947 to 1951 in Chicago over residential integration. In August 1947, integration of Fernwood Park public housing created a major stir in the white community and made black Chicago residents the target of brutal repression. The Fernwood Park Riots broke out for three days after the housing authority temporarily integrated black veterans into the housing project. A crowd of 1,500–5,000 assembled in the area and attacked approximately 35, possibly more, black citizens. It took over 1,000 policemen to quell the outbreak. The ferocity of the event triggered comparisons to the bloody 1919 Chicago riot.[84]

Two years later the Chicago community of Englewood underwent its own explosion with mob numbers as high as 10,000. In this case, false rumors of a home purchase by a black family triggered violent action. Unlike Fernwood, however, Englewood victims also comprised any person deemed an "outsider," which included some whites. The 1951 Cicero riot followed Englewood as another incident precipitated by the presence of a single black family in public housing. In this case, 650 National Guard and county officers stymied physical assaults though property was damaged. Historian Arnold Hirsch noted that in a sea of condemnation over the Cicero attack, one lone letter stood out as rather out of place for minimalizing the riot's effect. Its author, CORE founder Homer Jack, now executive secretary of the Chicago Council Against Racial and Religious Discrimination, noted that compared to previous incidents of mob violence, at least damage in Cicero was limited to vandalism.[85]

Chicago's upheavals were not new to Homer Jack. He'd already written an open letter telling the city it had "one more chance" after the Fernwood riots. City policy needed correction in order to calm black fears and prevent retaliation. Jack also acknowledged that during the Fernwood incident, the "Negro community acted with rare restraint, although on the fifth and sixth nights there were a few cases of counter-violence."[86]

Eventually Chicago CORE chair Gerald Bullock proffered his own proposal to deal with rampant violence against black residents, which included a proposal for a Racial Violence Emergency Council. He too pointed to the potential explosion inferred in Homer Jack's "last chance," declaring "unless a new method is devised to deal with this growing hoodlumism a major explosion is inevitable, and Chicago will become the scene of the bloodiest race war since the Fort Dearborn Massacre."[87]

Notwithstanding the frantic warnings of black reprisals, the two letters reflected a recurring problem for CORE as a whole, and in Chicago specifically. Without protection, self-defense was unavoidable. But, CORE leaders could only urge preventative action and alert city officials to potential open warfare. Chicago CORE was hard pressed to offer a goodwill solution to white assaults.[88]

The resulting gap led some CORE members to consider different options. As early as 1946, after fifty-nine home bombings, some members in Chicago CORE openly espoused self-defense squads to guard homes. Interestingly, although Chicago CORE's chairman was black, the self-defense plan received its greatest support from mostly white activists affiliated with the Socialist Worker Party. A white leftist organization with Trotskyist leanings, the group effectively hijacked Chicago CORE in 1946. Rather, Houser viewed it as a hijacking. In actuality, Gerald Bullock, black chairman of Chicago CORE, invited their participation despite warnings that the group had no allegiance to nonviolence tactically or philosophically. Bullock remained unperturbed even after the chapter disseminated a newsletter that argued the validity of self-defense over nonviolent protest.[89] Their presumed un-CORE behavior also spilled over to protest style. At the White City Roller Rink demonstration, one CORE leader complained that marchers waved signs that were "not exactly 'loving.'"[90]

Other chapters presumably dabbled in radicalism as well. Grand Rapids garnered FBI attention because of its union and communist affiliation. William Glenn, a staunch integrationist, was at the center of this controversy. Glenn's activism stretched as far back as the 1920s. He made several efforts to replicate the Communist Party's policy of popular front and worked with numerous groups including the NAACP, International Worker's Association (IWA), Communist Party USA, and CORE.[91]

Another CORE chapter based at Syracuse University came under suspicion for sedition—not an uncommon accusation against 1940s civil rights groups. Except along with the issue of purported treason, police accused Syracuse CORE of vandalizing the Red Cross Bank, and breaking the home windows of its executive vice president, the Reverend Dr. Ellsworth Reamon. Supposedly, this occurred because of Reamon's refusal to desegregate the blood bank.[92]

Houser devoted most of his attention to the SWP problem, which stemmed from CORE's excessively decentralized structure and federated style. SWP essentially represented an ideological break in the "CORE way," or more to the point, Houser's CORE way.[93] However, his inability to understand SWP as more than an aberration blinded him to ideological conflicts that shifted beneath his very feet, in Cleveland, Chicago, during the Journey of Reconciliation, and with other CORE chapters. National's failure to handle these differences also reflected the political difficulties of maintaining CORE within FOR. Muste feared, and rightly so, that nonpacifist CORE members could potentially lead the organization away from nonviolent action. CORE had to maintain its nonviolent face or its more than precarious status within FOR would be over.

Cleveland CORE began to peter out after 1947. Euclid Beach marked the chapter's last activities under Morrow. Even more detrimental, Morrow's new obligations on CORE's executive board and financial woes effectively brought her tenure as Cleveland CORE chair to a close.[94] To make matters worse, her radical beliefs and insistence on racial and economic equality, though it made for forceful and compelling reading, eventually affected her job. Morrow and *Call and Post* editor W. O. Walker became embroiled in dissension over her unionizing work. Walker, who had and would continue into the 1970s to be a seminal player in Cleveland economic and civil rights, ironically held the opposite position when it came to his own employees. Walker retaliated against Morrow and the other organizing writers by firing them, claiming he'd "tear the place down brick by brick" first. Morrow noted of this incident, "Of course, he had to take us back. [However], I wasn't there much longer than that . . . this was a pretty reactionary paper."[95] Though Walker rehired them to keep his paper running, it was the end for Morrow. Morrow left Cleveland for Chicago and then Cincinnati, where she continued to shake up segregation as a member of Cincinnati CORE with her life partner, Wallace Nelson.[96] Unfortunately, her departure left the Cleveland chapter flapping about without her presence to steer it in some form of direct action campaign. A year later, Lynn Coleman still complained that the loss of Juanita Morrow and those who followed left only members with lukewarm interest. The chapter did little beyond general activities and dues collections by socialist member and treasurer Tad Tekla.[97]

Cleveland CORE twice underwent leadership change to revive itself, but to no avail. Hortense Davis, leader of the CORE dependent children committee, took the job of chairman in 1950 with great reluctance. She wrote to Houser that "CORE in Cleveland was practically dead," but middle-aged Davis took the position despite her feeling that CORE should be a youth movement.[98] Unfortunately, her short tenure failed to ensure the group's survival. Davis called no meetings for a full year. Tad Tekla, Cleveland CORE treasurer, sent a letter to Houser on the chapter's progress, which basically stated that "Cleveland CORE seems to be dead."[99]

It was 1952 before the next formidable woman, Erosanna "Sis" Robinson, took Morrow's place. Sis, a young enthusiastic black woman, possessed the qualities Hortense Davis thought essential to Cleveland CORE's growth. A youthful resident at the Phillis Wheatley Association, Robinson aggressively and eagerly followed the tenets of nonviolent direct action. However, Robinson lacked the support she so badly needed. As a friend of both Robinson and Houser noted, "Sis herself is a fine person, dedicated, and courageous . . . if she could work with a stronger group elsewhere, [she] would be a tower of strength to CORE action."[100]

Even without experienced CORE members, Robinson was still quite a force to reckon. Robinson's solitary activism on behalf of CORE managed to move the group toward a small but immaterial uptick in activism. Aside from coaxing new

members, she lectured youth and church groups on CORE nonviolent philosophy. Although Robinson actively labored to generate interest in CORE, the group
lacked a galvanizing event and centerpiece for nonviolent action until the Skateland
demonstration.

Skateland was a known segregationist offender. Its discrimination history
directly tied to that of the Pla-more Roller Rink, a black skate facility. One person
owned both rinks as separate Jim Crow facilities for each community. In 1948, the
NAACP and the militant Reverend Wade McKinney led a boycott of Pla-more.
The owner was forced to sell out for the cost of taxes, but maintained his ownership
in the white Skateland rink.[101]

Despite Skateland's reputation, its selection as a direct action protest site
occurred unexpectedly. On May 24, 1952, Robinson, then a staff member of the
Mount Pleasant Community Center, accompanied three children, two black and
one white, on a visit to Skateland Roller Rink. The small group encountered no
obstacles with ticket purchase, but immediately ran into problems while acquiring
skates. A group of five white hoodlums attempted to trip Robinson and the children
several times while a guard looked on. When Robinson contacted the manager, he
refused to speak about her concerns.[102]

On July 13, over one month later, Robinson challenged Skateland's policy with
the aid of CORE member Michael Coffey, a white graduate student at Western
Reserve University. That action led to white male skaters tripping both Coffey and
Robinson at least twenty times. On this occasion they did meet with the manager,
but received no help.[103]

After negotiations broke down, Coffey, Robinson, Dean Fletcher (white), and
Thelma Warley (black) resolved to challenge discrimination at the skate rink. On
August 2, the group entered Skateland, and immediately white staff and skaters
began to harass them. Robinson, Coffey, and Warley waited forty-five minutes for
skates (Fletcher, who arrived earlier, had his skates). Upon entering the rink, white
skaters tripped Robinson again and again. The first time she scraped her knee. The
fifth time she fractured her wrist. Though the *Call and Post* featured Robinson's
story, neither she nor CORE went back to challenge Skateland's policies again.

Given Skateland's history, Robinson's assault should have functioned as a
major galvanizing force.[104] However, it did not. Much of the problem resided in
Robinson's decision to let the matter drop if direct action could not be brought to
bear. Both the NAACP and the Cleveland Community Relations Board (formerly
the Amity Board, now CCRB) offered Robinson legal support to sue for her injuries. Although the CORE protest generated interest, she refused help based on the
superfluous notion that a legal suit did not constitute direct action.[105]

Quite possibly, Caroline Urie, an adviser for Robinson and friend of George
Houser, influenced Robinson's view on this matter. Urie wrote that Robinson's

inability to gain broad community interest resided in the stance of the CCRB and NAACP for whom the "techniques of nonviolence are apparently incomprehensible."[106] Yet, this perspective was antithetical to CORE's short history of joint protests with groups like the NAACP and lawsuits under former chair Juanita Morrow. Further, such dependence on direct action required a larger membership, the very component Cleveland CORE lacked. As nearly the sole protestor for CORE, Sis Robinson eventually grew tired of CORE member and Cleveland community apathy. Sis Robinson declared in a note to Jim Peck, editor of the *CORE-lator*, that "Cleveland CORE has fizzled for a number of reasons . . . almost no one feels the real need for a group now. I never met so many people with so many other situations to respond to."[107] It took a few months for the national office to register Sis Robinson's statement, but it finally dawned on them that Cleveland CORE was inactive. In 1953, national CORE declared the Cleveland CORE chapter defunct, thereby validating what clearly had been the case over the last few years.[108] Erosanna "Sis" Robinson, however, said it best: "Cleveland CORE is dead. Gone. No more. Until, in some dim, vague future, an eager band of nonviolent direct actionists revive the movement."[109]

Cleveland CORE was dead, at least for now. But other chapters were dying too. In 1950, national CORE had approximately twenty chapters. It dropped the following year to eleven. Across the East, Midwest, and West, CORE chapters declined for various reasons. Some branches terminated after successful direct action protests, others from lack of direction, Red Scare and communist accusations, or failed direct action protests. Cleveland was also illustrative of a key aspect to CORE's demise during this and future periods. Some chapters deteriorated after the departure of key activists. Sometimes an exodus was voluntary, but more often than not the organization had a habit of culling its leaders from local sites and either moving them or expanding their CORE obligations. On the flip side, as CORE lost chapters, it failed to gain new ones, thus it appeared as if the national office was gushing vitality. Just as the civil rights movement stood on the precipice of massive action, CORE was slipping from its position as front leader for the nonviolent revolution. It was still mostly white, college-student-oriented, and sporadic in its protest activities.[110]

The cannibalization of Wallace Nelson became indicative of CORE leaders' anxiety about the organization's decline. Fearing Nelson's pro-anarchist leanings hindered chapter development, CORE acted against Nelson as an easy blame for the organization's stagnation. Wallace Nelson and life partner Juanita Morrow's June 1952 protest against Cincinnati Coney Island pushed the envelope on CORE rules of action. Nelson and Morrow chose to practice noncooperation and went limp upon arrest, refused to answer the questions of authorities, and instituted a hunger strike while in jail.

Nelson's protest style appeared again at the Rosedale playground in Washington, DC. The Cincinnati leader led another CORE affiliate, the Washington, DC, Interracial Workshop, and a neighborhood group, the Citizens Committee to Integrate Rosedale Playground, in protests against segregated playgrounds. The Rosedale Committee formed out of a mass meeting held by DC CORE in late 1951. The neighborhood group consisted of black community residents willing to use nonviolent techniques. However, Rosedale never quite acted independently from the DC Interracial Workshop and operated more as a black neighborhood arm of DC CORE. The two groups challenged playground segregation over several months from late 1951 to early 1952, but DC CORE participation dwindled overtime. Only three key figures from the chapter maintained ties, including Constance Perry, Lillian Palenius, and Albert Mindlin.[111]

The accidental drowning death of a black child who'd snuck on the playground to use the pool reenergized protests the following summer. Beginning in July, Nelson led group demonstrations with marchers who practiced noncooperation and went limp, but protests became increasingly aggressive over time. Black children and parents continued to picket after the Nelson-led demonstrations, or simply climbed the fence to allow black children to play. After several incidents of physical provocation, an altercation occurred between Rocco Colandreo and Walter Lucas, a member of the Citizens Committee. According to DC CORE member Lillian Palenius, Lucas lost his temper after hostile whites attacked local black children and their chaperones. Lucas left the protest and returned with his gun, which he then shot into the air. Both he and Colandreo were later arrested.

Though the Rosedale Committee intended to forward additional funds to CORE to allay the costs of the summer training workshop, Lucas's arrest obligated them to redirect monies to his bail. But, funding loss was the least of DC CORE's concern. Although the committee was a grassroots offshoot of Washington, DC, CORE, Lucas failed to remain nonviolent. His actions touched off a firestorm. Both organizations bitterly debated the use of violent tactics with Rosedale Committee characterizing DC CORE's condemnation and withdrawal of support as hypocritical. Plus, many believed that Lucas's actions pressed the Recreational Board to hastily desegregate both the playground and the pool at Rosedale. According to Mindlin, Rosedale residents viewed Lucas as a "symbol of revolt; even though they agreed on the surface, that his action was foolish and contrary to the spirit of the campaign."[112]

Although the organization's dissolution was purportedly precipitated by these events, it bares noting that Washington Interracial Workshop (DC CORE) aggressively acted to force Rosedale's disbandment. Mindlin claimed that the successful desegregation of the playground also facilitated the committee's disintegration. However, as he put it, DC CORE "engineered" its demise because support of Lucas implied tacit acceptance of violence, which badly implicated CORE. In his final critique of the success and failures of the Rosedale demonstrations, Mindlin concluded that "most of the neighborhood people never really absorbed the philosophy of nonviolence." And most importantly, "not only did an act of violence by one of our people create psychological conflicts that practically disrupted the group, but these conflicts exposed deep racial antagonisms towards the whites in the group. On the other side, the effort to preserve non-violent discipline created a harshness of spirit that did harm."[113]

Washington Interracial Workshop was not the only CORE chapter operating from of a harshness of spirit. Mindlin's evaluation of the Rosedale protest unknowingly implicated and reproached Nelson's philosophy and training methods. Nelson pioneered tactics of noncooperation within CORE and pushed the boundaries of civil disobedience. His ideological and tactical stance proved too much for other CORE leaders who felt that his pacifist anarchism painted CORE with the "crazy" brush. Peck argued that Nelson's hyper pacifism was ineffective and too "up in the clouds." Lula Farmer, James Farmer's second wife and a New York CORE member, referred to Nelson's going limp as too "far out" for the period. It didn't help that he refused to exclude communists or that he was also part of the Peacemakers, a militant pacifist group of draft and tax objectors. Lula Farmer succinctly described them as a bunch of "cultists" growing organic vegetables and refusing to pay taxes.[114]

Worse, CORE was also burdened with other militant pacifists, like Jeffre Sewart, whose "absolutist" pacifism and poverty empathy caused him to dress inappropriately for demonstrations in a get-up that included overalls and bare feet. Members in the New York and St. Louis CORE chapters felt that Nelson was too fanatical, too closely linked to FOR-styled pacifism, and too distracting from CORE's agenda. Washington, DC, CORE member Lillian Palenius purportedly believed the attack on Nelson was simply a power grab by New York CORE. Nelson's position as CORE fieldworker eventually led to an all-out fight. New York and St. Louis factions took the floor at CORE's 1953 convention to remove him as fieldworker. Nelson tried to fend off the challenge, and with supporters attempted to strike from CORE regulations the requirement to willingly submit to police arrest. But, he failed to stymy the tide of disapproval from persons like James Robinson, Lula Farmer, and indirectly James Farmer and James Peck in the New York chapter as well as Charles Odham, Marvin Rich, and indirectly Bernice Fisher from St. Louis—all of whom intended to ditch the pacifist tag once and for all.[115]

Houser disagreed with the New York and St. Louis members, but could do little to help Nelson. Houser had been CORE's executive director for ten years, but he was now on the way out of FOR. FOR continued to beat a dead horse and still questioned Houser's work on CORE. Houser argued that CORE was secondary or tertiary. Actually, he'd begun to protest apartheid in South Africa and was planning a trip to Africa that would last for months. Although the council claimed it did not wish to close off his relationship with CORE, FOR had harangued him for years about that relationship.[116] In April 1954, FOR officially requested that Houser no longer put any time into CORE as FOR staff. Houser submitted his resignation as executive secretary of CORE, and divided his duties among other CORE leaders and founders.[117] His resignation led to the 1954 reorganization of CORE, which eventually restructured Wallace Nelson out of his position—though it would be more accurate to say that his opposition found an opportune way to oust him.

New FOR executive secretary, John Swomley, was only too happy to speed removal of all vestiges of CORE. He instantly sent formal requests that it no longer hold an office within FOR space and that all CORE publication and mailing materials be removed. From the beginning Swomley felt the group syphoned personnel and resources from FOR, while never progressing in position and prestige. Additionally, CORE's failure to raise funding (a process Muste hindered) or gain black membership, added nothing to FOR's overall development. Swomley believed CORE's nonviolent position could be maintained as long as FOR staff continued as lay participants, but not staff. It was a miscalculation on his part, but no longer relevant.[118] CORE would sink or swim on its own.

In the meantime, Cleveland CORE had sunk. The chapter had to wait for over eight years before Sis's words materialized. Indeed, an eager band of CORE nonviolent activists emerged, led by yet another spit-fire diminutive black woman. From 1962 to 1965, she would be a central figure among black Clevelanders whose energies brought forth the chapter's second birth. She, along with other Cleveland CORE leaders, led a movement that eventually sent a quake through national CORE's carefully built goodwill foundation and shook apart its ideological underpinnings.

# 3

# An Eager Band

BILLIE AMES and her husband mutually agreed to a divorce. Still, the shock took a painful toll on her personal and professional lives. On March 29, 1955, she worryingly wrote to Geroge Houser, James Peck, and James Robinson, "the only thing right now I'm sure about is that I've got to get out of CORE—even if it means wrecking CORE."[1] Billie Ames's declaration was no small exaggeration. Her title, group coordinator, in no way reflected her central position in CORE. As an active member in St. Louis CORE, she participated in numerous demonstrations and edited the chapter's newsletter *Up to Date With CORE*. Ames took over Houser's duties and essentially rescued CORE after infighting over the Wally Nelson affair led to chapter implosions and member resignations. She also worked to resurrect chapters, which Robinson complained fell like a "house of cards" when leaders left. Thus, other CORE chapters suffered similar fates to Cleveland after Morrow's departure. CORE was coming apart at the seams; Ames told Peck "something had to be done—and quick."[2]

Political and social circumstances during this period further heightened Ames's sense of urgency. One year after national CORE declared its Cleveland branch defunct, the Supreme Court of the United States handed down its landmark 1954 decision ending de jure school segregation in the *Brown v. Board of Education of Topeka, Kansas* case. One year after that, a bus boycott some believe marked the beginnings of the 1960s freedom movement, emerged in Montgomery, Alabama. The city's black citizens, especially black women, depended on segregated public transportation that employed bus drivers who physically assaulted and dehumanized black riders. The arrest of activist Rosa Parks, who refused to submit to city segregation laws, inflamed community action. After previous fits and starts, Parks's decision became the impetus Montgomery's black community needed to launch a one-year bus boycott.

The event electrified the nation and galvanized those who'd fought so many years to utilize nonviolent direct action. Eager bands of activists cropped up around the south and CORE was their to usher them toward activism. CORE national stirred in the background both cheering these racially transformative events and planning to use the moment to highlight its long history in Gandhian nonviolence. However, its own advancement fluctuated throughout the 1950s. It was 1961 before CORE found its footing, and generated massive chapter growth, including the second incarnation of Cleveland CORE. Not surprsingly, the chapter again introduced competing visions about CORE tactic and relationship to the black community. But unlike the 1940s, this time it would not be alone.

Indeed, Billie Ames herself met similar contradictions during the 1950s as group coordinator. Ames had strategized successfully to link CORE philosophy with the burgeoning social movement. Her efforts translated as a financial and publicity boost that could transform CORE recognition into ground activism. However, not every CORE leader liked her approach. Ames attempted to launch a CORE community preparation program after the *Brown v. Board* case. The project readied local neighborhoods for school integration through nonviolent goodwill engagement. However, it created a "stinkeroo" among some CORE members, particularly James Peck and Katie Raymond. The two insisted that such a program could not utilize direct action method, and thus did not fit the CORE way.[3]

Despite efforts to stymy her agenda for CORE, Ames proved more than efficient at raising CORE from oblivion. She was sufficiently untouched by the political intrigue to cajole Wallace Nelson, Juanita Morrow, and other Nelson supporters back into CORE's fold. Marian Oldham joined Ames's effort to reinvigorate chapters. Leaders, particularly Robinson, credited Ames with reviving CORE's finances through her appeals. He also sought her approval for a meeting with Swomley to build a new relationship with FOR. Ames's importance to CORE became so clear that Houser recommended an official title change from group coordinator to national secretary. Ames's St. Louis home would serve as CORE headquarters, though publication and financing remained in New York. Lula Farmer, Peck, and executive committee member Ina Sugihara all agreed.[4]

Then the divorce came. CORE's renewal came to a short halt in spring 1955 when Ames exited. From 1954 to 1957, affiliates numbered at seven. Until 1957, CORE had no paid officers. Its staff was voluntary, and in the lean years between 1955 and 1957, it effectively managed to maintain only a small national staff with consistent participation from CORE founder James Robinson, CORE newsletter editor Jim Peck, Lula Farmer, Wanda Penny, Charles Oldham, and Marion Oldham.

Robinson, Peck, and Lula Farmer took the leading role in CORE after Ames departed. James "Jimmy" Robinson was one of the cofounders of CORE. In the early days, he established the Boys Fellowship House and participated in the early Chicago sit-ins. Jim Peck joined CORE in 1947. His association with George

Houser and Bayard Rustin resulted from his activities as a conscientious objector. One year after his participation in the Journey of Reconciliation, Peck became editor of CORE's newsletter, the *CORE-lator*. Lula, James Farmer's second wife, joined the Evanston CORE group in 1945. She spent her most active years with New York between 1945 and 1948, before departing and returning again in the early 1950s.[5] Together the three moved CORE forward.

Officially appointed CORE's executive secretary in 1957, Robinson followed Ames's example and linked the organization to the civil rights movement. As historian Aldon Morris remarked, Montgomery particularly assisted its quest for "organizational stability, national stature, and development of the [nonviolence] method."[6] In a phrase, the black southern movement generated for CORE public mention, money, and membership. Robinson smartly integrated Martin Luther King's name with donations letters. The association with King and Montgomery validated the organization's nonviolence work. No matter how tangential the relationship, the letter allowed CORE to assert that its nonviolence ideology was a proven method. Just the implication that CORE's work played any role in Montgomery helped it move from lifeless entity to reenergized interracial coalition. Within months, the King connection allowed Robinson to double CORE's mailing list and increase its annual fund.[7] Through his efforts and the images generated in the *CORE-lator*, these appeals garnered enough monies to bring on additional staff at a sustenance pay level. CORE began to grow again.

Nationally, CORE staff expanded to include St. Louis member Marvin Rich as community relations director. Rich's arrival from the St. Louis branch ensured the continuance of a goodwill-styled CORE. In 1947, Bernice Fisher urged Maggie and Irv Dagen to begin a St. Louis CORE chapter.[8] Early members included Charles Oldham, a US Army Air Force veteran and student at the Washington University School of Law; Marvin Rich, a Washington University student and activist in the Student Committee for the Admission of Negroes (SCAN) at Washington University; and other major St. Louis CORE members including Billie Ames, Evelyn Rich, and Henry Hodge. Despite its original association with Bernice Fisher, the St. Louis chapter emphasized negotiation and reconciliation, the goodwill aspects of CORE procedures. Its heavy reliance on the goodwill portion of direct action was the epitome of FOR-style CORE. As Dagen noted, "the whole idea of CORE from the beginning was to win over to our way of thinking people who, initially, for good and bad reasons, were opposed to some of the things we were trying to accomplish."[9] Vital to St. Louis's activist style was a dogged insistence on patience. As such, it gained a reputation for protracted, persistent successes against five-and-dimes, major department stores, and corner drugstores.

In the 1950s, St. Louis members rose to power within national CORE and its goodwill approach and chapter experiences dictated national's philosophy. After

1957, St. Louis members occupied the CORE Council and the national office. Charles Oldham served as council chairman, while Hodge became national vice chairman of CORE in 1959. Rich served on CORE's governing board, the National Action Council (NAC), in 1956 and later became CORE's first community relations director in 1959. Not surprisingly, the St. Louis chapter lost much of its fire when early leaders headed to the national office.[10]

Nonviolent direct action's victory in Montgomery allowed CORE to venture south. In Nashville, FOR members inspired by the Montgomery Bus Boycott formed the first Tennessee CORE, which became a flagship for southern affiliates. Headed by Anna Holden, her entrance to graduate school in Michigan a few years later precipitated an end to its short life. The bulk of its newly created southern chapters, however, came from the southeast including Florida and South Carolina. National's new financial apparatus helped it hire staffer James McCain. James McCain was a principal in Marion, South Carolina, before the board of education fired him for his NAACP activities. McCain later met a CORE affiliate who told him about its search for an organizer with southern contacts, networks, organizational experience, and community stature. One year after joining CORE, McCain's skills and background helped it attain an additional seven chapters in South Carolina.[11]

Gordon Carey followed McCain as CORE's second field secretary. He moved throughout the South, particularly Florida and North Carolina. Carey played a critical role in laying the groundwork for the 1960s freedom movement by coordinating and directing training institutes in Miami, Florida, that prepped emerging activists. The workshops, however, quickly fell by the wayside as national considered other projects and CORE chapters aggressively developed their own nonviolent direct action training.

The reduced focus on training by national had an unexpected consequence, however. It facilitated mass black membership, and did so in two ways. First, chapters asserted direct action campaigns over goodwill negotiations. Demonstrations garnered public attention and chapters attained participation at higher rates. Second, national allowed southern chapters to maintain their mostly/all-black character. Of course, this decision was partly a pragmatic acceptance that there were not likely to be southern whites willing to openly join the southern black freedom movement. Anna Holden and Robinson disliked the arrangement, and Gordon Carey prophetically noted "this tendency . . . could radically alter the nature of CORE."[12]

The issue of all-black chapters had not just arisen under Robinson's tenure either. Shortly after the Nelson fight, Billie Ames too met the challenge of what to do with unbalanced race ratios. Lincoln University, a Historically Black College and University in Jefferson, Missouri, had great difficulty acquiring white members in 1954. Ames solicited advice from Wallace Nelson on how to handle Lincoln. Now back in the fold, the militant pacifist insisted that CORE maintain its interracial character and Ames disband the group.[13]

Five years later, South Carolina COREs appeared to be the largest culprits in this transformation. The other associated problem was one of autonomy. In the black community, CORE worked closely with the NAACP and religious leaders to secure its position in the South.[14] Though Robinson argued that CORE had to distinguish itself from the NAACP, CORE heavily depended on community activists and members closely tied to it. It was difficult to cut ties or create clear lines of demarcation.

Jim McCain ran into other problems with the CORE way as well. Southern branches began to utilize methods not associated with CORE's nonviolent direct action. South Carolina chapters centered activism on voter registration, which Robinson contended was oppositional to CORE philosophy. McCain observed that "plenty of black people didn't feel like doing what CORE had in mind." Yet, CORE wanted SC members to take on its ideological bent and protest targets. Tensions increased between McCain, who insisted that CORE fall in line, and James Robinson, who insisted that the black community do the same. Nevertheless, Robinson had no choice but to accept the changing dynamics impacting CORE. The national office still depended on black southern activists to assert its position in the freedom movement.[15]

Fortunately, the organization also had Tallahassee CORE, a model goodwill chapter that gained CORE nationwide prominence. Tallahassee actually had its origins in the Miami nonviolent workshops. Tallahasseeans were among the over six hundred trainees at CORE's Interracial Institute. The seminars aided Carey and McCain's fieldwork and facilitated CORE formations throughout the South. Although national felt the project produced little result, a number of student leaders came out of its training program and shaped the southern freedom movement. Two of its participants—the Stephens sisters, Patricia and Priscilla—stimulated national CORE's nonviolent action agenda in innumerable ways. Also out of Tallahassee CORE was Gladys Harrington, who eventually left Florida for New York City to become the leader of Harlem chapter and a CORE Council member and most importantly, Richard Haley, who became field secretary and later executive assistant for James Farmer.[16]

Perhaps the most formidable and vital chapter in pre-1960s CORE, Tallahassee was a great boon to the organization. The branch heralded CORE's first major appearance on the national stage. They solidified its southern foothold and earned it more donations than any other local. This chapter was also disproportionately black, though national CORE tightly held the reigns. Robinson, for example, rejected a grant to Tallahassee CORE from the Southern Conference Education Fund (SCEF). Its association with southern white activists Carl and Anne Braden raised too many questions of communist affiliation/influence.[17] On another occasion, Marvin Rich was quick to advise the young women after their arrest to emphasize nonviolence as a method to reach the American conscious. He added that "it would also be well if you could say that you bear no malice or ill will toward your jailers, to those who arrested you, or to the owners of the store."[18]

With the advent of the student sit-in movement, the sisters became one of CORE's strongest commodities. They along with Henry Steele, William Larkins, Barbara and John Broxton, and other Florida A&M University students innovated protest tactics via the jail-in. Their decision to accept jail time garnered national attention and drew even more interest in CORE. Letters about prison conditions appeared in black newspapers, and the students received hundreds of responses.[19]

After their release, CORE sent them on a national tour to raise funds among northern liberal whites. Their tour schedule, which could include up to three states in just a day, so badly exhausted Barbara and John Broxton, William Larkins, and the Stephens sisters' mother that they returned home early. The sisters continued forth but Patricia Stephens suffered nervous exhaustion after her extended work travels.[20]

While black membership expanded in CORE via South Carolina and the Tallahassee movement, yet another event elevated CORE's stature. February 1, 1960, four students sat-in at a Woolworth's counter. Thanks to George Houser's pamphlet *Erasing the Color Line*, North Carolina A&T student adviser George Simkins called CORE for help after the local sit-in set off a movement. Carey, who was scheduled already to arrive in North Carolina within the week, immediately set about preparing area students for a mass sit-in. Additionally, Carey smartly hired students expelled from schools for their civil rights activism, thereby adding to CORE's staff and stature in the South.[21]

The black freedom movement was afoot. Throughout the region, students demanded an end to segregation. Not only had CORE advised the burgeoning student movement, but also its nonviolent direct action history and training made it the lead consultant group. More importantly, the student sit-ins led to a great deal of publicity, highlighted in the pages of the *CORE-lator*. The Woolworth protests additionally proved a powerful impetus for action outside the South for various CORE chapters who held sympathy sit-ins against the national chain.[22]

CORE played an important role for the young upstarts, and national leaders sensed the organization could do more. Yet as an interracially based group, the organization could not ignore one undeniable fact. The southern civil rights movement was black. Of course, white activists played an important role, but the *movement* was black inspired, black affiliated, black supported, black led. CORE chapters in 1960 numbered only twenty-four. If CORE intended to spread its chapters on the ground, it needed to revamp for southern realities in order to keep up.[23]

The reorganization also required new leadership at the top. Purportedly, Robinson lacked rapport with locals, micromanaged, lacked public charisma, and too thriftily controlled expenditures. Leading officers Marvin Rich, Charles Oldham, and Gordon Carey secretly planned to substitute Robison with someone who was a "leader of men" not a bureaucrat or administrative type. In 1961, CORE Council, now called the National Action Council, dissolved the executive secretary position and recreated the title as national director. NAC discharged Robison and replaced him with CORE creator James Farmer. NAC selected Farmer based on his activist background, charismatic leadership, and his black face—a component some NAC members felt situated CORE more properly among the freedom organizations.[24]

CORE officially designated James Farmer national director in February 1961, just in time for national office's first major direct action program since the Journey of Reconciliation. The Freedom Rides, remodeled from the original 1947 Journey of Reconciliation, aimed to test the 1960 United States Supreme Court decision outlawing discrimination in interstate transportation facilities. The Freedom Rides transfigured CORE and launched it among the big four 1960s civil rights groups.[25]

Tom Gaither scouted the Freedom Rides trail and members of New Orleans CORE ventured from Louisiana to Mississippi to test the route deeper south.[26] Unlike the earlier Journey of Reconciliation, Freedom Riders traveled past the upper South and into the deep southern states of Mississippi, Alabama, and Louisiana. The Freedom Rides started with a group of thirteen black and white students entering the South on two buses. On May 4, the first bus left Washington, DC, headed for Mississippi. They reached North Carolina and South Carolina, but suffered arrests and harassment. The riders arrived in Atlanta and then headed for Alabama. May 14, one bus got as far as Anniston, Alabama, when a mob met the bus. White rioters firebombed the vehicle, and activists barely survived. The second group made it to Birmingham but a mob dragged protestors out and mercilessly beat them. From that point, the driver refused to take them any farther. The violence and driver's refusal temporarily stymied the Freedom Rides. Riders traveled from Alabama to New Orleans and subsequently flew out of the South.

Youth associated with the Nashville Student Movement, however, vowed to take over where CORE left off. The students left from Nashville, Tennessee, on May 17 and advanced toward Birmingham. New Orleans CORE was equally adamant about continuing the rides, in fact, more so. New Orleans chapter took over Tallahassee's position as leading affiliate. Not only did it push national CORE to reinitiate the Freedom Rides, but its members were major players in the field, including David Dennis, Oretha and Doris Castle, Mat Suarez, Ronnie Moore, George Raymond, Jerome Smith, and Rudy Lombard. Indeed, Smith, Lombard, and Raymond had charted the path for riders from Louisiana to McComb, Mississippi.

As such, they had a great deal invested in the Freedom Rides' continuance. A New Orleans contingent rode to Montgomery as well with the full intention of continuing the Freedom Rides. Between Nashville and New Orleans, the national office acted quickly to control the action.[27]

Farmer hastily reassembled Freedom Riders and reasserted CORE's leading position. CORE members and Nashville students merged in Montgomery, Alabama. However, they met violence of such proportions that Attorney General Robert Kennedy reluctantly interceded and provided federal protection. The Freedom Ride movement ended on May 25, 1961, in Jackson, Mississippi, with arrests and imprisonment in Parchman Farm Penitentiary, but protests continued throughout the summer in local areas. Along the way, Freedom Riders forced local restaurants, lunch counters, and other public accommodations to desegregate. Eventually, Attorney General Kennedy, after considerable pressure, compelled the Interstate Commerce Commission (ICC) to create and enforce regulations that ended segregation in bus terminals and in interstate travel. November 1, 1961, the ICC officially terminated segregation in bus and transportation facilities.

After the Freedom Rides, CORE was stronger than it had ever been. It immediately launched its Highway 40 Project, which focused on restaurant desegregation from Washington, DC, to New York. Freedom Highways soon followed with a campaign to end hotel and restaurant segregation along highways. Howard Johnson's Florida hotels immediately desegregated, but others refused to do so. The protest stretched from Maryland to Florida, but CORE spent an exceptional degree of energy in North Carolina. It ultimately forced the chain to integrate throughout the state. Though CORE had literally transformed public accommodation access to hotel/motels along the United States eastern corridor, the demonstrations generated little national attention.[28]

Nonetheless, CORE had made its mark on the movement. Chapter expansion exploded to 68 by 1963 and 114 in 1964. Surprisingly, much of that increase emanated from the urban North and the West coast. Chapters exponentially grew in metropolitan New York areas and throughout California. Membership numbers markedly increased as well. Black Clevelanders were no different in their fervor to bring CORE to its city, partially in sympathetic support for the south but mostly because of its own difficulties.[29]

On the Cleveland home front, black residents of the city watched the media attention surrounding the Freedom Rides with their own problems knocking at the door. By 1960, Cleveland became the eighth-largest city in the United States. The black community ranked eighth in the nation as well. Their population steadily increased from 10 percent in 1940 to 16 percent in 1950 to approximately 28 percent by 1960. From 1950 to 1960, Cleveland experienced its greatest influx of black southern migrants in the city's history when the population increased by

Jarvis children's upstairs suite on Central Avenue. Central Avenue marked the main thoroughfare in the black community in Cleveland. The area eventually became the site of black Cleveland's most intensive poverty.
Photo: Glenn Zahn, December 15, 1954. From the Cleveland
Press Collection, Michael Schwartz Library, Cleveland State University

70 percent. The majority settled on the east side where approximately 98 percent of the black population in Cuyahoga County resided.[30] At the same time, white inhabitants in the city declined. One-fifth abandoned the inner city for the plush lily-white life of suburbia. From 1960 to 1963 an additional 44,500 departed leaving only Cleveland's west side and the ethnic enclaves on the east side as the last areas of white residency.[31]

The resulting ratio created an even harsher division of residential segregation. Despite circumscribed boundaries, the white exodus enabled the black community's advancement outside the traditional areas of the Central Avenue neighborhood. Previously all-white areas turned into all-black neighborhoods almost overnight. Kinsman, Buckeye, Hough, Glenville, and Mount Pleasant transferred from traditionally white, often Jewish, hands to black middle-class hands to black working-class and poor hands. In the case of Hough alone, the black population increased from 3.9 percent in 1950 to 73 percent in 1960.[32]

Homeownership rose, but only in the oldest sections of Cleveland, one-third of which classified as deteriorated or dilapidated. Homes were fifty years old or more and located in the oldest sections of the city. Subsequently, few houses were fitted with in-door plumbing or running water. For every dollar spent on homeowner-ship, the black community was four times as likely to live in homes of bad quality. In one area of 1,200 dwellings, Urban League researchers found that 99 percent of the housing fit the above condition.[33]

Renters faired no better. For every dollar spent, black Clevelanders were twice as likely to receive poorer quality housing. For those whites who left for suburbia but chose not to sell their home, they turned a handsome profit charging exorbitant rent. Former one- or two-family homes became rental property for three or more incoming southern black families. Thus the continuum of overcrowded housing that began in the Central Avenue area during the early 1920s spread in the 1950s and 1960s to neighborhoods such as Glenville and Hough, in particular. More importantly, the concurrent effort to "clean up" slum areas translated into a massive urban renewal in which the city removed dilapidated housing but never replaced it. The city of Cleveland exacerbated black people's housing circumstances by its refusal to end segregation in public housing and its allotment of fewer public hous-ing units.[34]

Black Clevelanders encountered employment difficulties as well. In 1950, Cleveland was among the first cities in the United States to pass Fair Employment Practice laws. That same year, black unemployment averaged 25 percent. In 1960, it reached 31.5 percent. The bulk of black labor consisted of unskilled occupations in manufacturing. Though these industries provided higher income, the work was hard and intensive. By the 1950s and 1960s, they faced additional job loss as corpo-rations left the area for cheaper labor in the American and global South.[35]

Nominal upward mobility hardly mitigated the overall deleterious affects of poverty. Among welfare recipients, three out of four cases appeared in low-income black communities. Two-thirds were likely to be located in Hough, Glenville, and Central. In fact, one newspaper article noted that Cleveland had more Alabamans on welfare relief than any other state but Alabama. Cleveland-born welfare recipi-ents only managed to top the former by forty. Three-fourths of the dependent child cases appeared in the same areas. And, 30 percent of Hough's residents received Aid to Families with Dependent Children (AFDC).[36]

If black southerners hoped an education provided a path to the middle class, they soon learned differently. The average black adult's education level in 1950 Cleveland approximated one year of high school at twenty-five years of age. In 1960, the statistic barely moved to two years of high school at twenty-five years old. The Cleveland School Board's decision not to build more schools drastically curbed educational opportunities. It created massive overcrowding with teacher to student ratios that went well over the recommended thirty. Some of the schools went without proper facilities, including libraries and playgrounds. For every $500 spent on white students in Cleveland schools, black students received $379.[37]

The political landscape of black Cleveland, however, fared much better. Black politicians, Republican and Democrat, moved into positions of power, most notable of which was the city council. The initial three representatives in 1950 multiplied to eight out of thirty-three members in 1960. The board of education, however, had no such voting bloc. Only one black representative occupied the school board and the relative absence became a problem that would implode in 1963.[38] Yet political representation, though important, meant little in the everyday life of poor black residents. And although the 1961 Freedom Rides reflected a new movement for black empowerment, black Clevelanders felt none of its successes. They would have to join the fray to redress the de facto segregation and poverty that restricted life in the North.

Nonviolent activism began in full swing with local small groups demonstrating for educational and employment opportunities. Organizations like the Freedom Fighters, Save Our Schools, local parent associations, and the Job Seekers appeared in the late 1950s and early 1960s, and worked alongside older organizations like the Urban League and the NAACP. Yet, none garnered enough strength to ignite a full-scale freedom movement in Cleveland.

In the spring of 1962, an eager band of activists stepped into this open field of freedom struggle organizations and reestablished a CORE Cleveland chapter. Spurred by the city's activist atmosphere and history-making events like the Freedom Rides, Cleveland CORE entered the city reborn. National field secretary James McCain first reactivated the chapter in 1959, but it quickly became defunct. For one year a small cluster of participants floundered about with Gregory Allen as its chairman. The branch eventually folded when Allen faltered after a series of personal family tragedies.[39] Older members like Eula Morrow, an activist in 1940s CORE and mother of Juanita Morrow, rejoined the group but refused to take up the CORE banner after Allen's failure to launch the branch.[40]

By 1961, the Freedom Rides brought the issue of a Cleveland chapter back to the fore, and interested parties wrote the national office for information. Only one person, Al Brent, successfully organized a CORE branch. Brent received permission on March 5, 1962, to begin Cleveland CORE. He held the first meeting April 15, 1962, in the *Call and Post* Africa Room. Shortly after the first meeting, the chapter descended into confusion. Power wrangling immediately ensued. Brent, whose initiative got Cleveland CORE off the ground, declared himself chapter chairman. His subsequent actions unsteadied the newly formed group. He selected an advisory board (local CORE chapters had no such body), assigned people to committee chairs who ostensibly should be selected through democratic means, and set about formulating a state CORE organization with the Dayton, Toledo, Cincinnati, and Columbus chapters—a move never authorized by national CORE.[41]

Needless to say, Brent generated quite some consternation for national. However, he was not altogether to blame for the confusion. Field secretary Fredericka Teer knew of his activities but never outlined correct procedure until members began to complain. To alleviate infighting, national dispatched field secretary Richard Haley. In the succeeding meetings, members elected John Cloud as chapter chairman and Brent vice president. Removed from power, Brent informed the national office of his intention to form another branch. National CORE instantly rebuffed the duplicate, and Brent and his second Cleveland CORE fell by the wayside.[42]

Lest his contributions be ignored as puerile antics, Brent played a crucial role in cultivating ties with other community organizations. Indeed, as "chairman" of CORE he allied with four organization leaders to produce a platform for black equality entitled *Targets for 1962.* The manifesto outlined pressing issues within the black community and demanded solutions for economic inequality, including apprenticeship training, minimum wage increase, and penalties for discriminatory businesses with city and federal contracts. The platform also issued a call for public welfare increase, better medical facilities and sanitation standards, and the establishment of drug rehabilitation centers. The proposal required policemen to participate in human relations education and testing for racial bias; called for allocation of public housing based on immediate need; stipulated prohibitions against subdivisions of one-family homes into multifamily units; insisted on aggressive enforcement of housing maintenance codes; and advocated for information centers to keep residents aware of future services.[43] George Kellon Sr., president of the Eleventh Ward Community Association; Charles Chavers, president of the Negro American Labor Council Cleveland chapter; William Turner, president of Cuyahoga County Voters League; and Lewis Robinson, president of the Freedom Fighters, joined Brent in signing the manifesto.[44]

Of the four leaders to put forth this proposal, Lewis Robinson and the Freedom Fighters played the most pivotal role in Cleveland CORE's development. In fact, Haley hoped they could step in as a ready-made chapter. The Fighters considered affiliation, but they chose not to join because officials felt their philosophy did not quite fit with that of CORE.[45] Failing in this attempt, the field secretary turned for assistance to William O. Walker, dean of civil rights in Cleveland. Haley had heard that "Walker had a very good reputation for being among the first well established Negroes in the city to support the Future Outlook League, a CORE type organization."[46] He also attempted to contact John Holly but was unsuccessful.

Haley could do little to help the struggling chapter, and consequently interested participants dwindled after the Brent affair. By the time John Cloud took over chairmanship in May 1962, there were only six participants. Nate Smith, one of those six, recalled this period as slightly tumultuous but the beginning of one of the most important CORE chapters. Smith remembered joining at the age of twenty-five or twenty-six based on his recollection of the car he drove, a blue and white '61 Chevy.[47] Roena Rand, a Freedom Rider who worked at Western Reserve; Phil Cloud, John Cloud's brother; and the Reverend Bruce Klunder and his wife, Joanne Klunder, joined Nate Smith as first participants.[48]

The small numbers were temporary. Cloud immediately began reconstructing Cleveland CORE, and the chapter made progress only weeks after Brent's removal. By the end of May 1962, Cleveland CORE could boast some success. Cloud completed the constitution and members participated in three protests: a Mother's Day demonstration against the arrest of Freedom Rider and Nashville student leader Diane Nash Bevel; a sympathy kneel-in with Freedom Fighters in support of the Albany, Georgia, movement; and a planned May 30 Freedom Rally.[49]

Even though John Cloud demonstrated rapid improvement in CORE numbers and activism, It was not enough for Mary Hamilton, the third field secretary to visit Cleveland, Hamilton was pleased with neither the leadership nor the membership. John Cloud maintained his position as chairman of Cleveland CORE while also serving as the state chairman of the Committee to Aid the Monroe Defendants (CAMD), an effort to assist militant black civil rights activists Robert Williams, Mae Mallory, and the Monroe Defendants against false charges of kidnapping. Hamilton saw this as a conflict of interest, since national CORE eschewed the organization's communist background.[50]

Hamilton also complained that there were no students, there was high turnover, and the group was "all Negro." She redressed this issue by collecting names, the bulk of which came from the mostly—if not all-white—Students for a Democratic Society (SDS) and the Student Peace Union (SPU). In June 1962, Hamilton sent another reminder to Cloud that included her admonition that he increase membership to at least thirty and that he find "more whites."[51] Perhaps Cloud's worse offense, Hamilton charged that Cleveland CORE had "not recognized the necessity for study of CORE methods and theory."[52]

Cleveland CORE hardly stood alone with an objectionable racial ratio or untrained membership. From 1959 to 1961, the national office documented northern chapters that contradicted the Rules of Action and proper picket line etiquette during joint demonstrations with other black neighborhood organizations. Complaints came in regarding picketers who sang or chanted, blocked entrances, verbally taunted disapproving crowds, and dressed inappropriately even though rules required the exact opposite behavior. CORE national finally felt it necessary to issue "suggestions" for protest etiquette that included being well dressed and quietly walking or occasionally chanting if absolutely necessary. As always, CORE protestors were to remain calm, courteous, and never verbally or physically abusive.[53]

After Farmer's arrival, concerns about protest behavior merged with apprehension over racial balance within the chapters. The massive increase in black recruitment tended to sway tactical direction. This could explain why Marvin Rich and James Farmer held conflicting views on enrollment goals. Farmer recollected his opinion that a mass meeting in Harlem's famed Abyssinian Baptist Church might help bring the black community "on the ground floor of this burgeoning new nonviolent movement." According to Farmer, Rich replied, "'we are not interested in the black community. We are interested in the activists in the black community.'" Farmer said of that moment, "I studied Marvin's face for a while and decided to defer this critical battle within CORE until a later date, after the Freedom Ride."[54]

The interaction exposed internal differences over the nature of what constituted "mass" membership. Marvin Rich, CORE's community relations director and a former St. Louis CORE chapter member, presumed that CORE membership consisted of an elite activist vanguard.[55] This, of course, flew in the face of Farmer's earlier belief dating back to the 1940s that CORE should be a mass nonviolent direct action organization. According to Marvin Rich, despite Farmer's original intention, CORE was not and would "never be a mass organization."[56] Though Rich likely intended to communicate a less clumsy distinction, the underlying question was, who determined CORE leadership, tactics, and membership? Rich assumed that CORE trained elite activists (black and white) in nonviolence. Farmer believed that the masses, if trained in nonviolence, acted as its own force for change. In short, the discussion amounted to who would tell whom what to do. As Farmer noted in the 1962 convention, "no longer a tight fellowship of a few dedicated advocates of a brilliant new method of social change, we are now a large family . . . of the method-oriented pioneers and the righteously indignant ends-oriented militant . . . our problem is the constant internal tension between means and ends."[57] Ultimately, an old question was coming to the fore. What kind of organization was CORE? Who would direct it if CORE invited greater black participation—means or ends?

Farmer's decision to postpone the discussion with Rich became a major misjudgment. It embodied a refusal to resolutely determine the organization's role within and relationship to the black community. Black members were bound to bring with them their own precepts for empowerment, whether they followed CORE Rules of Action exactly or not. Clarity might have helped CORE leaders manage or comprehend the organization's direction before the Freedom Rides dramatically changed its membership. But instead, the 1961 Freedom Rides catapulted CORE into the national spotlight leading black folk to join in droves. National headed into the 1960s freedom movement with problems epitomized by the reissue of action rules, the Rich/Farmer conversation and the concerns sketched in Hamilton's report on Cleveland CORE.

Hamilton's objections notwithstanding, the small group of six soon gained momentum adding on seminal players, including Art Evans, who became CORE chairman for most of its early years; Alex Weathers, a CORE picket captain, and his brothers Cyril Weathers and Malcolm Weathers; Bernard Mandel and David Cohen, professors sequentially at Fenn College and Case Institute of Technology; Don Freeman, head of the Afro-American Institute; Ruth Turner, executive secretary of Cleveland CORE; Antoine Perot, chairman of the action committee; Eric Reinthaler, socialist member, fund-raiser, and chairman of the treasury committee; and SCORE (student CORE) members Don Beam and Pauline Warfield.[58]

Art Evans led Cleveland CORE as chairman during its most active years. Born on May 20, 1932, in Wheeling, West Virginia, Evans's remembered that his family was economically poor but intellectually middle class. Early in life, Evans learned to "despise" his experience of racial discrimination and recalled that local whites often referred to him in derogatory terms. Raised no more than two hours away from Cleveland, Ohio, the city was a natural refuge away from his West Virginia hometown. After he served a stint in 1954 in the US Army, he moved to Cleveland permanently.[59]

Evans's parents introduced him to civil rights activism early in his youth, including information on the NAACP and the early 1940s CORE. Although he joined the NAACP when he came to Cleveland, he was more oriented toward the direct action strategy CORE offered. Evans also recollected that older members, simultaneous to Brent's interest, reintroduced the idea of a chapter and also played a strong role in its restart.[60]

Of the many black and white women involved, Ruth Turner was the chapter's most formidable leader. She became a "mover and shaker" on the issue of black power while on the National Action Council. Her impact on Cleveland CORE and its members was tremendous. Evans reminisced, "there was no greater spokesperson than her . . . it didn't matter if she was a woman or who, I had respect for that . . . She was extremely bright and had a vision that was most unusual."[61] James Farmer added his own insights in his memoir *Lay Bare the Heart*, recalling that Turner was one "of the brightest persons who had been my associates in CORE . . . a brilliant woman, sharp and tough." He went on further to note that while in CORE, "she and I had frequently been at odds," but she was "a formidable adversary, had integrity," and was "a tiger with sharp claws."[62] She also inspired future feminist and activist Barbara Smith. Her leadership was an impactful expression of women's power. Smith recalls that "one of the reasons we were able to do very interesting work with CORE [was] because the executive director was a black woman . . . and she was very open to having two young black women at the office."[63]

Raised in Chicago, Turner's family lived a middle-class life. Her grandfather owned land in Wilberforce, Ohio, and Turner spent her early childhood summers there. A graduate of Oberlin College, she majored in German and obtained a scholarship to the Free University of West Berlin. Turner subsequently returned to the

United States where she received a master's degree at Harvard University from the Graduate School of Education. It was at Harvard University that Turner was introduced and became a member of CORE. Upon receipt of her degree, Turner came to Cleveland, Ohio, to teach German at Collinwood High School until events of the freedom movement called her to action. Turner volunteered for CORE demonstrations and served briefly as CORE chair after John Cloud and before Evans took over. Months after the start of the Cleveland branch, Turner felt compelled to devote all of her time to CORE after the September bombing of the Sixteenth Street Baptist Church in Birmingham, Alabama, which killed four little girls.[64]

Out of the Cleveland chapter, equal to Turner and Evans in power, was her future husband, Antoine Perot. Perot also figured prominently in both Cleveland CORE and the national office during its transformation to black power. Born and raised in Lafayette, Louisiana, Perot's family was situated within the lower middle class. His father worked as a plumber while his mother worked as a housewife. Perot left Lafayette for the army and then migrated to Cleveland in the late 1950s where he attended law school.

Perot learned two early life lessons that influenced his involvement in the freedom struggle: the brutality of white supremacy and the charge by his father to never "lie down and take it."[65] Perot poignantly recalled one story his father shared about a brutal attack and murder in his hometown. White vigilantes targeted a black resident whose sister attempted to intervene in the attack. The vigilante leader also happened to be her baby's father. She hoped the child's presence would deter the lynching. Much to her horror, the baby's father dashed its head against the house and led the vicious mob to hang her brother from a nearby tree.[66]

The second story that loomed large in Perot's memory was an effort to coerce a black farmer into handing over his property. In reaction to the ultimatum, the black landowner along with his sons gathered arms to protect themselves. At the appointed hour, when armed whites arrived, the family ambushed the intruders and fired. Although the black farmer and his family made their point, they subsequently had to escape town after the violent skirmish. The two stories remained embedded in Perot's mind. These lessons left a strong impression on Perot's father and he passed the message to his son: "be a man in other words . . . if you have to go down, go down swinging. That's it."[67]

CORE's direct action method attracted Perot for this very reason. Once Art Evans introduced him to CORE, Perot immediately became immersed in the struggle for freedom. Though his experiential sensibility leaned toward self-defense, he joined the organization with the full understanding and belief in nonviolence strategy. He understood this usefulness, however, solely as a tactic and not as a personal philosophy.[68]

White members of Cleveland CORE soon followed after the Klunders, and also played essential roles. Some considered themselves socialists or socialist sympathizers.

Beth Robinson (wife of Lewis Robinson of the Freedom Fighters), Paul Younger, the Klunders, and Bruce Melville comprised some of the white members unaffiliated with the Socialist Workers Party. Eric Reinthaler, however, entered the chapter as a socialist in Cleveland CORE's early years and brought in additional members believed to have socialist sympathies—his wife, Judy Reinthaler, David Cohen, and Bernard Mandel being three.[69]

Cohen and Mandel, following the Klunders, held leading positions in Cleveland CORE. Both Cohen and Mandel were professors at local colleges. Mandel became well known for his leadership role in the curriculum committee for CORE's 1964 school boycott. Mandel was a well-recognized historian who wrote numerous journal articles along with the book *Labor, Free, and Slave: Workingmen and the Anti-Slavery Movement in the United States*, a biography on Samuel Gompers. A native Clevelander, he also headed the Cleveland Negro History Association. After CORE, Mandel went on to travel throughout Africa, where he became fluent in Swahili. Bonnie Holt, never a socialist, certainly had a socialist background. Holt, later Bonnie Gordon, initially joined the Freedom Fighters at twenty-two, but later linked with CORE. Born in Cleveland in 1942, Holt grew up on the east side with a middle-class family background. Her grandfather, a Hungarian socialist, immigrated to the United States. Her mother followed in the grandfather's footsteps and became a socialist as well. Holt lived with her mother until her death. At age fifteen, she moved in with her father and stepmother, Richard and Jean Tussey, both of whom were socialists and heavily active in Cleveland civil rights. Holt's earliest memories included an overnight visitation from the Monroe, North Carolina, freedom fighter—Robert Williams.[70]

The participation of socialists, however, proved a sticking point for some. Don Bean recalled that "they were not bad people," but the issue of who would control Cleveland CORE was still an early concern.[71] Nate Smith noted that part of the problem resided in public and media accusations that communist or socialist influences directed the ideological path of black organizations. It was a notion to which Smith took great offense. He declared, "I don't care what kind of rights was being denied us, they couldn't . . . tolerate no communists here in this country rallying people . . . like we were some dummies that didn't know the difference that we were being beat up and denied, and segregated and held back . . . we weren't smart enough. Like some communists had to come in and teach us that. That was an insult to me."[72]

According to Smith, members of CORE who associated with the Socialist Workers Party were just close enough to provoke outside accusations, but their participation created more benefits than losses to the chapter. As such, black leaders within CORE were unwilling to cut off important resources over concerns of socialist or communist membership.[73]

Art Evans also noted that the "communist" smear had no relevancy given the more pragmatic concern to obtain and utilize any and all aid. Evans likened the communist furor to drowning with no help from your white brethren while being told that black CORE members should say, no "Mr. communist," I don't need your help, instead "I'll [just] die."[74] Thus, when the Ohio State House of Un-American Committee came to Evans about Eric Reinthaler, CORE's chairman made it clear that as long as Reinthaler met the requirements for membership he and other communists would be a part of the group.[75] Antoine Perot backed this stance arguing for acceptance to any communist members who followed CORE guidelines. In fact, his speech on the subject landed him the position of vice chairman of Cleveland CORE.[76]

In 1963, Reinthaler's presence as a fund-raiser all but guaranteed CORE's strong start. The chapter chartered a bus to the March on Washington. The *Cleveland Plain Dealer*'s editorial was quick to note Reinthaler's "communist" involvement. However, the writer's attempt to out CORE backfired, and the organization garnered additional publicity for its project. The branch gladly added two more buses for its caravan to the 1963 March on Washington.[77]

Still, one year after the group's inception, national still showed displeasure at both the racial and socialist/communist character of Cleveland CORE. John Cloud, in particular, occupied the most troubling category as he was both black and suspected by national CORE to be a Socialist Worker Party member. Richard Haley noted in a report after his visit to Cleveland that the group remained mostly black and seemed unconcerned with CORE's interracial aspect. He went on to say that the chapter operated "as if they'd be more comfortable with an all Negro group."[78] Unbeknown to him, he was somewhat correct.

CORE's black leadership had no intention of handing over power. Art Evans, Nate Smith, Ruth Turner (now executive secretary), and John Cloud deliberately maintained a balance between resource needs that white socialists could provide and black control. As Smith stated, "we couldn't get more than chump change unless we involved these white people in fundraising."[79] But, black CORE leaders aggressively held policy-making positions along with loyal white leadership.[80] So as Smith put it, he was elected treasurer even though Reinthaler raised the money, paid rent, and managed to get wealthy socialist Max Wahl to give Cleveland CORE lots of money.[81]

Oppositionally, Bruce and Lynn Warsaw declared that it was the white membership that controlled the chapter, specifically himself, David Cohen, Eric Reinthaler, and Bruce Klunder. Or rather, whites "manipulated" the chapter until 1964 when black leadership was ready. According to Warsaw, Art Evans lacked the skills to develop CORE because he was "just a bus driver," and Ruth Turner relied heavily on him and Cohen. From his perspective, the two were indicative of the purported poor availability and unpreparedness of black leadership. Warsaw also believed that there were no internal racial tensions until the chapter's move to the "ghetto" or more specifically Hough. However, that belief did not quite mesh with the "pre-meeting" actions among black Cleveland CORE leaders at the chapter's start.[82]

Though whites were very much a part of the leadership, it was not without close watch, which particularly became clear in a later 1965 fight with socialist members. Additionally, although Warsaw believed Turner was not ready to take over CORE, it bares noting that Turner worked for CORE and had a full-time job before she became full-time executive secretary for Cleveland CORE in the fall of 1963. At which point, Cleveland CORE's protest momentum effectively took off. Meier and Rudwick also questioned (like Warsaw) the notion of black leadership given the positions of both David Cohen and Bernard Mandel as committee chairs. But committee chairs had little power. Power rested with the Action Committee, run by Tony Perot. Committee chairs for each CORE project sat on the Action Committee, which served as the policy and directive board to the subcommittees. Of the twenty participants on the Action Committee, six were white. The next most powerful body was the Executive Committee of which two (David Cohen and Bruce Klunder) out of eight were white. Thus, though whites served key roles (particularly Bernard Mandel, Eric Reinthaler, David Cohen, and Bruce Klunder), Cleveland CORE was still predominantly black controlled.[83]

This fact does not negate the relevance of all CORE's members. Other persons, aside from those previously mentioned, were essential to Cleveland CORE. All of these activists, black and white, added to the organization's existence and bolstered its status in the black community. None can be underestimated or relegated as insignificant, especially because their presence made Cleveland CORE among the largest and strongest chapters in the nation.[84]

Six months after its inception, Cleveland CORE garnered an impressive membership list. By the end of 1963, the Cleveland chapter had an active roll that numbered at 140 with 150 probate initiates seeking full membership. The chapter also consisted of over 60 members of the Student Congress of Racial Equality (SCORE). By early spring 1964, Cleveland CORE's membership was still mostly black with 300 members, 100 of whom were active, and associate member numbers that ran into the hundreds.[85]

During the early months when members hovered around thirty, CORE consisted of mostly working-class older black men. However, field secretary Richard Haley considered the women more militant than the men. The group did not receive an official charter from the national office until March 1963, but by then the organization had grown. Cleveland was one of only three chapters outside the South with an overwhelmingly black membership. Others included East St. Louis CORE and Oakland, California, CORE. Though whites joined in numbers enough to somewhat balance the racial ratio, by spring 1964 black members maintained the majority at two-thirds the membership.[86]

At its height, the organization's active and associate members included mostly working- and median income black folks. Many members were highly educated and solidly or transitioning toward middle class. John Cloud, for example, had a middle-class upbringing with a father who owned a flowershop. Though a young organization with a substantial middle-class membership, some considered CORE one of the few organizations to advocate for a working and poor black constituency.[87]

Its legitimacy as a militant Cleveland organization enabled it to meet in a variety of community and church spaces. In the early weeks, they met in one another's homes: Alex Weathers basement, Joanne Klunder's living room, and Phil Cloud's preschool rotated regularly. As CORE got larger, Nate Smith and Don Bean recalled that Corey United Methodist Church, Church of the Covenant (the most oft-used meeting space), the Unitarian Fellowship, and Greater Abyssinia Baptist Church were the most open to CORE's use. Community centers like the Phillis Wheatley Association (PWA) and the Bell Center also served as sites. When CORE finally solidified its headquarter space, the organization's office resided in Hough at the Luxor Building at 1740 Crawford Road.[88]

By summer 1962, CORE completed its constitution and committee set-up. The chapter had a total of five units: executive, membership, action, finance, and public relations. Action projects invariably led to more committees. Subsequently, they added housing, education, and legal sections. As Cleveland CORE incorporated other housing protest projects, it added a rent-strike subgroup. One of the more popular projects, the rent-strike subcommittees could get up to twenty actively serving participants. The last committee created in 1963 was the police action committee.[89]

Aside from funds raised by Eric Reinthaler, CORE received the bulk of its monies from dues, parties, and fund-raising events. The surge in funding and membership allowed CORE to hire their first full-time executive secretary, Ruth Turner, in 1963 at $50 a week. Prior to this position, she served as chairman of CORE from November of 1962 into the winter of 1963.[90] With Turner in as full-time spokesperson and executive secretary, CORE quickly moved from having only a few action projects to so many that major demonstration activities and events overlapped. CORE's growing prestige also reflected in the public's high attendance for "hot topic" demonstrations.[91]

Like most newly created northern chapters, Cleveland CORE spent a portion of its initial time in sympathy protests, forums, and fund-raising for national CORE action in the South. One particular forum illustrated the hampering hand that the national office could have on local chapter activities. In early winter 1963, Turner received a letter from Richard Haley regarding her question about CORE's participation in a forum on William Worthy's arrest. Although Turner viewed his arrest as more a civil liberties issue than racial inequality per se, Haley was quick to seize upon her hesitancy. Haley noted that CORE had no national policy on the William Worthy case, but that Cleveland CORE should remain "objective" or rather distant because of Worthy's pro-Castro leanings.[92] Thus, whatever Turner's proclivities were toward defending Worthy, the national office quickly squashed them.

Despite such a small start, Cleveland CORE transitioned from mostly lectures and sympathy protests to direct action specific to Cleveland issues. Cleveland CORE's first two major activities included a survey of discrimination in motels and a challenge of white residential housing developments, titled *Operation Window Shop*. In September of 1962, the chapter took a group of fifty "Negro buyers" into white neighborhoods to look at homes. The Operation Window Shop project proposed to dually halt the massive flood of whites out of the city while simultaneously providing those black Clevelanders with means to a path out of the crowded edges of the ghetto.[93]

One month later, the small CORE group found that of forty motels investigated, six were caught discriminating. The organization filed discrimination cases with the Ohio Civil Rights Commission. It, too, received little attention thereafter. Truthfully, neither of these actions created major interest from the black community. Indeed, its emphasis on middle-class issues had little relevance to the bulk of black residents in Cleveland, Ohio.[94]

Action against St. Luke's Hospital began shortly after the motel survey. Cleveland's history of discriminatory medical facilities dated back to the early 1910s. Although black Clevelanders finally managed to establish their own facility (Forest City Hospital) in 1939, the building was still too small to house all its patients. CORE acted on complaints of discrimination at St. Luke's Hospital and launched its first direct action project in December 1962. Four Saturdays in a row, CORE picketed. The Freedom Fighters, the Afro-American Institute, the NAACP, and the Federation of Ordinary People joined them. At the end of the month, the group counted its first victory. Though St. Luke's never met with CORE delegates, they capitulated to demands and desegregated the hospital. The victory was small, but a significant step toward enhancing CORE's pubescent reputation.[95]

Following the victory over St. Luke's, Cleveland and other Ohio chapters lobbied the Ohio Civil Rights Commission for passage of a Fair Housing Bill. The Commission for Civil Rights Legislation requested that Cleveland CORE join with other chapters to support a call for fair housing. In June and July of 1963, CORE members staged a sit-in in the Ohio House Chambers and at the governor's mansion, but the proposed measure was unsuccessful. Nevertheless, the demonstration was a crucial move for CORE. The Fair Housing Bill redirected Cleveland's focus from integrated neighborhoods to housing access.[96]

Additionally, Cleveland CORE actions turned aggressive in the state capitol demonstration. CORE members from the Ohio chapters, led by Reverend Arthur Zebb, scuffled to get on the capitol floor. Only Bruce Klunder managed to gain entrance; so, he staged a one-man protest in the middle of the capitol floor. Though the bill failed to pass, subsequent demonstrations followed the state capitol model of action—loud protests, refusal to leave, and blocking entrances. Although this mode of direct action was still fairly new to Cleveland CORE (they had employed the method only once before), other chapters had already begun the transition from quiet, well-dressed protests to loud raucous demonstrations. In fact, Columbus CORE members had chained themselves to the gallery seats in previous protests at the state capitol.[97]

Following the summer 1963 fair housing protests, CORE engaged the issue of housing for the poor. In an open letter to the "power structure," the organization listed the culprits for ghetto housing as the mayor, city council, housing, sanitation, urban renewal, county and welfare department, Cleveland Welfare Federation, banking and finance institutions, and the most egregious offenders, slumlords.[98] It was the organization's first public salvo in the battle against ghetto residency in Cleveland.

CORE eventually added rent strikes to its arsenal of direct action projects in December 1963. The rent strikes were designed to push the group ever closer to its constituency, and move CORE away from its middle-class focus. Hough resident David Owens headed CORE's housing committee. Owens divided demonstrators into teams of rent strikes, landlord research, and tenant displacement/relocation. CORE organized its first tenant council for a rent strike at 8503 Hough Avenue on December 10, 1963.[99]

Tenants at Hough Avenue perhaps had the most egregious problems. They paid an average rent of $90, though most were unemployed and on relief. Of the thirty-two rental units, twenty-five were vacant suites. At least twenty-six children occupied the left-over space averaging at least three children for each unit. Aside from the high cost of rent and overcrowding in small spaces, CORE found numerous maintenance problems. The chapter featured a flyer with rubbish in the alley, holes in apartment ceilings, and children peering between sections of missing banisters. Broken plumbing, cracked doors and windows, torn wallpaper, falling plaster, exposed electrical wires and, worse, children bitten by rats were also problems. In fact, to illustrate the gross nature of the conditions, Antoine Perot and Roger Young took a photograph shaking hands through a window pane entirely without glass.[100]

When CORE attempted to contact the rental agency, the employees threatened tenants with removal. The defiance of the agency led tenants along with CORE to stage a strike. CORE collected the rent money, which their lawyer David Moore held in escrow.[101]

A second rent strike at Longwood Apartments against the Bates and Springer management company followed soon thereafter. Residents complained of rats, roaches, broken laundry facilities, and inadequate building maintenance. CORE and the newly elected president of the tenant council (a neighborhood entity created from CORE tenant strikes), Geraldine Williams, led this strike. Others soon followed.[102]

Rent strikes, though a useful way to garner membership among low-income residents, ate up much of CORE's resources. CORE had to conduct fund-raising drives for persons evicted or who suffered utilities shut down, legal expenses, or relocation. Publicity/leaflets (10,000 copies for the Hough area alone), and a sound truck to bolster the rent strike also added costs. The organization even considered block strikes as opposed to individual sites to save costs and speed owner response. Perot particularly pushed this method with the insistence that CORE maintain a relationship with residents and build confidence in CORE's actions by being constantly *in* the building and in contact. Eventually, Ruth Turner remarked that "perhaps, some of us CORE people will move in with them" as a show of commitment. Though a clear indication of solidarity, this action proved to be an unnecessary step.[103]

The rental agency and management company capitulated to the tenants' demands as pressure mounted. Repairs on all the buildings under protest soon followed. Even the conservative *Cleveland Plain Dealer* was forced to question, "why does it take a crusade by CORE to bring these slovenly housing conditions to a head? . . . where was law enforcement before CORE came into the picture?"[104]

By early spring 1964, CORE had six other rent strikes along 78th Street, between Hough and Lexington Avenues. For each building, CORE set up a tenant council. For strikers who won their settlement, CORE designated a contact to ensure that maintenance of the buildings continued to occur. For each striking residency, they brought in city building inspectors, exterminators, and welfare inspectors. The CORE housing committee held a weekly meeting, developed a written guide for rent strikers, held open discussions with residents, ran a landlord check to determine ownership in other properties, history of violations, and approximate income. They even located landlords' places of home and church, contacted landlords, presented facts and standards for improvement, and issued a deadline for action. Landlords who did not comply could look forward to rent strikes, and were also subject to direct action protests in front of their suburbia homes.[105]

The rental strike movement was the second largest project by Cleveland CORE between 1962 and 1964. From late 1963 into early 1964, it successfully struck two buildings and was in the midst of rental strikes at seven others. The chapter was not successful in all cases. In part, this resulted from two situations. First, some of the slumlords simply could not be broken. Second, rising problems with the school desegregation fight took most of Cleveland CORE's resources and manpower and hindered total focus and funds toward rent strikes.[106] Nonetheless, the chapter clearly established a relationship and a reputation with poor black folks. Its developing aggressive tactics typified a growing inclination toward militancy in many of the CORE chapters across the United States, particularly the East coast.

Despite successes, the chapter met with some antagonism, particularly from Cleveland's black elite and ministerial leadership. Perot recounted that he was often told that he was simply a newcomer to Cleveland with few roots in the community of the same caliber as Cleveland's upper crust. As such, his and CORE's militant antics would end once they packed their one suitcase and departed town. Perot later noted with chagrin that the commentary held more truth than expected, but since he had nice things he actually had to pack two bags.[107]

Ruth Turner fared no better in assessments by Cleveland's conservative black leadership. This was no doubt made worse by the fact that she was a highly educated black woman who could be a pillar as opposed to "running around with those CORE people." As it were, she received poor treatment from middle- and upper-class black women who considered themselves among the better class of women's leadership.[108]

Cleveland CORE happily bore the derision and assumed the mantle of militant advocacy for Cleveland's black poor. Besides, the chapter had greater concerns than the criticism of Cleveland's conservatives, black or white. If Cleveland CORE and its leaders wanted to be part of a people's movement, it would have to maintain a delicate balance between the expectations of the national CORE office and that of the masses. Events in the fall 1963 and spring of 1964, however, would soon upset that delicate balance. The coming confrontation not only positioned Cleveland CORE as the leading freedom organization in the city, but also situated it on the precipice of transformation to black power. As Perot noted, previous demonstrations only served to prepare the organization for the real desegregation showdown. That face-off would not come over employment discrimination or access to public accommodation, but over the single most significant issue of the 1950s, 1960s, and 1970s black freedom movement—school inequality.[109]

# 4

# Lonely Are the Brave

BRIDGETT GILLIAM was a defiant young girl. She had to be. Bridgett attended the predominantly white Collinwood High School where she was susceptible to verbal and physical harassment from both students and teachers.[1] One such confrontation erupted after Bridgett's homeroom teacher, Miss Perkins, singled her out before the class as an example of the school's charity. When Bridgett challenged Perkins, the teacher defensively responded, "I am not prejudiced. Where do I show color?" Bridgett unexpectedly responded with a litany of offenses, which got her dragged out into the hall. Still within earshot of other students, Perkins screeched, "I don't know what to do with you. You are condemned; you'll have to get out of my homeroom!" For added measure, she slung one last parting shot to Bridgett to warn, "You have no friends." Bridgett waited for Miss Perkins's diatribe to end and then heroically replied with only four words.

"Lonely are the brave."[2]

Bridgett's mother had had enough. Ms. Gilliam came to Ruth Turner, executive secretary of Cleveland CORE, for help regarding her daughter's suspension from Collinwood. Turner wrote a report detailing the provocations perpetrated against Bridgett while she attended classes, which included the incident above. Mother Gilliam's choice to seek out CORE and Bridgett's courageous act represented two decided shifts in Cleveland's black community. First, it symbolized the emergence of an engulfing energy and movement for freedom. Second, it signaled the repositioning of Cleveland CORE from a small upstart group to a powerful direct action organization. CORE's leading position asserted itself during the most contentious period of the civil rights movement—fights over school desegregation. And though the school desegregation movement was hardly confined to Cleveland alone, its import lay in how the surrounding events transformed the city and the chapter. The traumatic ending forced members to reexamine the nonviolent direct action tactic, led to dissension within the United Freedom Movement, and propelled CORE toward an embrace of black power.[3]

School discrimination conflicts affected all CORE chapters in differing and myriad ways. Not all of them underwent such a wrenching reevaluation as Cleveland CORE, but some did. The school desegregation movement became so widespread that historians August Meier and Elliot Rudwick referred to the period as "the great school boycotts of 1963 and 1964."[4]

Originally, not many chapters emphasized school desegregation. Few had the resources or tactical know-how to challenge the de facto or de jure systems. During the 1950s, CORE slowly and indirectly made headway on the issue. St. Louis CORE submitted a proposal to desegregate and offered to mediate. Nashville CORE took a similar path in 1958 and attempted to inspire black parent participation in school integration though with little success. Soon thereafter, Wyatt T. Walker, who served as Virginia CORE state director and SCLC lieutenant under Martin Luther King, organized a 1959 march called "The Pilgrimage of Prayer for Public Schools."[5] In the early 1960s, a few East coast chapters demonstrated to end educational segregation— Bergen County, New Jersey, in February 1962, Long Island in August 1962, and Brooklyn CORE in September 1962. Cleveland CORE itself had good reason not to give its attention to the issue as the chapter was barely up and running that year. Secondly, the double dealing by the Cleveland School Board of Education did not fully unfold until the 1962–1963 school year.

In any case, school board protests generally emanated from black parent agitation then shifted to organization action. The tenor of CORE activism in the great school boycott protests depended heavily on local conditions and the catalyst for action.[6] Some circumstances drove CORE chapters to form coalitions with local groups, and many branches led citywide confrontations against school segregation. Chicago, for example, had similar problems to Cleveland. Residential segregation coupled with school board redistricting forced black children into an insufficient allotment of schools. To accommodate high student population, black kids attended schools in "double shifts," or half-day sessions. Eventually, the Chicago School Board of Education solved student overcrowding by adding over two hundred trailer classrooms while 50,000 seats in white schools sat unused. Protests actually began in early 1960, after which the board made a paltry effort to desegregate via voluntary transfers paid for by black parents. Fierce direct action protests broke out again in 1963 with Chicago CORE as principal co-organizer in the movement. Civil rights groups battled it out in demonstrations that degenerated into shoving matches, blocking police cars, kicking and cursing during arrests, and stone throwing at police. Ultimately, local alliances initiated mass boycotts when direct action failed to make headway.[7]

Milwaukee also grappled with the school board over classroom trailers. There, CORE joined an umbrella group called Milwaukee United School Integration Committee (MUSIC). Demonstrations in this city resulted from neighborhood school policies, which required students attend based on home location. Not surprisingly, segregated communities meant segregated schools. School marches in Milwaukee began in force by 1964, particularly when the city's school officials opted to integrate black children into white schools, but then segregated the classrooms in the receiving school. This was also a key issue in Cleveland and it eventually led, in both cities, to boycotts in 1964. Though protests continued in Milwaukee until 1965, the school board still refused to implement any desegregation plan. According to education scholar Jack Dougherty, MUSIC activists in due course circumvented school board recalcitrance and created an independent school in 1966. It was called Harambee Community School.[8]

In New York similar forces were at work. While black children crowded into ghetto schools, white children attended private and parochial schools. New York also began with a voluntary transfer program, which required black parents bear the costs. New York CORE failed to get much participation for the voluntary program. They soon learned that greater concerns lay in financial shortages, poor curriculum, and teaching quality. Despite policy differences, New York CORE joined Harlem Parent Committee and Parents' Workshop to create an umbrella group to integrate New York schools in summer 1963. Protests in Harlem got so hot that even Bayard Rustin helped organize a one-day school boycott.[9]

Around the same time, Brooklyn CORE became an active member of New York Citywide Committee for Integrated Schools. School board resistance in that borough led to cries for community control and the formation of a black parent/activist coalition school board in Ocean Hill-Brownsville. Brooklyn CORE, a central mover in the movement, joined what became the People's Board of Education. From their perspective, local control meant their right to hire and negotiate contracts with teachers, develop school curriculum, and set school budget. However, relations between the People's Board and the teacher union devolved into political machinations that summarily led to the parent-controlled board's dissolution. Ironically, the person most responsible for the failure of the Brownsville School Board was Albert Shanker, a former 1950s white New York CORE member and leftist, who historian Jerald Podair argued deliberately set out to destroy the Ocean Hill-Brownsville experiment.[10]

Seattle CORE got a late start in its school protest movement. In that case, the NAACP, the Urban League, and CORE triggered school action. Once again demonstrations started over a contentious voluntary transfer program. By spring 1965, the CORE/NAACP/Urban League coalition grew tired of board delays and began direct action marches. As was the case in Milwaukee, CORE and other groups remained integrationist in their goals, but black parents began to question the point of voluntary transfers that made them pay the costs of transportation. They too considered community-controlled schools, though Seattle CORE was unaffiliated with these efforts. The transfer plan actually dragged on until 1978 when it became compulsory because the city feared federal intervention.[11]

New Orleans CORE found the school desegregation fight to be a particularly galvanizing force for the city. Philadelphia's school movement successfully forced the school board to capitulate to integration demands. However, their school board reversed position and simply built another school. In St. Louis, CORE blocked school buses that transferred students to segregated schools. School board sit-ins also occurred in San Francisco, Englewood, New Jersey, and Cincinnati.[12] North, south, east, or west, CORE chapters rigorously fought to end school discrimination, sometimes individually, more often through community alliances.

Cleveland similarly reflected the coalition propensity of its sister chapters, though it was not without conflict. The last week of May 1963 Cleveland CORE leaders partnered with various grassroots groups to form the Cleveland United Freedom Movement (CUFM). Present at the formation of CUFM were Ruth Turner, executive secretary, and Art Evans, chairman, for CORE; Donald Freeman of the Afro-American Cultural Institute; Jim Russell, Lewis Robinson, and Leonard Hayes, leaders of the Freedom Fighters; Reverend C. T. Caviness of the Greater Abyssinia Baptist Church; and Baxter Hill, head of the Defenders of Human Rights.[13]

Before circulating a press release about the creation of CUFM, the group made the fateful decision to hold off announcement until Lewis Robinson's return from his travel south to assess direct action activities. During his absence, the NAACP publicized the formation of a rival umbrella group. Instead of a small coalition of Cleveland's most militant and radical entities, the NAACP gathered under its leadership a combination of civic and social-minded organizations under the title United Freedom Movement (UFM). Eventually, the number of participating organizations totaled over fifty.[14]

Cleveland's militant activists were livid. They charged into the first meeting of the United Freedom Movement and called out the NAACP for its duplicity. Associates of the Job Seekers, CORE, and the Freedom Fighters received no solace, and yielded to a United Freedom Movement over CUFM. In return, the NAACP gave CUFM leaders paltry committee positions. Nonetheless, the NAACP made its own error in judgment. Much closer to the black community's needs, the presence of those groups pushed the United Freedom Movement in ways that the conservative NAACP did not want to go.[15]

The United Freedom Movement kicked off its newly launched umbrella organization on July 14, 1963, with a massive interracial, interfaith rally in downtown Cleveland. Over 25,000 demonstrators listened to Roy Wilkins, executive director of the NAACP, and James Farmer motivate the crowd and inaugurate the new movement. UFM organizers considered the march the first major event in Cleveland to liberate the "soul of America" and "convey a sense of urgency."[16] Coordinated by Harold B. Williams of the NAACP, UFM chairs included Rev. Paul Younger, Rev. Isaiah P. Pogue, attorney Clarence Holmes, and Carriebell Cook. Ruth Turner of CORE served as secretary (this would be a recurring theme throughout her tenure with CORE).[17]

UFM's strong start, however, did not mitigate the organization's difficult search for a project that inspired community support. Their efforts toward unemployment, for example, dragged on for months with little impact. Worse yet, the tumultuous founding and the varied and major differences among UFM participants hardly made for an energetic association. Fortunately for them, their search for a galvanizing discrimination project came soon after black parents in the poor and working-class neighborhoods of Hough and Glenville made their presence felt in protest after protest over the issue of school desegregation.[18]

Grievances against the Cleveland School Board of Education (SBE) began as far back as the first influx of black southerners in the 1920s and 1930s. The NAACP sent it a complaint regarding curriculum reduction, low percentage of students taking math at Central High School, and the replacement of foreign language and bookkeeping with home economics and manual training classes—which included course subjects like laundry procedures.[19] By 1944, even CORE chairman Juanita Morrow felt the need to document school segregation as evidenced by the forced transfer of black teachers to all-black schools.[20]

Complaints came from all directions about the Outhwaite School for Boys and Longwood School for Girls. Black Clevelanders described both as dumping grounds for black southern children mislabeled retarded. Purportedly, the original directive for Outhwaite and Longwood mandated that the schools operate as an educational middle ground until black southern children could matriculate into their proper grades. Instead, students experienced pitiable treatment and the two institutions soon earned the moniker of "dumbbell schools" or the "penitentiary." Additionally, the number of black southern children classified for "special classes" continued to rise along with Outhwaite and Longwood's student population.[21]

As the years wore on, concerns increasingly grew over the lack of proper classes at all the schools. Worse, the addition of policemen to maintain discipline only aggravated parents' bad feelings toward the school board. Buildings grew old; students used poor equipment and had inadequate library and recreational facilities—presuming schools had a playground or library at all.[22]

The 1950s showed no improvement in the condition of black education. The school board refused to allocate funds to build new schoolhouses. From 1947 to 1952, the school board of education constructed schools only in white areas, despite the fact that mass exodus by whites out of Cleveland left a 6,000 drop in enrollment. By 1950, schools in the Central Avenue area had become overwhelmingly black. In the following decade, black school population from 1950 to 1965 went up from 98,000 to 149,655, with elementary schools experiencing the worse overcrowding.[23]

Simultaneously, school districts were drawn to maintain segregation. White neighborhoods too close to black wards were designated optional zones. For those white students who wholly fell within black school districts, the education board arranged "special transfers" on the basis that certain specialty classes were unavailable in black schools. Again the NAACP lodged a complaint but to no avail.[24]

In 1955, the Cleveland school board finally acted to alleviate the pressure of overpopulation, particularly in the elementary schools. The board initiated half-day attendance in what they called relay classes. Children attended school for approximate 3 ½ hours a day. Hough and Glenville were the first neighborhoods to feel the impact of these relay classes.[25]

Black parents were unhappy with the new solution. Before the entrance of CORE, they aggressively attacked the board of education for its mendacious mistreatment of their children. The Hough Area Citizens for Better Schools Committee, for example, investigated and reported on the relay system's harmful effects on teachers, students, and curriculum standards. Hough Area Citizens received no response. Little more than a year after relay classes began, black mothers demanded an end to the policy as a temporary solution to overcrowding.[26]

Parents also attempted to deal with overload by selecting alternate spaces in black neighborhoods for teaching. With parents' permission, the school board set up classes in churches, libraries, and portable classrooms—all of which were located in the black community. Parents additionally pushed for the purchase of a school bus that could transfer students to other less-crowded classrooms in black schools. As protests mounted over the relay classes, the school board sought passage of school building levies, but the referendums failed, and no new schools were built.[27]

Simultaneous to black parents' demands, the NAACP conducted an education survey in late 1961, early 1962. The group asked local organizations to back the investigation report's recommendations. The NAACP hoped to receive a response from SBE with regard to its suggestions for integration and better educational standards. However, the NAACP received no response.[28]

When community action waned, the school board shirked its responsibilities and allowed the problem to grow. In the early 1960s, de facto segregation in Cleveland schools impacted 93 percent of children in elementary schools, 78 percent in junior high schools, and 83 percent in high schools. Even more, 5,000 children in the Hough area alone were on relay. White classes stood empty and still more schools were built. Contrarily, black children continued to attend schools in overcrowded, dilapidated surroundings while Cleveland SBE claimed it acted in the best interest of Cleveland's children by maintaining a "neighborhood school" policy.

As a result, the beginning of the 1962 school year met with another round of protests from parents. On October 9, community folk attended the school board meeting to demonstrate again. Originally organized under the name Hough Parents, the group changed its title to the Relay Parents March to Fill Empty Classrooms. Headed by Daisy Craggett and Clara Smith, these women became instrumental in leading the school desegregation movement and were essential partners for CORE. As the numbers increased, the organization morphed into the Hazeldell Parent Association (HPA), led by Eddie C. Gill and then Mrs. Minnie Hill. HPA was joined by PACE—Plan for Action by Citizens in Education, the Citizens Committee to Support our Schools, and area council associations in Central, Hough, and Glenville neighborhoods. Previous to UFM's formation, these organizations held numerous rallies and marches on education inequality. [29]

After the school board refused to assuage black parents' grievances, the group came up with their own solution. Parents discovered available space in white schools, which the school board knew existed. If the school board would not construct new schools in black neighborhoods and increase educational access, then black parents would send their children where the system offered more education courses and where there was plenty of space—white schools. [30]

Under intense pressure from parent protestors, the school board folded and promised to transfer black children to white schools in the 1962 winter semester. Over fifteen hundred black children transferred from their schools to over nine white schools. The majority went to three receiving schools—Murray Hill, Brett, and Longfellow. All consisted of a predominantly white student percentage with Murray Hill ranking highest at 100 percent. Brett followed a close second at 97.8 percent. [31]

Community leaders additionally pressed for a levy that funded more schools for the black community. On the November 1962 ballot, education activists hoped the citizens of Cleveland would pass a fifty-five-million-dollar levy for school construction funds. Support Our Schools, an organization founded to assist relay parents, initiated a massive campaign of weekend calls and parades through the streets in alliance with neighborhood councils to garner support. The levy never passed, and the Hough and Glenville neighborhoods were dejected by the loss. [32]

Mere weeks after the school levy failed, the school board met with white parents to respond to growing anger over integration of their schools. Outraged white parents drove the board to maintain separation within receiving schools. Despite black parents' victory and much to their irritation, all the receiving schools divided black children into separate classrooms and either segregated or barred them from extracurricular activities. The first half of 1962, black Clevelanders struggled to force the school board to alleviate the new problem. [33]

Parents became further infuriated as reports trickled in detailing the egregious situation in receiver schools. School officials prohibited departure from the classroom, with one exception. Black students had a once-a-day bathroom break. Children, disallowed from sitting in the school cafeteria, ate lunch at desks in their assigned classrooms. Murray Hill Elementary forbade use of the pool. All the school administrators confined playground time to one period for all transferred black students or closed down any playtime at all. Fed up with administrative staff and teachers, the outrageous actions of the white receiving schools in the 1962–1963 school year goaded black parents to demand full and unconditional desegregation.[34]

Although the NAACP had previously addressed school inequality, angered relay parents were drawn instead to CORE. In late spring 1963, CORE and the Hazeldell Parent Association took their call to arms to the United Freedom Movement. UFM would serve as a launching pad for an all-out nonviolent assault against the Cleveland School Board of Education. Joined by the Job Seekers and the Freedom Fighters, Cleveland CORE and the Hazeldell Parent Association dragged a reluctant NAACP and the United Freedom Movement into direct action.[35]

UFM officially entered the school desegregation fight in the summer of 1963.[36] SBE grew concerned over mounting militancy by black parents and the new presence of civil rights groups. The administration consequently put out a policy statement on Equal Education Opportunity for All. The mission platform advocated for an outside entity to serve as a bridge between parents and the SBE. That liaison group became the Human Relations Council. Human Relations Council was charged with conducting a study on racial inequality, disseminating program resources and teaching materials, training teachers on human relations, and a directive to outline how SBE might overcome past educational deprivation.[37]

The SBE's Equal Education policy was met with derision. Black parents balked at the half-baked proposal, and immediately noted that there were no concrete deadlines nor did it deal with the treatment of black children in the receiving schools. Throughout July and August 1963, UFM met with SBE about the NAACP report that designated forty-four schools as predominantly white and eleven schools as predominantly black. School comparisons also indicated the obvious inequality in resource distribution. Further, the NAACP pointed to SBE's deliberate separation of black and white students, especially via special transfers.[38]

At the end of August, the United Freedom Movement submitted its own proposal of seven demands for integration of students, teachers, administrative staff, and curriculum materials. Not only would the school board follow its own edict to create a human relations committee, but UFM also insisted that it do more than a simple study. Instead, they revamped the Human Relations Council title (Bureau on Integration and Race Relations) and its function. UFM tasked it with implementation of a school integration plan, elimination of discriminatory practices, establishment of compensatory education programs, teacher training in human relations, and program creation for interracial and ethnic contact.[39]

The UFM also stipulated that the integration of all the transported classes must begin immediately. They served notice that the apprenticeship program at Max S. Hayes Trade School should be integrated or the whole curriculum outright discontinued. UFM also directed the school board to locate and use black real estate brokers to acquire and appraise property for school sites. Lastly, after selecting proper school locations, they stipulated that the school board must enforce construction contract requirements that prohibited discrimination as well as implement a no-discrimination clause within its own business and maintenance departments. The deadline for school response was set for September 23, 1963.[40]

In the weeks that followed delivery of UFM demands, the United Freedom Movement and the school board convened in closed door meetings. Cleveland SBE first claimed they kept classes segregated to keep the teachers with their students and to retain some of the neighborhood school atmosphere. The school board then argued that there were no incidents of segregation that hindered the educational progress of black students in the receiving schools. The United Freedom Movement contended that sequestering black students amounted to an internal segregation and the very nature of segregation limited black children's educational progress. Neither party found room for compromise.[41]

On September 16, 1963, before the deadline, the Hazeldell Parent Association met with the school board to discuss the UFM petition but the meeting ended badly. The deadline passed with no action by the school board. September 24, 1963, the day after the deadline, UFM called a mass rally of four hundred people at St. Mark's Presbyterian Church. Ralph McAllister, president of the school board, attempted to stall protest with another meeting. At the urging of CORE and the HPA, the UFM refused to wait and planned a picket of the school board of education building at 11:30 A.M. the following day.[42]

On September 30, a few days into protests, the school board capitulated to all UFM conditions and pledged to institute the program in January 1964. The only demand not met was the Bureau on Integration and Race Relations. Instead, they drafted another version of the committee and called it the Citizens Council of Human Rights (CCHR), a body that could study the issue of integration, but could not enforce it. Believing that their prerequisites would be fully met, UFM ended their protests. However, it touched off negative reaction by white parents from the receiving schools and their organization, the Collinwood Improvement Council (CIC). In the month of October, CIC roused the white community against integration. Over two hundred parents met at Memorial Elementary PTA to raise objections to SBE's plan. CIC brought to the next school board meeting a petition signed by thirty-four hundred residents.[43]

Under attack from white parents, the school board relented to their demands, and informed them that integration would be limited and would only take place where facilities were unavailable. Simultaneously, the UFM generated three work-ing papers on the necessity for integration. The first and third paper advocated the integration of classrooms and educators to chart a path toward ending discrim-ination. The second paper presented the idea of "compensatory education"—an affirmative action proposal that required the allotment of more funding to areas of historic educational inequality. In effect, a reverse flow of monies from white schools to black schools to equalize expenditures.[44]

Early in the winter school year 1964, transfer students began "diffusion" at receiver schools, but it did not occur as expected. When UFM received Cleveland SBE's blueprint for integration, the new plan failed to follow the agreed-upon deal. Instead of full use of the facilities and integration of at least the homeroom classes, the white receiving school barely reached 5 percent diffusion over the school week. Worse, students experienced episodes of harassment by teachers, including one white teacher who used a missing pencil to claim black people steal and needed training not to do that in white communities.[45]

Desegregation picketers Congress of Racial Equality and United Freedom
Movement, and counter protestors, North American Alliance for White
People, demonstrate outside the Cleveland Board of Education.
Photo: Bernie Noble, September 30, 1963. From the Cleveland
Press Collection Michael Schwartz Library, Cleveland State University

When Cleveland SBE renounced its agreement with UFM, it raised the ire of both Hazeldell Parent Association and United Freedom Movement. The parent association collected over 1,700 signatures for a petition to desegregate white schools. However, HPA concerned itself less with school-wide desegregation and more with specific student mistreatment. In other words, students and teachers could be kept in the classes together so as not to disperse the transported children and to internally maintain the "neighborhood" policy. However, it was not acceptable to wholesale and deliberately separate the students or block their use of school facilities and resources, acts that systematically produced unequal access.[46] Civil rights groups followed Hazeldell's platform, but further argued for SBE to desegregate Murray Hill, Memorial, and Brett elementary schools in accordance with the *Brown v. Board of Education* ruling. The newly created CCHR attempted to quell the animosity between the school board, United Freedom Movement, and the Collinwood Improvement Council. However, when school board members failed to attend a meeting, CCHR could not stop the progression toward a showdown.[47]

During the last week of January 1964, UFM and CORE began a multipronged protest at the school board of education building, and two receiving schools, Brett and Memorial Elementary. CORE and HPA provided the most manpower. During the morning 125 protestors marched at Brett and 75 appeared at Memorial in the afternoon. In both cases, demonstrators scuffled with angry white parents and the mob heckled or outright attacked protestors. Though the SBE issued another resolution, it was too little, too late. SBE modified its plan again to change receiving schools from white districts to "other" classroom spaces. Undoubtedly, this meant transfer to other black schools already hampered by overcrowding though less so. In effect, SBE clearly intended to circumvent the agreement and stall desegregation. UFM rejected it.[48]

On January 30, protests reached a crescendo at Murray Hill Elementary, a school located in the Italian ethnic neighborhood known as Little Italy. Murray Hill's white residents gathered around the school early that morning. Starting around 9:45 rioters became violent as rumors spread that protestors waited a short distance away to begin demonstrations. The angered throng struck anyone who seemed not to be a resident of the area. Agitators beat and threw bottles, eggs, and fruit at reporters, photographers, and innocent bystanders. Michael Antonucci, one of the few lone white voices who acted to calm the crowd, was beaten for his efforts. The rowdy crowd also vandalized the car of two black activists who missed the meeting point for the demonstration. Dissenters clubbed the vehicle with stovepipes, bricks, and cudgels.[49]

In the interim, marchers gathered in a parking lot off Mayfield Road near Western Reserve University approximately a quarter mile down a hill from the white mob. Before the march began, CORE activists listened to urgent pleas by ministers, priests, and black leaders who begged them not to go into Murray Hill. Harold Williams contacted direct action leaders in the parking lot by police radio and asked them to delay the picketing, claiming UFM was close to ending negotiations. Ruth Turner, opposingly, unwaveringly rejected the request and then staunchly made her opinion clear. Before anyone could stop her, Turner climbed to the top of a car and roared for protestors to hold firm! With fist raised, she shouted that they had come to face segregation at Murray Hill School, and they would not turn back now. They will charge up Murray Hill and face the mob! Turner's speech seemed to inspire the crowd onward. Meanwhile, fearful ministers and other worried participants grew horrified by the unfolding scene in the face of what they believed would be a blood bath.[50]

After Turner refused to halt the demonstration, advocates to end the protest quickly turned to Antoine Perot in hope that he might restrain Turner. Instead, Perot interceded with what he considered to be a middle-ground solution. If protests were to continue, he would only participate with all male demonstrators. Not only that, Perot further stipulated that those men who joined should be warned that this march was no longer a nonviolent direct action. In essence, any man going up Murray Hill had to be prepared to defend himself—violently.[51]

Perot's alternative certainly failed to address the ministers' concerns or that of other persons wishing to end the march. In fact, to their dismay, it only incited a showdown they hoped to avoid. Whether it was the thought of violence or the pleas to end the demonstration, the barrage of appeals prevailed upon Turner. She canceled the morning rally. Not to be outdone, however, Turner agreed only to a temporary halt and insisted that the possibility of an afternoon demonstration be left open.[52]

Violence temporarily dissipated around noon as white students came out for lunch (black children were kept inside for their own safety). The mob assumed a festival-like atmosphere when rioters passed around pizza and donuts. Reports spread that alcohol also went through the crowd, which precipitated the afternoon rise in violence. Police, who initially refused to quell the mass, now charged into the crowds to prevent them from entering the school and assaulting black children. Mob participants then headed down the hill to attack any remaining demonstrators. Fortunately, black activists had dispersed at 1 P.M. to another gathering point and barely missed the group coming toward them. After the afternoon melee, not one person was arrested. Rumors later abound that disgruntled white insurgents planned an excursion into the black community, but this was supposedly halted when number runners "sent word" that Murray Hill rioters who entered Hough did so at their own peril.[53]

Meanwhile, SBE called an emergency meeting with UFM that lasted from the morning and into the late afternoon. At 3 P.M. the Murray Hill demonstration was officially called off. The board ultimately yielded and gave an informal promise to have all transport students properly integrated into receiving schools but added the caveat that it would not begin until September 1964. September was an unacceptable date, particularly to CORE. It was just another stall tactic.[54]

The next day, CORE took lead in a protest and occupied the front of the SBE and its hallways up to the third floor. Forty-one activists spent the night at the SBE building in protest of its segregationist policies and police refusal to protect picketers at the Brett, Memorial, and Murray Hill. By evening, four demonstrators left, but others remained into the night. Twenty-five of the remaining overnighters came out Saturday, the following day, in order to plan and participate in a rally scheduled for Sunday evening at Cleveland's Antioch Baptist Church. The rest remained in the SBE building through Sunday.[55]

The following evening Ruth Turner gave a fiery speech at the Sunday rally in which she vehemently declared, "I'm going to change the tone of this meeting, because I'm angry—very angry." She went on to charge that, "I will tell you who is responsible for this mess and what we should do about them . . . McAllister: recall or impeach him. Board of Education, for its broken promises and backroom dealings with the Collinwood Improvement Association; support bond issues for integrated education and defeat those for segregated education."

Turner was also highly critical of Mayor Locher as well as black ministers and councilmen who wanted to avoid a fight and not take a stand. As far as she and CORE were concerned, UFM needed to "work for the election of those who want integration." Or else, "Why . . . continue to vote for people who do not speak for us?"[56] The crowd was more than receptive; observers noted that the audience leapt to their feet, shouted, waved, and applauded.

Baxter Hill, leader of the Defenders, was just as confrontational in his speech, if not more so. According to Hill, "Time has run out for the Negro to wait." Hill went on to say, to some amusement, that, "I'm a Mau-Mau . . . I've found out that the only way we are going to get anywhere is to believe in Mau-Mauism." Finally, he ended by saying that "Time has run out for anyone to mistreat us any more."[57] The words at the church didn't just reflect a dramatic oration by Hill and Turner, the most militant presenters. Frustrated by SBE's pendulum decisions and UFM's hesitations, the more militant organizations were now poised to take over UFM and push it toward more aggressive rhetoric and tactics.

UFM's coalition held another demonstration at the SBE building and discussed a massive citywide boycott. On February 3, the Freedom Fighters marched in front of city hall. On February 4, UFM picketed the SBE building, but this time with a difference. CORE had clearly ascended to leadership within UFM and moved to a more active sit-in protest.[58] Protests by CORE reached new levels as members trapped one woman in the restroom, blocked elevators, obstructed doorways—including

Demonstrators from CORE block door inside the Cleveland School Board of Education. Antoine Perot is center with his head positioned downward. Photo: unknown photographer, January 29, 1964. From the Cleveland Press Collection, Michael Schwartz Library, Cleveland State University forty who barred entrance to the office of the SBE superintendent—and hindered paths through which police tried to move. Even Harold Williams, coordinator for UFM and executive secretary for the UFM, had difficulty reaching the third floor.[59]

Response was brutal. Police dragged CORE members down the stairs from the third floor. One pregnant woman was nearly pushed down the stairs. At the same time, police barred journalists from reaching the third floor in order to view law enforcement's actions. Twenty-two protestors were arrested, among them Ruth Turner. All were charged with obstructing justice and, ironically, police assault.[60]

CORE's decision to forcefully take over the SBE building signaled three important developments. First, it indicated CORE's new position among UFM members. Second, it demonstrated a clear break from the hampering hand of the NAACP and conservative elements within UFM leadership. Third, it hinted at the inevitable division within UFM between the NAACP and CORE.[61]

As the school desegregation movement blossomed, the dynamics between Cleveland's militant organizations and the NAACP became strained. On the one hand, the NAACP's advocacy of negotiation over direct action constrained its ability to act in total alliance with CORE and other direct actionists in UFM. On the other, CORE's actions within UFM pushed the NAACP further than it had ever been before. Nevertheless, the NAACP's hesitancy about direct action during a period of constant deception by the SBE made it susceptible to power grabs within UFM from more assertive groups, particularly CORE.

A confidential report in February 1964 by the Jewish Community Federation summarized the brewing internal strife between CORE and the NAACP." The power, however, has increasingly been assumed by the more militant groups and the 'respectable' organizations have either stopped attending at all or have played an unimportant role and have directed their efforts to other channels. Even in the Negro community, only those organizations and individuals ready to lay it on the line for direct action of increasing intensity retain standing and influence . . . CORE representatives, a number of local newly emergent groups, and hitherto unknown individuals (most of them quite young) have in large part taken over, although the NAACP, which has grown vastly more militant, remains the leader."[62]

Although the NAACP seemed to retain its leadership over UFM—as its founding organization—CORE's increased standing, larger demonstration participants, and respected relationship with the Hazeldell Parent Association greatly energized UFM. More important, CORE compelled UFM's embrace of direct action and the school boycott as protest methods against the Cleveland School Board of Education. CORE's influence was not greeted well by everyone within UFM. Frustrated by the influence of CORE, one informant revealed to the FBI that conferences and controlled picketing had always been successful for their organization and that CORE was to blame for racial violence. The NAACP, for its part, responded with aggravation over CORE's action against the school board. Their executive secretary and coordinator for UFM noted that the "sit-in at the Board was peaceful and according to plan until some participants against the agreed plan took matters in their hand and trapped the elevators, blocked stairs and held hostages in lavatories." The NAACP, however, was clear in its condemnation of the police action that followed, noting, "this was a job they [police] intended to enjoy."[63]

After the SBE police beatings, Mayor Locher hoped to avoid further demonstrations and asked the Cleveland Community Relations Board to intercede. The evening of February 4, SBE and city officials once again agreed to meet the demands of UFM. UFM temporarily suspended its demonstrations until member organizations could vote on the proposal. This time, the integration of students would occur during the second period of the winter semester beginning March 9, and the SBE would review plans for new schools to alleviate overcrowding.[64]

UFM formally approved the stipulations, but also added that it would not accept, under any condition, relay classes, overcrowding, substandard classrooms and schools, rented spaces, or any other temporary educational spaces. UFM further stated that they would not allow the neighborhood policy to become a red herring that reinforced the unequal share of resources. The organization went on to state, "We accept the agreed upon settlement with the understanding that the re-segregation of our children must not be a consequence . . . We will now watch carefully to see that the new pledges which we and the Board are agreeing to will be carried out faithfully."[65]

Turner, however, responded much more negatively to the proposal, stating, "It was nothing. It should have been rejected last Tuesday. The community interest has subsided now. We will have to start all over again to get community interest."[66] In spite of Turner's fears, Cleveland's black community was in no danger of losing interest. However, it was more likely that her issue revolved more on the NAACP's insistence on engaging in back-and-forth negotiations that stalled direct action momentum than an actual lack of interest per se. Additionally, there seemed to be no point in accepting a proposal with SBE since it was prone to rescinding its agreements in the first place.

Not surprisingly, the SBE proved to be anything but faithful. It translated this agreement as a decision to re-segregate via newly built schools while receiver schools temporarily integrated black students. CCHR had planned to produce a report in March for school sites. However, SBE ignored this arrangement, and skipped to its own previously discarded plans. The costs were great. The expenditures for building a new school equaled $1.25 million while the fees for bussing to nearby empty classrooms amounted to $35,000 a year.[67]

Two architects formerly hired to build proper schools were fired. SBE rehashed discarded plans and used them as the basis to begin immediate school construction before its own CCHR finished its proposal. SBE scheduled three elementary schools for construction in the black community of Glenville—all of them on substandard sites. CCHR discussed their concerns about building schools at the selected sites, and it along with UFM requested that SBE cease its construction. The City Planning Commission rejected the first school site, Woodside, for two reasons. The first was its substandard size (no space for playground and would have to be three stories to accommodate small space). The second related to location; it was a mere two and half blocks away from Hazeldell Elementary School. The second school spot, Lakeview, suffered the same problems as the first site—substandard lot opposed by the City Planning Commission. Further, improper planning situated the school next to a planned widening of Lakeview Road, which stripped down most of the playground and possibly part of the building. Children would have to cross a heavy traffic thoroughfare in order to get to school, and it too would be built only four blocks from another elementary, the Louis Pasteur School. The third place, Rosedale, was no better. This site extended an already large elementary school. Worse, the school served an area scheduled for demolition in two to five years for the expansion of Western Reserve University. Clearly, the school board was prepared to do anything to maintain racial segregation in Cleveland.[68]

Late in February, UFM asked for a moratorium, but McAllister and the school board ignored these appeals. In the midst of the conflict, school superintendent William Levenson buckled under pressure and resigned. Still, McAllister and the SBE saw no reason to change its plans. The transport students were integrated again while the SBE accelerated its school building plan, though white school districts had over twelve hundred empty classrooms.[69]

CORE also attempted to sway the school board with a full-page article in the *Plain Dealer*. The ad addressed several aspects of the school crisis and gave particular attention to addressing the fallacy of "neighborhood" schools. "Some people feel a local school focusing on local educational and cultural needs can be a valuable center for community life. But when such a school is located in a racial ghetto, its special assets become liabilities. The same emphasis on neighborhood distinctiveness only serves to tell the Negro child every day that he is a second class American. Dr. John Fisher, President of Teachers College, Columbia University, stated: 'When the effect of a neighborhood school is to create or constitute a ghetto-type situation, it ceases to sever the purpose of democratic education.' . . . We need consolidation of resources to make sure that all children have access to good libraries, science laboratories, special teachers and teaching methods. We suggest the educational park as a way to do this."[70]

The educational park solution served both students and parents while also voluntarily integrating the Cleveland public school system. Unfortunately, maintenance of the "neighborhood" policy and the rash endeavor to end protests and complaints by white parents meant the go-ahead to construct schools on sub-standard plots. CORE called for a picket of the first school under construction, Lakeview. In preparation, CORE inaugurated school construction demonstrations with a rally at Corey Methodist Church on April 3, 1964. The theme was *The Negro Revolt— What Comes Next?* The mass meeting brought together two speakers, Louis E. Lomax and Malcolm X, who occasionally debated each other over their different approaches for ending racial inequality for black people.[71]

Louis Lomax, a famed journalist, became the first black American to appear as a television newsman. A writer for the *Chicago Defender*, *Harper's Ferry*, and other national magazines and papers, Lomax eventually gained a position as a host for a weekly news program. However, he was also known for his production, with colleague Mike Wallace, of a five-part documentary in 1959 on a little-known group called the Nation of Islam. *The Hate That Hate Produced* also highlighted the group's national spokesman, Minister Malcolm X.

Malcolm X came to national spotlight after the news documentary featured the black "hate" group that came out of the pressures of white racism and dis-crimination in America. However, black Clevelanders hardly accepted this version of the Nation of Islam or Malcolm X. Activists and residents alike were drawn to Malcolm's fiery rhetoric, militant condemnation of white supremacy, and call for black nationalist solutions to American oppression. Many in CORE already admired Malcolm X, despite viewing somewhat differently the role of nonviolent strategy. Ultimately, Turner recalled that most in CORE were quite mesmerized by Malcolm and agreed with him in many ways. Personally, Turner found him to be gentle, soft spoken, even appearing shy, and "very respectful of everyone he encoun-tered, especially women . . . a real gentleman!"[72]

Listeners packed Corey Methodist to hear the debate. CORE members recalled being enthralled by Malcolm X's speech the "Ballot or the Bullet." In it, he argued that ". . . in 1964, it's time now for you and me to become more politically mature and realize what the ballot is for; what we're supposed to get when we cast a ballot; and that if we don't cast a ballot, it's going to end up in a situation where we're going to have to cast a bullet. It's either a ballot or a bullet."[73]

Antoine Perot was slated to give the "CORE" position after Malcolm X, but happily conceded to end the rally, which had gone past its original end time. Ruth Turner climbed the platform to announce plans for a demonstration at the new school on Lakeview Road and Saywell Avenue in Glenville. Civil rights leaders led a procession of over two hundred marchers who carried a wooden box to "bury" Jim Crow. The march to bury the Jim Crow effigy ended at Lakeview school site where the box was subsequently buried.[74]

On April 6, CORE and UFM lived up to its promise and picketed the Lakeview school site. The first day of picketing at Lakeview, protestors managed to break through the line and block bulldozers and other construction equipment. CORE chairman Art Evans crawled under a cement truck after site leader Antoine Perot asked him to stop the vehicle. Three others assisted Evans in stopping the truck and refused to move until police carted them off. Six demonstrators, including blind CORE member Chuck Burton and a very pregnant Mrs. Beth Robinson, wife of Freedom Fighters Lewis Robinson, laid face down in a trench that stretched forty feet long, fifteen feet wide, and five feet deep while construction workers dumped dirt on the protestors. Police lifted activists out of the ditch and arrested them. Robinson was placed on a stretcher and carried off to a paddy wagon. Most, if not all, of the demonstrators seized by police were CORE members and residents of Hough and Glenville.[75]

Undeterred, they went back again the next day on April 7, 1964. Like the day before, protestors at Lakeview managed to break through the police line and block construction machinery. Among the protestors, this time was the vice chairman of CORE and an original founding member, Reverend Bruce Klunder.[76]

Born in Greeley, Colorado, son of Everett and Beatrice Klunder, Bruce Klunder moved with his family to Oregon where he received his education at Oregon State College. While at Oregon State, he met and married Joanne Lehman on December 22, 1956. Two years after the two married, they left for New Haven, in order for Bruce Klunder to pursue a degree at Yale University Divinity School.[77]

During this period, the Klunders spent relatively little time participating in social justice action; most of their activities were relegated to sympathy marches here and there. After graduation in 1961, he and his wife left for Cleveland where he became associate director of the Student Christian Union, a ministry of several denominations and the YMCA, housed at the Church of the Covenant.[78]

Sometime in early spring 1962, the Klunders chaperoned an integrated youth group interested in understanding the South's racial segregation. They met students in both Nashville and Atlanta and conducted a sit-in in Tennessee. This activity received media attention in Cleveland and situated the Klunders as racial equality activists.[79] Subsequently, both Bruce and Joanne Klunder were drawn to Cleveland CORE and its direct action style. Strong leaders within CORE, the two actively participated in most of the demonstrations held by the Cleveland chapter. The Lakeview protest certainly was no different. Originally Bruce Klunder planned to be absent from the second day of protests to avoid arrest, though it certainly was not a case of fear. He planned to lead a YMCA trip to Peru, and an arrest in April stood the possibility of interrupting his travel arrangements. That morning Klunder met with a ministerial alliance group hoping to garner some participation by more ministers on the Lakeview picket line. They refused to act. So, Klunder stepped in to man the picket even if the reprisals potentially hindered his trip out of the country.[80]

When the demonstrators broke through police lines on the second day of the Lakeview demonstration, Bruce Klunder followed suit. Two women threw them- selves in front of a bulldozer to stop its movement. The women lay face down out- stretched in the muddy construction site. Bruce Klunder, alone, headed to the back to block it from behind. He positioned himself three feet in back of the bulldozer. Klunder told the worker, "I'm behind you," and then he also lay with his face in the mud, hands stretched over his head. Antoine Perot signaled a CORE member to inform the driver that activists lay in front and behind him.

Construction worker John White, driver of the bulldozer, froze in his seat for a couple of moments. He then maneuvered the excavator from the protestors in front by reversing. Several people screamed to White that Klunder was behind him, among them protestors Janet Hanson and Benjamin Gibson. Despite their frantic efforts, White didn't hear them. Or, he refused to listen. Maybe, it was an accident. Maybe, he did it on purpose. John White reversed direction. Before anyone could move, the bulldozer ran backward over Bruce Klunder. The weight of the machine crushed his body flat, face into the ground.[81]

A CORE member, also a nurse, ran to give him first aid. As she moved to turn him over and check his vitals, it became clear he was dead. She knew he was dead. His body felt like a bag of sand. Every bone was broken into so many tiny pieces. Sitting back on her knees she savagely screeched and wept. Suddenly she ran screaming to police, "They've killed Bruce! They've killed Bruce!" She then fell limp in the arms of a friend before succumbing and prostrating herself on the ground. Another demonstrator turned away from the scene, pain etched deep in her face. As the horror of Klunder's death became clearer, some demonstrators went into shock, others became hysterical. All were devastated. Police removed his body on a stretcher as more spectators became aware of the gruesome scene. In shock, Ruth Turner silently wept.[82]

Pandemonium thereafter ensued. CORE member Ben Gibson grabbed John White by the collar and tried to jerk him out of the seat. Police started toward Gibson to stop his violent reaction. Gibson scrambled over the bulldozer and leapt midair off the machine hood, with police in pursuit. Cleveland's law enforcement followed for only a few feet, but then backtracked when they realized the driver was now under eminent attack by others in the crowd. White was beaten until the police abruptly intervened. Afterward, the driver claimed that Klunder had somehow jumped in front of the machine. Klunder was taken to Lakeside Hospital where he was pronounced dead on arrival.[83]

Although the group dispersed, it was too little, too late. Hundreds began to gather as word spread that Bruce Klunder had been killed. The gathering storm increased in number and vehemence over the hour. Repeating, "We want Malcolm! We want Malcolm!" the protestors heckled community and CORE leader attempts to redirect the crowd to an impromptu memorial. The chanting eventually broke. The crowd of few protestors increased into the hundreds. They threw bottles, bricks, and other site debris. Mounted police charged into groups of people. Patrolmen jumped on protestors three to five at a time. Tony Perot and other members of CORE attempted to stop the hysteria, but failed. Some civil rights activists and neighborhood residents redirected the rocks, bottles, and other objects from the site toward law enforcement.[84]

As word reached CORE headquarters, Student CORE (SCORE) member Pauline Warfield let out a shriek, threw her body backward, and collapsed in grief. It was as if, in that moment, my mother lost her mind. She was not the only one. The violent outbreak after Bruce Klunder's killing lasted for twelve hours. Riemer Drug Store was destroyed. The night was filled with flying rocks, bricks, bottles, sporadic violence, broken windows, and "looting." Police from neighboring areas gathered in riot gear, and dispersed crowds using tear gas. It took three clean-up crews to clear

On April 6 and 7, 1964, United Freedom Movement picketed at the Lakeview construction site to protest the school board's plans to build three elementary schools to avoid desegregation. CORE member Reverend Bruce W. Klunder died after a bulldozer crushed him while protesting at the Lakeview school construction site. Photo: photographer unknown, April 8, 1964.
From the Cleveland Press Collection, Michael Schwartz Library, Cleveland State University

out garbage the following day. Twenty-six people were arrested. Thirteen people, eight of whom were police, received minor injuries from flying objects.[85]

The weekend before Klunder's death, CORE and rally participants paraded to the Lakeview school site carrying a coffin to symbolize the burial of Jim Crow. The coffin was buried near the site of Bruce Klunder's death. Joanne Klunder later recalled her husband said that morning, "The only way to stop that school is to put our bodies between the workmen and their work."[86] Joanne Klunder, her father, Russell Lehman, and the Klunders' two children were at the Cleveland zoo when she heard her name called over the intercom. Active CORE member Margaret Grevatt met the family at the zoo to give them the news. Klunder's three-year-old son turned to his grandfather and said, "I hope Daddy isn't dead."[87] Tragically, her son was right.

The death of Bruce Klunder quickly made the evening news and spread across the United States. *Time* magazine featured stories about the demonstration with fault laid at the feet of Cleveland CORE and horrifically even Bruce Klunder himself.[88] *Ebony* featured a story of Joanne Klunder's bravery and her decision to continue her work on behalf of racial equality. Malcolm X, still in Cleveland after Klunder's death, was soon peppered with questions upon his return to New York during a speaking engagement at the Militant Labor Forum. The black nationalist leader was quick to downplay the media storm surrounding Klunder's sacrifice, particularly when matched against the many black leaders assassinated in the fight for freedom. In Cleveland, accusations went back and forth as to who was at fault—the city officials and SBE's recalcitrance or CORE and UFM's "irresponsible" protests.[89]

However, the media sensation mattered little to CORE members. They were all angered and devastated by Bruce Klunder's demise. He had been among what Turner called the white committed. White CORE member, Dave Cohen had a different take wondering aloud in an interview whether Klunder's death had been for naught. Even among the CORE members there was indecision about whether the school protest had been worth the personal loss. To the broader public, Klunder was known as the first man to die on the civil rights battlefield in a northern city.[90]

Over fifteen hundred attended Bruce Klunder's memorial; the people spilled into the church hallway and outside down its front steps. They sang from the Presbyterian hymnal, #373: "Once to every man and nation, comes the moment to decide, / In the strife of truth with falsehood, for the good or evil side."

His wife, Joanne, and children Janice and Douglas sat along with his sister Barbara Baker and his parents, Mr. and Mrs. Everett Klunder, in the front pew. The memorial address given by Reverend Eugene Carson Blake of Philadelphia was followed by words of remembrance from CORE member Walter E. Grevatt and other chapter members. Over 150 ministers from more than half a dozen denominations came to pay homage as Blake recounted how Klunder was "a private soldier in the battle for racial brotherhood," and called for his death to "mark a new beginning" in racial brotherhood.[91]

James Farmer and activist comedienne Dick Gregory came to mourn his death as well. Gregory had a different take on the possible repercussions of Klunder's death. The *Cleveland Plain Dealer* newspaper quoted him as saying, "the negro is not seeking a fight. But if he does fight, it probably will come after one of his white friends is killed. That's why the situation here is so potentially dangerous. You people aren't living on a day-to-day basis. It's hour to hour." Two pages over, the newspaper announced that the city suspended Lewis Robinson's employment for organizing the Medgar Evers Gun Club, formed directly after Malcolm X gave his Ballot or the Bullet speech.[92]

April 8, the day after Klunder's murder, three hundred people assembled on the mall for memorial services at noon, and then later marched to city hall and sat-in for hours to support UFM negotiations with the mayor and SBE about relocation of the three Negro schools. Mayor Locher became fully invested given his relationship to Klunder, who also happened to be assistant minister at his church, Church of the Covenant. In the meantime, police officers ominously removed badges, displayed

Antoine Perot prepares marchers and reporters for protest
at the Cleveland School Board of Education.
Photo: unknown photographer, April 9, 1964. From the Cleveland Press
Collection, Michael Schwartz Library, Cleveland State University

clubs, and strapped riot helmets on to their heads.[93] The next day, April 9, Bruce Klunder was cremated.

In the following days, Mayor Locher interceded and managed to get a judge to issue a temporary halt to both demonstrations and construction of schools for four weeks. SBE agreed, again, to the terms of a proposal to halt construction temporarily on two of the schools, end contract negotiations on the third school, and form a panel to study the integration issue and negotiate with UFM. Ruth Turner left the meeting, noting, "this is the first time that I have come away from one of these meetings thinking I had an agreement I could live with."[94] But, that feeling was short lived after William McKnight, assistant law director, called to have the Lakeside school property surrounded by an eight-foot-tall steel fence with barbwire and heavy floodlights during the night.

Ralph McAllister left the meeting early for another appointment. The day after, he reneged on yet another "final" agreement. McAllister opposed UFM's participation in SBE discussions with an outside consultant and remarked that it was highly questionable that it had any "responsible groups" with which to negotiate. McAllister's statements came much to the surprise of Mayor Locher, who noted that McAllister was fully aware of the agreement and had volunteered the consultant's name. Still, McAllister single-handedly refused any decision reached previously by the board. Instead of accepting the accord, McAllister called a secret session of the SBE. He finally agreed to the settlement, but only if he could include the addendum that SBE would hear any interested parties who could help. That same day, buses carrying black children to Collinwood were pelted with rocks.[95]

McAllister's last antic was the final break for Cleveland's black community and the UFM. UFM called for a mass boycott. Black ministers and leaders who previously vacillated on whether to join the movement were incensed and backed a boycott. Black leaders who previously refused to support the UFM reversed their decision and endorsed the organization, its call for a school boycott, and its downtown business boycott campaign. They also called for the implementation of the CCHR plan and the resignation of school board members who refused to comply.[96]

Initially, UFM only "studied" school boycotts as a possible protest tool. However, it became clear that discussions were underway to begin a boycott as early as January 1964. A delegation from Cleveland headed to New York to discuss a proposed simultaneous six-city boycott of public schools. The New York conference of activists unanimously voted instead to hold boycotts according to each city's timetables, especially because Cleveland CORE expressed concern over the likely slow response of black conservative groups back in Cleveland.[97]

Nonetheless, Cleveland did receive assistance for how to prepare a one-day boycott. New York, Syracuse, Cincinnati, Chicago, and Boston already had moderate to large boycotts. New York CORE was the most successful with its 44 percent absentia rate. About 25–30 percent of Boston and Cincinnati's black students boycotted, while Chicago managed to get a huge participation of 172,350 out of 470,000 students. Syracuse CORE even managed to get 900 out of 1,100 elementary children to boycott Washington Elementary School.[98]

Though boycotts were underway in a number of cities, some within UFM appeared reluctant to validate such a plan in early February. The Hazeldell Parents Association and CORE were not. In fact, the same day UFM issued a statement that school boycotts would not be "ruled out," another article announced that Ruth Turner of CORE would go to Chicago on behalf of the Hazeldell Parent Association to review the city's school boycott plan in preparation. The Hazeldell Parent Association further noted that it would contact UFM for backing, if necessary, but that HPA had already canvassed the school district and voted in support of the strategy. Turner returned from Chicago with film and a manual on how to generate a school boycott. In a later interview, she noted that if sit-ins failed, she would urge black Clevelanders to begin boycotting. CORE and Hazeldell were clear, even if the UFM was not. There was going to be a boycott.[99]

By the beginning of April, neither CORE nor the Hazeldell Parent Association had cause for worry. The death of Bruce Klunder ensured that there would be no opposition. Ruth Turner announced at Corey Methodist Church that in two weeks—Monday, April 20—the school boycott would begin. CORE would run freedom schools during the day for children to attend. Leaders and members of the black community backed the demonstration. Cleveland's black physicians and dentists announced support for the boycott, denounced the school board, and offered to give a doctor's note for every child. Each note would read exemption granted from school on the basis of being "sick of segregation."[100]

McAllister responded with denunciations and threats that participating parents were guilty of a crime and threatened prosecution for anyone who chose to take their children out during the boycott. McAllister's assertions only served to drive the final wedge between SBE and the black community.[101]

Monday, April 20, 1964, over 90 percent of Cleveland's black students boycotted all schools.[102] Meticulously planned by CORE member Bernard Mandel and organized by the leaders of SCORE and the youth council of the NAACP, the boycott was an all-out effort by every segment of the black community.[103]

Children arrived between the periods of 8:30 A.M. to 9:00 A.M. for registration and schools were dismissed at 3:45 P.M. Freedom schools were divided into four sections of first to third grades, fourth to sixth grades, seventh to ninth grades, and tenth to twelfth grades. Each supervisor of a freedom school was given a sheet of emergency numbers, hospitals for emergency treatment, and fire procedures. There were over sixty-two sites selected to hold classes for the freedom schools, most of which were in local churches, but also included such places as the Friendly Inn and the Phillis Wheatley Association.[104]

A thirty-five-member committee with Mandel as chair crafted the curriculum. Subjects included American civics and the civil rights movement, black history and culture, and freedom songs. Children defined and discussed American ideals such as the Declaration of Independence, the Constitution, the Bill of Rights, the flag and the Pledge of Allegiance, personal freedom, and the Fourteenth and Fifteenth Amendments. These concepts were framed within the broader meaning and context of the civil rights movement. Classes also explained how these ideals reflected in the work of groups like the United Nations, UNESCO, and UNICEF.[105]

Locally, students received information on the United Freedom Movement and its leadership. Students were also given short summaries and histories on the leading organizations within UFM, including CORE and the NAACP. Teachers even explained various direct action methods and concepts including negotiation, rent strikes, sit-ins, nonviolence, Negro revolt, and civil disobedience. At the end, students were granted a freedom school diploma.[106]

Of the seven school boycotts across the United States including Chicago, New York, and Cincinnati, Cleveland's was the most successful.[107] Arguably, this was in no small part precipitated by the tragic death of CORE's vice chairman, Bruce Klunder, and the audacity of McAllister to add insult to such injury by threatening black parents with prosecution. Even the newly founded Emergency Clergy Committee for Civil Rights (ECCR)—a group of over two hundred Christian and Jewish clergymen—called the boycott a repudiation of SBE's decisions and demanded that all members of the board resign. The NAACP was quick to give itself credit for the boycott's victory, claiming, "the recent Cleveland school boycott was a tremendous success and a show of unity in this town. It served notice on all sources that the distance between the masses and the NAACP does not exist. In Kansas City where a boycott was carried on during the same week it failed because the NAACP did not support it."[108] Hardly an equal analogy, the boycott would have succeeded in spite of NAACP participation. The reality was that the NAACP had to be pushed, prodded, and nearly knocked down and dragged into the school board fight by HPA and CORE. The NAACP's real power lay in its legal assistance, a crucial component of the school desegregation fight, which inevitably became UFM's last strategy of redress.[109]

The NAACP filed a temporary injunction to halt construction on the Lakeview school site, but Judge Kalbfleisch denied it. NAACP and UFM lawyer Louis Stokes filed an appeal in federal court. The NAACP followed the school desegregation fight with education lawsuits on behalf of Charles Craggett and twenty-one black children against the Cleveland School Board of Education on May 22, 1964. SBE and

UFM argued against McAllister's claim that the suit was baseless and that the fault lay with black southerners who decreased educational standards in black schools.[110]

In the meantime, McAllister busily rushed to place a school construction levy on the ballot for additional funds for school buildings. UFM and CORE initiated a protest against the May 5 levy on the basis of its inherent intention to maintain segregation. The referendum passed overwhelmingly in white areas and failed miserably in black neighborhoods. Nevertheless, the numbers were high enough to engender the passage of the levy and passed with a 55 percent vote in favor. CORE staunchly opposed the levy, and even pushed the UFM to do so as well in spite of internal opposition. The Urban League, for example, was hesitant to oppose the levy, and thought it more "statesman like" for it to publicly announce support instead.[111]

During the months of May and June 1964, UFM still attempted to negotiate with the SBE, but board members refused to meet. June 5, the judge handed down a ruling against the plaintiffs in the Craggett case. In it, the judge claimed that the NAACP had not proven that the SBE deliberately attempted to segregate schools or that the neighborhood schools were discriminatory in nature. The loss of the Craggett case officially ended the city mass movement against school segregation

Though neighborhood school policy supposedly marked the paramount goal of the SBE, it did not hold to its own district boundaries. Hazeldell parents received notices that their children would attend the Lakeview elementary, though many passed by two schools or over three major traffic arteries to walk the long distance to Lakeview. In fact, the construction was incomplete on the school. Windows on one side of the school were not in place. A major stairway case had yet to be erected and heavy machinery still occupied the property.[112]

Black parents angered by the substandard school building at Lakeview, now Stephen Howe Elementary, initiated a last attempt to obtain proper and equal education for their children. September 6, the Hazeldell parents met to express outrage and anger over the long walk and partial completion of the school. Though the new superintendent, Paul Briggs, delayed opening the school, there was no solution presented to deal with the parents' concerns about the long-distance walks to the school. Three days later, they met again along with leaders from various freedom organizations including Ruth Turner and CORE members Joanne Klunder and attorney Stanley Tolliver. Some organizations (particularly the NAACP) steered away from "inflammatory" language and carefully crafted support statements that alluded to a suggestion that the Hazeldell Parent Association retreat from another school desegregation fight. Only CORE pledged to stand by HPA and give aid in any way possible. In spite of having received less aid, black parents refused to stop their fight and made their position clear at a mass meeting. An observer remarked, "The dramatic feature of the evening was the profound change and emphasis that occurred from within the ranks of the membership. One after another, mothers and fathers, began to stand and say one way or another, 'I will never let my child attend that school.' Some vowed willingness to run neighborhood schools and face arrest if necessary . . . *This meeting was notable for its indigenous control, lack of attention to leaders of the past, and simple strength of what one might call the black person's voice"* (emphasis not mine).[113]Anger over the Lakeview/Stephen Howe Elementary School would not be silenced. The Hazeldell Parent Association planned to stage another boycott, this time with only one organization for community support—CORE.[114]

Aside from the notable absence of UFM, Hazeldell faced other opposition from within the black community as well. Reverend Isaiah Pogue advocated for mediation and the use of legal means to deal with the situation. George Forbes, city councilman, issued a press release stating his dissent against the boycott, but then recalled who his constituents were and retracted his statement. Articles from the major papers featured grandiose fallacious stories of a new school with new books, all the more insulting to the Hazeldell parents as workmen were still crafting an entranceway, plastering exterior overhangs, laying concrete, and hanging windows. By the opening of the school, the only question for the Hazeldell parents was whether the boycott would be a temporary measure or permanent.[115]

The school opened with a 75 percent absentia of black children, and lasted a full three weeks before black children assigned to Stephen Howe trickled into the school. In response, the NAACP issued a press statement of "understanding and praise for the plight of children attending the school."[116] However, it did not lend encouragement for another school boycott of Lakeview due to its belief that a second boycott lacked potential. As an alternate suggestion for the UFM education committee, the NAACP advised it to study future placement of a black representative on the school board.[117]

The UFM gave limited support during the second parental boycott, and only acted in the role of negotiator on behalf of the Hazeldell parents. CORE was the only organization to facilitate the parents' resolution. For several weeks the chapter kept a freedom school open for boycotting parents, and even did so when the number of boycotting children dwindled down to only ten. CORE gave its last remaining aid to the parents of the ten children, but they too eventually stopped. SBE later remarked that though the boycott ended, attendance was still down at Howe. It was later found that some parents moved, enrolled their children in private school, or simply kept them at home.[118]

In September 1965, UFM leadership hesitantly recognized that Briggs rhetorically supported improved education for black children but noted also their concern that he unrelentingly followed neighborhood policy. Later that fall, UFM endeavored to meet for the last time with the SBE to suggest a ten-step plan, but the meeting degenerated into a series of personal attacks and accusations. Although there were a couple of meetings here and there, most of them ended with no solution. Parents could send their children to school or not.[119]

The last endeavor of the school desegregation movement ended in the fall of 1964. By January 1965, the NAACP cautiously announced that progress and new proposals seemed forthcoming based on Superintendent Briggs's six-month report. They too found no specific effort by Briggs to integrate the school system, but the NAACP continued to watch the Cleveland SBE. In the final analysis, it was not CORE who broke the back of the school board of education, but a successful lawsuit sponsored by the NAACP almost a decade later. *Rhodes v. Reed* was among the most comprehensive judicial decisions on education in the nation, and it forced the SBE to institute integration and improve educational quality on a myriad of levels.[120]

Battered by the school desegregation movement's failure and Klunder's killing, Cleveland CORE's Ruth Turner laid out the lessons learned from the school deseg-regation fight almost a year later. She wrote, "The passing of the school levy (which we wanted to defeat) taught us these lessons: Lesson I—Just because we had a successful boycott does not mean other projects automatically will succeed. . . . Lesson II—We can not rely on the existing political machines to get our message across. If we want the job done well, we must begin organizing our own political machinery."[121]

Mayor Locher and SBE president McAllister had to go! And, CORE intended to help them to the door. After the devastating results of the previous year, the chapter tenor and tactics drastically changed. Simultaneously, a new slogan emerged to give voice to Cleveland CORE and other freedom movement activists. It was a battle cry for agency and empowerment. Cleveland CORE joined the rising movement, utilized it, and turned it into a weapon for political power—black political power. The tragic irony was that it was no cry from the Deep South or damning speech by Malcolm X that sparked this revolution. Distinctively, it was the shatter-ing event of Bruce Klunder's death and its broader meaning for Cleveland CORE. In the same way that John White crushed Bruce Klunder's body into the earth, Cleveland's white political and legal structure rolled over the city's black freedom movement. In all its gruesomeness, the minister's death signified an end to aspira-tions for interracial integration and heralded the overthrow of nonviolent direct action methods. The similarities and implications were brutally uncanny. Plus, the paradox was meaningful in more ways than one. For on that fateful day in April— when one white man died—black power in Cleveland became ineluctable.

# II

# 5

# New Directions to Black Power

"THE PROMISED LAND! . . . Who promised me this land . . . Goddamn it!"[1]

That protestation came from the potty mouth middle child of Rufus and Lillian Robinson. In the 1930s, the Robinsons and their thirteen children ventured from their Decatur, Alabama, home to the Midwest city of Cleveland, Ohio, in search of a better life. A typical migration story, they experienced all the highs and lows of being black living under northern de facto segregation. Of their thirteen younglings, little Lewis turned out to be the most vocal about these experiences, hating the subtle racism. Young Robinson developed at an early age a "bitterness and . . . growing knowledge" that, "all I had to help me was me."[2]

Robinson's outrage and self-help beliefs reflected a cultural and historical reality for black southerners migrating to the North. They experienced in northern urban spaces an oppressive system of inequality, patronage, and paternalism. Southern-born black folk brought with them fundamentally different ideas for how to operate within these restrictions, and on whom they could depend for their livelihood. It nurtured among them a belief that empowerment came through self-help and internal community building. Their arrival to Cleveland pushed the complacent black elite into further militancy and led to a vigorous challenge of city segregation. This working-class style of group consciousness, self-help, and militant protest found expression in groups such as the Future Outlook League, when Robinson was still a pre-teen.

Predictably, this broader self-help milieu intensely affected 1960s Cleveland CORE, particularly with its larger black affiliation. Publicly, black nationalist philosophy appeared to burst onto the freedom movement scene in 1966 with the shout "Black Power!" But within Cleveland CORE, it actually emerged from 1962 to 1965 as philosophical and tactical deviations from the CORE way. These developments—association with nationalist groups, sympathetic views toward armed resistance, and dual membership in groups with methods antithetical to CORE—fed growing beliefs that nonviolent direct action was dead. The new freedom frontier required intensive political, social, and economic community organizing. Cleveland was not the only chapter to learn this lesson, and together these branches along with other national events motivated national CORE in a new direction.

The 1961 Monroe, North Carolina, incident became Cleveland chapter's first transformative agent. Shortly after the Freedom Rides, NAACP chapter leader Robert Williams requested riders visit Monroe in a joint protest against Jim Crow. On August 21, 1961, Williams and his followers staged a march that surprisingly met with little aggression. Five days later, another demonstration turned violent when a KKK motorcade pursued protestors back to Newtown, a nearby black neighborhood, and repeatedly threatened to run them off the road.[3]

Days later, a segregationist mob estimated from two to five thousand assembled, attacked black marchers, and beat many mercilessly. Most activists escaped the rioting and returned to Newtown in preparation for another assault by white residents. While black citizens planned a self-defense strategy, a white couple somehow wandered into the area. Apparently, Williams sequestered them in his home for protection until they could safely leave.

Notwithstanding his good intentions, law enforcement used the incident to accuse him and his associates of kidnapping. One of these confidantes, New York activist Mae Mallory, had joined Williams after his open request for aid to the Monroe freedom struggle. While Williams avoided imprisonment and escaped along with his wife to Cuba, Mallory headed first to New York and then to Cleveland, Ohio, where she subsequently came under arrest. Mallory fought extradition for over two years, arguing that the charges were false and North Carolina would never give her a fair trial.[4]

National CORE maintained a file on the Mallory case, but appeared decidedly ambivalent about the situation. Freedom Riders were all but integrated into the very fabric of the incident—since twenty-year-old Freedom Rider John Lowry also faced kidnapping charges. CORE had to protect its own, and thus argue the accusation's fallacy. Still, Williams's steadfast belief in armed self-defense had no place in the CORE tactical handbook, and certainly not as a philosophy. The organization intended to hold on to its newly acquired status as a big four civil rights group, but only as a *nonviolent* civil rights group.

The Monroe incident was an uncomfortable problem in other ways as well. Since the 1940s, CORE systematically avoided any implication of communist association. Yet, leftists forcefully led community and funding relief efforts for the Monroe defendants. The socialist influenced Committee to Aid the Monroe Defendants (CAMD) provided legal assistance and covered associated fees via a national public relations and fund-raising effort. When John Lowry joined the committee, it greatly complicated CORE's ability to remain aloof. Additionally, local CAMD operations were asking CORE chapters for defense aid. National CORE quickly sent a memo to all its chapters noting that they were "advised that a number of CORE chapters have received in recent weeks requests for contributions and joint sponsorship of meetings for the Committee to Aid the Monroe Defendants." The letter then stipulated that "CORE chapters should refrain from any official endorsement whatever of CAMD."[5] National director James Farmer, backed by NAC, unequivocally denied CAMD financial assistance.[6] Despite this decision, Farmer still participated in fund-raising activities sponsored by the organization. Nearly three weeks after the memo, he joined panelists Malcolm X and William Worthy in a fund-raising event on the theme, "Challenge of Racism."[7]

Conversely, national CORE's ambiguity did not at all manifest in Cleveland CORE. Realistically, the chapter had little choice but to fight extradition in the Mallory case. Her actions, along with those of Robert Williams, became renowned nationally and internationally. More important, their symbolic show of pride, self-defense, and human rights inspired black people throughout the United States. Even the conservative Cleveland NAACP added its name in February 1962 to the long list of groups opposed to Mallory's expulsion. One month later, NAACP members rallied for a mass march sponsored by another legal aid group, the Monroe Defense Committee (MDC).[8]

Inescapably, Cleveland CORE could hardly be the lone nonparticipating organization. The chapter lent its forces beginning in fall 1963. They demonstrated with other local groups for her release, announced meetings of the Monroe Defense Committee, and called for a joint Christmas boycott.[9] The group also sent a telegram to Attorney General Robert F. Kennedy and Governor James Rhodes in which they noted: "We regard your decision to send Willie May Mallory back to North Carolina to be a shameful betrayal of the Negro community."[10]

In December 1963, the chapter notified NAC of its intention to give monetary assistance to the Cleveland Monroe Defense Committee for bond money. James Farmer, however, submitted a motion to turn down the request, seconded by Alan Gartner and passed by unanimous vote by NAC. Also by unanimous vote, NAC prohibited all CORE chapters from participation with other groups connected to the Mallory case. Although NAC advised chapters on the new decree, Cleveland CORE failed to respond to the national office's demand and continued along the same path. Why Cleveland chose to contact NAC regarding Mallory remains a mystifying move. It had no choice but to involve itself, had been for months, and former chair John Cloud already served as chair on the leftist leaning Cleveland CAMD.[11]

National CORE's conflicted messaging appeared again after a complaint from Dayton CORE regarding Cleveland's joint march at the governor's mansion. Although other Ohio chapters contributed, W. S. McIntosh, Dayton CORE's executive secretary targeted the Cleveland branch. To alleviate McIntosh's anxieties, Richard Haley, associate national director, directly contacted Ruth Turner. Haley assured McIntosh by letter that the Cleveland chapter's participation in the proposed demonstration would conform to CORE standards and was not an effort to simply embarrass the governor. He wrote, "CORE has maintained a cautious attitude about this case because both Mrs. Mallory and the Monroe Defense Committee seem to have firm leftist connections. However, she is a human being, and we must think of that before politics when such a thing as extradition to Monroe is involved."[12] Haley had no intention of forcing Cleveland CORE to disavow its work on behalf of Mae Mallory, notwithstanding her "leftist associations."[13]

Other leaders in CORE were not so quick to let Cleveland chapter govern its own alliances. James McCain, then director of organization, tried to revoke the leftist association pass Haley granted in the Mallory case. McCain received an article that inferred that communists easily infiltrated Cleveland CORE. McCain wrote to Turner and pointed out that Article III, Section 3 of CORE's constitution prohibited membership with any other group or organization that expounded a philosophy inimical to the fundamental principles of CORE. McCain also requested that Turner contact him about the article, though there was no documentation that she did.[14]

Cleveland's connection with the extradition case ended March 1, 1964, but national did not determine that closure. Mallory and her supporters faced a disappointing defeat when Ohio governor Michael Disalle denied her appeal after twenty-eight months of struggle. Although Common Court pleas judge Thomas J. Parrino accepted the extradition order, he granted a temporary stay of thirty days. The stay was short lived. Over the period, Ruth Turner and Pauline Warfield kept close ties to Mallory until her release and return to Cleveland.[15]

Monroe unavoidably sat at national's steps, but other radical associations raised difficult questions as well. The Nation of Islam (NOI), for example, had a profound impact on CORE branches, and many chapters informally interacted with NOI members. Malcolm X appeared at numerous New York area CORE demonstrations. He gave his famous "Ballot or the Bullet" speech at Cleveland CORE's rally. New Orleans CORE developed very close ties to the mosque in its city. The organization and its followers ubiquitously appeared in and around CORE as a visual black nationalist alternative to the CORE way.

Among these chapters, and others like it, Malcolm's argument that self-defense was a natural dignified response for a prideful people psychically resonated.[16] Many were hard pressed to argue the point when he questioned nonviolence "in Mississippi and Alabama, when your *churches* are being bombed, and *your* little girls are being murdered."[17] Malcolm X's vocal denunciations of nonviolence disconcertingly interrogated any movement that might concern itself with transforming the

spirit of an intractable foe. According to James Farmer, Malcolm X's critique seriously challenged nonviolent philosophy, especially given the ferocious white brutality that protestors regularly faced. The unrelenting violence and the government's
lackadaisical response began to needle at some within CORE (black and white)
and lay bare Sue Thurman's original query to Gandhi many years ago. How do
you apply nonviolence where there are guns, no real trials, and no courts to protect
people? .[18]

Malcolm's forceful assertions of black manhood and armed protection represented no small subsection of the black community. Rural, small-town versions
of Malcolm X's self-defense philosophy surrounded southern CORE chapters.
Distinctly, theirs was a not a question of ideology, but their very survival. Though
the public face of the movement eschewed weapons, its muzzled presence soon
became openly recognized. While acceptance of self-defense was obvious for many,
it was slow and pained for others—especially within CORE. Leaders began to wonder what had happened to the nonviolent spirit in the movement.

The national office conversation on nonviolence vacillated in 1964 among
its leadership. Norman Hill, national program director and ever the intellectual
pragmatist, noted that nonviolence had to produce victories to hold its position
as the leading method. Farmer insisted that CORE's history required a minimum
commitment to nonviolence and that it was not just an interchangeable tool. Rich
countered that nonviolence was more than a strategy—it was meant to be a transformative ideal that enabled people to respect one another. Despite devotion to
nonviolence—philosophy or tactic—events on the ground continued to hem in
their choices on the matter.

In 1964, SNCC, CORE, NAACP, SCLC, and COFO launched a summer
voter registration and education project across the South. Each organization handled particular regions with joint operations in Mississippi. The Mississippi Summer Project, also known as Freedom Summer, began as a two-week orientation
at Western College for Women in Oxford, Ohio. It brought trainees to the Deep
South to help expand voter registration efforts and enhance community organization through freedom schools, local centers, and citizenship workshops. One week
into volunteer training, Mississippi SNCC organizer Bob Moses shocked student
volunteers with the announcement that three CORE members, Michael Schwerner,
James Chaney, and Andrew Goodman, were missing, likely dead. After civil rights
groups forced the FBI to investigate, it became hopelessly clear that the missing
three workers bespoke a larger story of unchecked violence and murder in the
South. As the search continued, various other bodies were unearthed—including
a young fourteen-year-old Hubert Orsby, who was found floating in the Big Black
River wearing a Congress of Racial Equality t-shirt. Eventually, the activists discovered Chaney, Schwerner, and Goodman were also dead.

For David Dennis, New Orleans CORE member and national's representative in Mississippi, nonviolence—especially at night—was no longer an option. While SNCC had been in talks over the use of self-defense, CORE continued to beat back the problem. Resultantly, Dennis simply chose not to alert national of his decision (and that of others) to carry a gun. He also determined never to tell another black Mississippian again not to defend themselves.[19]

While the nation turned all eyes to Mississippi, they missed other parts of the South burning with its own heated viciousness. The extreme level of violence experienced in CORE's Louisiana Voter Education Project base made 1964 a tortured summer and drove southern CORE staff toward violent self-protection.[20] Historian Joe Leonard referred to the Louisiana movement as "catchin' hell down here." And hell it was. The secluded parishes of Louisiana brought with it nightly raids, drive-by shootings, attacks, and general harassment of CORE offices and the black community. Well into 1965, Louisiana protestors faced dog attacks and brutal beatings. In the month of April 1965 alone, there were over thirty-three violent incidents. An eight-year-old was severely beaten during a children's march in July 1965, and from March through July 1965 there were over a dozen bombings. Even James Farmer had his own harrowing experience when nightriders surrounded a funeral home and threatened to burn it if Farmer did not leave. Thinking quickly, the local funeral director managed to smuggle Farmer out in a casket and hearse so that he could escape Plaquemine, Louisiana. In that moment, there was no question in anyone's mind. Had Farmer stayed, he would have met his maker that night.[21]

Violence so jarred one community that black men in the Jonesboro, Louisiana, area stepped in to provide the protection that federal, state, and local law enforcement refused to deliver. Armed security details soon followed CORE workers as they traveled throughout the area. Once the summer ended, the patrollers remained in action. When CORE sent additional workers in fall 1964, the defense group was already on hand. Charles Fenton, newly arrived CORE member, initially balked at the idea of weaponry in the CORE Freedom House. However, the local intimidation soon convinced him otherwise. What was an unofficially named but organized black defense patrol, under Fenton's suggestion, became officially structured into the Deacons for Defense. Naturally, national CORE was more than a little confused as to how to handle the public revelation about the Deacons. The office dodged the whole issue even after the *New York Times* featured CORE's role in the Deacons' formation. Local chapters, however, heralded the Deacons' rise or rather, cheered it with abandon.[22]

Local militancy via armed protection was not the sole domain of southern rural towns. In Cleveland, Lewis Robinson began target training in a nearby farm outside of Cleveland for the Medgar Evers Gun Club. He formed the patrol group shortly around the time of Malcolm X's "Ballot or the Bullet" speech. However, Cleveland

CORE expressed uncertainty over Robinson's self-defense group. Eventually, Turner stated publicly that it was a bad idea and unnecessary in Cleveland.[23] In the end, Robinson was suspended from his city job for his activities. The city's action came as no surprise to Robinson, who long suspected the city's intent to fire him given his leadership of another militant Cleveland group, the Freedom Fighters!

The Freedom Fighters became *the* premiere freedom group before Cleveland CORE arrived on the scene. The organization often worked as a direct action option in tandem with the NAACP, though the partnership often came after repeated urging. Founded and led by southern transplant Lewis Robinson, it was the closest in organizational character to Cleveland CORE, and thus influenced the chapter's early development. Freedom Fighters formed from a youth coalition within the Cleveland NAACP. After a series of meetings, the activists—all male but for one woman—reconstituted themselves into the Freedom Fighters on December 1960. Their membership consisted mostly of former southern black males in their late twenties and early thirties. Participant numbers ranged from thirty-five to forty-five persons, and most were factory laborers. Relatively few were college students.[24]

From the outset, leaders insisted that the group fund itself through organization fees and community donations. Robinson premised his decision on the belief that the association must remain autonomous and in their hands. He also repeatedly urged his members to redirect their finances toward the purchase of a home, preferably with space enough to produce rental income. Robinson arguably had good reason to advocate for autonomous revenue, since his militant leadership of the Freedom Fighters made him a distinctive and easy target for Cleveland officials.[25]

Constitution guidelines required members to nonviolently demonstrate; it advocated black economic uplift, political independence, and alliances with other black militant groups. Freedom Fighters prohibited whites from service as officers of the organization, although they could participate in supporting roles as committee chairpersons (a similar outcome within Cleveland CORE). Leaders of the organization also sided and interacted with groups that followed the Freedom Fighters' pattern of relegating whites to the fringes or outside, illustrated by Robinson's decision to deliver a speech about black unity at Nation of Islam Mosque #18. Thus, their political philosophy was a mix of black nationalism with tactical nonviolent direct action.[26]

Despite its nonviolence regulation, the question of self-defense methods (which Fighters viewed as separate and unrelated) took months to decide and was the sole item to delay the constitution's completion. Many founders promoted physical retaliation and wanted permission, as Lewis Robinson put it, to "in fact, beat the hell" out of attackers.[27] After some time, they settled on a verbally stated compromise that would not appear in the constitution. Fighters disallowed solo picketing, and any person who met with physical confrontation must first alert nearby persons and their picketing partner. Guidelines required protestors to document the incident and provide detailed description of the culprit. If after receiving aid, the assault continued or if no assistance appeared, then picketers could proceed with the unwritten policy. All persons trapped in the above circumstances had permission to defend themselves. Although some members suggested this would darken FF's public persona, Robinson frankly responded, "to hell with our image and what the newspapers thought of us. We were fighting for freedom and not for an image."[28] It was that image, however, that deterred national CORE from making the Freedom Fighters a local branch.[29]

Despite Fighter's stance on self-defense and black self-help, it could not be said it lacked an integrationist bent. Three years before Cleveland CORE entered the equal housing fray, Freedom Fighters pioneered Cleveland's first sixties demonstration against white flight. The group sponsored Sunday jaunts into white suburban areas for black couples seeking homes. In Robinson's words, "[We] let the whites know that 'blacks will be here too.' Run! You can run, but you can't hide!"[30] However frightening for whites, his tactic principally centered on those persons who could in fact purchase a home. Other activities included southern movement sympathy protests, fund-raisers for Greensboro sit-in demonstrators and Tennessee's tent-city sharecroppers, and participation in CORE's 1961 Freedom Rides.

The Freedom Fighters eventually branched into demonstrations that primarily dealt with employment discrimination, occasionally winning two or three jobs here and there at retail stores. The Central Cadillac protest was the Fighter's most aggressive job campaign. It also marked the first major cosponsored demonstration between themselves and Cleveland CORE. Previous joint events garnered only minor recognition from the black community, but this protest proved the most impactful. The Central Cadillac demonstration took place before CORE's fall 1963 rent strikes. It spurred the chapter's first growth spurt of membership and contributions and introduced it to regional partners in the freedom movement.[31]

Central Cadillac was the largest outlet for automobile sales in northeast Ohio, and it received a high percentage of profits from Cleveland's black middle class and wealthy. With such strong economic support from the black community, the Freedom Fighters argued that Central Cadillac should at least hire one or two black salesmen. The dealership refused, so the Fighters' initiated action against Central Cadillac for discriminatory hiring practices in spring 1963.[32]

Initially, Central's owners and Cadillac's national corporation headquarters received letters requesting these hires. However, Ancusto Butler, head and solo member of Job Seekers, soon became impatient with the negotiation process and began a one-man picket of Central Cadillac the first week of May 1963.[33] To much surprise, Butler's solo demonstration actually met with some success in that his presence began to influence purchases by black customers. By mid-month, Cleveland CORE joined the Central Cadillac demonstration at the Freedom Fighter's invitation. The NAACP also cooperated with the protests but limited participation to solidarity marchers.[34]

The alliance picketed the dealership at the height of its sale season. New to the demonstration scene, Cleveland CORE initially followed the rules of action—no arguments and no blocking the entrances. CORE leaders directed marchers to "remember the instructions of National CORE: 'No matter what the provocation we remain cool and courteous to all. We do not respond to hoots or to jeers.' Of course, if attacked, we never hit back. Our strength lies in moral force."[35] However, Rules of Action soon dissolved under the Freedom Fighters and Butler's influence. As the spring and summer dragged on, tactics by both CORE and the Freedom Fighters aggressively progressed. Aside from being quite loud events, some protestors were now cursing at and loudly talking against black consumers who crossed the picket line. Those who chose just to "look" at the cars immediately made their intentions clear so as to not raise the ire of the picketers.[36]

Most protestors worked in the day, so the daily blockading usually took place in the evening until closing. However, night marches missed a crucial period of attack. Freedom Fighters/Cleveland CORE resolved this weakness with the help of black car jockeys who gave the names and license numbers of black Clevelanders who shopped during the day. The Freedom Fighters/CORE coalition then located these potential day buyers and attempted to dissuade vehicle purchase. The result was a decline in both the day and evening sales.[37]

Protest at Central Cadillac continued unabated by the formation of the United Freedom Movement. Though it took weeks for UFM to support the Central Cadillac protest, the project got a boost from a myriad of segments within the black community. One noted supporter included one of the biggest number runners in Cleveland, who not only refused to trade up his car for the new edition but also sent some of his runners to man the picket line.[38]

Local support, however, was not enough to win the Central Cadillac demonstration. By fall, the company still refused to hire even one black salesman. Consequently, Fighters/CORE further stipulated that the dealership must now hire black mechanics, office clerks, plus additional salesmen beyond the initial one request. The coalition also determined to access a larger platform by which to force acceptance of their employment demands. In fall 1963, CORE and the Freedom Fighters headed for a regional conference of grassroots organizations. They intended to turn their protest into a national crusade. On November 9, 1963, the Cleveland coalition appealed to the delegates of the Northern Negro Grass Roots Leadership Conference in Detroit, Michigan. The alliance campaigned for a nationwide boycott resolution against General Motors and its Cadillac division for unfair hiring practices. The delegates resolved to organize an economic boycott of Cadillac in solidarity with the Cleveland call for jobs. Eventually, the conference passed the proposal in a second plenary session.[39]

Despite positive regional and local responses and a discernible decline in Central Cadillac sales, CORE pulled out its members in late fall. This decision had less to do with the now lengthy fight with Central Cadillac and more to do with Cleveland CORE's own burgeoning organizational independence with the rent strikes and school protests. Abandoned by CORE, the Freedom Fighters brought their protest methods to a new level. In December 1963, leaders of the Central Cadillac protestors ominously claimed that if negotiations, which had stalled for weeks, failed to begin it could no longer guarantee that windows would not be kicked in. Needless to say, negotiations restarted. Though the Freedom Fighters "Freedom Now" mentality took decidedly menacing tones, nonviolent direct action and negotiations ultimately prevailed and Central Cadillac hired a black mechanic, receptionist, service salesman, parts write-up clerk, and a black car salesman, who unexpectedly claimed he received the job only because he was qualified.[40]

Despite CORE's departure from the Central Cadillac demonstrations, the alliance held together in other areas. CORE members and leaders were in high attendance when the Freedom Fighters invited famous Detroit pastor and black liberation theologian Albert Cleage to speak on behalf of the dealership protests. Reverend Cleage delivered his speech, *The Future of the Negro in America-Power Through Unity*. The speech centered on three topics: black political power, black economic power, black spiritual power. Cleage's discussion of nonviolent philosophy was of particular interest, as he proclaimed that "even right down there with Dr. King, walking up and down and in and out of the pool rooms, *they're not all non-violent in Birmingham!* You know, it's un-American, this non-violence, really. I'm not advocating violence, I'm just saying non-violence is un-American" (italics in original).[41] Cleage believed supporting southern nonviolent marchers was important; however, it should not come at the expense of black life. Self-defense meted out by any demonstrator was justifiable. Cleage visited Cleveland often and CORE members had numerous opportunities to hear him speak. Art Evans remembered that his fascination with Cleage's message stemmed from the minister's ability to highlight issues particular to the northern struggle. He also had a "militancy about him," which led many to highly regard the religious leader.[42] Evans later described Cleage as far ahead of CORE, and a man who just made sense though—at the time—Cleveland CORE held to national policy.[43]

While some had a strong affinity for Cleage's nationalist ideas, the self-defense issue remained a sticking point. Nonviolent direct action was the heart of CORE philosophy and strategy. Neither local nor national CORE could tactically support armed protection. According to national CORE, that also meant eschewing any association with groups who purportedly believed in self-defense. The former—nonviolent methods—remained at the heart of Cleveland CORE's beliefs, but not the latter—association with proponents of self-defense. This was particularly evidenced by Cleveland CORE's connections to Mae Mallory, Malcolm X, Freedom Fighters, and Albert Cleage. The self-defense issue reared its head over and over even if Cleveland insisted on sustaining its core values. These self-protection philosophies and nationalist ideals drew members into ideological conflict with the organization, which most solved by joining other groups.[44]

John Cloud, though no longer CORE chairman, was not the last member to serve dual membership with more radical entities. Art Evans unquestionably symbolized this dual dynamic. He served with the Monroe Defense Committee and ensured that Cleveland CORE sustained strong relations with the Nation of Islam. While CORE's second chairman, he also held dual membership in the Afro-American Institute. The institute comprised a group of black men (Henry Glover, Nate Bryant, Hanif Wahab, and founder Donald Freeman) dubbed the Soul Circle. The Afro-American Institute was a Cleveland-based think tank, which worked with civil rights groups throughout the community. It firstly centered its demonstrations on the Mae Mallory case, but later diverged into other protest areas.[45]

More telling than the institute's association with militant causes, however, was its "unofficial" history. The Afro-American Institute served as the public policy arm of Revolutionary Action Movement (RAM). Don Freeman, a Cleveland schoolteacher and founder of the Afro-American Institute, was its intellectual impetus. RAM started in spring 1962 after Freeman encouraged students at Central State University to form a working-class, direct action, and nationalist-based movement for the North. These students, primarily led by Max Stanford and Wanda Marshall, spread RAM from Ohio to Chicago, Philadelphia, New York, and Detroit. Revolutionary Action Movement ultimately became an anticapitalist advocate of urban guerilla warfare, a strategy that extended beyond armed resistance for self-defense and into revolutionary overthrow of the government to establish a black socialist republic.[46]

According to Stanford, the organization purposefully infiltrated CORE chapters to "push the bourgeois reformers as far up-tempo as fast as possible, while at the same time laying a foundation for an underground movement."[47] Indeed, some RAM participants found themselves in CORE chapters. However, CORE members reversed the flow and also joined RAM. Brooklyn CORE activists moderately made up New York RAM, along with writers, poets, and other black artists. John Bracey of Chicago CORE noted that Stanford and Freeman had ties with the chapter there. And, a Cleveland grand jury later accused Lewis Robinson, who floated in and around CORE, of being a member of RAM. Cleveland CORE had a close affiliation with RAM through Evans, who noted that he had strong ties to Freeman and Stanford. Additionally, the two visited and occasionally stayed in Evan's home. Finally, David Cohen confirmed chapter association by remembering that "Max" and "Don" hung around at meetings.[48]

The organization's ties also led the chapter to defend Freeman in the spring of 1965 when the Cleveland School Board of Education fired him for his political leanings and organizational associations with RAM. CORE contended that the school board unconstitutionally invaded Freeman's personal life, and argued that the board only had jurisdiction to judge classroom performance. When SBE ignored appeals, CORE urged black residents to sign support petitions. Still, as usual, the school board remained unmoved.[49]

The inclination to embrace alternate tactics and groups appeared among other members as well. After the March on Washington, a cadre of CORE folks including Tony Perot, Judy Reinthaler, Alex Weathers, Roger Younger, and later Charles Snorton, Betty Renter, Edward Durden, along with other local activists co-organized a political party called Freedom Now. This was not peculiar to Cleveland. This third-party platform first achieved notice from journalist William Worthy at a street rally in Harlem in June 1963. During the August March on Washington, organizers issued a formal call to create an independent black political group titled Freedom Now Party. Freedom Now leaders intended to garner at least a million voters and bring forth a massive surge in black political representation. Unfortunately, the party only took off in Detroit, Michigan, though there were numerous attempts across the United States, Cleveland being one.[50]

In December 1963, the Cleveland committee outlined a platform for an independent political group. This Freedom Now Party (FNP) consisted of a large cross-section of activist organizations. The group insisted that only the black community and its representatives should elect candidates. It, like MOWM long ago, encouraged "support from as many white persons as possible," but "of necessity and out of responsibility to . . . the Negro population" noted the need to prevent domination or manipulation by white political interests. The group was adamant in its disclaimer that it was a matter of self-determination and declared that "the sooner we learn to give more leadership and less excuses, and have something people can VOTE FOR, we'll really be on the way."[51]

Cleveland's Freedom Now's Party also proposed to encourage dignity, self-respect, and Negro leadership, as well as to provide the machinery needed to help the masses "become aware that Freedom, Justice, and Equality must come by revolt: a total economic, social, and political change."[52] The party platform also demanded federal enforcement of the Fourteenth and Fifteenth Amendments, federal troop protection in the South, and a national education system with federal controls to assure total integration and uniform teaching standards. The education mandate consisted of free schooling at all levels from elementary to secondary, college, and technical, and an immediate demand to subsidize higher education for poor youth. Unemployed workers incapable of being retrained and relocated would receive permanent pensions to avoid economic destitution.[53]

The party additionally advocated for a national health program from "cradle to grave," a revision of tax structure to exempt the poor from income tax, reduction of the work week to thirty hours, development of a full-scale federal public work program, new job creation, a minimum wage increase, and a uniform national system for unemployment compensation to cover the entire period of joblessness. The government must also ensure housing for persons of low- and middle-class income, plus pass and enforce residential antidiscrimination laws as felony offenses punishable by lengthy imprisonment.[54]

Perhaps the most interesting aspect of the political proposal was its discussion related to foreign relations. "We repudiate the United States' neo-colonialist imperialist foreign policies in Asia, Latin America, South Africa, Portugal, and Afro America . . . We fervently support the Pan African goals implicit in their policies. We denounce the . . . hypocritical policy of the United States toward the fascist regime of Verwuord in the Union of South Africa stemming from the enormous investments of American capitalists, which help to perpetuate the denial of basic human rights to the Black Africans in the Union of South Africa."[55] In the final version, the committee reduced the long section on foreign relations to "no support of colonialism abroad. End colonialism of 15 million Negroes at Home."[56]

Although CORE members clearly had a heavy hand in the party's mission statement, the political entity never achieved any success. At some point a flyer from an organization called the Cleveland United Negro Party and Work for Freedom did advertise a candidate, but nothing seemed to come of it. In fact, it was unclear if the political parties were separate entities or the same one with an official name change.[57]

Whichever the case, the Freedom Now Party signified diverse endeavors to align Cleveland CORE with the most militant, sometimes black nationalist, ideologies in the city and region. Cleveland CORE metaphorically saw in Mallory, the Freedom Fighters, Reverend Cleage, the Job Seekers, the Afro-American Institute, and the Freedom Now Party the uncompromising demand for self-determination and liberation. And because CORE members held prominent positions within these organizations, they would soon move these ideas from Cleveland to the national office as they moved up the organizational ladder.

Rising black nationalism, extreme violence, and intractable structural racism overwhelmingly pressured and destabilized the nonviolent direct action movement. The Kingian years of nonviolent demonstrations and boycotts declined. Freedom activists aimed to attack the very political and economic structures holding African Americans in the lower stratum of American society. They insisted that a new strategy for black empowerment could end the difficult problems of political and economic exclusion, which kept the masses of African Americans locked in poverty and barred from power. Despite the many changes taking place in the southern movement, the public image of the black freedom movement appeared to converge on the problems of America's urban and northern cities where empowerment ideas gained momentum as an alternative to direct action protest.[58]

Simultaneously, Lyndon Johnson pledged to tackle the high poverty rate with a series of government programs designed to target the "other America." Johnson's 1964 State of the Union unveiled these government initiatives as a War on Poverty. During the same year, Johnson's administration established the Office of Economic Opportunity (OEO), a government agency responsible for the administration of these programs. In tandem with the government, wealthy nonprofits like the Ford Foundation emerged to facilitate antipoverty programs with large community grants.[59]

Concentration on the urban North also occurred because current events demanded it. As soon as OEO started, it met with the first in a series of small rebellions in cities like New York and Philadelphia, which demonstrated black disenchantment and frustration with America's urban decline. Cities imploded from unemployment, dilapidated housing, declining municipal budgets, and the general deterioration of inner-city life. However, the August 1965 outburst in Watts, California, underscored a change in the American public's attention and the black freedom movement. With thirty-four dead, over one thousand injured, and three thousand instances of arson, Watts highlighted and coincided with the movement's intensified focus on structural inequality. At the same time, it emphasized and justified Johnson's "War on Poverty" programs.[60]

National CORE entered this space with experiments of its own. Those who wanted "freedom now" were willing to substitute direct action for another path to freedom. Given this determination and the national focus on poverty, Farmer acted to bridge the gap between CORE's die-hard nonviolent direct action integrationists and its equally die-hard goal-oriented activists. Inevitably, local chapters also needed this "new direction" given the barriers that structural racism posed, direct action's inadequate response, and their rudderless sense of how to handle these more complex issues.

Added to that, Farmer became increasingly concerned that this lack of direction spilled over into chapter skirmishes that came more frequently and produced "splintering and internecine warfare," as "victories [came] more laboriously." CORE acted to halt dissension and address direct action's falling relevance by tightening its administration and offering an alternate stratagem for freedom. CORE's survival, according to Jim Farmer, now depended on its ability to incorporate ghetto voices and transition into community organization. For CORE, it was a "New Direction."[61]

Problematically, many members had little understanding of how to follow this new direction. Others were unprepared for the differing ideological perspectives within the community when they did. Though some branches relocated to urban black neighborhoods and worked well within those areas, other chapters failed to evolve with the new changes. Ultimately, national failed to prepare chapters for more grassroots involvement.

Farmer believed that most of this failure to embody the new CORE concept stemmed from a clash between the ends and means oriented. Farmer acknowledged the diverging sentiments among CORE members that highlighted the divide between old guard integration direct actionists and black community-based activists. He couched the issue as a simple conflict between ends- and means-oriented members, contrasting approaches, which could work to the organization's national interest—if regulated. Nonetheless, such adjustments also meant a fundamental reshuffling of power toward the black community. Thus, some old guard unfairly tagged the new direction toward black empowerment as an extension of black nationalism. Despite the obvious friction characterized in this dichotomy, community involvement was much more complicated than two philosophical poles of integration versus black nationalism.

Norman and Velma Hill, national leaders within CORE, especially reflected this complexity. The Hills had an extensive background in labor and civil rights. Norman Hill, a labor activist and Chicago-based organizer, built a national reputation from his activities in Chicago and the Route 40 restaurant desegregation movement. He also became known for his organizational work around the 1963 March on Washington. Likewise, Velma Murphy Hill had also gained standing for her participation in demonstrations. In 1960, she and her then fiancé, Norman Hill, protested with the NAACP youth council against segregation at Chicago's Rainbow Beach. She paid the ultimate sacrifice when a head injury from mob attack made her miscarry. Velma Hill went on to become a fieldworker for CORE.

The Hills' broad background in labor and civil rights activism shaped their intellectual acceptance of other protest approaches and enabled them to suggest new avenues for CORE activism. Norman Hill's status as national program director especially positioned him to promote an alternative plan for CORE, which involved a new community-involved strategy. The proposal pressed for a program that built coalitions with labor, civil rights groups, and Democratic Party politicians. Hill grounded his idea of community transformation on this relationship. Yet, this diverged from the agenda of chapters like Cleveland, which intended to create community empowerment through unified racial action.[62]

Hill's distinctive method for community organization, though different from Cleveland chapter, failed to take hold as a national policy. This had less to do with ideological differences than internal CORE politics in the national office. Farmer

broke with the strategist over accusations that Hill tried to oust the national director and replace him with Bayard Rustin. Included in the supposed cabal were A. J.
Muste, married couple Norman and Velma Hill, and socialist activists Tom Kahn
and Max Shachtman. Although rumors circulated that Hill was the master mind
behind Rustin's attempted takeover, much of it amounted to hearsay, back history,
and guilt by association. But it gained traction for a variety of reasons.[63]

Bayard Rustin (and A. J. Muste for that matter) were the key factors in this
particular episode. Hill along with Tom Kahn had worked closely with Rustin in
organizing the March on Washington. Plus, both Hills had personal and ideological
ties to the former FOR leader. However, tensions between Rustin and Farmer dated
back to the 1940s, and Farmer became highly sensitive and suspicious of people
within CORE associated with Rustin. Hill, however, felt Farmer overreacted to his
suggestion to bring Rustin in as a consultant on CORE's changing policy. Still, even
if Farmer overreacted, his feelings were substantially based on what other observers
pointedly note was Rustin's deliberate habit of upstaging Farmer.[64]

Additionally, Rustin's association with Kahn and Shachtman made matters
worse. Rustin and Kahn were not only close, but also worked intimately under
Shachtman to move the black freedom movement toward an aggressive affiliation
with the Democrats. Shachtman insisted on leading a "realignment," of liberal/civil
rights within the Democratic Party that would culminate in a coalition dominated
by labor. Shachtman was by no means subtle in his intentions to do so, which
increased suspicion of Rustin, and by extension, the Hills.[65]

The tensions around realignment arose most glaringly over whether to back the
Mississippi Freedom Democratic Party (MFDP) at the Atlantic City Convention
or throw support to Lyndon Johnson to avoid discord with the movement's main
(though barely) political supporters. MFDP challenged the seating of the Mississippi
Democratic Party delegates at the annual Democratic Party Convention—arguing
that the state party delegates could not represent Mississippi's citizenry while black
Mississippians were disenfranchised. Johnson feared southern democrats would
leave the party if MFDP received delegate status. Through backroom dealings
and negotiations, Johnson offered to give MFDP two at-large seats but keep the
Mississippi delegates in place. Johnson and other Democratic officials pressured
civil rights groups to accept the compromise, which created conflict among these
organizations.

CORE's National Action Council passed a referendum August 8, 1964, throw-
ing its backing to MFDP in a steering committee vote of 8 to 5, in support of
MFDP's seating at the convention. Once CORE insisted that it would stand with
MFDP, Hill left CORE believing that there was no room for coalition building
between labor, civil rights, and the political left. Ironically, SNCC broke with Max
Shachtman over his insistence that it should also accept the Johnson administration's

two at-large seat compromise, an effectively symbolic position. SNCC was not too happy with Rustin either after he too insisted they backed the compromise.[66]

Many in CORE were hard pressed to accept Hill's coalition argument as a useful avenue to black community empowerment, particularly after the Atlanta Convention. First, the Democratic Party had refused the seating of delegates from the Mississippi Democratic Freedom Party—a counter interracial political party to the exclusively white segregated Mississippi State Democratic Party. Second, Democratic president Lyndon B. Johnson exasperated the situation when he suppressed media coverage of MFDP representative Fannie Lou Hamer. Both actions gave credence to the belief that the Democratic Party was not a trusted partner and it inevitably led to a rejection of a labor-Democrat-civil rights alliance. Because many activists viewed the Atlantic City Convention as a failure of white liberalism, community organization transmuted as a strategy that centered upon independent action, and self-empowerment by the black community within existing structures or, if necessary, outside of them.[67]

Shortly after Hill's resignation, Farmer moved forward with CORE's "New Direction" an organization plan designed to heighten mass black involvement and community growth. Farmer initially announced the new proposal at CORE's 1964 annual convention. The plan emphasized community engagement in three areas: economic, cultural, and political.[68] The cultural department addressed issues of self-identity, and self-esteem, plus a new thrust toward black consciousness. Under the economic department, CORE aimed to encourage small black businesses and farm cooperatives, while political action allowed CORE to venture into partisan politics.[69]

The political component within New Directions was a contentious model of action for some within CORE. For years, CORE struggled internally with members who wished to cross the divide from direct action into political activism by outwardly endorsing, working for, selecting, or running as candidates. New Directions cleared the way for chapters who had long since advocated this switch in CORE policy. The 1965 Director's Report further highlighted CORE's intent. Farmer argued that CORE had to harness "the political potential of the black community in order to effect basic social and economic changes . . . to alter meaningfully the lives of Black Americans."[70] Brooklyn CORE was well on its way, and ran one of its chapter leaders, Major Owens, as a candidate for city council after it set up the Brooklyn Freedom Democratic Movement. Farmer acknowledged that such a move was a far cry from CORE's earlier policy, but the former requirement was "no longer applicable to the needs of the movement." In fact, Farmer claimed that CORE might as well "admit that old policy is dead, and move boldly on with the new" even if some were hesitant.[71]

The New Directions economic program was not as troubling for many. In some ways, it rehashed the Brotherhood Mobilization Plan. The proposal permitted local branches to create agricultural and home-based cooperatives, the original basis for CORE's financial independence. CORE approved and held as model examples economic cooperatives like the Tote Bag project out of Haywood County, which sold leather bags to provide an income for displaced farmers, and the Louisiana sweet potato cooperative. The cooperatives were both defensive and offensive strategies. First, these entities provided alternate income for agricultural workers penalized for civil rights activities. Second, it incorporated themes of institution building and black economic independence, which allowed CORE to argue that it embraced some elements of nationalism even though the cooperatives were initially conceived as solutions to pragmatic realities.[72]

Despite a difficult, and sometimes, confusing start, Farmer intended for New Directions to steer rising militancy among chapters and bridge the gap between this new radicalism and CORE's constructed identity.[73] However, many saw New Directions either as a partial "rescue" for the old CORE or as a capitulation to rising challenges to interracial nonviolent direct action. Either way, community organizing—and its intensive focus on the black community and black leadership— still became a proxy for black nationalism in the minds of CORE old guards.[74]

The differences between community involvement advocates and their opponents played out during the 1965 Durham convention NAC meeting. Turner captured the period's atmosphere by insisting that integration was dead and that community power was the new goal. However, CORE would have to determine whether it intended to build power for itself or for the people. Turner contended that the nature of the freedom movement had changed, and that the direction no longer consisted of desegregation or integration thrusts but issues related to unemployment, inferior housing, displacement from urban renewal, poor schools, and low motivation. CORE's reputation within the movement amounted to "exposing civil rights problems but not solving them."[75] According to Turner, CORE ultimately failed to affect fundamental economic and political conditions because it was ill equipped to address more complex social problems. Turner reserved most of her criticism for the national office, which she maintained fell short of helping local chapters to meet these new realities. Too many CORE chapters unsuccessfully comprehended the nature of community organization and expected instant results. Additionally, a substantial number of branches interacted only with organizations that reflected CORE's own mission, but that attitude excluded alliances with a variety of local groups. More to the point, CORE chapters were "unrepresentative of the people they claim to represent."[76]

Other NAC members and chapter leaders joined Turner's complaint against the national office. Milwaukee CORE's Cecil Brown repeated Turner's admonition to move at a faster pace from direct action to community action. National's unorganized and noncommunicative relationship with locals hindered their ability to properly transition to community-oriented strategies. Some NAC associates also reproached CORE headquarters for being too heavily led and influenced by office staff who ignored local needs. Questions came to the fore regarding undue influence in CORE's programmatic thrust, unconnected reality to the ground-level freedom movement, and continued allegiance to interracialism. The national staff's hesitant acceptance of community organization and its slow implementation (much of which was actually a reflection of poor internal structure) led Turner to staunchly demand national staff just "take orders" since they had no basic understanding of chapter needs.[77]

Turner's reaction partly reflected her own fears about Cleveland CORE's status after the school desegregation letdown. Beginning late fall 1964 and early 1965, demonstrations precipitously declined and direct action activities were sporadic and small. Projects like Sympathy protests, a co-directed workshop with the Urban League, and supply (food, clothing, funds) drives during and after Freedom Summer were among these efforts. Cleveland also initiated a letter-writing campaign against *Call and Post* on behalf of striking members of the International Typographical Union, AFL-CIO. The chapter voted unanimously to support the workers, and asked sister chapters in Columbus and Cincinnati to join its action against *Call and Post*'s antiworker stance in their perspective cities.[78]

The chapter launched its last major direct action campaign from summer 1964 to spring 1965 against the Cleveland police. CORE's initial position on police brutality stemmed first from its ill treatment during school desegregation demonstrations. However, it soon blossomed as a broader community issue. CORE actually picketed the police headquarters and City Hall as early as February 1964, but demonstrations kicked into high gear over the summer. On one occasion, CORE canceled the weekly membership meeting and directed activists to meet at the steps of City Hall to combat excessive police force. The chapter also planned a rally in mid-July titled "Trial of the Police Department" to expose police abuses. It subsequently issued after the "trial" several demands for an immediate end to brutality, automatic suspension of accused officers, a Citizens Police Advisory Board, improved police procedures, and human relations training.[79]

Various black activists along with Cleveland CORE also lobbied the Ohio Civil Rights Commission to investigate police officer transgressions, which included refusal to arrest whites who perpetrated crimes against black residents, false arrest, property destruction, verbal and physical beatings, shootings, and permanent injury. When the commission examined CORE's complaint, it found that unknown persons mysteriously edited the only visual proof, television news film, of the most violent police scenes during the school desegregation movement. Despite efforts to hide evidence, testimony before the US Commission on Civil Rights bolstered Cleveland CORE's accusations of excessive force and confirmed police misconduct.[80]

Although sit-ins and other protests quieted in the fall, animosity toward the police department reignited May 1965 when Mayor Locher refused to disavow the city police chief's testimony before an Ohio State congressional committee. Chief Richard Wagner incited the black community with incendiary allegations that Cleveland's black freedom organizations justified the need for a death penalty. Wagner testified, "In Cleveland . . . we have people saying they intend to overthrow the government of the United States and incidentally, shoot all the Caucasians. One of those groups is RAM (Revolutionary Action Movement)."[81] UFM petitioned for a meeting with Mayor Locher and Chief Wagner, both of whom rebuffed their requests. UFM responded with a wait-in at the mayor's office for four days. Nonetheless, the office obstinately rebuffed their appeals. UFM refused to leave City Hall, and consequently the police arrested five people. Wait-ins and marches continued unabated for days afterward. CORE, no longer satisfied with UFM's wait-in at the mayor's office, intensified the demonstrations, and staged a march directly in front of Mayor Locher's home.[82]

Notably, Ruth Turner's picket sign read, "Why Fight? Let's Switch Mayors." The poster powerfully signified Cleveland CORE's growing intent to switch from direct action to the new directions political component. Other Cleveland CORE members also welcomed the change in agenda. Perot argued that the chapter had not devoted enough time to community organizing. The group missed a major opportunity when it failed to sustain the tenant councils since community involvement prompted deeper commitment to the movement.[83] For Turner and Perot, their failure to consistently employ community organization policies and projects reduced the chapter's effectiveness.

In spite of this critical evaluation, not every chapter leader agreed with Perot or Turner's insistence for greater community involvement. Fall 1964 to early 1965 saw internal challenges within the chapter that temporarily destabilized its membership and its "new directions" agenda. Conflict surfaced between SWP members/ black direct actionists and black leadership/community organization proponents. The direct action faction, led by Art Evans and championed by Bernard Mendel and Eric Reinthaler, ran a slate of officers in opposition to CORE's new direction. Community organization advocate Ruth Turner, backed by Pauline Warfield, Tony Perot, Dudley Woodard, Chuck Burton, Don Bean, and David Cohen, ran a counter slate.

At stake was the question of whether Cleveland CORE intended to confront police and ramp up community protest or move more vigorously toward community organization. The Evans faction pushed for more marches against Cleveland police, and argued that direct action was more important for CORE's survival. Protests generally produced unsolicited income during and after every campaign, attracted additional membership, and garnered media attention.[84]

Members of the Congress of Racial Equality picket outside the home of Mayor Ralph Locher. CORE members were protesting Locher's refusal to meet with representatives of the United Freedom Movement. Ruth Turner Perot holds sign in back ground, "Why Fight, Let's Switch Mayors," representing CORE's turn to community organization and eventually black political power. Photo: James Thomas, June 12, 1965. From the Cleveland Press Collection, Michael Schwartz Library, Cleveland State University

The Turner faction contended that CORE's paramount goal should be the immediate needs of poor black people. Demonstrations had little applicability for transforming the nature of the system and the black community had to liberate themselves in a fundamental way. Most significantly, Turner and the community organization group also believed that the SWP used the front of black leadership via Evans to propagate its own proclivities of violent confrontation with the government, or in this case, the state's enforcers, the police.[85]

Whichever the case, the Evans-SWP group faced a major loss to the Turner alliance. CORE member and SWP sympathizer Bonnie Holt later recalled that she saw more voting members than ever before when the two slates came up for vote.[86] Purportedly, conflict degenerated to such a state that both Evans and Turner were accused of being dictators. Evans later noted that the chapter had almost become matrilineal in terms of the leadership control that Turner wielded within the group. Clashes within Cleveland CORE became so problematic that Ruth Turner skipped the February 1965 NAC meeting to instead deal with the chapter's issues. She attended an executive committee retreat to hash out the chapter's new program, but also to deal with personality conflicts that halted the organization's progress.[87]

After Turner reasserted control over Cleveland CORE, she and other Cleveland members moved to firmly position themselves in the national office. In fact, as early as summer 1963, Art Evans, Tony Perot, and Ruth Turner had served already as regional fieldworkers or National Action Council members. The group sought to enhance its standing by submitting its leadership for officer positions on the NAC. Summer 1965, only days after Turner told national staff "to take orders," Cleveland CORE pressed its political aspirations. The chapter expected to run Ruth Turner for the slot of second vice chair of NAC thereby moving her previous year's general membership on the NAC board to a more powerful position. However, the group reversed its decision and internally negotiated to bolster Long Island CORE chapter chairman Lincoln Lynch's bid for the seat. Turner instead ran for secretary of NAC with support from his faction. Despite the political trade with Lynch, Turner only lost her bid for second vice chairman 78 to 86. After the loss, Fran Crayton of Brooklyn CORE immediately moved for a unanimous vote to slot Turner for NAC secretary. It passed without dissent.[88]

With her power reaffirmed and climbing the ladder to national influence, Turner produced a newsletter that emphasized the political component of the "New Directions" proposal. Ruth Turner noted:

> For the past month we in CORE have been talking about political action and the civil rights movement . . . and so for a month now we have thought seriously about getting into political action here in Cleveland. But what does this mean? . . . CORE's political goals must be unselfish as our goals in direct action have been; to help develop in the Negro community the power to make full equality and justice a reality . . . CORE must try to involve in political action those who have not cared before . . . involvement means helping people feel that their registering and voting makes a difference.[89]

Cleveland CORE's first political activities included voter registration and political education. The chapter got over two thousand residents of Ward 27 (Hough and Glenville) listed on voter rolls, and planned a drive in the Central Avenue West area. CORE provided information on candidates who refused to give aid during the school desegregation crisis as well as listed the names of black Clevelanders running for state and local offices.[90]

The chapter regained momentum in 1965 with its new political activism thrust. In the summer of 1965, the chapter went all out for Carl Stokes's mayoral campaign. Stokes, a well-known black lawyer and politician, ran in the 1965 Cleveland race as an independent. During the latter half of the summer, the chapter spent a good deal of time engaged in voter registration campaigns with other organizations.[91] By the fall, it unofficially converted to volunteer quarters for Stokes's campaign. CORE also sent letters and flyers urging black residents to type, stuff envelopes, pass out Stokes campaign paraphernalia, and visit "barber shops, beauty parlors, and pool rooms."[92] Even the national office noticed the activities on behalf of Stokes, declaring, "Cleveland CORE is solidly behind Stokes . . . the other members of the civil rights unity group have not endorsed him, the chapter is now working with a group of women, 'Domestic Workers of America' who have just organized."[93]

The "other members of the civil rights unity group" undoubtedly referred to the United Freedom Movement. After the school desegregation fight, UFM created few waves as an organization except for the brief boost it received from the Wagner-related protests in May 1965. In the latter months of 1964 and into 1965, UFM conferred to determine its new agenda. But, workshop participants disputed the organization's future relevance and suggested that its survival partially rested on the ability to endorse and influence specific candidates.[94] The NAACP, however, stood in constant opposition to this notion. Internal pressures finally boiled over when the NAACP refused to accept a constitutional change giving organizational endorsement to Carl Stokes. After Klunder's death and the city's repression of the school movement, CORE and other militant organizations found the NAACP's attitude unacceptable. An NAACP member soon thereafter noted, "we are now in the showdown phase of whether UFM should be or not or whether it will be with us or without us."[95]

On August 1965, that showdown occurred when James Russell, Freedom Fighter's cofounder, initiated a motion—seconded by Antoine Perot—that UFM endorse candidates after careful screening. The motion carried, but that vote led to the immediate resignation of three leaders: the Reverend Sumpter Riley, Wendell Erwin, and Armond Robinson. Both Erwin and Robinson sat on the Executive Committee of the NAACP.[96] Although the vote instigated squabbling between the NAACP and CORE/Freedom Fighters, the NAACP did not immediately leave. But in February 1966, the NAACP eventually decided that the barely functioning UFM should go on without them. Remaining members within UFM issued a press release stating that "the NAACP withdrawal will not result in acrimonious competition. Everyone has a role to play in the civil rights struggle," and that suggestions of UFM's decline were "without foundation." Nonetheless, the NAACP departure and the internal instability of Cleveland CORE proved to be the final blow to an already weakened UFM. The organization broke apart thereafter.[97]

The internal bickering within UFM notwithstanding, Cleveland CORE continued its political activities on behalf of Stokes. However, Stokes lost his bid for mayor by a mere 1 percent of the vote. Cleveland CORE's first major foray into partisan politics fell short of its goal, but his close victory gave the black community and Cleveland CORE hope. Indeed, many believed Stokes had won, and pointed to rumors that his loss resulted from disappearing ballot boxes from black wards.[98]

After the heightened activities associated with the 1965 Stokes campaign, Cleveland CORE hardly functioned at its previous direct action levels. Mass letters no longer included letterhead and address information. The November newsletter spelled the chapter's circumstances in quite circumspect language by noting that "while you have not heard from Cleveland CORE often this past year, we have been active in many areas." Those areas included voter registration, community organization of housing projects, and the Stokes campaign.

This is not to say that Cleveland CORE lacked a presence or disappeared from the city. Throughout 1965, the branch deepened its activities in the area of community organization and still remained one of the better-known freedom groups. Cleveland CORE expanded its housing initiative and tenant councils into the Central-West area—a section of Cleveland weighed down by poverty since the 1930s. The activists focused their attention on the Longwood Housing Project and other public housing developments in the Central Avenue area. CORE also modified its official mandate of school desegregation and formally promoted better school quality and higher educational standards for under-resourced, ill-equipped schools. By early fall 1965, Cleveland CORE celebrated the opening of the Bruce Klunder Freedom House (a memorial and education space dedicated to Klunder) on Woodlawn Avenue and hosted James Farmer for its dedication. The event served to highlight a fair housing rally planned later in the week.[99]

In the latter months of 1965, Cleveland CORE planned several fund-raising activities including an award banquet with Dick Gregory and greeting card sales. However, these efforts did not mitigate the chapter's financial fall. By late 1965, CORE moved from its office in Hough to the Klunder House. Turner eventually lost her paid post as executive secretary, though as a volunteer she maintained the title. The financial loss paralleled the chapter's drop away from direct action and the departure of SWP activists.[100]

Baxter Hill, formerly head of the Human Rights Defenders, briefly took over the chairmanship of Cleveland CORE in October 1965. The chapter restructured its executive committee so that there were only three offices elected at large—Hill as chairman, Max Schoenfeld as recording secretary, and Jennie Coles, treasurer. Ruth Turner still served as executive secretary of Cleveland CORE.[101]

Under Hill, Cleveland CORE's "new direction" focused on an economic program that confronted unemployment and work discrimination. Cleveland CORE utilized a number of protest methods including marches and boycotts. It held a sympathy boycott on behalf of grape workers in California, and urged Cleveland residents not to purchase Scheneley Liquors and Delano Grape Products. The chapter also listed job openings and training information in its newsletter.[102]

CORE's largest employment demonstration launched on February 1966 under the name "Operation Breadbasket." It included multiple direct action protests and boycotts against Kroger Grocery Store. For six Saturdays, CORE protested discrimination at Kroger. Activists demanded an immediate expansion in black employment: 39 percent increase in cashier and management positions, transfer of all part-time workers to full-time positions, and the current manager removed for failure to integrate. Picketing was small but consistent and eventually spread to other grocery stores, though it remained unclear what gains the chapter managed to garner.[103]

The Research Committee headed by former SCORE, now CORE member Pauline Warfield, also directed focus toward employment discrimination. Initially the committee sought to study Cleveland's handling of War on Poverty funds, and ensure its proper distribution.[104] It then branched out, and investigated racial discrimination in all government departments including the Internal Revenue Department, the Navy Department, the US Postal Service, the National Aeronautics and Space Administration, and the Veterans Administration.[105]

Concurrent with Cleveland CORE's focus on employment issues, the chapter attempted to augment its community organization activism among the unemployed. It coauthored a joint proposal with Students for a Democratic Society (SDS) and its Economic Research Action Project (ERAP), which suggested ways to craft a movement of the unemployed. Workers without a job would provide the core membership and leadership within a loosely constructed organization. The proposal recommended that the government not just enforce antidiscrimination laws, but also actively guarantee employment for poor black residents. The short- and long-range goals of the program incorporated job retention programs, expansion of apprenticeship programs, uninhibited membership in unions, a shorter work week, relaxed requirements for unemployment compensation, and shared decision making in the allocation of government resources.[106] Though long-range goals were amorphous and expansive, the proposal represented Cleveland CORE's first effort to gather the unemployed as an organizational force.

The working paper, though a small effort, was not Cleveland CORE's only work in this area. Norman Hill, no longer with national, consulted with Midwest regional chapters in December 1965 regarding the economic barriers in the rust belt region. Defense industry needs during World War II generated a massive semi-skilled and unskilled workforce. As companies automated, the demand for labor precipitously dropped. CORE now had the task of not only ending discrimination, but also filling an employment gap. Such circumstances became exasperated when more and more black southerners migrated to the urban North and West. This was particularly the case for Cleveland, where unlike many cities, the largest portion of black settlement into the city actually occurred in the 1960s after the second great migration.[107]

This predicament led Cleveland CORE to more actively address issues of working poverty and underemployment, especially as reflected in the new members it recruited. Lula Primus, member of both CORE and the Domestic Workers, joined Hill in regional training to outline how other chapters could emmulate Cleveland CORE's work with the Domestic Workers. Membered by mostly working poor women, Domestic Workers helped the chapter restructure its techniques for economic advancement. The alliance fought for minimum wage increase, multiple membership levels in black organizations for those on welfare, vacation and health benefits advocacy, clothes and food collection, and assistance to senior citizens as well as the disabled.[108]

Cleveland CORE maintained its activist character in other nuanced and subtle ways as well. The chapter allied with SDS and other civil rights groups to form the Citizens Committee for an Adequate Community Action Program (CCACAP). The committee opposed the local Council of Economic Opportunity—War on Poverty's local policy panel—for its exclusion of poor people. CCACAP stopped funds for six months, before the city received a grant. Unbeknown to CCACAP, the NAACP managed to get two of its representatives appointed to the board in backroom negotiations despite the group's mandate to position only local poor residents. [109]

Turner's experience in Cleveland undoubtedly led her to write a report for NAC, which rebuked and censured any action by CORE that resembled Cleveland NAACP's departure from community empowerment. Turner concluded that federal programs superficially addressed poverty's symptoms, fell short of creating the large-scale employment needed, and systematically refused to place poor people in control of the resources meant to help them. She further proposed that all COREs operate as a watchdog organization to ensure proper representation on these policy-making bodies. According to Turner, CORE was better positioned to apply pressure from the outside, a feat that Cleveland CORE demonstrated in its own city.[110]

Her objections to any relationship to the War on Poverty beyond overseer were hardly without merit. In 1965, many CORE chapters suffered the slow leak of experienced personnel from its chapters and national office into these federal programs. Such actions hit at CORE's community organization efforts. Notably, it exposed the obvious problem of how to engage in community action systematically and long term with no long-term volunteers and no funding. As it were, even Cleveland CORE was slow going on the endeavor to create long-term change through community action.[111]

Despite Cleveland CORE's successful implementation of new directions, in both political and economic areas, the local chapter did not fair as well as it hoped. The branch's financial debilitation affected Turner's position and eventually forced her to seek part-time employment with the *Call and Post*. Ruth Turner now actively served as an officer of the National Action Council, but only as a volunteer worker for the local chapter. Cleveland CORE's community organization also suffered from the constant rotation of CORE staff and committee members. For example, 1965 marked the beginning of an almost annual replacement of the Cleveland CORE chairperson, further undermining its stability. According to a Ford Foundation report, "by 1967, CORE's membership had dwindled to 300 . . . [though] it continued to exert considerable influence in Cleveland as well as in National CORE."[112] Thus, Turner and other Cleveland CORE leaders still had power to affect change even as other Cleveland chapter leaders rotated and membership dropped.

During the 1966 annual CORE convention, Arthur Evans, who led Cleveland CORE as chairman took the position of first vice chairman on the NAC. Donald Bean, former SCORE activist and later Cleveland CORE chairman, became a representative on the North Central Regional CORE committee.[113] Tony Perot, formerly CORE Midwest field officer, became program director for the national CORE office.

After Turner's election to secretary of NAC in 1965, she stated that she would "continue to be a pencil pusher to the best of my ability."[114] Turner greatly understated her power, and was more than a "pencil pusher," by any measure. In fact, it was Turner who provided the convention's theme "The Black Ghetto—An Awakening Giant."[115] The Durham 1965 convention signified a new direction for CORE and its chapters. No longer focused predominantly on the southern movement, CORE sought to address the needs of millions of black people caught in poverty and contained in urban slums. Their new direction would help harness "the tremendous economic potential of the ghetto and . . . [develop] political movements."[116] Ultimately, Durham finalized CORE's slow transition from southern civil rights to the northern ghettos and from direct action to community organization. By 1966, Ruth Turner retained her title of secretary, not on the NAC, but as assistant to the new national director and leader of CORE's black power era, Floyd McKissick.

Cleveland CORE members leaving from Bruce Klunder Freedom House
at 5120 Woodlawn Avenue to participate in March Against Fear.
Photo: Bill Nehez, June 10, 1966. From the Cleveland Press Collection,
Michael Schwartz Library, Cleveland State University

# 6

## Breaking the Noose

"WHAT do we WANT?
Black Power!
WHAT do we WANT?
Black Power!
WHAT do we WANT?
Black Power!
WHAT do we WANT?
Black Power!"[1]

THAT SHORT, 2-LINE CHANT shook the global grounds of black conscious-ness. June 16, 1966, Student Nonviolent Coordinating Committee leader Stokely Carmichael climbed the podium to address demonstrators from the Meredith March Against Fear. That night, he roused the crowd with his powerful speech and intro-duction to a new expression for freedom: black power. Before Carmichael delivered his now famous speech, Martin Luther King Jr. begged the SNCC leader not to use the phrase, arguing that it undercut the movement's moral standing. Carmichael refused, but King hoped that he might persuade Floyd McKissick, CORE's recently elected national director, to join him in deferring SNCC's decision to shout black power. Much to his dismay, McKissick was anything but cooperative. The orga-nization had undergone similar changes as SNCC in rethinking the role of direct action, nonviolence, and integration. Close to a month later, delegates at the CORE Baltimore convention endorsed the slogan. Ultimately, both groups were on a road that SCLC could neither stymie nor follow.

Notwithstanding the speed with which CORE supported such an undefined phrase, endorsement of black power was no great ideological jump for the orga-nization. Of the major civil rights groups, CORE was especially primed for this evolutionary transformation and urban focus. Among the "big four" (aside from the

NAACP whose northern chapters were not known for their militancy), CORE had more chapters outside the South and a longer history of activism in these regions. Additionally, national circumstances, internal and external, augmented local metamorphoses to create a perfect storm for black power's arrival. Locals had thrust the national office into conflict over black nationalist associations, armed self-defense, and community organization. The resulting fights led to a struggle with white members over power and resources within CORE that damaged its stability. Black power triumphed, and advocates got their way with a concentrated program of new direction now labeled Target City. Yet as they struggled to determine what Target City meant strategically and programmatically, the resulting fall-out over "white money" left some black nationalist supporters disaffected from national's early version of black power.

White national staff and chapter members ruled CORE's council for most of its life. In 1962, the committee underwent a formal change in title (National Action Committee to National Action Council) and with that came an astronomical overhaul in representation. Originally composed of national office staff and four outside chapter members, NAC increased in number to twenty-two including now the national director, *CORE-lator* editor, five elected officers, two members from each region, plus five director appointees.[2] The alteration gave unprecedented power to the locals, and the change triggered a racial rebalance that substantially made it interracial. The 1963 Convention Constitution Committee exampled some of this rearrangement with its black composition that included Patricia Due, Oretha Castle, Clarence Funnye, Lincoln Lynch, John Cloud, and Rudy Lombard. Though some of these members did not avidly advocate black nationalism, a smattering of black nationalist adherents were among them and more soon appeared.

National CORE received reports from local chapters beginning in 1962 that indicated its nagging, unfocused but persistent presence. The typical response from national office was to suggest enhanced training and remind chapters about CORE philosophy. Yet, this affected little of the growing sentiment among black CORE activists. CORE members fluidly vacillated between black nationalism as a strategy or ideology, and it was not long before some openly advocated for racial pride, black leadership control, and/or the ouster of white members.[3]

Julius Hobson, in particular, characterized this quintessential fear of an all-black CORE. Hobson was part of black power's parental lineage as an important mentor for Stokely Carmichael during his Howard University years. Carmichael reminisced that Hobson had been an "experienced struggler, a good strategist, an uncompromising militant, and a man of selfless devotion . . . whom we were prepared to listen and whose direction in matters of struggle we would accept."[4] Hobson challenged Farmer on CORE's acceptance of the 1964 civil rights bill, which he viewed as watered down. Hobson also advocated all-black leadership and ran afoul of many members—black and white—for his dictatorial rule over Washington, DC, CORE. He ultimately left to become part of the larger movement toward black power, though he later critiqued its too slow movement to the left.[5] Still, Hobson's presence added further angst about CORE's estrangement from interracialism.

In 1964, NAC's racial balance converted to a black majority and with it pressure mounted. Power struggles ensued over who was in charge, especially as the movement itself transitioned. The schism between NAC, local chapters, and the national office became particularly acute with white national staff perceived as unwilling to recognize the coming new order.

Farmer got caught in the crossfire when he unsuccessfully charted a middle path between the two groups. Some CORE means-oriented/nationalists believed Farmer unprepared to guide and direct CORE into the new militant era. Simultaneously, actions meant to appease the burgeoning nationalists and navigate both the freedom movement and his own ideological transformation, created antagonisms with old guard members of CORE who wished to retain the organization's former mission.

It became a major confrontation in 1965 when Charles Odham (NAC chair), and Marvin Rich (community relations director) designated white staff member Alan Gartner (national treasurer and former Boston CORE chairman) heir apparent to the CORE chairmanship. Farmer charged that the three dismissed him as a "figurehead." Farmer went on to argue that "there is no way that a white man can be titular head of what Louis Lomax has called the 'Negro Revolt' at this point in history."[6] Needless to say, the national director opposed the selection, and demanded Odham retract Gartner's name or prepare for an open challenge at the 1965 convention with Floyd McKissick, black lawyer and chairman of Durham, North Carolina, CORE as Farmer's nominee. McKissick unquestionably ranked high in CORE national. Although he officially began legal work for CORE in 1960, he actually rode one leg of the Journey of Reconciliation in 1947 when it traveled through North Carolina. In the 1950s, McKissick participated in nonviolent direct action protests, and by the mid-1960s, he was a highly well known and favored veteran activist for CORE.[7]

Farmer's choice to go for McKissick over Gartner created a major hullabaloo, but he held out based on two objections. First, Gartner's undemocratic selection ignited charges of white paternalism and questions of who was in charge. Second, Farmer correctly assessed that the atmosphere required an assertion of black leadership. Both ideas implied black nationalism to some, and a dangerous trend that could undermine the true heart of CORE. It certainly contradicted Farmer's earlier stance that MOWM's racial chauvinism had no role in embracing true brotherhood. However, the changing dynamics of the movement gave him plenty reason to rethink his initial thoughts. Tactical necessities now took precedence over his earlier philosophy.

Opposition to Farmer's reasoning led to an immediate reprisal for his choice of McKissick over Gartner. In the process, some old guard in national office and NAC began to accuse him of becoming a black nationalist or latent Garveyite. The characterization was absurdly inaccurate, and ignored the obvious pragmatic reasons for such a decision. The freedom movement was under transformation, and CORE encountered derision as an organization presumed mostly white led. Even more, control by white members in the national office raised questions about CORE's ability to comprehend black needs, or even respond to its own local chapters, many of which operated under black leadership.[8] Finally, there was the simple irony that Farmer only followed a similar strategy that Rich, Odham, and Carey employed to install him as national director of CORE.

Farmer's maneuver situated McKissick as CORE chairman, and directly placed him in line for national director. It hardly surprised anyone that McKissick became a frontrunner after Farmer resigned in late 1965. McKissick's opponent was associate national director of CORE and later founder of the National Welfare Rights Organization, George Wiley. Wiley's support came from those who yearned to retain CORE's interracial goodwill character, but also from southern chapters with whom he'd crafted a very good rapport. His opposition, to the contrary, claimed he could not take CORE to the next level of its development.[9]

Many McKissick backers also rebuffed Wiley because of his white wife—a relationship that they argued had no place in the new era of black pride. Turner was among those who disputed Wiley's nomination on this matter. The disagreement stemmed from her belief that the symbolic impact of a black male with a white wife during a period of heightened black militancy continued to make CORE look disconnected from the black community. Noticeably, she did not hold this position two years prior when it came to Cecil Brown, Milwaukee CORE leader, whom Turner nominated for service on NAC. Thus, her issue with Wiley's wife appeared to partially boil down to one of image.[10]

Turner was not the only one who complained about CORE's "too interracial" persona. Contention over black leadership and interracial marriage occurred with Farmer when Gladys Harrington, according to Jim Peck, raised the same misgivings. Black-white sexual intimacy also created friction among chapters. Several times, mixed-race sex became a proxy for power relations or a symbol of ideological allegiance. Such certainly was the case in New Orleans, where the chapter purged all members who engaged in interracial liaisons.[11]

The New Orleans chapter ranked among CORE's earliest and best branches in the 1960s. Out of it came a cadre of activists who strongly defined the southern movement's development. Early member Jerome Smith was among those who helped to chart the Freedom Ride from New Orleans into Mississippi. Ronnie Moore came to lead CORE southern regional, and later became executive director of the Scholarship, Education, and Defense Fund (SEDF)—the nonprofit arm of CORE. David Dennis, CORE staff in Mississippi during Freedom Summer, famously gave the eulogy for James Chaney. Oretha Castle not only represented CORE throughout the state of Louisiana, but also held membership on the National Action Council during the early 1960s. They represented the heart of New Orleans CORE's leadership. However, the introduction of newer members, particularly white students from Tulane, into this tight-knit relationship inevitably created skirmishes for chapter power. Castle noted that white students who joined CORE made the chapter a space for their ideological control and rule changes, which aggravated black members. One small example included a ban on prayers before CORE meetings.[12]

Second, some interpreted CORE's interracialism as both a political and a social interactive philosophy. Castle noted that New Orleans CORE became a meet-and-greet space for interracial sex. Indeed, as she bluntly stated, it was an opportunity for white men to easily find some "black meat." Castle was hardly alone in her belief that the parties distracted from the chapter's real intentions. Matteo Suarez was equally upset, noting that "most of the white boys who were coming in were looking for black chicks, and we had a big meeting one night in which all this was thrown out, and one guy said 'you damn right I came here to get me some black pussy,' and he said 'that's the only reason I'm here.'"[13]

Eventually, condemnation surfaced from the black community itself. Local leaders approached Castle about CORE's interracial parties, and the city's black newspaper, the *Louisiana Weekly*, chose to editorialize its disapproval. In response, black leaders within New Orleans CORE removed those perceived as distracted from the movement and too presumptuous about their own position. The purge created so much dissention that national office dispatched Richard Haley to mediate the conflict.[14]

Though the purge in New Orleans appeared to be an easy example of sex taking on political dimensions within CORE, it also reflected in less subtle ways. As Jim Farmer noted, one California chapter also had its problems with black/white intimacy. The issue culminated with a black male CORE member who complained about "white bitches" trying to run the organization. Subsequently, a white female CORE activist jumped up and exclaimed she must have been a bitch, since "I'm sleeping with you." Although the emotional outburst was only one among many that evening, clearly, night activity found its way into a politically charged daylight.[15]

Whether New Orleans, a random couple among the California CORE chapters, or George Wiley, fights over interracial liaisons and marriages acted to disrupt the old image of interracial brotherhood for the new black is beautiful identity. Wiley symbolically and ideologically seemed unsuited to CORE's new black militancy. However, Wiley later argued that it really amounted to political machinations and intrigue. According to him, Farmer and Turner supported McKissick because he was easily manipulated and directed by them both.[16]

Whether that was true or not, Turner was unquestionably instrumental in the election of McKissick to the office of national director in January 1966. She used her influence among NAC and chapter leaders to gather undecided support in his direction.[17] Turner's political acumen led insiders to also credit her with national CORE's shift in policy—first to the North and then in relation to black power. Indeed one historian argued that Turner crafted CORE's black power policy though she held none of the perceived power positions within CORE.[18] Turner's forceful arbitration of the McKissick nomination, confrontation with local peers and national staff unwilling to accept community organization (later black power), and open defiance of CORE's interracial portrayal steered many to believe that Turner was a rabid black nationalist separatist and the main culprit in CORE's downfall to black power. In a real sense, she became CORE's proverbial boogey-woman of black power.

Several national staff presumed that Turner's animosity toward whites was pure separatist in nature. However, Turner had a long history with black leadership from the moment she took over Cleveland CORE. It was no surprise she would extend that into the national office. It would be more correct to say that her strident insistence on black leadership manifested as resentment toward white control of CORE. Discord over the *CORE-lator* exemplified these antagonisms. Turner acted to remove Jim Peck from the editorship of the *CORE-lator* at the April 1965 NAC meeting. Although the first maneuver failed, she ultimately succeeded. By midsummer, NAC abolished CORE's national media organ, the *CORE-lator*, after its editor Jim Peck refused to change the format. The council claimed Peck insisted on presenting black activists with "their heads bashed in," as opposed to exposing inequalities in the North or promoting CORE's community organization efforts. Peck rebuffed NAC's request to shift the newsletter from southern direct action to "new directions."[19]

Rather, Peck was known for his dogmatic, sometimes bombastic insistence on the "CORE way." His refusal to change the *CORE-lator* ran head long into a challenge of black leadership. Peck's later castigation of black power in general essentially meant there was no place for him. NAC abolished the *CORE-lator*, which amounted to Peck's dismissal, though members actually intended to keep him in CORE (Herb Callendar asked him to join a CORE rally not even a year later). He ultimately left embittered by the whole experience, and a number of CORE members were hurt by what they viewed as ill-treatment of this longtime stalwart of civil rights activism. It was a painful moment for many old guard supporters in CORE.

Even historians August Meier and Elliot Rudwick added to the overall sense of Ruth Turner as black power shrew. The two asked Marvin Rich in an interview if he thought Turner's stance stemmed from ideology, anti-administration, or personal ambition. Rich responded that he generally felt it was a measure of all three, and distrusted her willingness to heavily criticize James Farmer and then later work for him in the Health, Education, and Welfare Department.[20] Of course, that presumed Turner's criticisms were actually directed at Farmer alone. She, and others, had an enormous distrust of Marvin Rich, who most CORE staffers and activists actually believed ran CORE. Rich handled day-to-day administration and CORE policy, while Farmer served the function of CORE spokesman, adviser, and civil rights leader—a rank not unlike Martin Luther King Jr.'s position within SCLC. However, Rich supporters insultingly referred to Farmer as a front man, while his opponents believed Farmer overly shielded Rich because of personal loyalties. While various white and some black CORE members referred to Rich as the "brains" of CORE, others viewed him as its paternalistic director. Thus rightly or wrongly, Rich came to represent white dominance within CORE in the same way that Turner symbolized black control. And yet, ironically, both downplayed their roles in spite of clear indications to the contrary.[21]

Marvin Rich held a similarly innocuous sounding title as Turner's "secretarial" positions. As national office community relations director his duties included fund raising and budgetary administration. Among newly selected NAC members, Rich represented the old guard. He sanctioned and reinforced CORE's continued focus on the South and argued that the foundation of CORE's financial donations depended on an interracial notion and a southern focus. When it became clear that the tide toward community organization was changing CORE, Rich left in April 1965 to become director of the CORE Southern Education and Defense Fund (CORE-SEDF)—a tax-exempt branch.[22]

Before Rich's departure, many viewed him as holding too much power, which translated as part of a persistent past of white paternalism in CORE. Jim McCain, for example, pointed to this history when counter strategies to direct action emerged among black South Carolinians who wanted to do voter registration. However, James Robinson ignored the request. Farmer recalled in an interview with historian Aldon Morris that "my friends in CORE at that time did view CORE as being their property . . . it was paternalistic, very paternalistic . . . they viewed the black brother as the junior partner in the alliance."[23] Although Farmer named no names, Richard Haley had no compunction leveling this accusation toward Rich, whom he perceived as emblematic of this problem. However, white CORE member Anna Holden countered that these feelings really flowed from a resentment of capable whites.[24]

Yet, black response to CORE national still hinged on the feeling that paternalism existed, and this perception was the deciding factor. Accordingly, animosity openly broke out during and after Rich's tenure in the national office. Farmer, national staff, and NAC appointees all claimed Rich hobbled CORE's financial footing. Turner first blamed Rich for partially withholding information on CORE's damaged state too late for NAC to act. Conversely, her husband, Tony Perot, contested this viewpoint and suggested that the organization's high debt and runaway budget stemmed from its position as a crisis organization. Additionally, when NAC motioned to hire a professional fund-raiser in 1963, both Peck and Rich raised objections—Peck who argued that such professionalization was not the CORE way and Rich who pointed to empty reserves and the limitations of linking fund-raising to special projects (although that was the reason for CORE-SEDF's existence).[25]

However, the biggest dispute revolved around CORE-SEDF and CORE's mailing list. CORE-Southern Education Defense Fund originally formed in 1961 as a nonprofit arm of CORE after the IRS denied it tax-exempt status. CORE-SEDF provided legal aid, scholarships to activists expelled or returning to school, and community leadership training. Its mission was to raise money and manage the budget of various CORE ventures. CORE-SEDF was specifically created to funnel funds in from government and foundation sources, as well as to allow small and larger givers an opportunity to classify their donations as tax-free. While the nonprofit SEDF pulled from multiple fund sources, CORE depended on the mailing list to raise monies. That list served as 60 percent of CORE's fund-raising source. Loosing such a list would hit CORE hard, which is why personal relations between CORE and Rich deteriorated when Ollie Leeds, Farmer, and others noted that Rich took the mailing list for CORE-SEDF's use.[26]

The accusation added to already strained relations between the two organizations. CORE had created SEDF, but had no dominion over it. SEDF was a separate nonprofit that held fund-raisers in CORE's name and based off its southern activities, but then distributed the funds as it saw fit. Turner and others also feared that SEDF's coverage of some CORE salaries shifted employee obligations away from CORE. (This was exampled by Carl Rachlin, who later departed CORE for SEDF.) Rich countered these allegations by noting that SEDF intended to develop its own constituents and that it did not raise money via direct mail. It still covered CORE's legal costs, but other programs had to be negotiated since every project could not be funded. And finally, SEDF continued to see itself as a service organization to CORE. Despite Rich's assurances, the former director could not avoid suspicions that he appropriated CORE's funding. Farmer expressed agitation on several occasions, because he believed that SEDF siphoned off CORE's donors. Though Farmer and Rich agreed to ban mailing-list use, various persons testified that Rich reneged on the agreement and in the process undermined CORE's financial footing.[27] Farmer went on to note that "SEDF has been doing competitive fund-raising—61,000 pieces out the day after we were told there was no direct mail fund-raising to be done by SEDF."[28] According to Farmer, SEDF's board promised no further competition after being confronted. Ollie Leeds also claimed that he caught Rich photocopying materials for direct mailings. Jimmy McDonald mentioned a similar incident, and recalled that Rich asked him for the large donor list. As far as McDonald was concerned, Rich took "the whole damn thing and set it up over there . . . bringing all the wealth ya' know, white money to SEDF." Bob Curvin also reflected on the general sense within the organization that Rich had abandoned CORE and left it in financial straits.[29]

Although Rich seemed to escape NAC's ire before he left, it clearly followed him to SEDF afterward. According to Norman Hill, Rich could feel the heat in CORE even if he was not in immediate danger of removal. He also believed that without him or Rich, Turner's rise to power advanced unfettered. Arguably, Hill also meant black power's ascension as well.[30]

However, Ruth Turner was not the only Rich critic and her presence alone hardly determined CORE's transition to black power. She was among a cohort that included chapter leaders across various regions including Oretha Castle, Will Ussery, Cecil Brown, Bill Bradley, Gladys Harrington, Louis Smith, Ollie Leeds, Bonnie Barrow, and numerous others. Turner was never the only black power supporter. Ollie Leeds of Brooklyn CORE and Cecil Brown, for example, both submitted position papers on black power as a CORE strategy. CORE national staff Jim McCain, Robert Curvin, Jesse Gray, and George Raymond sat on a panel to discuss black power's deeper meaning. Locally, the new Cleveland CORE chairman Baxter Hill claimed, "Black Power is selling newspapers. The Negroes here don't care about it at all, they just want more opportunities." But then Frank Anderson, a known black nationalist proponent, soon replaced Hill.[31]

And while many white CORE members saw Turner as a ready example of the new black nationalist strain, some proponents within CORE considered her not nationalist enough. Roy Innis, for example, argued that Ruth Turner, Wilfred (Will) Ussery (San Francisco CORE chairman and NAC member), and Antoine Perot were actually militant integrationists with black consciousness. Allegedly, Innis constantly fought off both Turner and Ussery in order to pursue a nationalist agenda for CORE. Certainly, she and Tony Perot drew a sharp distinction between what they considered black nationalism versus black leadership as well.[32]

Innis's wife, Doris Innis, also rejected the notion of Turner as a nationalist, and suggested she was unused to dealing with "real" black nationalist men. Doris Innis also noted that Turner had a distaste for Innis, "as Roy was a strong man, and thus intimidates a strong woman." Innis held this belief despite the many ways Turner's own words reflected patrilineal expressions of black uplift.[33]

Indeed, Doris Innis raised some interesting questions about the attitude of male CORE leaders toward black women. Though Turner noted she never felt gender bias, she recalled that Innis and McKissick used language that clearly pointed to patriarchal proclivities within the national office. McKissick occasionally used patronizing language, which Turner shrugged off as "just being Floyd." However, Roy Innis could be particularly crude and was infamous for attending rallies where he'd ask male CORE staff "where's the beef?"—referring to the absence of attractive women.[34] Innis was also infamous for his Harlem Black Male Caucus, which deliberately aimed to keep out whites and black women from leadership. Michael Flug, another CORE follower, went so far as to suggest that fear of Turner's power and her gender prevented her designation as a Washington, DC, political liaison for CORE. According to Flug, questions arose as to whether a woman could "deal with problems on a governmental level."[35]

Institutionally, national CORE also articulated this gendered vocabulary in its 1966 resolution at the Baltimore convention. Their declaration stated that "Black Power is effective control and self-determination by men of color in their own areas."[36] Despite the obvious assertion of black power as synonymous with black male uplift, these patriarchal proclivities hardly hindered the influence Turner wielded within the organization. Her impact on NAC members placed her in the leading position to influence and then articulate CORE's black power.

She along with Lincoln Lynch wrote CORE's "Constructive Militancy," a document presented to the Senate Sub-Committee on race-based uprisings and civil disorders. The focus was to "rebuild men, not merely rehabilitate buildings. To that end there must be a reconstruction of the institutions of the ghetto."[37] The testimony outlined a series of programmatic solutions to poverty and racism in areas of education, housing, welfare and antipoverty programs, and employment. Though it too equated black empowerment with male empowerment.[38]

Turner was not without a cohort when it came to expectations about white participation in CORE either. National CORE fully transitioned to a black power organization June 1966. The 1966 convention officially changed CORE's constitution to include the ideal of "racial co-existence through black power" as the only method through which to attain equality.[39] The 1966 convention also marked the first time that CORE outright supported self-defense. Otherwise, the organization defined black power primarily by what it was not. Black power was not hatred, but racial pride. Black power did not mean exclusion of whites, but inclusion of all in a common moral and political struggle guided by black leadership. Black power was a psychological, political, and economic tool for change. Most important to CORE's definition, black power did not translate as separatism but an effort to create a new society.[40]

Though dubbed a black separatist, Turner was one of many who articulated black power as a pluralist sentiment. Turner's essay best explained her position and that of many in CORE. Black power was born out of an organizing experience in the black community. More importantly, it was "an audacious prideful affirmation of self, without which Negroes cannot assume a respected position in an integrated American society."[41]

Turner's affirmation of black power never negated participation by white activists. To the contrary, she actually believed that white activists provided valuable functions within CORE. She observed, "there is a definite role for the white committed person, the person who is willing, as the Reverend Bruce Klunder was, to lay down his life. There certainly is a role for that person."[42] The "committed white," however, had no role controlling the black freedom movement, and the very point of black power meant that black people determined their own destiny and fight for human rights.

Before CORE declared black power, Arthur Evans, soon to be CORE vice chairman, expressed the same sentiment. The Cleveland CORE organizer proposed that the national office create a Friends Service Committee. Friends Service Committee operated to stem the tide of white departure after the New Directions agenda by providing white activists an alternative to community organization work in the black community. CORE did not implement Friends, and white members continued to trickle out CORE throughout 1965. Still, Milwaukee CORE's Cecil Brown insisted that even in the midst of black power, CORE was interracial.[43]

Brown, Evans, and Turner's black power version created space for the "white committed" and assumed black power existed within the same geographic, political, and economic system of the United States. It meant "the reaffirmation of the concept of a pluralistic American society, respect of an individual's heritage and contribution, and a respect of difference in a nation that tends too readily to become amorphous, dull, and conformist . . . Black power [could] build cities, communities, institutions, and men worthy of American ideals."[44]

Turner effectively gestured to American idealism but held ethnic collaboration and contribution as a pathway to freedom. This is not to say that Turner advocated full assimilation into the American body politic as that misses the more compelling aspects of her and other CORE members' thoughts on black power, especially with regard to the American economic system. Turner's take on capitalism partially determined her support for McKissick, whom she pointedly asked to reconfirm the "need to reevaluate the capitalistic system."[45] Thus, underlining the social and political pluralism was a growing critique of capitalism, which made their version of black power just a little bit different over time.

Notwithstanding Turner's enmity toward American capitalism, the organization still needed funds to do community work. National and locals suffocated from a choked financial stream. Turner learned through personal experience (low funds had one year prior halted her full-time service as executive secretary for Cleveland CORE) that CORE chapters could no longer depend on volunteer staff. Community organization and economic development necessitated long-term commitment and intensive labor to create and implement projects. Without paid workers, local branches were at the mercy of sporadic participation. Concurrently, national could not afford to allocate resources for aggressive community action, hence the financial effect on programming became a serious distress for staff and NAC members.[46]

CORE's 1966 budgetary state was part of a longer history of financial problems. Actually, CORE had always suffered instability. The latter 1950s and early 1960s provided a short period of stabilization, but the organization was constantly in debt. Between 1963 and 1965, CORE's debt substantially increased while its donations decreased. In 1963, CORE's debt equaled $62,000. Two years later, it was $295,000. By 1966, the sum amounted upward to $400,000. Donations, which started strong under the Freedom Rides period, declined after 1964. From 1961 to 1962, funding equaled $607,000, and in the budget year 1964, it amounted to $886,000. In 1965, it dropped to $803,272. NAC noted in 1966 that the income in the first few months equaled about $94,000—and historians Meier and Rudwick estimated that its budget for that year likely summed $400,000. The decline suggested that CORE's move to the less media-driven New Directions began to cripple its finances, but it also indicated that cross fund-raising by SEDF might have impacted CORE's income.[47]

CORE national also noted that donations partially decreased because there was less "blood money"—funds gathered after a violent confrontation against nonviolent activists. In other words, as CORE began to engage in programming that garnered less limelight and media images altered from black victims to black perpetrators, the organization's donations decreased. NAC also blamed Farmer for not foreseeing, and thus preplanning, for a curtailment of funds once CORE turned from blood money to the subtler New Directions. The *CORE-lator* got thrown in at the June 1965 meeting as an example of a costly expenditure, which did not serve the new CORE. Finances, then, became another basis for the suspension of the *CORE-lator*, which followed a month later.[48]

Simultaneously, creditor calls kept CORE tremendously weakened. The debt partially originated from the Freedom Rides project. According to Farmer, CORE had huge financial losses from court costs. Though they won, Mississippi deliberately sent out individual checks to the Freedom Riders' last known address. Most of them came back to Mississippi, which promptly kept the returned monies. This seized money, compounded by budget expansion as CORE's size enlarged, undermined northern programming.[49]

Although NAC claimed Farmer failed to notify them about CORE's financial situation, the reality was quite the opposite. Staff informed NAC of a downturn in finances after 1963. NAC member and associate national director George Wiley explained that "the organization fell off the financial ledge after the summer of

1964. Marvin Rich left the organization . . . we had overspent and the crisis stayed with us through the summer of 1965." Wilfred Ussery (NAC member and San Francisco CORE chairman) even feared the possibility of bankruptcy.[50]

Farmer sent a fretful memorandum in spring 1964 begging task workers to limit expenditures because CORE needed money badly. Not two months later, he sent field staff another anxious missive explaining that CORE's situation had become "desperate," to explain delayed paychecks. Only three months after the December 1964–January 1965 NAC meeting, Farmer declared, "the critical nature of our financial plight became evident . . . expansion plans, therefore, was held in abeyance while we wrestled with the problem of survival."[51] NAC actually mentioned that Farmer's stature within the movement helped CORE eke out some donations and loans that carried them through the 1965 summer. Thus, the council clearly had some foreknowledge of CORE's situation.[52]

CORE's financial state also forced national to set the southern chapters adrift. As CORE began to withdraw focus on the South, SEDF continued to focus on the region in direct contradiction to CORE. SEDF dropped CORE's name in April 1966, and after CORE declared black power, made the break formal. SEDF changed its name to Southern Education and Defense Fund for Racial Equality (SEDFRE) and retained tenuous ties with CORE paying for legal fees and assisting southern staff. However, the two organizations shortly broke all ties with each other the following year.[53]

SEDFRE was a sticking point for black power NAC members. Its independence from CORE was a slap in the face to its new black power agenda. Added to that, the majority of SEDFRE's staff and board consisted of mostly white liberals and activists, which meant that SEDFRE continued to circumvent the call for black leadership (until Ronnie Moore's chairmanship in 1969). Even worse, the organization effectively made money off CORE's work and by holding to the Southern interracial agenda while the whole of the black freedom movement took a different track. CORE's upper echelon, particularly Innis, began to argue that CORE should commandeer SEDFRE's board. Instead, CORE reduced its spending, refinanced its bills, and partially reduced the debt. But, that was not enough. The organization's debt spiraled upward while contributions took a downturn.[54]

Still, NAC militants ridiculed national for concentrating on self-sustaining institution building without consideration to local leadership and community activism. Some aspect of the New Directions had to move forward. Initially Farmer outlined a multicity community center idea which required an estimated yearly commitment of $10,000 to be coproduced by locals. Farmer noted that such a move was "unprecedented for CORE, but it is now a necessity . . . if we lack funds, we lack muscle."[55] But branches were ill equipped to raise the monies needed and the national office considered other funding alternatives. Lacking the necessary cash flow, CORE narrowed its effort to one start-up city—Chicago. Summer 1964, CORE determined that it would establish three community centers in the north, west, and south sides of the city in what it called the Northern Summer Task Force Project. Their goals included initiating tenant strikes, assisting welfare recipients, protesting public accommodation, providing unemployment benefit information, and creating work brigades among the unemployed. By summer's end, the project was over but CORE intended to try another one-city community-organizing program.[56]

A year later, CORE's New Direction singular site transformed into what it called a Target City. Tony Perot, then field secretary for Midwest regional CORE, initially proposed several cities for Target City, from Chicago to Los Angeles, Baltimore/ Washington, DC, and Newark. Eventually, it came down to Chicago or Baltimore. NAC declined Chicago because Martin Luther King and SCLC were there. CORE had little inclination to share the spotlight or have its project overshadowed by the presence of King. NAC's choice was Baltimore.[57]

Baltimore's selection also hinged on the Maryland Freedom Union. In late fall 1965/early 1966, field secretary Toney Riley, Columbia CORE Michael Flug, and Bronx CORE Howard Quander submitted a proposal for CORE to emulate Cesar Chavez's United Farm Workers and SNCC's Mississippi Freedom Labor Union with a northern version of its own. The trio called its proposal the Northern Freedom Labor Union and chose Baltimore as the location to begin its recruitment. Baltimore was a nexus of activist support and identifiable targets, including a very large CORE chapter, Jim Crow unions, low wages, and a substantially sized black ghetto. Herb Callendar, director of organizing and former Bronx CORE member, formally approved the measure and Riley, Flug, and Quander went to work.[58]

The three temporarily settled in Baltimore and requested that any unorganized workers visit CORE. In the midst of union preparation, nursing home workers set off an impromptu strike when its organizers were fired. This central group of nursing home aides became the basis for the Maryland Freedom Union (MFU). As word of MFU spread, other low-wage laborers came to CORE for assistance. CORE and MFU successfully unionized workers. The coalition helped get increased pay, and spurred Baltimore steelworkers in one company to form the Bethlehem Steel and Shipyard Workers for Equality.[59]

Spring 1966, CORE formally designated Baltimore a Target City based off Flug, Riley, and Quander's union activities. CORE gave the Baltimore Target City Project (TCP) the designation, "Breaking the Noose." Although TCP focused solely on grassroots action, in many ways, it was an outgrowth of northern chapter protest activities, though with one notable difference. The northern model became a CORE national project. Voter registration, union organizing, community activism, police brutality demonstrations, direct action protest, and job training became cornerstones of "Breaking the Noose." Baltimore TCP also desegregated local restaurants and bars, built community confidence, opened freedom schools, and made forays into black political power by running and supporting candidates.[60]

Internal strife wracked the venture from its inception. Target operated separately from the local chapter, but Baltimore CORE soon became aggravated with what it viewed as national's takeover. Meanwhile, some TCP staff and national CORE officers targeted Walter Brooks, head of the Baltimore Target City Project, with accusations of manipulation and incompetence. The Target Project infighting seeped in among the staff, between the Baltimore CORE chapter and national office, and from Baltimore TCP to the national office.[61] However, the greatest strength and stumbling block was the decision to orchestrate a project that depended greatly on organic action by residents. The approach could engender a sustained mass movement or operate in short bursts without long-term action. CORE achieved success with MFU, but the rest of the black community suffered from apathy and fear, evidenced by the Klan's open marches and meetings close to black neighborhoods.[62]

National eventually dispatched Tony Perot to assist Walter Brooks with stamping out conflict and increasing community action. Under Perot's direction, the project developed a freedom school and created committees in the area of housing, welfare, education, political action, and fund-raising. Baltimore Target also received an additional influx of Ohio CORE workers like Pauline Warfield and Ed Boston, who had quit high school to join Target City. Turner was occasionally present, but much of that related to visits to see Perot—her future husband—and last-minute organization of the national CORE convention in Baltimore.[63]

Although personnel issues were no longer as acute, Target still had no initial start-up funds, and became constantly burdened by financial instability. At one point, the office electricity shut down, forcing staff members to use candles. TCP workers who were supposed to be paid received no funds for weeks.[64] Pauline Warfield recalled going hungry because pay came sporadically at best. She went on to say that she and Brooklyn CORE member Danny Gant actually competitively made a run for a can of sardines during one low point. There were instances of malnutrition, cramped quarters, unsafe living conditions, and periodic unchecked illnesses. Toward the project's end Danny Gant, Ed Boston, and Danny Underwood were sleeping on the floor. Baltimore wanted to keep Warfield on as director of Maryland Freedom Union but national had no funds to keep her there.[65]

Without a cash flow, the program operated ineffectively. Committees did not consistently function, national office provided no back-up support, and numerous duties stretched Target City activists thin. The project and its staff were further hampered by national's last-minute decision to hold the 1966 annual convention in Baltimore to showcase the new Target City Project, thus imposing time, resources, and energy.[66]

Over time, Baltimore Target's budgetary situation improved. The group got an important boost from the Department of Labor after Tony Perot along with another CORE member developed a youth employment proposal. The Labor Department allotted $70,000 for their job training program. Though the first employment program concentrated on males, they also planned to incorporate young women. The women's project fell through, but the young men's venture proved to be the most financially stable and successful part of Baltimore TCP after the Maryland Freedom Union.[67]

Labor organizing, eventually, fell to the wayside. Baltimore TCP's program depended heavily on MFU, but the group's relations with CORE wavered. National and local labor unions pressured CORE national office to disassociate or disband the group. Flug believed that McKissick, Turner, and Lincoln Lynch (CORE associate director) viewed MFU as only a "way station" to politics, businesses, and government-funded programs within large interest areas. Flug rightly argued that MFU's slow disassociation from national represented a lost opportunity for CORE to link black power with workers.[68]

As Target stabilized, it successfully launched aggressive campaigns against segregated public accommodation. Increased political action set the ground for more black representation in various offices, including city council. And most importantly, a community that was plagued by fear found courage and self-worth, as Klan members who once unabashedly marched through black neighborhoods ended their terror tactics when black residents jeered them out of the community and TCP staff maintained armed night guards.[69]

Thus, despite the many conflicts and financial troubles, Baltimore TCP sufficiently turned the corner for national CORE to consider a second city for its Target City Project. But before national CORE could select a second site, questions arose about the very meaning of the Target City Project and its utility as a black power program. Perot attempted to provide a broad description, stating that it was a "concept in which people see themselves as catalytic agents in an attempt to move other people in the community."[70] Others suggested that Target City Project was simply community organization geared toward the needs of the black community, or a stimulus for action. This vague explanation of Target City partially explained why national CORE devised no plan with a specific outcome. It was clear Baltimore TCP would include direct action, community organizing, and political activity. However, CORE implemented the details of a Target City as it created the mission. Clearly, Maryland Freedom Union, as a grassroots organization, was crucial to TCP's conception, and outright unsuccessful without it. But beyond that, unspecific goals and the extensive time and energy it took to transform a community immobilized by fear hampered robust outcomes. Though NAC remained unclear on how to define TCP, it *was* clear that no other would follow without sound financial and administrative footing.[71]

Paradoxically, TCP funding quickly became a prickly issue. Federal funding from the Department of Labor made Baltimore a viable project, but rumblings began almost immediately among CORE's more radical membership regarding this subsidy. In fact, NAC itself questioned the wisdom of such an idea only months earlier when San Bernardino CORE appealed to national for help with attaining OEO funds for a tutorial program. Several NAC activists felt that such grants set a dangerous precedent, and argued for a partnership with another nonprofit for that purpose.[72] Funding sources aside, other denunciations arose over slotting newly trained black youth into low-wage, dead-end employment (the teen employment program trained young men to work in a gas station). Despite these legitimate criticisms, Perot charged forward on the next Target City Project.

Once again, national CORE kicked around location options. Both Newark and Chicago came up. Don Smith, CORE staff in public relations, explored Newark, New Jersey, as a possible Target City Project given its 50 percent black population. But, of the many towns visited, only Cleveland, Ohio, emerged victorious.[73]

CORE designated Cleveland the second Target City Project (TCP) for a number of reasons. First, Cleveland CORE members held powerful positions within the national office. Antoine Perot was program director, Ruth Turner served as special assistant to Floyd McKissick, and Arthur Evans held the position of national vice chairman.[74] Their close ties to Cleveland, Ohio, better positioned Target City to navigate the political, social, and economic terrain. And—it was simply the right time.

Cleveland was ripe for political change. The six-day Hough riot the previous year situated it among the major cities on the precipice of increased racial violence. While national CORE took its first steps toward black power, the residents of Hough demonstrated their own brand of black power in the summer of 1966. In early July, Ruth Turner told Bob Curvin, former CORE Newark leader and NAC member, "Hough was about to blow" and predicted the summer months would bring a riot in Hough.[75] She was right. Monday evening, July 18, black residents gathered at Seventy-Niners' Café at the corner of Seventy-Ninth and Hough Avenue. The owners, the Feigenbaum brothers, angered black residents when they refused to give a black Hough patron a glass of ice water. This was not the first time the owners ran afoul of black Clevelanders. Six months prior to the summer incident, an unknown assailant attempted to set their car on fire for an unknown perceived slight. As news spread of yet another offense by the Feigenbaum brothers, black Hough residents began to gather in a crowd. Eventually they stormed the bar. Police arrival on the scene only exacerbated the situation.[76]

Don Bean was director of the Target City Project, Congress of Racial Equality, Cleveland, 1968–1969. Outlined above was national CORE's black power trajectory.
Photo: Herman Seid, 1968. From the Cleveland Press Collection, Michael Schwartz Library, Cleveland State University

Donald Bean and Will Ussery in the Cleveland Target City Project Office.
Photo: Karl J. Rausckolb, September 1967. From the *Cleveland
Plain Dealer*, Cleveland Public Library

The mob dispersed throughout Hough and began looting, rioting, and setting area businesses on fire. Policemen and firemen who entered the area were hit with bottles, rocks, and other objects. Although black community leaders launched a door-to-door effort to stop the violence, it continued unabated. Police and National Guard sealed off Hough from the rest of Cleveland while National Guard patrolled the area. The riot lasted six days. By its end four black Clevelanders were dead. Damages and costs to the city were in the millions.[11] The riot was over, but anger still simmered. Political discontent paralleled grassroots rage. Black Clevelanders backed a second mayoral run by Carl Stokes after the many slights of the city's previous mayors. The Hough rebellion additionally stimulated interest in Carl Stokes among Cleveland's white business owners and philanthropist who feared another flare up. More importantly, black Clevelanders were of one accord, due in no small part to Cleveland CORE and its role during the school desegregation fight.

Finally, the national office chose Cleveland because Tony Perot wrote the proposal, located the funding, and the final decision landed in his lap. This latter issue proved a particular sticking point given that NAC required staff to submit various cities for selection. Yet, it was hard for NAC to put up too much of a fight for one obvious reason—money. National managed to start its second Target City Project based on a small but significant grant from the Ford Foundation.[78]

CORE first submitted a proposal in late summer 1966 that funded Cleveland Target City and provided overhead coverage to clear some of CORE's massive debt. Ford turned down the group because it lacked tax-exempt status, and included a request to cover CORE obligations. Perot and Turner, who played a leading part in negotiations with the foundation, rewrote the proposal. Meanwhile, Ford investigated CORE's history in Cleveland and found many in the community impressed by early Cleveland CORE's past leadership. And of course, they also found that local businessmen were concerned that Cleveland might "blow-up."[79]

Perot submitted a second draft in spring 1967 for $300,000, which ran only a Cleveland Target City Project. July 1967 Ford granted the organization $175,000, half its request. However, it was CORE's first major donation during its black power period and inspired a glimmer of hope for its declining economic situation. Although most supposed these funds went directly to the Cleveland chapter, the monies were actually earmarked under a special purposes fund of national CORE. Cleveland CORE and Cleveland Target City operated separately within the city.[80]

The foundation greatly underfunded Cleveland TCP, in spite of its stated needs. CORE leaders were particularly aggravated to learn that local Cleveland groups received larger amounts than had a national organization. The Catholic Conference for Interracial Justice, for example, obtained a grant of $200,000, the Businessmen's Interracial Committee got $250,000, and NIEU, Negro Industrial Economic Unions, received a whopping $520,000. In reality, the funds were actually given as a last-minute move to avoid any potential controversies related to Ford's support of an avowed black power organization. The reduced grant forced national CORE to revamp the program, and focus on voter registration, youth leadership training, and literacy tutorial classes.[81]

Even with some funding success, national office came under heavy fire for accepting money from Ford. The foundation had gained a dubious reputation as a financial reservoir for black power organizations. During the 1960s, it simultaneously held a position of leftist radicalism in the minds of white conservatives and corporate manipulator in the thinking of radical black activists. Created in 1936, the foundation's reputation changed over time. In the 1950s, white leaders began to view Ford's philanthropy as an enemy to the cause. Their reputation for "radical" funding decisions ballooned when McGeorge Bundy entered as its new president in 1966.[82]

Brooklyn CORE was among its many recipients, though chapter leader Sonny Carson later came to regret Ford's largesse. Other black power groups and organizations also received large grants, including community development corporations and other nonprofit organizations serving the black community.[83] Bundy's decision to fund these groups, however, raised a great deal of conflict among the foundation's advisory board, particularly Henry Ford II, who wrote in his resignation letter that Ford Foundation was "a creature of capitalism . . . [and] It is hard to discern recognition of this fact in anything the Foundation does."[84]

Despite Ford's developing persona as a financial well for black power, not every CORE member was thrilled. National CORE's acceptance of Ford Foundation funds created a firestorm. In the first instance, a number of leading members, particularly Brooklyn CORE's Sonny Carson and Ollie Leeds, believed succor from corporate philanthropy amounted to CORE becoming a "tool to blind black people" and a "vehicle for personal fame."[85] Divisions arose over (1) the use of white funds, (2) the use of white funds to keep CORE afloat, and/or (3) the use of white funds for programming that essentially sustained the capitalist system. There were also questions as to whether CORE should save itself at "the price of support and subsidy by Ford." Additionally, internal arguments developed over whether the grant should go to local chapters, regional offices, or the national office. Finally, some argued that if CORE was committed to building a movement, then the focus should not be on saving CORE at all, regardless of who funded it.[86] In all cases, the argument hinged on the legitimate fear that financial dependence became a mechanism for controlling CORE and the black community, to the detriment of both.

Carson raised his concerns at the 1967 CORE convention in Oakland, California. He claimed, "I've since changed my whole feeling about allowing a self-perpetuating mechanism like . . . the Ford Foundation to finance anything. But then, I still thought there was some way of using them without being dependent on them. I was wrong, though: it's just like you are on welfare. A sound cooperative economic plan must be created if we are to survive."[87] Carson challenged CORE's direction and claimed that the organization had to make a decision—would it be a reform movement or a revolutionary catalyst? Carson contended that "people in the black community were talking about community control," but that in the case of Brooklyn CORE's school fight, "Ford (the Foundation, that is) and other co-conspirators from respected circles of education got together and came up with a form of decentralization."[88] In other words, Ford had actually acted to dilute and limit control efforts by the black community. As such, neither he nor others would support CORE's dependence on Ford for its TCP plans or as an avenue for black empowerment.

Carson was not the only displeased member. Conflict within CORE turned nasty at the convention's NAC meeting. The group divided between Will Ussery (former chairman of San Francisco CORE), Floyd McKissick, Roy Innis, Art Evans (second national VP), and Bob Lukas (chairman of Chicago CORE) versus Sol Herbert (first national VP), Bonnie Burroughs (national secretary), Ollie Leeds (chairman of Brooklyn CORE), and Bill Bradley (chairman of San Francisco

CORE). The latter group opposed the Special Purposes Fund (the holding entity for TCP grants), opposed the Ford Foundation Proposal for the Cleveland project, opposed the use of any white financial backing, and ultimately opposed the current leadership within CORE. At this particular meeting, questions regarding the Special Purposes Fund became particularly heated. According to the notes of one observer, debate became "especially bitter and vituperative and almost led to violence when the Staff Western Regional Director responded angrily to provocative statements by Roy Innis."[89]

Purportedly, Innis "taunted the insurgent group with political naiveté and hypocrisy in opposing the Special Purposes Fund and foundation grants to the organization while at the same time they were 'taking the orders' of Marvin Rich, white Director of the Scholarship and Education Fund for Racial Equality."[90] Innis went on to imply that most of the Ford Foundation opposition refused to explain how CORE would develop without money and he insisted that CORE could, in fact, take funds from white structures without allowing strings. Leeds took immediate exception to this and argued that the local chapters were not concerned about funding the national office. Innis, in turn, charged Leeds with hypocrisy—an accusation that did not go unnoted by the eyewitness who remarked that programs out of Leeds chapter received funding from the Office of Economic Opportunity and the Department of Labor.[91]

Crude as Innis might have been, his argument was not untrue or half-baked. Although activists and scholars alike questioned the role of "white money" in the movement, it was a rather misdirected discussion because it focused on external intentions and not internal dynamics. Black agency within an organization could powerfully determine its direction. Additionally, foundation money was not a new presence in the black freedom movement and had appeared in the early 1960s, well before black power came along. Groups like the Taconic and Phelps-Stokes Foundations heavily funded voter education projects. Thus the notion that foundation funding automatically translated into outside control or that it diluted militancy among civil rights organizations was dubious.[92]

Instead, the circumstances of leadership and project choice determined the potential for foundation influence. Moorland Spingarn interviewer Robert Wright specifically confirmed this case during his 1968 interview with Floyd McKissick. McKissick recalled that at every step, CORE considered the implications of a Ford grant—from its initial application to final approval. He also stated that CORE leadership sought to avoid any sacrifice of black power principles. Interviewer Robert Wright later inserted his own recollections regarding the negotiations between Bundy and McKissick. Apparently, the two met at Eleanor Holmes Norton's apartment, and conversation became rather tense. Bundy had a number of demands that McKissick refused to accept in exchange for the funds. Ford Foundation's evaluation also mentioned that the grant's conditions so antagonized CORE, the organization almost told Ford to "take its money and 'shove it.'" But, after negotiation and debate, CORE accepted the grant.[93]

McKissick argued that CORE had hoped to make Cleveland its model city for black self-determination, but they could not get enough funds to follow suit. At the same time, McKissick wished to undo some of CORE's financial burden. In the Convention NAC meeting, McKissick told Leeds that the organization owed creditors close to $400,000 and that he took the position of national director with the platform to reduce debt. He also noted that the "program being proposed for Cleveland would be the kind of substantive action which in effect could begin to revitalize the entire CORE organization."[94] The Leeds/Carson group continued to charge that CORE could not possibly call itself a black power organization while using white funds to achieve black empowerment. The meeting finally ended with neither party satisfied, and the McKissick faction worried that the dissident group could prove a bigger problem than just in a NAC meeting. It became clear two days later that the opposition faction had every intention of leading a debate on the convention floor over the Special Purposes fund and the inclusion of whites within CORE. Additionally, the Northeast region submitted its own slate of officers with the intention of ousting Evans from vice chairman with Herb Callendar as his replacement. Sol Herbert aimed for vice chairman, and Innis, who sided with McKissick, was locked out without the support of the Northeast region chapter leaders. Their attempted takeover, however, failed.

Despite accusations of cooptation and internal arguing regarding the Ford Foundation, Cleveland TCP put the Ford Foundation grant of $175,000 to good use. McKissick explained that CORE intended "to move politically at first."[95] CORE's first order of business was to register Cleveland's black voters days before the deadline in preparation for the second Carl Stokes mayoral run. Thanks overwhelmingly to the Ford Foundation grant (Ford also gave monies to SCLC for voter registration in Cleveland), of the over 25,000 newly registered voters—close to 75 percent were black.[96]

As the 1967 Democratic mayoral candidate, Carl Stokes was clearly the man to beat. The massive registration project by Cleveland CORE overwhelmingly determined Stokes's position as a leading candidate. The Hough Riots also helped catapult him to the political forefront as a solution against the occurrence of any more uprisings. Certainly, the summer push to keep things "Cool for Carl" helped situate Stokes as a viable option. According to Cleveland CORE member and lawyer Stanley Tolliver, Stokes's mayoral candidacy really amounted among whites to "fire insurance."[97]

Nonetheless, it would be immensely erroneous to assume that only external funding and riot fears placed Stokes in the position of lead candidate. In actuality,

Carl Stokes's charisma and good looks were legendary. As *Time Magazine* noted, he "could beguile white suburban clubwomen at tea and rap with soul brothers in Hough."[98] Born in the Central Avenue neighborhood, Cleveland's poorest section, Stokes dropped out of high school and joined the army. He returned to Cleveland where he acquired an early introduction to politics through his association with John O. Holly, former leader of the Future Outlook League, and later as a political organizer for the Democratic Party. His relationship with Holly earned him a state job that eventually led Stokes into law. In 1957, he passed the Ohio bar, and by 1962 he was a representative in the state legislature. In 1965, he announced his decision to run for mayor of Cleveland.[99]

Stokes's first mayoral run in 1965 could not have been a better time for Cleveland CORE, who at that point latched on to the campaign as a political action arm of its community organization program. Additionally, Stokes's 1965 campaign represented both the black power philosophy national CORE came to espouse and the change Cleveland CORE and its members craved since the school desegregation fight. Cleveland CORE's hope that Stokes could bring change actually mirrored the whole black community's attitude. By the time Stokes announced his intentions to run again, the black population in Cleveland had reached 38 percent. Housing remained a major issue with the same problems from previous years exacerbated and still unattended to by Cleveland's local government. And, poverty increased throughout the east side, but particularly in the Hough area as exampled by the $1,000 decrease in Hough families' median incomes.[100]

The day of the mayoral election, it snowed heavily in Cleveland. Despite snow, voter turnout was high in both black and white neighborhoods. During the night, votes for Stokes and Republican candidate Seth Taft remained equal and too close to call. Toward the late morning it was discovered that there were still wards that had not reported. All of them were in black neighborhoods. By five the next morning, Stokes pulled ahead of Taft to become the first black mayor of Cleveland, Ohio, and of any major city in the United States. Stokes won by a mere 1,644 votes.[101]

With Stokes's victory, the target project powerfully and appropriately seemed to embody its new name. Cleveland Target City Project was now called *Harambee*, a Swahili word meaning "all pull together." The word aptly described the Cleveland community spirit during the political campaign. Yet, it was also the perfect term for the next phase of the Target City Project—communal capitalism.

# 7

# Harambee City

CLEVELAND WAS TO BECOME a new black utopia. McKissick vowed that, "after politics, economic power automatically flows. We are going to work on a total program."[1] Carl Stokes's mayoral win was only the first step. It was one thing to educate, organize, and vote in a political administration predisposed to black civil rights. However, it was another matter altogether to address the structures that kept black Clevelanders in poverty. The job-training program in Baltimore, though successful, had already revealed one weakness in CORE's approach to black economic power. Desertion and mass divestment wracked inner cities like Cleveland, Gary, Detroit, Pittsburgh, and other rust belt towns.[2] In such instances, job training or discrimination became almost moot in an economic climate where no jobs existed.

Solutions to economic disparity varied in this period. A veritable hodge-podge of ideas emerged in the latter 1960s that paralleled CORE members' thinking. Some nationalists acted to build economic power through separate spheres of "black capitalism." Others saw the capitalist system as an impediment to black empowerment. Sonny Carson, for example, argued that the very essence of capitalism created a class of laborers trapped in place and beholden to an owner class. It was a corrupt system where poor blacks could never achieve freedom. According to Carson, black activists had to destroy capitalism "if black people are to be free."[3]

Neither side fully reflected CORE. The organization resided within a nexus of voices on black economic power. From 1967 to 1969, CORE launched a nuanced and pragmatic program that paralleled a larger movement afoot for economic empowerment. CORE used a second grant by Ford Foundation to construct a strategy for financial uplift not quite capitalist nor Marxist/Socialist. Leaders like Ruth Turner, Tony Perot, and especially Will Ussery, chapter leader of San Francisco CORE, keenly felt the problems inherent in capitalism, and recognized that it was not enough to train black Clevelanders to be workers in a dying municipality. CORE had to rebuild the economic base of a deserted city. It had to become an innovator and business creator. It had to bend the capitalist system to allow black folk to become more than low-wage, sustenance laborers. CORE had to face the reality of America's economic system, and still find the keys to its access.

To find the answer, key figures within CORE guided the national office toward a middle solution. CORE's 1967 convention set the tone for this economic plan. Workshop resolutions insisted national office "plan, design, and develop proposals for the economic development of the community."[4] The proposal had to incorporate land purchase cooperatives, construction companies, and credit unions. Additionally, until such time as unions ended discriminatory policies, the committee advocated for parallel black labor unions. Finally, all ventures had to reflect "dual, parallel, or separate possibilities from the American business system."[5]

CORE leaders were not the first or only activists moving along this trajectory. Those who supported the middle approach to economic empowerment trailed after neighborhood groups who began setting up nonprofit entities known as community development corporations (CDCs). In the post-King era, CDCs assembled all across the United States. Cities like Rochester, Oakland, Newark, and Selma were among the first to experiment. They created enterprises that employed job trainees, redirected business income toward community programming, and trained workers for middle management. As not-for-profit community based groups, CDCs facilitated greater trust by serving a wide-ranging coalition of residents and neighborhoods. Thus, these institutions also served as the local partners OEO needed for the War on Poverty.

Some CDCs also devised an open styled, communal form of capitalism similar to CORE's request for "dual, parallel, or separate" systems. Community capitalism, or rather shared group ownership, operated within the current economy but also acted to disrupt hierarchical differences between owner and laborer. Those few CDCs who embraced community capitalism sought to transform employees from "cogs" in the capitalist machine to beneficiaries in the system.[6]

Compared to other municipalities, Cleveland occupied a unique position during this period. First, it was the only city to host CORE's nonprofit CDC. CORE Enterprises Corporation, planned to generate mass ownership participation for Cleveland's black poor. CORE proposed to nationalize the program utilizing the policies laid forth by Louis Kelso, an economist known for his advocacy of universal capitalism. While national advocated the middle route from above, Cleveland chapter supported it from below. As a member of Operation Black Unity, an umbrella black power group, the local branch openly insisted that OBU's franchise boycott lead to broad models of ownership.

Secondly, Cleveland-based CDC-Hough Area Development Corporation (HADC)- ranked as one of a few neighborhood development groups to receive a large multimillion-dollar grant from the Office of Economic Opportunity. HADC backed CORE's community capitalism strategy and locally mirrored CORE

Enterprise's communal capitalism plan. HADC also happened to include CORE members among its staff who had either worked with the Cleveland TCP, the Cleveland CORE chapter, and/or the Baltimore Target City Project.

The previous year's political victory and CORE's local alliances amplified its black economic program and effectively inaugurated Target's second phase. November 1967, national hired its first official Cleveland TCP director, Phillip Carter. Carter, a native of West Virginia and former basketball player at Marshall University, sponsored the Civil Rights and Human Rights conference. Workshops focused on the recently released Civil Disorders Report authored by the Ohio Civil Rights Commission. Seminars also addressed economic advancement and employment, welfare and health systems, housing, police, media, and causes and preventions of civil disorders. Carter condensed conference research papers and produced a large report, assisted by various academics and consultants, on poverty and economic development.[7]

The TCP's investigative report was more than a mere study; it set the basis for a new initiative. Spring 1968, McKissick announced that CORE had created a new black power program, which would tap the sources of American wealth to help black people "become full partners in the capitalist system."[8] The TCP position paper recommended CORE initiate a community development corporation as an independent spinoff of Cleveland Target City. CORE Enterprises Corporation (CORENCO), CORE's CDC, operated as an economic-based research, education, and development entity that endeavored to own economic structures within and produce goods and services for the black community.[9] CORENCO officially opened its doors at 10616 Euclid Avenue in the summer of 1968. Wilfred Ussery, CORENCO cocreator and CORE's current national chairman, came in to personally handle the nonprofit's progress.

CORENCO measured its success based on the culmination of eight outcomes:

1. Employment programs must enable company or corporate share purchase by new employees
2. Purchase white owned small businesses that service the black community
3. Identify enterprises willing to assist management or franchise purchase by black employees
4. Provide general job training and placement services
5. Prepare labor workshops and skill enhancement training for upper-level management positions
6. Expand small black businesses
7. Offer consumer education; and
8. Engage "in such other activities as may facilitate Black people becoming the legitimate constituents—that is, employees and/or shareholders, and preferably both—of the business community of the Cleveland area."[10]

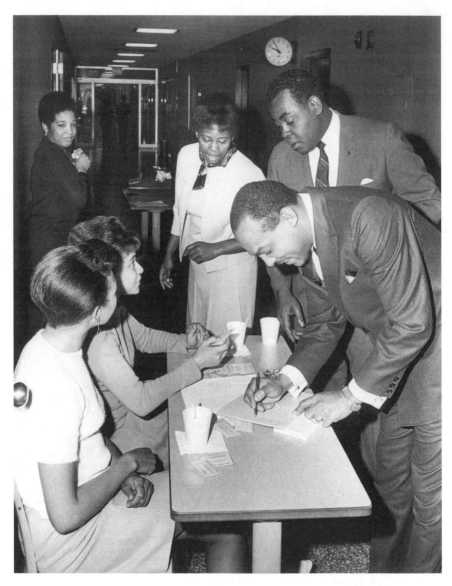

Mayor Carl Stokes signs in for the CORE Target City Conference.
Municipal judge Lloyd O. stands next to him.
Photo: Ted Schneider, March 30, 1968. From the Cleveland Press
Collection, Michael Schwartz Library, Cleveland State University

CORENCO pulled heavily from the ideas of lawyer and economist Louis Kelso.[11] Kelso argued in *Capitalist Manifesto* and *Two-Factor Theory: The Economics of Reality* that capitalism did not necessarily obviate participation by the average wage earner. It simply failed to democratize itself. Kelso offered a theory, which allowed all wage earners to participate in wealth building while it suppressed concentrated affluence. He maintained that production emanated from two different sources—capital (land, structure, etc.) and labor (mental and physical).[12] Within the current American system only those who had capital could acquire more while wage earners depended on labor alone to build wealth. The United States had to revamp the capitalist economy, and eliminate its dependence on wage employment, tax breaks, and traditional growth strategies. Kelso also argued that the government needed to end welfare, and "initiate a program to achieve universal capital ownership."[13]

Kelso contended that universalized capitalism provided the basis for economic justice, if the government realized economic parity through three principles: The Principle of Distribution, the Principle of Participation, and the Principle of Limitation. Within these principles, Kelso cited the rules of capitalist exchange and development. Under the principle of distribution, each person who generated wealth received a "distributive share" based on his or her individual contribution.[14] Second, through the principle of participation, every person had a right to achieve and maintain a standard of living. In other words, no person could be denied access to the capitalist economy. And finally, the principle of limitation determined that no one person could usurp the second principle and own wealth to such an extent as to exclude others "from the opportunity to earn a viable income."[15] If the American economic system followed these principles, insisted Kelso, it would "hardly come as a surprise, therefore, that in a truly capitalist economy, economic freedom and justice will be as widely diffused as the ownership of capital."[16]

Employee share ownership plan (ESOP) became Kelso's most highly regarded economic theory. Though corporations presently employ the concept, during the late 1960s, CORENCO was among the first to actualize Kelso's ideas. ESOP emanated from a larger assertion that Americans needed a "second income." Kelso and his partner Patricia Hetter theorized that through broad ownership in expanding enterprises individuals could produce real affluence with little labor, and "with the concept of economic justice." Thus, workers built wealth from their labor and a second income acquired through group ownership in corporations.[17]

Ussery had Kelso meet with CORE as early as October 1967—before Stokes's victory in Cleveland. He and Patricia Hetter presented their concept for second income to the National Action Council. Thus, it was no surprise that the forty-five-page CORENCO proposal all but reiterated Kelso's second income strategy.[18] Wilfred Ussery, national chairman of CORE, bolstered Kelso's ideas with his own thoughts, and insisted that "80% of what makes money in America is owned by 3% of Americans. Negroes . . . are in the white structure of industrial sharecropping, just earning enough to survive, and remain tied to the system."[19] Floyd McKissick also rubber stamped the second economy hypothesis in his essay, "CORE's Program: Building a 'Second Economy.'" McKissick similarly suggested that the black poor can become economically productive through the buying and selling of stock, particularly in companies that serve them.[20]

This is why CORENCO gave minimum wage earners management training to augment promotion opportunities, while it also advocated share purchases for employee wealth building—regardless of job level. Any parent franchise or corporation could place its plant or company within the black community, but only if it hired and trained black employees for middle and upper management, and guaranteed technical help and other assistance until solvency. Once the corporation recovered costs, the parent company turned the business or franchise ownership over to employees through stock and shares in the company.[21]

CORENCO hoped to extend beyond well-known firms and involve a broad range of businesses in manufacturing, including appliances, furniture, food, cars, pharmaceuticals, clothing, and building materials.[22] The plan additionally provided for community-related services in the area of home maintenance and repair, automotive service, mental, dental, and eye care centers, day care nurseries, employment services, funeral and memorial societies, group insurance plans, hotel and restaurants, trucking and moving services, and finally a development and land holding company to improve land use. These companies would also serve as wealth share businesses and example prototypes.[23]

CORENCO insisted that financial institutions partner with the black community to enhance independent ownership. Banks and credit unions that established associations with African governments received particular consideration. It also crafted economic alliances with other industrialized nations from which the black community might glean technical skills, goods, and resources. Outside of Africa, Japan figured prominently and CORENCO recommended that black companies manufacture Japanese items- specifically televisions and automobiles—for sale within the United States.[24]

CORENCO's proposal integrated an African-styled cultural and business center into the project as well. "Shops specializing in products imported from African countries" both reinforced positive black self-images and provided "profitable economic activity." The shopping center also consisted of a travel agency, entertainment booking company, an export-import distribution complex, restaurant, and other businesses that provided jobs and investment possibilities for black Clevelanders. Finally, the proposal called for media outlet control, noting that "the need for black ownership of a radio and TV station has never been greater than it is now. A black press could combat confusion, rumors, and misinformation. It could also engage in meaningful educational programs to raise the level of living and achievement in the black community."[25]

Comprehensive and detailed, the plan nonetheless departed from CORE's original community organization approach. Will Ussery argued that CORE was "no longer interested in developing 'community groups and projects' that 'float off on their own thing.' We are talking about things that are tied into CORE and that are controlled by CORE."[26] Essentially, CORE altered its program of grassroots activism, and became an entity for community organizing in and of itself.[27]

Though CORENCO's program potentially had a transformative effect on poverty in Cleveland, CORE lacked the capital with which to achieve its goals. For help building its new multimillion-dollar nonprofit, national office turned to Cleveland's political and business elite. Late summer 1968, CORENCO headquarters sent out letters, which requested participation in an economic conference scheduled for October 29, 1968. In the letter Ussery urged city bosses to remember that "White society is deeply implicated in the ghetto. White institutions created it; white institutions maintain it and white society condones it."[28] He also added that "our intention is not to establish a new welfare burden for present property owners and wage earners, but rather a series of self-sustaining economic institutions whereby black residents can be owners of capital instruments and wage earners."[29]

To that end, national CORE leaders Roy Innis; CORE's economic adviser, Donald Simmons; Kermit Scott, director of chapter development; and CORE chairman Wilfred Ussery, met with over seventy business leaders and requested a pledge of $10 million. These funds would help CORENCO spread from Cleveland into New York, San Francisco, and Washington, DC. The idea generated heightened public interest, but did little to empower the national office or the CORENCO idea. CORENCO as a national development corporation never fully got off the ground.[30]

Ostensibly, the project should have appealed to white business leaders and politicians locally, and nationally. President Richard Nixon, for example, had begun to tout the positive attributes of black capitalism in early 1968. March 1969, Nixon even established by executive order, the Office of Minority Business Enterprise. According to Nixon, the concept of black capitalism promoted participation in the economy, investment within the community, and "dignity, pride, and self-respect."[31]

However, Nixon refused to embrace communal forms of capitalism even as he accepted black participation in capitalism. This incongruence emerged for a couple of reasons. First, the Office of Minority Business was built around attracting favor (and more to the point—votes) from the black middle class, while appearing to support aspects of black power.

Secondly, and most important, Local and national politicians were still smarting from the Stokes defeat. Nixon and Congress were horrified that a nonprofit determined the selection of a mayoral candidacy and denounced what they believed to be Ford's arrogance.[32] The White House actually considered the foundation "left-wing" radicals. Although it was anything but that, the Ford Foundation and McGeorge Bundy earned a place on Nixon's infamous "enemies list," a catalogue of persons, organizations, and institutions that the administration intended to suppress through prosecution, investigation, IRS probes, and various other means of harassment. Nixon directed aide Tom Huston to investigate Ford. Huston was no ordinary White House staff. He authored the infamous *Huston Plan*, which authorized illegal surveillance and intelligence collection on people and organizations perceived as subversives. Huston unreservedly followed Nixon's directive to probe Ford and noted that "certainly we ought to act in time to keep the Ford Foundation from again financing Carl Stokes' mayoralty campaign in Cleveland." Nixon's response was that he should "follow up hard on this."[33]

Ford's decision raised the ire of enough government officials that Congress not only penalized it, but also all other foundations. Not two years after Stokes's victory, Congress passed a punitive law that levied enormous taxes against nonprofits. Ford and every other private foundation paid a massive price for the perceived intrusion into politics. Congressman Wilbur Mills, who headed the House Ways and Means Committee, led hearings into nonprofit organizations accused of "social engineering." Ford Foundation was a particular target, but all major charities were scrutinized. Congress passed the Tax Reform Act of 1969, legislation that enforced a 4 percent tax on annual investment income for all foundations. Purportedly, Congress designed the tax act to cover the costs associated with government audits of private foundation expenditures. For Ford, that penalty approximated $10 million. Congress also prohibited tax incentives for private charities and increased donation rules, which effectively acted to hinder and discourage philanthropy. Additionally, as a direct response to Cleveland CORE's successful voter registration drive, Congress prohibited all major nonprofit donors from funding one-time municipal voter registration drives.[34]

Five years later, foundations were still fending off the 4 percent penalty. In 1973, the collected total from all these private institutions averaged $76 million. Ford along with various other groups testified before a congressional hearing to lobby for a decrease to 2 percent. The Lilly Endowment, Brown Foundation, U.S. Steel Foundation, Jonssan Foundation, and the J. E. and L. E. Mabee Foundation, among many others, all petitioned for a reduction or a set accounting fee.[35]

Years later, the Ford Foundation annual report painted a rosy perspective on what it called "the troubles of 1969." The account claimed that it was "not all that bad," though they took "greater pains, since 1969, to avoid the appearance of hubris." They also noted that the current regulations and its enforcement had been "consistently fair," and that "the sentiments of the President's men toward organizations like ours had very little effect." This, of course, assumed that a ten-million-dollar loss and no grants for voter registration could actually be deemed a "little effect."[36]

The Cleveland voter registration project dampened CORENCO's long-term advancement, and hindered external partnerships among Cleveland's financial sect. However, the foundation renewed national CORE's grant to the Harambee Project in August 1968 for its black power economic program. Similar to the previous year, the allotted $300,000 fell well under national office's requested $800,000. National CORE sent a letter blasting Ford's grant decision. Staff members Innis, Perot, and Carter were particularly disturbed that the second year's monies barely equaled the amounts given to local organizations from the previous year. The group argued, "Our track record cannot be questioned and neither can the quality of our performance . . . We, therefore, request the funding of our program within the original amount. In addition to the original amount, we are requesting discretionary funds in the amount of $50,000."[37] CORE's complaints went unheeded and the organization launched its second year of TCP again with limited funds.

The small grant undermined CORENCO's operation, but it was also likely that CORE's internal issues impacted its effectiveness as well. Unbeknown to Ford, national CORE barely maintained the existence of the Cleveland TCP without continuous internal strife and national's waning organizational strength. TCP again suffered from internal antagonisms—in this case—between national CORE and Cleveland TCP or between Cleveland CORE, TCP staff and TCP advisory board members, and just general squabbling among TCP personnel.

Initially, national office hoped to head off such problems by having the local branch man the Target City Project. On August 5 and 6, 1967, national staff Ernest Howard and Kermit Scott met with Cleveland CORE regarding the implementation of the Target City Project. The original plan created a subcontractual relationship between national CORE and the chapter. However, the two consultants raised questions about consistency and conflict of interest by allowing chapter members to hire themselves. After the meeting, Scott and Howard issued a report that advised a separately run project and a TCP advisory board that incorporated Cleveland CORE's chairman.[38]

Howard and Scott also suggested that national set policy and standards for implementation. Thus, if voter registration made up one aspect of the Target Project, CORE should outline a specific number of voter registrants it expected to have in a given period. The two strongly counseled national CORE to provide written operation policy for the administrative staff. Finally, they suggested that Target Project and Cleveland CORE maintain separate offices in order to avoid confusing project and chapter activities.[39]

National CORE followed only two of these suggestions—establishing a board and maintaining separate offices. The TCP advisory committee included Cleveland chapter leaders along with national and regional officers. The council regularly submitted reports to the national office to document TCP's progress. Thus, national could justly contend that Target project progressed well, though it had set no specific outcome as per the report's request.[40]

However, the other recommendation national accepted led to contentious exchanges. Separate offices strained the relationship between TCP and Cleveland CORE—or specifically, the directors. Though Harambee staff endeavored to form stronger relations with Cleveland CORE, they generally stalled action in this department. Discord broke out after TCP staff rebuffed requests by Cleveland chapter for program funding. On another occasion, Carter failed to meet with the executive committee of Cleveland CORE, in spite of his agreement to do so. He insisted that Cleveland chairman Frank Anderson never formally invited him, to which Anderson tersely replied "consider himself invited."[41]

Further, national CORE neglected to delineate differences between the advisory board and the administrative office. The two groups sometimes overlapped duties or overstepped boundaries. Perot was particularly weary from infighting and stated in the spring of 1968 that there was "a basic misunderstanding about the role of this board. [He was] tired of coming to meetings which degenerate into 'gripe sessions' . . . Unless we can put these things aside and get seriously down to business—[he] intends to resign in September."[42]

Phillip Carter was not far behind Perot in this feeling, and also threatened to leave the job. Indeed, relations in the Cleveland CORE Target City Project degenerated so badly that Carter forced Donald Bean, his associate director, to take a leave of absence. Carter claimed that pressures had apparently become too great for Bean, and that his "insubordination" partially forced the issue. However, Donald Bean was the least of Carter's problems, as he actually had disputes with the leadership of Cleveland CORE, other staff members, and the Cleveland TCP advisory board.[43]

Carter finally left in June 1968 along with two other staff members. Though he submitted a resignation along with Patricia Austin, his executive assistant, and Boyd Puryear, an administrative assistant, all three later claimed they were fired. National CORE was then hit with a letter from their lawyer threatening a lawsuit based on breach of contract. Whether the three were forced to leave or left on their own accord remained unclear, but whichever the case, Carter's departure ended the first phase of Harambee.[44]

National CORE quickly replaced Carter with Arthur Evans. As acting director, Evans effectively held the office during the first grant wrap-up. Roy Innis, appointed associate director of CORE in 1968, promoted Donald Bean to Harambee director after Evans's departure. Bean, a graduate from West Virginia University with a BA in sociology, had served with Cleveland chapter since the early 1960s). Before his transition to TCP, he served as acting associate director of CORE in 1967 and also held the position of chairman for the North Central Regional CORE. He joined Harambee TCP in July 1968 where he worked under Wilfred Ussery on the CORENCO project.[45]

Bean directed Harambee from fall 1968 to winter 1969. As a member of CORENCO's staff and later as Harambee's director, Bean strengthened ties between Cleveland chapter and TCP, beginning with a joint economic boycott against General Electric's vacuum cleaner plant.[46] This event ignited Cleveland chapter's most notable direct action project of the year. On June 30, 1968, Cleveland chairman Frank Anderson and TCP director Don Bean subsequently urged a boycott of all GE products.[47]

GE Corporate complained that the boycott was unwarranted and that it had ninety black employees out of six hundred persons working for the company. GE and CORE failed to come to an agreement, and chapter members walked out the second meeting. The company claimed that Cleveland CORE threatened and coerced local business owners, and on one occasion informed a store owner he could desist from carrying GE products, get out of business, or be "burned out."[48]

CORENCO staff member Donald Bean insisted that they simply contacted fifty stores located in the black community and requested removal of GE products.[49] Additionally, given Cleveland's large black population (38 percent), the group hardly found GE's black employee numbers comforting. Cleveland CORE and TCP also charged GE with hiring black laborers for menial jobs, denying advanced training and job promotion, and allowing racially hostile working conditions. CORE went on to claim that GE's union only mimicked the actions of the corporation by supporting discriminatory behavior.

The protest failed to engender a Cleveland movement. Consequently, the chapter requested at the 1968 Columbus, Ohio, convention that CORE begin a nationwide boycott. In fact, the only resolution that passed with ease at the contentious conference was Cleveland's suggested GE protest. The resolution made national news. But after a few weeks, little was heard from CORE either locally or nationally.[50]

Only months into Bean's tenure, Innis ascended to national director of CORE in September 1968. Innis transferred Bean to the national office, but he refused and decided that "after careful consideration of this promotion, I have decided that I would prefer to remain in Cleveland."[51] By May 1969, Bean had a position as an administrative assistant to city properties director Edward J. Baugh under the Stokes administration.[52]

Cleveland CORE member Charles Cook headed Target City after Don Bean. Cleveland CORE had again undergone a short-lived transition.Grady Robinson replaced Frank Anderson as chairman. Nate Smith returned to the chapter, once again as treasurer. Carl Murray was installed as first vice chairman, Aubrey Kelley as second vice chairman, Connie Webster became recording secretary, and Charles Cook was named communications secretary. Cook also had held a second position as voter registration coordinator in the Cleveland TCP.

Cook's background was rather mysterious. Described as a large man with a soft voice, he never named his place of birth except to say that it was "some insecure place in the South. I left so fast I can't remember it." He attended Bowling Green State University but later joined the marines. After leaving the armed services, he worked odd jobs at the post office and manufacturing companies. Cook joined CORE some time around 1968, where he gained quite a reputation. Apparently, he evicted federal staff in Cleveland from their offices, and placed their desks on the sidewalk "where the people were" as a challenge to Nixon's disregard of the black community.[53]

Roy Innis replaced Don Bean with Charles Cook January 1969. Cook maintained the Harambee TCP office and voter registration operation. During his time, CORENCO (what was left of it) became a plan of the Innis and Cook administrations. Instead of a formal corporation, TCP reconfigured CORENCO as smaller, more manageable economic development projects. To that end, CORENCO and TCP jointly set up two companies, Target Food Services and Target Maintenance Services. William Hicks, a TCP staff member, managed Target Food Services. Target Food Services delivered catered and prepackaged food for hospitals, airlines, and other companies. Larry Bailey, Cleveland CORE chairman after Grady Robinson, directed the Target Maintenance Services. Target Maintenance Services provided cleaning and building repair assistance.[54]

According to Cook, "basic CORE policy assumes a broad-base ownership of all its economic undertakings." This meant that both businesses were stock companies. Supposedly, Target Food Services had a total value of $150,000 and Target Maintenance Services' worth was $60,000. Though the companies started under TCP in the summer, national CORE hoped Ford Foundation would fund the two companies according to their assigned total value, $210,000. Meanwhile, TCP set about obtaining agreements for each company and building their value. Eventually, Target Maintenance Services contracted with A&P Grocery Store, Case Western Reserve University, and Giant Tiger department store. Still, Ford Foundation granted no monies to Cleveland TCP for 1969.[55]

Without Ford funding, Cleveland chapter initiated direct action protests at Cleveland Trust and Central National Bank on behalf of TCP and the CORENCO plan. Picketers demanded that local financial institutions help create and support black banks—another key component of CORENCO. But, demonstrations got nowhere. Harambee TCP and CORENCO were dead.[56]

Charles Cook remained in place as titular director of Harambee until 1970. In June, Cook was shot three times in both the head and neck in an incident, which he

*Left to right:* Target City director Charles Cook; deputy director Clarence Todman; general manager of Target Maintenance and Services, Larry Bailey; and general manager of Target Food Services, William Hicks Jr. Photo: unknown photographer, September 18, 1969. From the Cleveland Press Collection, Michael Schwartz Library, Cleveland State University

claimed to be an accident. Purportedly, the unnamed associate improperly handled a handgun and it went off—three times. Police, however, had information that a verbal altercation occurred moments before the shooting. Cook recovered from his injuries and went on as leader of Cleveland TCP, though he barely sustained it.[57]

Instead, Cook spent the majority of his efforts on Cleveland CORE as its new chairman, following Larry Bailey. Though CORE did little in the way of direct action protests, the chapter participated in one last major movement campaign—a multi-organization demonstration against McDonald's under the auspices of Operation Black Unity (OBU). While the CORENCO idea of communal capitalism drew to an end for Harambee Target City, the concept reemerged within OBU's direct action protest for McDonald's franchise ownership.

Operation Black Unity formed on June 21, 1969. The organization consisted of various black power and civil rights organizations in Cleveland, Ohio.[58] To a certain extent, Operation Black Unity was a rehashed black power version of the

United Freedom Movement. Early members of Operation Black Unity included CORE, NAACP, Urban League, Afro-Set, Council of Churches, Ohio Black Concern Committee, Welfare Grievance Committee Poor People's Partnership, the Federation of Black Nationalists, Community Fighters for Housing Large Families, July 23rd Defense Committee, United Pastors' Association, SCLC, Federation of Black Nationalists, Pride, Inc., House of Israel, Greater Cleveland Welfare Rights Organization, Hough Development Corporation, and Domestic Workers of America. Eventually OBU grew to twenty-three local black organizations.[59]

The group had several committees to address racial issues around the city. Initial OBU projects were small unnoticeable events. The organization planned a Christmas boycott of all Cleveland stores in December, but only handed out flyers that urged black consumers not to purchase during the holiday season. OBU's Christmas boycott eventually concentrated on Sears and Roebuck at East 83rd Street and Carnegie, which lead to minor decreases in the store's profit.[60] OBU also demanded more black hires in the fire department, staged sympathy rallies, and investigated brutal attacks of black students at the Collinwood High School.[61]

June 1969, Operation Black Unity began its first and only major project, a local boycott of the McDonald's food chain. It began late February 1969 when the Reverend Ernest Hilliard, affectionately known at First Spiritualist Christian Church of America as Prophet Thomas, applied to McDonald's for a business franchise. Rabbi David Hill, ministerial leader of the House of Israel, attended the meeting as support. McDonald's required Hilliard visit its Chicago headquarters and operate a local franchise for a week. McDonald's also claimed that it could not facilitate a franchise unless local owners agreed to sell.[62]

In early April, Hilliard and Hill learned that McDonald's chose to grant black Clevelander Charles Johnson a franchise. It became clear that the corporation intended to circumvent their original request. In late June, Hilliard and Hill brought their case before Operation Black Unity. The organization accepted their request for aid and demanded a July 5 meeting with Edward Bood, McDonald's vice president.[63]

Events grew more strained after the mysterious killing of Rev. Ernest Hilliard on July 4. Presumably, an assassin fatally shot Hilliard in the driveway of his home in Warrensville Heights, a suburb of Cleveland. Conflicted accounts surfaced about Hilliard's dying statement. His wife reported that he stated that "white folks" shot him. The police insisted that Hilliard actually referenced a white car that neighbors saw flee the scene. Either way, many activists believed his murder directly resulted from his and Hill's pressures on McDonald's.[64]

Bood refused to meet with Hill or Operation Black Unity, and wrote back that Hill encumbered "meaningful and rational dialogue." His strident, emotionally charged rhetoric, bodyguard/entourage presence, and unfamiliarity with "sound business practices" prohibited negotiation. Bood also rejected OBU's accusation that McDonald's rebuffed black investors. The company had reached out to potential black investors but found relatively few who had business training or enough financial resources (especially since McDonald's charged black business owners more). The vice president then compounded bad relations by staunchly insisting he would not bow to threats, harassment, coercion, intimidation, and violence. Finally, he accused Operation Black Unity of extortion after the organization requested that perspective buyers donate to its programs.[65]

Bood's letter offended OBU, particularly his assumption that the black community lacked persons of business acumen or that OBU coerced contributions. Dissatisfied, OBU began a boycott five days later. On July 10, OBU members (most of whom came from the local black nationalist group Afro-Set) demonstrated in front of four McDonald's chains on Cleveland's eastside. Two days later, McDonald's restarted negotiations. However, McDonald's shut down talks again when it learned OBU appointed Rabbi Hill negotiation chair. Activists walked out of the meeting and pledged to maintain picket lines in front of the four restaurants.[66]

On July 24, the organization submitted a position paper, with substantial assistance from Carl Stokes and his administration, listing five demands. One, McDonald's must submit to the purchase of at least five restaurants in Cleveland's black community. Two, future McDonald's franchises within the black community must be granted to black owners. Three, franchise payments from all five restaurants (the fifth was slated to be built as the first sit-down McDonald's in Cleveland) go to OBU as opposed to McDonald's. Four, purchasers receive irrevocable franchise rights—in order to prevent any double cross or betrayal by McDonald's corporation. And finally, OBU had the right of approval for franchise buyers.[67]

While McDonald's and OBU haggled, local owners turned to Carl Stokes's administration for help against the demonstrations. All four chains experienced financial losses. Owners irrationally feared that nonviolent picketers presented a violent risk. The mayor responded by placing a police officer at each restaurant and promising to assist the talks. Meanwhile, the boycott immobilized all four restaurants.

Bood pointedly noted that McDonald's financial losses created job loss for over 150 black employees.[68] However, many employees openly supported OBU's boycott. Walter Johnson, McDonald's shift manager on East 83rd Street remembered that, "Shortly after the boycott began, the management and crew of the East 83 Street unit met ant [and] voted to support Operation Black Unity by closing down operations. It was the first unit to close during the boycott . . . the incident had a large impact on many lives."[69]

In mid-August, McDonald's owners took matters into their own hands. All four acted outside the behest of the parent corporation and hired lawyers to negotiate with OBU directly. Unlike McDonald's headquarters, all agreed to give 2 percent of their sale price plus $2,500 to OBU for programs in the black community. However, McDonald's corporation shrank from the agreement and nixed final approval. The last stalemate forced Stokes's administration to directly mediate. McDonald's refused to concede to any other demands but one. It would facilitate sales, but stipulated that it and OBU must have co-approval for potential buyers. The final agreement forced McDonald's to release four of its east Cleveland franchises and a fifth future sit-down restaurant. Negotiations were underway for two fast-food sites on East 104th and St. Clair, and 9101 Kinsman. Charles Johnson, the previously approved buyer, received the East 142nd and Kinsman McDonald's. The last restaurant and the largest on East 82nd and Euclid Avenue went to the newly organized Hough Area Development Corporation (HADC).[70]

OBU had good reason to accept HADC's offer. The organization had credible standing among black activists and the community. Over forty community leaders and professionals had formed Hough Area Development Corporation. It began in April 1967 as a watchdog organization concerned about the distribution of federal revitalization funds for Hough neighborhood. It soon became a collaboration for economic development. Within one year, it received a grant of $1.6 million from the Office of Economic Opportunity (OEO) and $62,000 from Carl Stokes's Cleveland Now!, which made HADC one of the most well funded community corporations in the nation.

Despite its large budget and good standing, conflict soon arose between McDonald's, HADC, and OBU over mutual approval for specific restaurants. McDonald's legal representative James Davis (lawyer for Squires, Sanders, and Dempsey) solicited Hough Development's purchase of a second McDonald's soon to be constructed. The franchise was the first sit-down restaurant in Cleveland—a venture speculated to bring in over a million dollars. Davis, on behalf of McDonald's, also contracted with HADC to train managers and allocate 25 percent interest in the units to the newly hired managers.[71]

With such a large profit at stake, OBU determined that it would select the purchaser for the sit-down McDonald's. OBU allotted the future 107th and Euclid sit-down McDonald's to Fred Benbow, OBU secretary and the St. James A.M.E. Church representative. McDonald's ignored OBU's decision and handed over the fast-food business to HADC. Hill immediately complained that the original agreement stipulated OBU's right to determine black ownership for specific McDonald's branches. Even though OBU approved HADC's ownership of one McDonald's, it did not approve of the nonprofit's purchase of any other.[72]

Hill went further to say that as negotiation spokesman for OBU all prior agreements were now null and void. Hill, however, held only a committee chairmanship. Rev. Donald Jacobs, W. O. Walker, and Jonathan Ealy directed OBU. As such,

Hill could not overturn any decision the organization made as a body though he implied he could. Hill's assumption of OBU leadership notwithstanding, Donald Jacobs and Jonathan Ealy agreed that OBU should determine both purchaser and specific allocation.[73]

Though Jacobs and Ealy publicly appeared to support Hill, internally members argued back and forth over the contract. HADC leader DeForest Brown and his supporters pushed OBU to rescind its agreement with Fred Benbow. When Brown's attempt failed, HADC threatened to drop both franchises. Jay Arki, member of the local Federation of Black Nationalists, accused Brown of double-dealing with McDonald's. Despite disagreement, OBU eventually realized via its own legal team that, indeed, the organization could not specify franchise ownership. HADC would retain both restaurants.[74]

HADC won, but OBU remained annoyed with DeForest Brown though it could say little about it internally or publicly. HADC was well on its way to building a reputation in community development. Their projects consisted of a credit union, six hundred housing units, a rubber manufacturing company, the Handyman Maintenance Company, and its biggest business project—the Martin Luther King Jr. Plaza—a shopping center located securely within the heart of Hough community. The Martin Luther King Plaza plan incorporated town homes on the second floor, while the first floor remained commercial. The organization had deep ties to Hough, which also made it untouchable. Its board members comprised only neighborhood residents and black Clevelanders who advocated community control. Most of its employees lived in the community. The Handyman Maintenance Company, for example, provided work to twenty-six inhabitants. And, Community Products, Inc., the rubber company, specifically employed welfare recipients.[75]

Perhaps most significantly, its community control philosophy incorporated broad community ownership of HADC businesses. For example, much like the CORENCO plan, the profits from the Martin Luther King Plaza provided for daycare services, entrepreneurial and job training, and technical assistance to local businesses. Also, HADC planned to set aside stock in some of its businesses in a trust for welfare recipients, though it had yet to figure out ways to divvy up employee profits.[76]

To what extent CORENCO's plan influenced HADC was unclear. Certainly, former CORE members and associates were well represented among HADC's founders and staff. Franklin Anderson (former chairman of CORE and second director of HADC after Brown's departure) cofounded HADC along with Daisy Craggett, who worked closely with CORE through the school desegregation fight. Pauline Warfield (SCORE and CORE member), Nate Smith (former treasurer for Cleveland CORE), and CORE members Mason Hargrave and Katie Dixon all worked for HADC. Geraldine Williams, who led the rent-strike movement, also

joined. Because CORE members and associates figured prominently in the organization, its leadership and staff had to be familiar with the CORENCO plan.
HADC's attendance at Target City's economic development conferences also
pointed to some degree of cross-fertilization.

Although HADC struggled to create group ownership in its other enterprises,
Hough Development structured its McDonald's as a communally owned business from the outset. Most of its employees had to live in Hough. The CDC also
intended to distribute the restaurant's future earnings, which approximated a million dollars, through community service programs and employee stock. As such, the
restaurant symbolized a significant model for profit sharing between itself and the
black community. However, the potential monies earned also raised arguments as
to whether HADC should have both franchises.[77]

HADC had few supporters for its two purchases. However, Cleveland CORE
validated HADC's group ownership approach. Cleveland CORE chairman and
TCP director Charles Cook reaffirmed that "we're not talking about making a half-
dozen millionaires. CORE is interested in a structure in which profits from the
restaurant will benefit the total black community."[78]

*Left:* Charles Cook, CORE chairman, *center:* David Hill, *right:* Perry Holloway
from Bradholl-Moore Associates press conference at the CORE office.
Photo: Glenn Zahn, August 6, 1969. From the Cleveland Press
Collection, Michael Schwartz Library, Cleveland State University

Roy Innis (*center*) was the only national leader to
appear for the Operation Black Unity Rally.
Photo: Timothy Culek, August 27, 1969. From the Cleveland Press
Collection, Michael Schwartz Library, Cleveland State University

The project also garnered national CORE's attention. Roy Innis came to Cleveland to encourage the local chapter's participation in the McDonald's boycott. He spoke at OBU's August 1969 rally before a crowd of five hundred at Antioch Baptist Church. Innis criticized black leaders from the NAACP and the Urban League for their absence and signaled that Cleveland had national CORE's backing. However, local dynamics between CORE and OBU were different.[79]

The chapter ideologically sided with HADC, but it had no stake in the arguments over the 107th Street McDonald's. CORE held no committee positions within OBU and it had no funds to buy a franchise. Moreover, OBU inclined toward individual ownership, a direct contradiction to CORE's philosophy. Resultantly, Cleveland CORE kept a peripheral position in the organization. January 1970, four months after Innis's appearance at the rally, the chapter no longer affiliated with the group.[80]

Equally, CORE's relative silent departure might also reflect OBU's perception of CORE as a questionable partner. More to the point, rumors circulated in late fall 1969 that allegedly CORE had backdoor dealings with McDonald's. Whether the national CORE office or local chapter stood accused was uncertain. Former

CORE chairman Baxter Hill chose not to name a specific party, but expressed his disappointment with the unauthorized contact with McDonald's.[81] Although no proof seemed to exist that CORE was the culprit, theoretically it paid the price for the suspected deception. On October 26, 1969, the Cleveland CORE branch office went up in flames.[82]

To make matters worse, CORE chairman Charles Cook believed that neighborhood firemen deliberately delayed arrival by forty-five minutes. The office also took heavy water damage as firemen fiercely quashed the flames. The fire chief claimed trucks arrived two minutes later and that the blaze consumed the building because it was set in four different places. Thus, the extensive burn was not due to the firemen's negligence but to arson.[83] In either case, CORE representatives were conspicuously absent from OBU meetings and off the OBU roster thereafter.

OBU went onward after CORE's departure, and spent the early part of 1970 fending off the indictments of its members. State charges stemmed from alleged requests to perspective McDonald's buyers for $6,000 donations to cover OBU operation costs.[84] The grand jury intended to prosecute multiple members of OBU, particularly those associated with the Cleveland Black Panther Party and the House of Israel. However, only two were accused. An all-white grand jury handed down secret indictments on October 1969 against Rabbi David Hill and his associate and

Cleveland CORE office decimated by fire. It was believed
that CORE betrayed OBU and retribution followed.
Photo: Herman Seid, October 25, 1969. From the Cleveland Press
Collection, Michael Schwartz Library, Cleveland State University

House of Israel parishioner, James Raplin, on charges of black mail.[85] Officials set Raplin free on bond, but held Hill.[86]

OBU angrily asserted that "the action of the Grand Jury was carried out with the sanction of the racist courts and a racist prosecutor, prompted and aided by commercial interests which bleed the black community and fail to put anything back. The real extortionists are the commercial interests who have profited by the millions."[87] OBU provided money for Raplin and Hill's defense, but the state convicted both for extortion. Hill received a sentence of one to five years; however, he escaped custody and became an expatriate in Guyana where he rebuilt the House of Israel under the name Rabbi Edward Washington. Raplin was not so lucky. The state incarcerated him for several years.[88]

The boycott's power can not be underestimated. As a direct result of OBU's protest, McDonald's issued a directive requesting that white owners in inner city areas sell to interested black owners. Over twenty-one stores in Detroit, Oakland, Kansas City (MO), St. Louis, Los Angeles, Chicago, Dayton, and Denver transferred to black hands. The corporation also hired a director to oversee the transfer. Further, HADC staff member and former CORE representative Nate Smith claimed that once Burger King witnessed the affect on McDonald's, they too looked for black owners. Thus, though short lived and individually focused, the McDonald's boycott and its subsequent effect on HADC's community development work had a greater impact than CORENCO and the Target City companies. Yet even so, it was Cleveland CORE, Harambee Target City, and Cleveland CORE members who substantially led the way to black economic empowerment in the city.[89]

While CORE leaders morphed into economic development or dispersed into similarly minded organizations, Ford Foundation felt compelled to assess its own role in the Harambee Target City Project. In a final report, the philanthropist giant received a damning internal evaluation. According to Lisle Carter and Edward Sylvester, Ford misconceived, misunderstood, and misstepped at every turn. So concerned that its association with CORE would backfire, the foundation understood little of what CORE proposed. As a result, expectations were unspecific and the foundation was equally content if CORE's proposed goals were just as general. The foundation never fully examined its potential impact on Stokes's candidacy, because staffers never believed Stokes would win.[90]

Internal dynamics within Ford added to the problem. The organization missed an opportunity to critically examine the first project because the first assessor was too familiar. The evaluation standard seemed only that the project not "blow up." Since it did not, that became the basis by which Ford gave more funding. But, this perspective clearly set the foundation's main concern as its own interest over helping the project. Carter and Sylvester further added that when Ford's initial relations with CORE did not flop, the foundation then became concerned CORE was not doing enough.[91]

The report condemned Ford's attempted meddling in internal CORE dynamics without consideration of inside politics among the national staff, within the local chapter, and between the local chapter and national office. And while it unsuccessfully endeavored to influence CORE, it ignored CORE's financial state. In doing so, it botched the Target City operation by not embedding special overhead provisions to deal with the economic circumstances that hindered CORE's success in the second phase.[92]

Ford's second small grant stymied the organization's ability to get from "here to there." It provided no technical training, did not consider that the movement from direct action to community programming needed lead time, failed to recognize that conditional funding could not sustain a community organization engaged in such complex processes, and "improvidently" financed a community "super structure" (CORENCO) on an untenable meager amount. The final assessment of Ford was a stinging rebuke.

Simultaneously, national CORE's project was too broad in scope. According to the report, Phillip Carter was ideologically tone deaf and out of step with CORE. Even Roy Innis referred to him as "politically a bull in the china shop." In the second phase, TCP fell down in its community outreach and effectively became inactive. It suffered from too many personnel rollovers. Internal bickering also diminished the project's development. The project itself collapsed with little funding. Innis's takeover of CORE was the final death knell for Target City. CORE's black separatist stance turned off many supporters in Cleveland. Oppositely, radicals accused the black separatist, and by extension CORE, of being bought off by Ford. In the final estimation, the report stated that there was no pathway for Target City Project to follow. The combined circumstances made the grant an overall inexcusable failure.[93]

*But . . .* CORE could not be written off so easily. The authors admitted that voter registration by CORE made an undeniable impact, and ironically created a hopeful environment that left the black community less open to its more "radical" economic message. From their perspective, local groups like Hough Area Development Corporation were influenced by CORE's economic development work (evidenced by their hire of Frank Anderson). And TCP's former director Phillip Carter accurately noticed that work in Cleveland stimulated economic development efforts in Pittsburgh. As such, CORE could frankly say that its black power strategy became synonymous with economic development. And more telling, many within Target City moved on to leadership roles throughout the Cleveland community and Stokes administration.[94]

The report was a harsh critique of both parties. But while Ford had the luxury to hesitate, revise, and rethink its decisions, CORE could not rest on its economic development laurels. Left with the clear understanding that grant aid from Ford was finite, the organization had one last strategy. National turned to the only institution large enough to financially facilitate its economic development plan, funded enough to wipe out its debt, and powerful enough to expand CORENCO across the nation. That body was the United States federal government and its leader—the 1968 presidential winner, Richard Nixon.

# 8

# A Nation under Our Feet

CUYAHOGA RIVER was on fire. Opening and closing your eyes a hundred times could not stop that sight from searing into the public's collective conscious. It was an outrageous oxymoron: water on fire. The fiery polluted river wound its way into Lake Erie in 1969 as the symptomatic embodiment of urban deterioration that hit Cleveland in the 1970s. The story was a standard theme in most of America's urban spaces. Cities abandoned by industry, tax losses, forfeiture of city services, rising crime, deserted buildings and residential blight, increased vermin populations, unemployment, family disintegration, transportation interruption, and fiscal crises.[1]

Black mayors, like Carl Stokes, undertook herculean tasks with none of the previous decades' resources. Cities like New York pleaded for federal intervention to halt default, to no avail. It was a circumstance captured mightily by the *New York Daily News* infamous 1970s headline, "Ford to City: Drop Dead!" Urban problems were immense, made worse by the brain drain of everyday black activists and other residents beating a hasty retreat from the city. Even community activists John and Pauline Frazier experienced their own final straw. While away on vacation, robbers broke into their east Cleveland home, and in a rather twisted take on Goldilocks and the Three Bears, proceeded to live in their house, sleep in their beds, eat their food, and drink up their best wine.

The year not only signaled the unavoidable and undeniable signs of city decline, but it was also national CORE's last chance to pivot toward a black power solution that could stay economic destitution in black communities. As Roy Innis once wrote, "the division between reformist and revolutionary" were false binaries. Given the circumstances, CORE needed an ideology reflective of black community needs, whether it was socialism, capitalism, or a measure of both or neither. Innis simply boiled the idea down to "liberation."[2]

CORENCO's proposal actually promised something more concretely defined than the broadly termed "liberation" implied, but it lurched back and forth due to its dependence on Ford funding. CORE needed to codify this Cleveland blue-print, and nationalize it to actualize black power's true potential. Simultaneous to CORENCO's opening, the national office began preparations to craft a bill for a federally backed CDC. The Community Self Determination (CSD) Bill converted capitalism into collective ownership through a massively funded development corporation.

The plan fit within a larger black historical milieu of economic interdependence and post-slavery collective-owned endeavors. But CORE's leadership failed to har-ness this history and prove community capitalism's viability. Opposition worsened because CORE solicited aid from the Nixon administration, which elicited deep misgivings about CORE's intentions.

CORE's government-based funding scheme led activists and academics to misconstrue its intentions as bourgeois black capitalism. But black capitalism, like black power, conceptually defied definition and came to mean many things to many people. Stokely Carmichael argued that "Black ghetto residents demand . . . a shop that they will own and improve cooperatively" and that "the society we seek to build then, is not a capitalist one." In *Black Power,* he, along with Charles Hamilton, further teased out the vision of economic empowerment, arguing that 40 to 50 per-cent of net profit should return to indigenous communities and would take various forms, including scholarships, charity services, and jobs.[3]

Concurrently, the state, embodied by Richard Nixon's administration, deified free market capitalism and gave little consideration to any other variations. Nixon's 1968 campaign speech, "Bridges to Human *Dignity*," contended that the govern-ment had a role in helping black Americans obtain their "piece of the action," or place in the American dream. Nixon constructed civil rights and freedom as an outgrowth of economic participation in laissez faire capitalism. William Safire, speechwriter for the Nixon administration, purportedly dubbed this "piece of the action" black capitalism—much to the frustration of some in the campaign who felt the phrase too narrowly defined the scope of their intentions. Ultimately, however, black capitalism Nixon-style characterized the administration's eventual solutions to black inequality. The Small Business Administration (SBA) and the newly estab-lished Office of Minority Business Enterprise (OMBE) expanded federally backed loans for individual companies and focused almost entirely on the fiscal develop-ment of the individual businessperson.[4]

On the ground, black activists embraced both old-style black business models or furthered the cry for group ownership. Organizations like Cleveland's Hough Area Development Corporation, Oakland's Operation Boot Strap, and Rochester's nonprofit CDC FIGHT turned capitalism into community ownership, employ-ment training, and in some cases nonprofit manufacturing. The National Economic Growth and Reconstruction Organization (NEGRO) and the Cleveland-based

Black Economic Union (BEU) became national groups geared toward individual enterprise and business training.[5]

Though most organizations leaned toward the traditional black business model, hybrid institutions diversified capitalism's structure and operated through collective distribution, nonprofit community ownership, and worker training. These entities transmuted black capitalism into economic development. However, the idea was not always clearly separated from conceptions about black capitalism—particularly when these groups depended upon corporate, foundation, and government funds. Often, black capitalism became weighted by presumptions that the goal of its advocates and their financial backers were one and the same—when more often they diverged. As a result, these efforts came under heavy fire from black radical claims that these groups were greedy and disregarded capitalism's degenerative and degrading impact on the black community.

Perhaps the most well known militant challenge came from the 1969 National Black Economic Development Conference in Detroit. James Forman issued forth his Black Manifesto, which denounced black capitalism. The manifesto demanded $500 million in reparations for the establishment of cooperative businesses in the United States and in Africa.[6] At the same conference, presenter activist James Boggs argued that the underdevelopment of the black community and structural racism were inseparable from the capitalist structure. Thus, any advocacy of black capitalism amounted to re-enslavement, or, at minimum, an acceptance of one group's exploitation of another. In order to counter capitalism as Boggs defined it, black development had to embrace six guidelines of economic uplift. First, the black community had to acknowledge that capitalism was a system of exploitation. Second, by virtue of financial need and historical exploitation, the black poor had a right to direct community improvements. Third, participants had to learn through civic engagement and a struggle of "grievances" to cultivate decision making. All neighborhoods required a large influx of resources for rapid growth in education, health care, housing, and new technology training. Finally, "any program for the development of the black community must be based on large-scale social ownership rather than on private individual enterprises."[7]

Many of the goals found in Black Manifesto and Bogg's "Irrationality of Capitalism" articulated ideas already in action by local community development corporations. And though CORE was often thrown in under the bourgeois black capitalist umbrella, CORENCO's plan followed both proposals' guidelines. While the manifesto called for out-right reparations, CORENCO's demands for funding rested on specified set asides or what Roy Innis called "recoupment of earnings" from government, banks, and the private sector. All three demanded cooperative investment and group ownership in the black community, a key element for all these doctrines. Thus, CORENCO's platform was not unlike black radicals' demands or that of other past efforts for cooperatively owned businesses. By extension, this rendered CORE's black economic power projects (CORENCO and the Community Self Determination Bill) populist in nature.[8]

Historically, American populism emerged as a political movement for fiscally strained and destitute farmers in the 1890s. Rural-based populists formed cooperatives, challenged corporate controlled public transportation, and confronted company monopolies. However, wealth share or cooperative economies in the black community stretched back further than the 1890s. Historian Steven Hahn's *A Nation Under Our Feet: Black Political Struggles in the Rural South from Slavery to the Great Migration* suggested that slave economy—the exchange of goods, service, and labor served to "redistribute . . . to those in need [and] to reinforce ties of kinship and friendship," thereby creating a sense of community.[9] Because of slavery's character, African Americans could not incorporate conventional norms of power and authority (wealth). Resultantly, Hahn explained that slave economy and community ownership played out based on labor contribution that entitled "members of the household to a roughly proportionate share of the produce."[10] South Carolina slave Charles Ball exampled this sensibility when he offered his adopted family his labor earnings in return for a portion of the funds and proceeds from the family's garden.[11]

Historian Jessica Nembhard's *Collective Courage: A History of African American Cooperative Economic Thought and Practice* researched the emergence of cooperatives among free blacks before and after slavery. According to Nembhard, cooperatives operated based on values of self-help, self-responsibility, equality, democracy, and solidarity. These collectives inclined toward three cooperative types: consumer, producer, or worker owned. Worker cooperatives allowed laborers to share profits, and offered "economic security, income and wealth generation, democratic economic participation," and environmental and communal stability.[12]

According to Nembhard, Chesapeake Marine Railway and Dry Dock Company, formed in 1865, was the earliest worker-owned company. The business allotted shares at $5 each. Within five years, they paid off their mortgage, and afterward paid out 10 percent dividends per year. Long term, black caulkers became part of the white union and the company's existence dampened efforts by other trade groups to lock out black workers given the possible competition of black independent industriousness. Similarly, another enterprise, the 1901 Mercantile Cooperative Company located in Ruthville, Virginia, also set share prices at $5 each. No investor could have more than twenty shares, and purchase could occur in installments.[13]

W. E. B. DuBois's edited volume, *The Negro in Business*, examined the persistent presence of collective worker-owned businesses. C. H. Fearn's paper, "A Negro Cooperative Foundry," reviewed the short history of his company, Southern Stove Hollow Ware and Foundry. Southern Stove, which opened in 1897, sold stock only to colored people and at the price of $25 a piece. The foundry lasted a few years until it went out of business in the early 1900s. However, Fearn firmly believed in the company's mission. His conference paper reasoned, "if we are able to become the masters of the different trades and to employ our own capital, direct and control our own industries, then the time will come that we will cease to be the serfs."[14]

Throughout the 1890s cooperatives also appeared as part of the populist revolt by farmers. According to Lawrence Goodwyn, populists were neither capitalist reformers nor socialists. Populists "sought to redesign certain central components in the edifice of American capitalism" to create a cooperative commonwealth that respected "individual striving."[15] Equally central to this rebellion, protest and political empowerment gave populists a sense of "somebodiness."[16]

According to DuBois, collectives declined in the early 1900s. Many failed due to poor management, no expertise, low levels of capitalization, and racial discrimination. However, they made some resurgence after 1917. The UNIA certainly reflected this cooperative comeback. Most UNIA businesses were consumer based— buying clubs, credit unions, or coop housing.[17]

Populism among whites reappeared in the Great Depression as a broadly defined capitalist reform movement. Then Louisiana congressman Huey Long led a futile but wildly popular campaign to "Share Our Wealth." Long's assertion made, as he often put it, "every man a king." Otherwise, if the United States failed to redistribute wealth from the massively rich to the poor, the nation faced societal disaster. Long intended to grant the poor a basic annual income and housing, veteran benefits, free college education to all, and pensions to senior citizens sixty or over. Both the 1890s and 1930s populist perspectives embraced collective ownership and decried capitalism's limited accessibility for all to enjoy. However, Long eschewed any form of state wealth distribution, and acted to "save" capitalism through a more encompassing alternate vision similar to Kelso's second income theory.[18]

While Long argued for monies to be seized from the wealthy, historians Hill and Rubig point out in the *Business of Black Power* that other forms of collective wealth appeared during this same period in the religious populations of Father Divine and Daddy Grace, whose devotees divested and donated worldly possessions. Monies rematerialized as businesses, heavens (Divine's reference for his followers' homes), and banquets in which all shared in the church's riches.[19]

Both churches were private self-sustaining institutions, dependent first on contributions by its flock and second upon business patronage by the black community. Indeed, the description self-sustaining was rather an understatement, as the two groups profited handsomely. Father Divine and Daddy Grace generated a combined wealth worth millions. For over two decades, Daddy Grace's church, United House of All Prayer, was renowned for its multiple property ownership in thirteen states and six foreign countries estimated at $10 million—though it was partially unclear whether it was part of the church's portfolio or constituted Grace's personal estate. Others claimed that its wealth was much greater when the numerous Grace products were added, including *Daddy Grace* toothpaste, *Daddy Grace* cold cream, *Daddy Grace* hair straightener, and *Grace Magazine*. The church even created senior pension plans for its members. Collective ownership made Daddy Grace rich, made United House of All Prayer among the wealthiest black religious institutions in the United States, and gave its members food, work, housing, and a retirement plan.[20]

Historian George Frederickson characterized this period between the 1920s and 1930s as part of a rising tide of populism in the black community. Frederickson argued in *Black Liberation: A Comparative History of Black Ideologies in the United States* that populism found expression in a more expansive language of *peoplehood* or *people-ness*, which broadened the Marxian conception of working class to include the petit bourgeois. The interclass nature of such a group meant that they held no allegiance to capitalism or socialism, but an inclination toward a "third way." They often supported institutions or structural reform that included cooperatives, employee-owned businesses, limitations in individual stock and property owner- ship, and prohibitions on large concentrations of wealth.[21]

Of course, not long after the 1930s period of black populism, James Farmer propagated the importance of economic cooperatives and income independence for the black freedom movement. The Brotherhood Mobilization memorandum argued that financial independence was necessary to sustain and protect any organization against potential repercussions. Though homespun goods provided a method for generating profit, this portion of the Brotherhood memo never took root in 1940s CORE. But by the 1960s, southern CORE chapters turned to economic cooper- atives to aid black farmers and tenants who suffered punitive economic attacks for their freedom movement activities.

Farmer suggested as early as 1962 that southern community work with black rural laborers might serve to reconcile conflict among the means and ends members. According to the former national director, CORE had to extend program areas and membership into other protest forms, and that the "current experiences in the rural South indicate that programs of self-help for economic survival must accompany expansion of the drive for civil rights."[22] The rural program reflected a larger effort to move toward producer and consumer coops, along with the creation of credit unions. Thus, in some ways the rural transformation of the movement served just as forcefully to craft a program toward black economic power as the urban North.[23]

In the late 1960s, other economic development voices came through. On the East coast, Ollie Leeds pushed McKissick to move in this direction suggesting that CORE-created cooperatives and credit unions would allow the organization to take a militant stand while still transforming the financial existence of the black commu- nity. But according to Innis and Leeds, McKissick failed to follow through. On the

West coast, Louis Smith's Operation Bread Basket successfully pointed to a manufacturing and corporate alliance in the form of Shindana, a short-lived black doll
company that employed black residents in south-central Los Angeles and whose
proceeds funded community service projects, including day care.[24]

Yet despite CORE's ideological progress toward black economic development
from the Brotherhood Memorandum to CORENCO, some perceived CORE as
more like the Daddy Grace of black power, in its most negative sense.[25] Scholar
Manning Marable held up Innis and McKissick as typical styled supporters of black
capitalism. In part, this perspective stemmed from his belief that collective programs still amounted to capitalism in that it failed to challenge its underlying racist
structure. Meaning, any change to capitalism was irrelevant, because it accepted the
very premise of capitalism's existence, and all forms of capitalism amounted to the
same thing—just capitalism.[26]

But, this perspective left black activists with few solutions to black inequality
in American society. Realistically, CORE's critics were no less sucked into capitalism's machinations than anyone else, and the larger black community was certainly
stuck in its clutches. All citizens and noncitizens earned income, paid for services,
and few—if any—joined the hippies in free commune living out in the woods.
Capitalism was absolute. CORE's black populism emerged as a crucial alternative
that acted against and upon the system, sometimes outside its parameters to make
it tenable.

Though CORE perceived America's financial system as an unavoidable reality,
it did pose a challenge to this economic structure. Sociologist James Jennings pos-
tulated in *The Politics of Black Empowerment* that many scholars erroneously classify
the "'noise' produced by black interest groups [as only concerning] inclusion within
a given economic and social status quo." However, by flattening these differences,
this school of thought "dismissed the political impact and potential of black activism that does not automatically opt for economic integration and political inclusion into the mainstream American polity."[27] Further, this perspective ignored how
the state acted against full black participation or how demands from a socially and
economically subordinate class equated to a confrontation with the state. In other
words, even black reform efforts translated as heretical.[28]

Still, CORE, Floyd McKissick, and Roy Innis metamorphosed as examples
of black power turned black capitalism. Yet, McKissick Enterprises—the former
national director's newly formed business post-CORE—and national CORE
hardly operated in tandem or with the same perspective. Will Ussery made this
clear when he noted, "I think . . . there ought to be important new models of
community ownership of the services and the institutions within that community
rather than simply vehicles for how to provide more entrepreneur Horatio-Alger
type opportunity for some black businessman who has the resources to move in on

a situation like that. . . . I'm not sure Soul City provides important models for how we ought to get at that."[29]

While director of CORE, McKissick in fact embraced aspects of black power populism. He explained Kelso's second income theory, how it potentially empowered the black community, and outlined the concept as part of CORE's development stratagem. And though many insisted that Soul City reflected only free-market principles, they actually ignored Louis Kelso's presence as McKissick's spokesman on collective ownership, thus missing Soul City's partial effort to incorporate group wealth.[30]

Roy Innis confused the matter further by articulating these ideas as "separatist" ventures, which reflected territorial self-determination as opposed to economic transformation. Though he initially represented CORE's black populist policy, the long-established nationalist insisted on framing the Harlem Commonwealth, a community development corporation backed by OEO funds; CORENCO, a nonprofit focused on broad-based ownership, employment, and distribution of goods and services; and CORE's upcoming Community Self Determination Bill, legislation designed to nationalize local economic development efforts—as CORE's intention to build autonomous nation-states. Although all these entities operated independently within and directed by the black community, each sought to reorder the financial structure operating against the poor and working class. To say these infrastructures represented a separatist bent by CORE missed the subtlety of their methods and hid the groundbreaking potential of shared wealth.[31]

Whether due to Innis's nation-state framing or McKissick's Soul City, activists in and around CORE eventually rendered efforts like CORENCO immaterial. Criticisms boiled down to two streams of thought about CORE. First, once CORE accepted capitalism on any level, it purportedly situated itself as bourgeois middlemen co-opted to quell the masses. Accepting Kelso's "every man a capitalist" appeared to many as if CORE drank the free market kool-aid. Nevertheless, CORE and Kelso fundamentally entered from two different spaces and motivations when it came to the two-income theory. Kelso's theories, like Huey Long's, resulted from his belief that capitalism needed saving and served as a legitimate alternative to communism's appeal. Black power populists in CORE, however, held no ideological allegiance to either communism or capitalism. They simply wanted something that worked.

Second, CORE became synonymous with betrayal when it accepted funds from foundations and the government in order to push forward its black economic power programming. Brooklyn CORE's Sonny Carson was especially enraged and lividly told CORE leaders that talks with foundations and the government opened CORE's black power program to cooptation and control.[32] Finally, he contended that CORE had—in effect—"negated its responsibility to black people. They were talking about reform, black capitalism, and repairing a structure that had humiliated, dehumanized, and murdered black people."[33] Unsatisfied with the proceedings of the 1968 Columbus, Ohio, convention, Carson and his chapter members left. Sixteen other chapters walked out with him. Carson and many others blamed McKissick and Innis for CORE's change in direction.

But, McKissick and Innis were not alone. There were other contributors who espoused black economic development or what Carson assumed was black capitalism. National staff and NAC members crafted CORE's black economic projects with and without McKissick and Innis. CORENCO, for example, was the brainchild of Will Ussery. The CORE black power committee—Roy Innis, Ollie Leeds, and Bonnie Barrow—encouraged the creation of a credit union. Ruth Turner and Tony Perot considered the Maryland Freedom Union the best expression of black power in the Baltimore Target City Project and supported Cleveland's CORENCO.[34] These members took a populist approach to capitalism that, to a certain extent, Innis correctly articulated as liberation.

Yet Carson insisted that national just wanted the money, and that he did not believe that increased funding necessarily prevented CORE's demise. Caron's critique was partially true. CORE wanted the money. National's financially unstable status endangered Harambee. From 1966 and into March 1967, circumstances grew so desperate that one month after CORE's black power declaration, the associate director, Lincoln Lynch, claimed that the Internal Revenue Service was about to padlock the door. McKissick and Lynch failed to obtain financial assistance from unions, and staff salaries were in arrears. Urgently, the organization asked for a loan from the Nation of Islam (NOI) for $10,000 and later $35,000. The Honorable Elijah Muhammad, NOI spiritual leader, turned them down unless some form of financial security could be produced.[35] Despite grasping at straws, by December 1966, the debt of $300,000 was decreased by $70,000 and national CORE operated on a reduced budget of $30,000 down from $45,000. Simply put, CORE needed large-scale funding for its very survival.[36]

Its survival also hinged on producing victories through black power programming. Farmer, chair of CORE's national advisory board, attempted to articulate CORE's black power agenda, and simultaneously free the organization of financial constraints. He and McKissick courted various donors and unsuccessfully tried to consolidate CORE's debts. CORE was fundamentally undercut, and some members of its honorary advisory board felt the organization should more aggressively court white liberals back into the fold. David McCall (later known for his role in producing the well-known 1970s short educational series, *School House Rock!*) lambasted the suggestion, charging that white liberals, though he himself was white, had been "sliding away" for some time. He went on to argue that during the age of black power, "liberals would not be much help anyway." Turner had sarcastically argued the same in "Organizing the Black Community for the Purpose of Promoting the Interests and Concerns of the Black People." She declared that without black power how would white liberals "have rationalized their disenchantment with a civil rights movement they could no longer lead nor understand?"[37]

Donor criticisms aside, CORE banked on foundation and governmental assistance from white liberals who held greater access to resources. McKissick had built much of his directorship on reducing CORE's financial obligations, and he could say he halved CORE's debt at tenure's end. But staff and NAC were increasingly frustrated that in the interest of cutting costs, McKissick did not build the organization. NAC's assessment of McKissick, however, was somewhat unfair. In order to successfully sustain Target City, CORE needed to shore up its financial footing. It was not an easy task, especially given Ford's insufficient grant. There were few entities with the monies to financially back CORENCO, let alone create multiple versions of it, except one—the American federal government. This was why CORE chose to deal with Nixon despite the divisions and criticisms that came from members like Sonny Carson.[38]

In late winter 1967, the national office decided to send Associate Director Roy Innis to Harvard's Institute of Politics at the John F. Kennedy School of Government. Innis was CORE's rising star, particularly after the earlier formation of the Harlem Commonwealth Council in 1967—a New York–based, all-male-led community development corporation. Innis had risen from among the ranks of Harlem CORE and became a mover and shaker among its leadership in the mid 1960s. In 1965, he accepted Harlem CORE's chairmanship. Two years later, at the 1967 convention in California, he became the national second vice chairman. Six months later, Floyd McKissick made him associate national director. It was presumed that McKissick eventually intended to hand the top position to Innis.

At the Harvard Institute Innis met with Gar Alperovitz and John McClaughry. Alperovitz and McClaughry were two political counterparts who came to economic development via different models. McClaughry was a lifelong Republican and Alperovitz, a similarly dedicated Democrat. Miami University granted McClaughry his bachelor of arts in 1958. In 1963, he received his master's in political science from the University of California at Berkeley. Vermonters elected McClaughry to its state house in 1968 and 1970. Before becoming a Vermont state senator in the 1980s, McClaughry held a position as senior policy adviser and speechwriter for Gov. Ronald Reagan for his 1980 campaign.

Gar Alperovitz was nothing short of a die-hard leftist. He received his bachelor's from the University of Wisconsin-Madison, his master's from the University of California, Berkeley, and his PhD in political economy from the University of Cambridge. His first book, *Atomic Diplomacy: Hiroshima and Potsdam*, shocked the academic world in 1965 when he suggested that the decision to use atomic weapons was unnecessary and emanated from cold war political maneuvering. Alperovitz became legislative director in both houses of Congress shortly after receiving his doctorate degree. He subsequently spent his intellectual career challenging capitalism and arguing for alternative models to economic development.

Alperovitz and McClaughry crafted with CORE a bill for a government-sanctioned community development model. Southern black activists, northern black power advocates, legal experts, tax attorneys, economists, businesspersons, graduate students, and campaign staffers from Richard Nixon, Hubert H. Humphrey, and Robert F. Kennedy joined them at the institute and added more elements. There they cultivated a legislative plan that provided financial and structural support for this federally backed economic development corporation. The legislative proposal, entitled the Community Self Determination Bill, became CORE's second step toward black economic liberation.[39]

After weeks of debates, arguments, and late nights, the group hammered out a basic concept for a national CDC proposal. The authors initiated a call for a federally funded entity with regional headquarters, and subsequent city-based community corporations. Federally charted CDCs were authorized only for populations between 5,000 to 300,000. Resident branches determined services and defined neighborhood needs through a localized referendum process. The law prohibited profits from any business going to one or a few individuals. Instead, branch CDCs would finance community service projects (health care, nonprofit housing, legal aid, day care, and education) and/or disperse profit acquisitions among the community. The bill also authorized the creation of community development banks as well as a secondary financing institution—similar to the Farm Credit System. Attached to the bill was a tax amendment that granted unique status to community development corporations.[40]

Development corporations were designed to provide welfare, health care, consumer education, business ownership, homeownership, neighborhood renewal planning, and community representation regarding public policy. All CDC businesses had to be 10 percent owned by residents in the area. Ownership went only to residents whose median income fell below national level. Corporation stocks sold at $5.00 each for cash or sweat equity and each member had a vote regardless of holding. CDC management was led by nine board of directors selected by the 10 percent owners. Most importantly, all community nonprofits aimed for eventual self-sufficiency.[41]

In order to garner further support for the Community Self Determination Bill, CORE's black power leadership turned again to the 1968 presidential candidates. Surprisingly, they received the most feedback from Republican candidate Richard Milhous Nixon. John McClaughry, Institute Fellow and special assistant to

Community Affairs for Richard Nixon's campaign, played a key role in setting up a meeting between CORE leaders and the candidate in late spring 1968. Ultimately, Nixon offered additional legal and technical support. To some, the secret meeting and the subsequent help left a nefariousness impression of CORE as bought and sold to the Richard Nixon campaign.[42]

However, Nixon was not the only candidate to give CORE aid. Floyd McKissick and James Farmer met numerous times with Robert F. Kennedy from 1966 to 1968. Despite Kennedy's publicly expressed outrage and distance from Floyd McKissick/CORE's black power message, the presidential runner helped CORE with is debt out of political gratitude to Farmer. The former national director gave Kennedy major assistance during the New York judge "Surrogate Fight of 1966," a political free-for-all in Harlem, which Kennedy used to assert total dominion of the New York Democratic Party.[43] According to Farmer, Kennedy frankly asked him what he wanted in exchange. Farmer used the opportunity to discuss CORE's financial status and asked for help wiping out the organization's debt.

Kennedy had Farmer and McKissick set up a tax-exempt arm for the organization, and instructed them to call all creditors and "offer them 25 cents on the dollar. Be prepared to go up to 35, 40, even 50." Kennedy then noted that "their alternative is to get nothing because you'll be forced into bankruptcy. They'll take it." Finally he told Farmer, "let's do a dinner. Have McKissick's guys, whoever he is, get in touch with my guys and pick out a ballroom, a big ballroom, and $100 a plate and we'll fill it. Let's get to work on it."[44]

Thus, it was Kennedy who helped CORE dig out from under its debt. Additionally, most political insiders viewed Harvard Institute of Politics as a think tank for Robert Kennedy's campaign. As such, Kennedy's debt reduction aid and the Harvard Institute's resources combined with Nixon's technocrats to facilitate the next phase of CORE's existence. Until the presidency was decided, it appeared as if CORE was the winner.[45]

The bipartisanship, which marked the bill's creation carried over to its sponsorship. The community self-determination bill was introduced in the House by thirty-six Republicans and twelve House Democrats who signed off as sponsors. On July 12, 1968, several senators across party lines (nineteen Democrats and fourteen Republicans) backed the bill. Advocates included Republicans Charles Percy, Jacob Javits, and Howard Baker, along with John Tower, an extreme conservative from Texas, and Democrats John Conyers, Gaylord Nelson, Edmund Muskie, George McGovern, and Fred Harris.[46] Once in Congress, Presidential candidate Richard Nixon urged consideration but not endorsement, Nelson Rockefeller was silent, and Eugene McCarthy endorsed its basic principles. Kennedy likely would have backed the bill, but had been assassinated a month prior.[47]

Despite bipartisan backing, Congress contentiously debated the legislation's merits. The bill was numbered at over 180 pages, a size that led co-contributor John McClaughry to suggest that many condemned it without having read it. For those who did read the bill, political reasons for or against were varied and many. Due to its large structure, the community development corporation potentially knocked out any competing CDCs by forcing one local unified entity. This appeared to some congressmen as antithetical to free market principles of competition. A few registered concern over what they believed were separatist implications within the bill after a decade-long fight for integration. Others contended that participation by the poor potentially skewed the organizations away from expert management and opened the door to too much democracy. Some challenged the premise of wealth share and ownership as a viable alternative given the more immediate need of economic security via a paying job.[48]

Not many members of the congressional black caucus supported the act. Representative John Conyers, who helped introduce the bill, also expressed some later concern about Nixon's commitment to the bill after his presidential victory. Yet ironically, the caucus submitted a similar list of recommendations to the president for consideration. They called for a publicly funded development bank, a federally backed entity that provided loan guarantees and security for CDC firms, an increase in funding for development corporations, and provisions for technical assistance.[49]

The final political blow came from congressmen who claimed that the community self-determination bill smacked of communism. Community capitalism and profit sharing dispersed funds and overturned individualized free market profiteering. Second, community development banks undermined individual enterprise by giving CDCs first pick to business loans. Worse, community businesses could become competition to already established local companies who likely could not compete. What was more disconcerting was that these federally backed nonprofits indirectly made the state the arbiter of wealth redistribution. As far as these proponents were concerned, the CSD bill was a prelude to mini communist states.[50]

While politicians raised concerns from one direction, civil rights activists also failed to grasp CSD's potential for national transformation. The Reverend Franklin Florence of Rochester, New York, snidely suggested that the legislation be torn up because "you can't start out wrong and end up right," and also referred to it as "smooth honky talk." The underlying premise was that government mandated community control was, in fact, not community control. Peter McNeish in his piece "Where Does the Money Come From?" implied that such centralized power was a run-up to clunky bureaucratic structures and power struggles within the black community.[51]

Former Harlem CORE chairman Clarence Funnye also condemned the bill. Funnye criticized Innis's formulation of CSD as separatist economics. In an essay called "We Don't All Have to Be in the Ghetto Just to Be Brothers," he recounted the story of one activist who proselytized that ghettoization of the black community would not lead to economic development. Manufacturing plants had left the city, but some resided a short distance away in suburbs. Instead of relying on a black economic enclave, the black community had to follow the jobs out of the city. He also insisted that ultimately separatism (and by extension the CSD Act) was a tool of white supremacy.[52]

Former CORE program director Norman Hill took a different approach in his criticism of the bill. Hill argued that community control and self-determination depended on a "commitment from the majority of Americans to provide the economic security that is the basis for social justice and political freedom." Hill was actually right in his assessment. Whether one supported CORE or the Black Manifesto, both depended upon the state or institutional grants for reparations. Harkening back to the Civil War, Hill argued that America made its position clear when it said no to "forty acres and a mule" for newly freed slaves.[53]

Most of the antagonism among activists flowed from Nixon's association with the bill and their fundamental mistrust of the newly elected president. Nixon's relationship to the black community was more than strained. Individually, his racist ideas about black inferiority dramatically hindered personal relations with many black leaders, including those in his own administration. Second, Nixon's 1968 and 1972 campaign manager, John Mitchell, crafted a voter strategy aimed directly at folding in disaffected southern and western conservative Democrats into the Republican Party. These courted constituents, whose major political goal included undoing the victories of school desegregation and civil rights, openly challenged hard-fought federal laws for black equality. Added to that, Nixon's Supreme Court nomination of segregationist judges, lackadaisical enforcement of school desegregation, and political ties to staunch racist congressmen essentially terminated any possibility of good relations for most black leaders.[54]

Of the various other opponents, many believed arguments coming from economists and academics were the most damaging. Arthur Blaustein was particularly caustic in his condemnation of the CSD bill. Blaustein, like other detractors, continued to incorrectly tie the bill to bourgeois "black capitalism" and enrichment of the few, arguing that "when a Republican administration backs a community control bill, we need to take a hard look."[55] Although this patently ignored how the bill was created and the fact that Democratic congressmen also backed it, there was something to be said about the uneasiness of any association with Nixon. Blaustein also pointed to the presence of Title I-D in the Economic Opportunity Act, directly geared toward economic development of the ghetto. Poignantly, he drew attention to Hough as an example of existing community development projects already in operation. He also maintained that there were similar policies already reflected in OEO's mission as well as other nonprofit national groups. Potentially Blaustein might have been referring to the National Economic Development and Law Center (NEDLC), who over its first few years under his leadership facilitated the creation of close to five hundred CDCs in urban and rural areas. Thus, Blaustein's argument was not without self-interest as any federally backed national CDC potentially competed with, even challenged NEDLC's work.[56]

Andrew Brimmer, first and only black member of the Federal Reserve Board, took the opposite view to Blaustein, and claimed that protected ghetto markets were too poor and too narrow to support profit levels. Thus, CSD could not stymie affluent black consumers' integration into the national market. In "The Negro in the National Economy," Brimmer insisted that the black community had no capital, no skill, a small market, high potential for small business failure, and faced big business competition. Instead, black Americans had to enter all levels within conglomerates, increase technology sophistication, and become a managerial class. Any future black business had to make the shift from individual proprietorship to corporation.[57]

Problematically, Brimmer's approach locked out black poor people, and thus would condemn any civil rights group to the same charges CORE unfairly faced. Additionally, it did not solve the more essential problem of industrial and business loss in urban cities. There were no corporations in which the black working or middle class might become a managerial caste. Economist Courtney Blackman also disputed Brimmer's perspective, and noted that he failed to account for the "psychological and institutional aspects of black economic development." Similar to historian Goodwyn's "somebodiness" concept, Blackman suggested that noneconomic factors (racial pride, community solidarity, etc.) could play an important role and facilitate economic growth with equal impact to facts and figures.[58]

Sar Levitan in *Community Self Determination and Entrepreneurship: Their Promises and Limitations* agreed with Brimmer's supposition that outside competition hindered separate based economies. Additionally, even if the federal government moved to create a protective market, there was no guarantee that those who profited would remain in the community. Levitan asserted, "once a resident of the ghetto collects enough green power . . . he would be likely to move out." Finally, the ghetto economic development approach with one empowered entity ignored community diversity.[59]

Sociologist Martin Rein acknowledged that the bill incorporated broader community participation and profit distribution, but cogently noted that middle-class expansion eventually fed into an overall capitalist system. As black middle-class markets increased, predominantly white businesses would become increasingly attracted. Thus, in cases of sudden competition, there was bound to be a future conflict between "black and white capital."[60] Black businesses with less capital were likely to lose in such a race.[61]

Moreover, Rhein pointed out that repetitive reference to taxation decrease and profits allocated to social services appealed to conservative elements by exempting the federal government from its duties to the people. The bill also required the eventual phasing out and repayment of government funds. The CSD built reimbursement into its guidelines to create an alliance with the Republican Party and push through the bill with bipartisan support. However, most small businesses tended to die off quickly. Thus, the probability of repayment was likely weak.

It does bear noting that the erratic rise and fall of businesses could negatively effect group ownership as well. This certainly proved to be the case with HADC's ownership of McDonald's in Cleveland. The business failed to maintain a profit for a variety of reasons. As the franchise operated in the red over the next two years, the HADC board voted to sell it to an individual proprietor, thus ending its concerted effort to realize community ownership. Still, had CSD passed, its national apparatus might have provided aid to HADC's McDonald's project, which effectively had little support for its solvency problems.[62]

And, of course, any repayment plan also meant that CORE did not receive recoupment funds but simply a governmental loan. For Rein, CSD surreptitiously reinforced ideas of blackness as social burden and allowed the state to ignore the political and social demands of the reparations movement. It appeared to Rein that the CSD effectively acted as an apology for black people's presence in the United States.[63]

The *Georgetown Law Journal* provided an alternative view to Rein's contention that CSD failed to take into account market constraints or encouraged an image of black burden. It argued that the bill provided economic and educational opportunities, ownership of productive capital and property, improved health, safety, and living conditions, and enhanced the opportunity for meaningful decision making for poor residents. This process was especially enhanced by the requirement for a minimum 10 percent pledge to community stock. Additionally, all shareholders— comprised only of community residents—had a right to elect a board of directors responsible for the day-to-day operation of the organization. The elected directors appointed CDC officers, but at any time displeased residents could select new board members.

The law journal's major concern rested not in the notion of capitalism or CORE but rather the structure of the CDC itself. According to the author, there was too much potential for CDCs to take over municipal duties. As such, it potentially left any group vulnerable to judicial or legislative attack. Nonprofits could not just be economically inclined but also had to be politically adept as well. To avoid the political maneuvering required, the journal suggested augmenting programs already in operation.[64]

Intended or not, the journal's suggestion amounted to a dual approach that merged black protest with economic development. The decrease in direct action— now transmuted into community organizing—forced few companies to invest in neighborhoods or increase employment. Poor black communities were left with neither the opportunity to create or acquire businesses for economic development nor the energy to fight businesses that maintained racial status quo. Thus, the actual unfortunate aspect to CORE's move to economic development and professionalized community organization was its withdrawal of direct action as an arsenal for black empowerment.

Arguably, this tactical decline was also responsible for why the bill languished in Congress and the White House. Congress remanded the act to the Committee on Finance for discussion. The Committee on Finance consulted with the Department of Agriculture, HEW, HUD, Labor, Treasury, SEC, and the Federal Reserve. The reviews coming from various government departments were similarly mixed. The director of the Office of Economic Opportunity, Donald Rumsfeld, claimed that in the OEO's opinion, Bill S-33 was "worthy of careful consideration" but they were unable to recommend its enactment, "since we do not as yet have the information necessary to know whether the approach has been sufficiently developed from a conceptual or technical standpoint."[65] Rumsfeld's missive went to Senator Russell Long, who also held the position of committee finance chairman. The bill effectively fell flat, lost in committee evaluation.

Along with congressional indecision, the president-elect also wavered on community ownership. The bill's passage greatly depended on Nixon's willingness to follow through on his campaign promise to push for collective capitalism via the CSD bill. However, Nixon's support was lukewarm after his election. His advisers assumed few would back it, though politicians like Secretary George Romney had "expressed considerable interest in the ownership theme, dating back to his profit sharing plans at American Motors in the fifties, and continuing throughout his relations with the black community while Governor of Michigan."[66]

Nixon's insistence on individually owned businesses created further trepidation about his intentions toward economic development. Even John McClaughry, Nixon's own consultant, worried whether the new president would follow through on the bill's original design. He also greatly despised the term "black capitalism," since the phrase undermined and discredited the efforts represented in the act. In the same memorandum to Len Garment, Bryce Harlow, John Mitchell, and the President-elect Richard Nixon, he also challenged the appointment of Daniel Patrick Moynihan as a consultant on the black community given he was the "man who told Negroes their family structure was the source of their problems."[67] Indeed,

James Farmer had leaked surreptitiously the infamous memo that advocated "benign neglect" of the black community.[68] Thus, McClaughry's critiques further solidified the notion that Nixon was out of touch with black folks.

Nevertheless, Nixon permitted White House staff from various agencies to evaluate CSD's potential. David Kennedy, then secretary of the treasury, opposed the Community Self Determination Bill. Still, he liked certain aspects of it, particularly tax incentives to promote community development and community development banks. Kennedy's main point of objection stemmed from his concern that the CSD granted too much power to an alternate governmental body. There were too many subsidies, and he also disagreed with the allowance of Federal Reserve earnings as a resource, insisting that such an endeavor likely added to the overall deficit.[69]

Secretary of Commerce Maurice Stans claimed that even if CSD was successful, it ultimately failed "to integrate the disadvantaged into the business enterprise and social systems enjoyed by the majority. The bill would, instead, result in separate economic and social systems for the disadvantaged by operating independent of the mainstream of American life."[70] Stans was not far off the mark, in that Roy Innis certainly intended it that way.

Despite opposition, the secretary of housing and urban development, George Romney, embraced the idea—as the Nixon campaign assumed—though he too felt there were parts that needed revision. HUD also noted that the cost of undertaking CSD would be high but argued that "the attempt can and should be made. The alternative is to allow further decay of our tormented cities, and further despair and bitterness among its poor and minority citizens."[71]

As the idea circulated in early 1969, responses within the White House to CSD eventually boiled down to questions about costs and effort. White House aid Charles Williams noted that the proposals to expand ownership, as exampled by CSD, took too narrow a view on economic development and current markets. "Mom and pop" businesses were too small in impact and "ownership of a few five dollar shares in a community development corporation" actually did not offer much in the way of financial stability. Most of Williams's criticisms hinged on the inability of these programs to immediately eliminate poverty and remove the poor from public assistance. Proposals had to move the poor from "public assistance to economic independence," or it was not worth the try.[72]

Nonetheless, Williams did suggest that CSD be rewritten to reflect a "bolder, more imaginative approach." The new plan had to be an adequate scale, must meet standards for long-run economic feasibility and decrease public subsidy, include some stake in society like direct employment, synchronize national development with growth policies, consolidate capital into one national institution, provide technical and managerial expertise, and ensure maximum employment and participation of minority persons in job training. Williams wanted business equity held in trust, stock transferred first to creditors and then employees, subsidy based only on a production design that culminated in independence within ten years, and a budget no more than what it took to get to the moon (NASA's budget was less than 1 percent of the federal budget under Nixon). The absurdity of Williams's expectations reflected a broader attitude of political expediency that pushed for an easy victory over economic inequality without community contribution or self-determination, government investment, a workable timeline, and with creditor pre-eminence, which stymied employee buy-in.[73]

McClaughry took the opening left to him by White House staff and rehashed the 1968 CSD bill. The second and third iteration came in the form of the Community Corporation Act of 1970 and 1971 (never introduced). However, each of these suffered the same fate as the Community Self Determination bill. Arguments still continued to revolve around the fear that such entities were too expensive and bureaucratic to create or might become "semi-political units of government."[74]

Ultimately, the black community suffered most from the failed passage of the Community Self Determination Bill. Individual nonprofits became susceptible to the vagaries of presidential administrations that cut financing or obliterated OEO—their main funding source. Neighborhood groups had no national apparatus by which to lobby in Washington, DC. Local development corporations had no central mechanism for creating best practices models by which to compare or borrow successful project ideas. Individual groups were left to pursue local banks for funding support—an exercise without guarantees of success in either obtaining monies or receiving loans at a good rate. Small CDCs lacked power or influence with larger corporations, and could not induce a reversal of manufacturing and industrial loss. It effectively forced economic development on an incremental scale. The bill's failure terminated budding community transformation and ended the opportunity for mass shared wealth.

CORE's communal wealth plan depended greatly on an honest partnership with government and an internal leadership with clear standards and objectives. But, neither of these components were in place. Campaign promises dissolved under Nixon's presidential administration. On the one hand, Nixon appeared somewhat open to black leadership concerns. His commentary about black capitalism, the extension of affirmative action, and the hiring of liberals into advisory and high government positions implied the possibility of a moderate Republican administration. Yet, what Nixon did with the left hand, soon came undone with the right—literally—as these two forces viciously vied for position and influence. Often, the administration's duplicitous nature stemmed from political expediency and which of these two factions—liberal or conservative—made the better constituency case.[75]

Because the administration incorporated a liberal faction, the community self-determination bill did not die dramatically on the congressional floor but instead became part of a larger movement that morphed into what Nixon aides called Expanded Ownership (EO). Expanded Ownership appeared in Nixon's 1970 State of the Union Address. In it he called for reforms that allowed each citizen a chance at the "American dream." According to Nixon, this meant voting rights, equal employment, and "new opportunities for expanded ownership. Because in order to be secure in their human rights, people need access to property rights."[76] In fact, a number of CORE former affiliates and associates found a place in the files on Expanded Ownership. The EO files included references to CORE's CSD bill, McKissick Enterprises, Kelso's Second Income, and even Hough Area Development Corporation. Leonard Garment, who became EO's steward in the Nixon administration, essentially got saddled with the "minority" detail, handling all manner of events associated with civil rights concerns from the American Indian Movement (AIM) to economic development programming for urban communities. It was Garment who took up the mantel of CORE's CSD bill and linked it with Kelso, CDCs, HUD housing, and black capitalism—Nixon style. Garment explored the possibility for a revamped CSD bill and pushed the administration to more seriously consider "expanded ownership."

Garment investigated various iterations of expanded ownership. At his behest, the assistant secretary of commerce researched "democratic nations" engaged in expanded ownership. Garment also visited Deforest Brown, executive director of Hough Area Development Corporation, and hoped to gain clarity on how to improve federal program coordination with local groups. Garment requested and reviewed publications on expanded ownership, community development, urban and rural cooperatives, second-income (Kelso plan), and universal capitalism.[77]

But aside from Cleveland and CORE associated EO projects, Garment also deemed groups and ideas like FIGHTON, a Rochester CDC, the Harlem Commonwealth Council (Innis was executive director), and the A. Philip Randolph Institute's Freedom Budget as best practices. Even the small efforts of individual companies found their way into these materials. Rotodyne Manufacturing, a company that produced devices that reduced air and water pollution, bypassed SEC rules and distributed stock to its black and Puerto Rican workers through a third party nonprofit entity. Rotodyne designated a nonprofit CDC group to act on behalf of its workers and their community and serve as a conduit for scholarships.[78]

As Garment built a case for expanded ownership, special assistant to community affairs, John McClaughry, joined the White House aide in advocating for an enhanced position for expanded ownership in Nixon's policies. Though McClaughry was hardly a CORE associate, he articulated CORE's agenda via the bill and assertively situated his consultant company into position as the lead policy adviser on CSD, especially after the White House determined that CORE leader Roy Innis was too volatile.[79]

McClaughry distilled the 180-page Community Self Determination bill into a five-page missive and brochure on community economic development as the key to expanded ownership.[80] McClaughry surmised that capital acquisition might be obtained through cooperative or community development banks. He recommended regulatory amendments to the Security and Exchange Act to facilitate stock sale by community corporations; outlined potential sites of joint private/public ventures; and suggested policies which might "encourage the creation of profit-seeking community corporations with a broad base of ownership."[81]

As a Nixon insider, McClaughry tried again and again to focus the administration on economic self-determination, a concept he learned from black conservative and Newark Black Power Conference organizer Nathan Wright. According to McClaughry, the Nixon campaign requested his assistance because of his work on the Home Ownership Foundation Act of 1967 and his knowledge about issues affecting the black community—something McClaughry attributed to his association with Wright. Still, McClaughry noted the irony and recalled that "it occurred to me that there might be some mordant symbolism in the Republican presidential candidate having to obtain counsel on inner city minority issues from a Harvard Fellow who had grown up in an Illinois farm town and built himself a log cabin in the back woods of northeastern Vermont."[82]

Yet, McClaughry became one of expanded ownership's most ardent advocates and kept the concept on Len Garment's radar. He wrote to Garment, "I would naturally subsume the remains of black capitalism and minority enterprise under this new rubric . . . I could not possibly be more convinced that the party that grasps the significance of expanding ownership will be the *party of the future*." McClaughry believed that if Garment set up a meeting with Nixon, he could convince the president to "comprehend the historic potential."[83]

While Garment pushed the idea through various government departments, McClaughry submitted proposals to other funding sources including the Ford and Sabre Foundations. Additionally, McClaughry suggested that Garment turn EO into a department or agency as a better substitute to the Office of Minority Business, which had no real sources, high personnel turnover, narrow scope, and was not inclusive of all.[84] But, the agency suggestion came off as an even worse idea to White House officials who saw it as too unwieldy a bureaucratic structure.

Expanded ownership as an ideal did not end with Nixon's removal from the White House. However, changing dynamics, which paralleled the rise of the far right in the Republican Party, perverted expanded ownership. EO, like other aspects of the 1960s, underwent a transmutation by far right conservatives that grossly rearticulated movement goals as hyper-individualized, capitalist-inspired, personal freedoms. Ronald Reagan's July 1974 speech to Young Americans for Freedom, titled "Expanded Capital Ownership: The Only Answer," argued the positive attributes of his version of expanded ownership. According to Reagan, the concept undermined labor union control by granting employees direct ownership within the company. Without government controls, such companies represented the best form of democratic expression. And more important, expanded ownership facilitated mass consumption. Reagan used the idea again, this time for more nefarious reasons, in an August 1987 speech to justify the expansion of "people's capitalism" in Central America as an alternative to communist governments.[85]

If Richard Nixon was suspect as tricky "Dick," Ronald Reagan was the devil himself. And therein lay the explanation for why expanded ownership never received attention from civil rights groups. Undoubtedly, without CORE and the Community Self Determination bill, the likelihood was slim that anyone within the Nixon administration would have given black economic development a second thought. However, allegorically speaking, the Community Self Determination bill and expanded ownership unequivocally exemplified the metaphor of a prime steak and potatoes dinner served on a trashcan lid. Presentation was everything. No matter how good it appeared, no civil rights organization or activist would touch it.[86]

Of course, none of this represented the intentions of CORE or CDCs. For that matter, it did not characterize the intentions of Kelso either, who believed that singular ownership should be limited to allow for broader participation. And ironically enough, Reagan's conception even ignored the Nixon administration's understanding of expanded ownership. While Reagan believed expanded ownership disrupted the role of government in American lives, civil rights activists linked government and private corporations as essential to equalizing economic equality. Few activists could embrace expanded ownership after it took such wayward turns from the original grassroots idea.

In the end, the Community Self Determination bill's abortive attempt to revitalize CORE or garner governmental aid fell flat. In many ways, it was the best of the black populist sensibility within CORE. Despite the many criticisms, the CSD legislatively crafted a pragmatic pathway for economic equality. The bill sought to force economic concessions from the government, generate jobs, and rework the capitalist system. Its creation was not a symbol of backroom political deals or bourgeois ascendency by CORE, but a genuine effort to transform the everyday lives of black poor people. As Sar Levinson noted, it was never a "magic solution to the vast problems of the ghetto . . . but an experimental program."[87] Its innovation was a worthy effort by CORE that ultimately failed.

# 9

# Until . . .

IT WAS ALL ABOUT a pretty girl. That's why Roy Innis became a member of CORE. He originally came to Harlem chapter meetings to impress Doris Funnye. This original happenstance transcended from local activism to the national directorship in 1968. Dominance in CORE had turned into a competition of the last man standing, and Roy Innis stood atop a pile of would-be leaders.[1]

In January 1968, McKissick's appointment of Innis to associate director greatly upset NAC. McKissick soon came to believe it was a bad idea too. June 19, 1968, he rebuked Innis for asserting his name as the new national director before McKissick officially retired. Although he originally intended to name him as a successor, he now believed him unfit. He also accused Kermit Scott and Tony Perot, along with their wives, for being involved in Innis's attempted coup for national director. He went on to note that he had "no desire to leave a divided organization," and he hoped that Innis would "redirect [his] efforts toward developing unity and building CORE."[2]

Despite McKissick's willingness to leave the national directorship to Innis, many CORE leaders wanted no part of a future CORE with him as national leader. To no surprise, the 1968 Convention in Columbus, Ohio, became tumultuous and ended badly on an undecided note.[3] Aside from the issue of CORE's financial woes, delegates had to choose who would continue CORE's path toward black power. However, convention participants had relatively few, if any, options.

Ruth Turner Perot's father fell terminally ill in the summer of 1967. She subsequently left CORE right after Cleveland received the Target City grant. The Ford Foundation lamented her absence, noting that Turner had kept the Cleveland chapter together and was well regarded in the black community. Her resignation was a "blow." Months later, Turner landed the job of James Farmer's special assistant at the Health, Education, and Welfare (HEW) Department, the last bastion of liberalism within the Nixon administration. Though the two had "frequently been at odds in CORE," he brought her to HEW, because he needed someone with political acumen. According to Farmer, Turner, "a tiger with sharp claws," managed to usher through the appointment of six minority regional directors of Head Start, out of ten, at the Office of Child Development.[4]

Tony Perot, whose proposals and negotiations led to funding for all three Target City Projects, also resigned. May 29, 1968, a month before Ford Foundation sent its second allotment to national CORE, Perot informed McKissick of his decision. The national director responded, "I accept your resignation with much regret and mixed emotion . . . useless to say, I do not want you to leave the organization as I have said numerous times before." Perot worked with CORE as a consultant, but soon thereafter, the Urban Institute, a nonprofit think tank on social and economic issues, offered him a job.[5]

The likeliest candidate, Will Ussery, made it clear he would not run. According to Ford, Ussery was "a planner by inclination," who desired a degree in urban planning and community development. His decision to pursue graduate education led to his short time with CORENCO. Ussery had brought "prestige and expression to the project" but his departure and that of others effectively terminated for Ford any interest in CORE projects.[6] The former CORE national chairman also planned to marry, and felt disinclined to fight Roy Innis for CORE.

Art Evans went to work for the state of Ohio. Don Bean served in the Stokes administration in the Office on Aging where he oversaw the completion of urban gardens for Cleveland renewal projects. Nate Smith and Frank Anderson left CORE and then HADC to become independent businessmen. Floyd McKissick created McKissick Enterprises and worked to build Soul City until the early 1980s. Herb Callendar changed his name to Makaza Kumanyika after traveling throughout Africa. He received his master's degree in agricultural science from Cornell University, and moved to North Carolina to help black farmers. Lincoln Lynch, former associate director, had already departed before Turner, frustrated from no pay and infighting. He became vice president of the New York Urban Coalition, an organization devoted to the end of poverty and racial conflict. Sonny Carson and the black revolutionary nationalists insisted CORE had become a "tool to blind black people" and a "vehicle for personal fame"—no doubt partially referring to CORE's dependence on federal funds and foundation grants.[7] When it became clear that Innis would lead CORE and continue on this path, Carson and Brooklyn withdrew in protest. Other chapters followed.

The second CORE meeting in St. Louis ended horribly as well. Innis pushed through a constitution that diminished the autonomous status of local CORE chapters. In protest, Chicago CORE leader Robert Lucas opposed Innis. This time, he and his chapter left CORE. A total of forty-seven representatives followed from chapters in Illinois, Pennsylvania, Wisconsin, and Ohio. Their faction later regrouped and formed the Black Liberation Alliance.[8]

Battle weary, economically overwhelmed, and preoccupied by personal and familial affairs, many populist and revolutionary proponents took jobs or joined other movements that reflected other iterations of black power, economic and community development, antipoverty work, or social service. In every case, these positions reflected the spirit of their civil rights activism in CORE. And, Roy Innis remained.

Innis's ascension to power marked a transition away from the more inclusive aim of CORENCO to a more conservative style of black nationalism. As Meier and Rudwick noted, "ironically, CORE now unequivocally committed to separatism, proved unable to harness the surge of black nationalism. CORE stood transformed, but it was no longer on the cutting edge of the black revolt."[9] The black populist agenda lingered on under the Innis administration, but the national office devoted relatively little attention to Cleveland as a national project thereafter. Under Innis, CORE solidly espoused black separatism and placed heavy emphasis on autonomous nation-states.[10]

Under new leadership, CORE presented a three-part program for black liberation, the third of which—redraft of the U.S. Constitution—never occurred. Phase I involved passage of the Community Self Determination bill. The bill failed to move in Congress or the White House. However, Innis made one last effort in 1972 at the Gary Black Political Convention. In a surprising turn of events, delegates not only endorsed the bill, but also added it to the black agenda platform.[11] CORE shortly thereafter followed up with another legislative bill entitled the Rural Development Incentive Act (RDI). RDI effectively served as the rural version of CSD. The act was designed to bring industrial and commercial firms to rural areas and facilitate employment and collective ownership. It, like the Community Self Determination Bill, went nowhere. Thus ended Phase I.[12]

Phase II proposed to control institutions that "materially affect" the black community. Innis incorporated police, schools, government, and capital instruments under this rubric. Phase II programmatically took the form of a unitary school plan, a proposal designed to give black parents independent and separate control of black school districts.[13] Problematically, his insistence on district separation reminded many of school segregation, making it difficult to claim "black nationalist" status when it appeared to sync with the philosophies of people like segregationist George Wallace. When CORE filed an amicus curiae against bussing, the organization's reputation worsened.[14]

Still, Innis's position was not a solitary attempt. Inevitably, the slow process of integration and its deleterious effect led many to advocate for an independent black school movement. Innis thus articulated a growing feeling throughout the black community that it was better to maintain community control of education. He officially received backing from the Gary National Black Political Convention in 1972. Though some resented the idea, Innis managed to push through a resolution, which was subsequently backed again by a post conference steering committee. CORE later attempted to establish an independent Harlem school. Although it failed in Harlem, CORE did establish a school in the Bronx.[15]

Although nearly defunct, local Cleveland CORE still supported the national office. From 1970 to 1972, Cleveland CORE attached its name to various events, but the chapter remained relatively quiet.[16] The local branch sponsored a literacy project, advocated for a separate school system in Cleveland, and promoted a fashion benefit show for the local chapter.[17] Interestingly, the CORE "women's committee" sponsored a fashion show. What this gender distinction meant for black female membership or leadership within Cleveland CORE remains a question. Notably, up until this point, no CORE chapter maintained such a body or distinguished women's activities in CORE actions. Despite the implications, the local organization remained mostly immobile during this period.

December 1972 brought a revitalized local chapter. Charles Cook re-chartered the chapter under the leadership of Rev. Alvin E. Ward, a former CORE member. Cleveland CORE reactivated a third time.[18] The third formation of Cleveland CORE engaged in direct action demonstrations and agitation against police brutality. Throughout the year, it served as the lead organization in the struggle for a citizen's police review board and better officer training. Cleveland CORE also held a hearing detailing police brutality accounts and installed a hotline to report incidents. The chapter eventually acquired assistance from Black Unity House, the Black Affairs Office of Cuyahoga Community College, SWP, Families United for Prison Reform, the Episcopal Dioceses, and the Lutheran Metropolitan Ministry.[19] The police brutality demonstration was the last civil rights project by Cleveland CORE. Despite renewed activism, it failed to sustain itself, and the chapter died yet another time—this time not to be revived.

While Cleveland CORE surged briefly back into the civil rights scene, Charles Cook became an officer in national CORE. While still Midwest regional director, he traveled with Roy Innis to Uganda to observe Idi Amin's government. Cook proselytized Uganda as the only African country offering dual citizenship to black Americans. He also explained CORE's agreement to recruit doctors, dentists, technicians, and other skilled professionals to help Idi Amin's government rebuild Uganda.[20] Like Cleveland CORE, however, Cook remained relatively inactive after his 1973 trip to Africa.

CORE continued to advance other programs and policies after Cleveland CORE's demise. Economic development did not disappear under Innis, but it generally failed to materialize. In the later 1970s, CORE planned a job venture with Prudential International Commodities. The company would establish plants in Harlem and the South Bronx. However, few believed CORE could complete such an immense project—equated to be $40 million. It never did.[21]

Innis's CORE also established an official Department of African Affairs. The national director visited political officials in Kenya, Tanzania, Liberia, and Guinea. He assured them that CORE would send domestic assistance and arms. He claimed the organization also planned to lobby for trade agreements. None of these proposals came to fruition.[22]

Although the Department of African Affairs enhanced CORE's black internationalist program, other policy positions on Africa disastrously created fissure with former CORE leaders, and black activists broadly. Innis's stance on the Angolan conflict centrally defined this conflict. The Angola civil war began as a fight for independence. In 1975, the nation divided between two previously unified factions, the communist-backed People's Movement for the Liberation of Angola and the National Union for the Total Independence of Angola (UNITA). Western governments (including the Apartheid South African government) interceded on behalf of UNITA. In early winter 1976, Innis vowed to send recruits to back the pro-Western/South African rebels in Angola. But the notion that Innis intended to help any group supported by the apartheid government created quite a stir. It also led to accusations that he worked for the CIA. Protestors in California halted his speech, and James Farmer insisted that if Innis continued along this path, he would resign from CORE's advisory board. Mary Dennison, associate director of CORE, referred to Farmer's actions as "hysterical envy," claiming much of the reaction was much ado about nothing. But Farmer made it clear that Innis's latest decision was the final straw for him. He withdrew from CORE's national advisory board.[23]

While Innis made political decisions many activists found suspect or outlandish, he faced additional heat for his alleged gangster persona. As a matter of fact, Innis was renowned for it within CORE. It eventually exploded into the public after police brought charges against his associates and alleged Innis's collusion in physical assaults. In 1972, student peers beat Innis's son. Innis purportedly retaliated by having three CORE members beat the attackers. However, he claimed these accusations were lies meant to destroy him and CORE. Nevertheless, three convicted CORE members received probation for their actions. Six years later, Innis faced denunciations once more when associates claimed he put a hit out on his adversary, Waverly Yates, a competitor for the national directorship. According to newspapers, Innis allies planned Yates's assassination but never carried through on his orders. Innis was not convicted for this alleged crime either.[24]

Innis's erratic decisions and questionable character as leader of CORE eventually led former members to call for his ouster from office. In 1978, Farmer and

McKissick protested Innis's usurpation of CORE and his refusal to call a national convention, which inevitably kept him in place as national director. One of the dissident voices also came from Charles Cook, who broke with Innis and sided with Farmer and McKissick. As Farmer and McKissick moved to push Innis out, the national office also came under fire for extortion. [25]

The situation in CORE festered in 1979, when Attorney General Louis Lefkowitz brought charges against Roy Innis and his aides Wendell Garnett and Mary Dennison for defrauding the public. Innis charged that the state's harassment and decision to freeze CORE's assets forced the organization to close its local elementary school. In January 1979, Innis or the state—depending on your perspective—ended the school career of 175 students at CORE's South Bronx School on Washington Avenue. [26]

Meanwhile, former CORE members picked up their pace to remove Innis as national director. In March 1979, Val Coleman, Lincoln Lynch, and Herb Callendar (Makaza Kumanyika) met with Farmer to design a program for a counter organization to CORE. The journalist wrote, "participants—now in their mid 40s to late 50s and aging, balding, or putting on weight—met in a suburban home after a testimonial dinner for Farmer the night before."[27] The imagery undercut the idea that they could bring vitality to the organization. Though previous CORE leaders made every attempt to remove Innis from the directorship, their efforts officially came to an end July 1983. A New York judge found that Waverly Yates, who declared himself national director of CORE in a parallel CORE convention, was not CORE's duly elected officer. The judge officially designated Innis the legitimate head of CORE, and there he has remained. [28]

By the early 1980s, Innis had changed his philosophy from black power advocate to Republican conservative. He no longer advocated for Swahili education. Instead, he lobbied for the removal of sex or race from school education, and pushed for more privatization of the workforce. Ultimately, he eschewed black power altogether and turned CORE into a national organization on behalf and in support of conservative, Republican philosophy. Altered so dramatically from its early origins, divided and broken, CORE became a shell of what it once was.

The special relationship that Cleveland had to CORE and CORE to Cleveland —the events that led to and inspired my mother's CORE—is chronicled here. In telling this story, this book by no means captured all of what CORE was or what it meant to the thousands who labored on its behalf. It only filled the historical gap on CORE and black nationalism, and depicted the complex interplay of local and national dynamics that pushed CORE from its early start to fight off, ignore, and eventually embrace black power. The ebb and flow of this struggle for "ownership," and the centrality of Cleveland, both city and CORE chapter, is the key to understanding CORE's larger history.

CORE never reflected one clear ideological path, and along the way, many entered and left, agreed and disagreed, politicked and negotiated. The process, sometimes painful, transformed CORE from direct action to community organizing and interracialism to black power. Though many members perceived it as a veritable defection from the organization's early roots, in many ways, the first years of 1940s Cleveland CORE hinted at and created room for black power's arrival. Early founders struggled for institutional and philosophical independence from its pacifist sponsor, Fellowship of Reconciliation. What appeared as small ideological skirmishes with FOR masked critical points of power struggle and submerged disagreement over the long-term strategic practicality of nonviolence.

Few chapters reflected this repressed discontinuity like Cleveland, Ohio. Its sizable black membership hinted at the possibilities of philosophical challenge when racial ratios tipped toward numbers, which reflected CORE's constituency. The presence of militant whites in other chapters exacerbated ideological incongruences as well. National CORE managed to suppress or ignore these aberrations, partly because FOR's guiding authority pressured and steered single-mindedly toward pacifist styled goodwill direct action.

From the 1950s to early 1960s, intensified black activism pushed CORE to operate as an interracial organization within a black movement. This is an important distinction and major moment. The assertiveness of black agency via the southern freedom movement forced CORE to play nursemaid. It was too small, decentralized, unstable, and white to direct or lead the black freedom movement. Instead, it took its cues from the prevailing winds of protest. In part, this is why CORE members moved to replace its white executive director, James Robison, with African American CORE founder James Farmer.

However, this positionality situated CORE in such a way as to foreshadow who would eventually tell whom what to do. By the mid-1960s, black membership overran CORE and militant tactics overrode FOR perpetuated convictions. Still interracial, CORE's internal creed changed dramatically in order to attain and retain relevance in a period of exploding protest. Urgent calls for Freedom Now! left room for interracial alliance and nonviolent strategy, but not interracial brotherhood and nonviolent philosophy. The distinction was crucial. Alliances and strategies altered and shifted when either ceased to have applicability. As appeals for black political, social, and economic uplift mounted, 1966 ushered in new coalitions and protest methods that translated into black power. Meanwhile, white leadership retreated voluntarily or by force, and so did nonviolent direct action protest. Officially, black power took over CORE in the summer of 1966.

As if on cue, Cleveland CORE swept into national power and brought with it ideological challenges reminiscent of its 1940s period. Its members propelled and encouraged CORE's black power policy. Their approach targeted local cities for structural transformation and used government and foundation funds to politically change and economically develop two cities, Baltimore and Cleveland. In Cleveland, black power activities by CORE exposed a decidedly distinct path to black power—not quite black capitalism, not quite separatist, not quite Marxist revolutionary, but somewhere in the pragmatic middle. Black power populism hailed from a longer tradition dating back to slavery and connected with the periodic rise and fall of cooperative movements. But this transition came much to the consternation of other CORE chapters and members who felt their own kinship, owning of, and vision for CORE.

The rise and fall of Harambee was an important moment in national CORE's black power period. The success of the Stokes win and the potential of Cleveland's Target City's economic program made community development more conceivable as a CORE direction. CORENCO opened up new possibilities for community wealth distribution and a financially rejuvenated national CORE. However, business leaders, government, and the Ford Foundation rebuffed funding requests. Internal bickering added to CORENCO's woes and greatly diminished its potential. Though TCP suffered from financial strain and personnel upheaval, it signaled for CORE a different path to black power and economic stability. TCP and the CORENCO model also set parameters for a different style of operating within American capitalism. It was an idea that certainly gained traction, as exampled by Hough Area Development Corporation, which localized many of the ideas behind CORENCO.

However, the failure to nationalize CORENCO forced the national office to reconsider the funding of its community development model and to seek out other sources. Ford Foundation had systematically shorted the organization and hampered its ability to make meaningful, substantial, and sizable changes. Although CORE attempted to persuade (or threatened, depending on your perspective) banks to aid some plan of improvement for the black community, the endeavor stalled. Lack of funds, then, limited CORE's progress and maneuver into other cities and left the federal government as the last possible resource.

The Community Self Determination bill and its subsequent iterations powerfully impacted the Nixon administration's liberal and moderate faction. It motivated an exploration of expanded ownership, and generated a larger focus on economic development that included cooperatives, community development corporations, corporate ESOPs, and communal wealth. Despite CSD's concerted effort to lobby for federal monies, the many criticisms from all sides halted the experiment in place despite its great potential.

For many, CORE's association with Nixon and the federal government was intolerable. Marxist revolutionary black nationalists within CORE charged America's capitalist system with debilitating the black community and rebuked the assumption that black Americans should imitate such a structure, no matter the variation. The organization failed to challenge the American economic system, and to protect itself from outside control from governmental or nonprofit sources—all of whom were white. CORE leaders from the East coast, like Brooklyn chapter leader Sonny Carson, particularly reflected the anger and disappointment of CORE's flirtations with white money and economic systems.

Their departure along with black populists left Roy Innis to articulate a new platform for black separatism. Innis and his colleagues advocated total black control, no white membership, and separate spatial spheres of control within the United States. In other words, black communities acted as governmental, societal, and economic nation-states separate from the United States. The black power populist approach fell behind.

Thus, paradoxically, CORE actually had many owners, but not all accepted black power or the kind of black power that Cleveland CORE represented. The divisions over black power style and the personal/personnel changes among CORE members eventually took its toll on the organization and smoothed the way for Roy Innis.

It would be easy to say that black power or government financial appeal began CORE's decline and/or right turn. It was easier still to blame Roy Innis's personality and political machinations for CORE's demise. But the truth was that many forces were at work to end CORE and the movement. As Farmer noted, "It's true civil rights organizations are not nearly as influential or as effective as they were in the 1960s. We were so busy concentrating on emergencies and things immediate that we made no long range strategy. Then the erosion came, caused by economic problems and disagreements with allies."[29]

Realistically, there were other undercurrents at work as well. The 1970s depression hit cities and the black community hard. CDCs partially began to fail when government funding decreased and conservative politicians took control. Additionally, many of these institutions were too small and could not successfully make the leap to self-sufficiency and community ownership. Inflation, increased operation costs, white backlash, and a financially undercut constituency all played a hand. Black economic development, in and of itself, was not a marker of ineffectual or callous leadership. Rather, it was an experiment laid waste in an era where the black freedom movement itself gave way to social, cultural, and political dynamics.

SNCC and MFDP dissolved, and the government's counterintelligence programming wiped out militant groups like the Black Panther Party. SCLC essentially limped along with no major civil rights campaigns. Returning Vietnam soldiers, massive economic depression, drug influx, oil embargos, city deterioration, and the commodification of blackness from the "hippest trip in America," to Superfly and discos, soon replaced much of the movement. Black political power achieved massive successes with the election of black mayors, congressmen, and the first black woman to run for president on the Democratic Party ticket, Shirley Chisholm. Real and visual expressions of black freedom existed alongside structural inequalities that appeared immovable.

CORE sustained itself but in the worst ways by its transition into ultraconservatism. In its current incarnation, national CORE has few existing chapters. Direct action and community engagement, the organization deserted years ago. It sustains itself with small programs and an annual Martin Luther King award dinner that honors conservative personalities. Niger Innis, Roy Innis's son, frequently appears as CORE spokesperson and political pundit on the conservative news channel, Fox News. Whether black power advocate or integrationist, CORE has become unrecognizable to many former members. According to any and every CORE member one met, the refrain was the same as that of my mother. There ain't no doggone CORE. CORE is dead.

But that was not how I saw it. CORE was not dead. It lived through my mother's work at Southeast Raleigh Community Development Corporation. It lived in Matteo Suarez's preschool and its mission to inspire stronger, positive self-images among black children. It lived in George Wiley's National Welfare Rights Organization. It lived in Uncle Makaza's nonprofit Agricultural Teams, which provided resources to black farmers facing land loss. It lived in my uncle Tony's community and business associations in Ghana and Nigeria. It lived in Louis Smith and Shindana's black baby doll, Tamu. It lived in Aunt Ruth's current nonprofit work on black health disparity. It lived in all those CORE members who carried their experiences forward still building a path to black freedom.

In coming to understand how my mother came to be, I learned that CORE forever lived, and to some extent, so had black power. And so, I wrote this book. Because for me and the millions who benefited and still benefit from CORE, . . .

CORE is not dead.

It is not gone.

There will be more.

Until . . .

# Notes

## Preface: The Wiz behind the Curtain

1. Nishani Frazier and Laura Hill, "The Business of Black Power," Panel presented at the annual Association for the Study of Afro-American Life and History, Richmond, VA, October 5–9, 2011.

2. Raymond Arsenault, "Ploys in the Hood," *New York Times*, Sunday Magazine, March 19, 2009, BR 15.

3. Patricia Hill Collins, *Black Feminist Thought: Knowledge, Consciousness and the Politics of Empowerment* (New York: Routledge, 2000), 19.

4. Since this is a preface, my goal is not to recount the history of relativist vs. objectivist debates, but to note important benchmark texts. Carl Becker and Charles Beard offered some of the earliest arguments for a relativist approach to history. Carl Becker, "Everyman His Own Historian," *American Historical Review* 37, no. 2 (January 1932): 221–36; Peter Novick, *That Noble Dream: The "Objectivity Question" and the American History Profession* (Cambridge: Cambridge University Press, 1988), 252–58. Perhaps the most well known text to address the objectivity issue in historical writing, *That Noble Dream*, was followed by a spate of rejoinders. For other associated texts, see James T. Kloppenberg, "Objectivity and Historicism: A Century of American Historical Writing," *American Historical Review* 94 (October 1989): 1011–30; Thomas Haskell, "Objectivity Is Not Neutrality: Rhetoric vs. Practice in Peter Novick's '*That Noble Dream*,'" *History and Theory* 19 (1990): 170–81; Joseph Levine, "Objectivity in History: Peter Novick and R. G. Collingwood," *Clio* 21, no. 2 (Winter 1991): 109–27; Henry Turner Jr., "Peter Novick and the 'Objectivity Question' in History," *Academic Questions* 8, no. 3 (Summer 1995): 17–27; John Zammito, "Are We Being Theoretical Yet?: The New Historicism, the New Philosophy of History, and Practicing Historians," *Journal of Modern History* 65, no. 4 (December 1993): 811–13; Thomas Haskell, *Objectivity Is Not Neutrality: Explanatory Schemes in History* (Baltimore: Johns Hopkins University Press, 1998); John Lewis Gaddis, *The Landscape of History: How Historians Map the Past* (New York: Oxford University Press, 2004); Tibor Machan, *Objectivity: Recovering Determinate Reality in Philosophy, Science and Every Day Life* (Burling, VT: Ashgate Publishing, 2004), 41–70; Robert Perks and Alistair Thomson, "Introduction to Second Edition," in *The Oral History Reader*, ed. Robert Perks and Alistair Thomson (New York: Routledge, 1998), 3–6; Howard Zinn, *Politics of History* (Chicago: University of Illinois Press, 1990), xvii–xviii.

5. For more discussion of the human impact on objective research method, see Thomas Khun, *The Structure of Scientific Revolutions* (Chicago: University of Chicago Press, 1970); Novick, *That Noble Dream*; Martha Howell and Walter Prevenier, *From Reliable Sources: An Introduction to Historical Method* (Ithaca, NY: Cornell University Press, 2001), 143–50; Satya Mohanty, *Literary Theory and the Claims of History: Postmodernism, Objectivity, Multicultural Politics* (Ithaca, NY: Cornell University Press, 1997); Alan Spitzer,

*Historical Truth and Lies about the Past: Reflections on Dewery, Dreyfus, de Man, and Reagan* (Chapel Hill: University of North Carolina Press, 1996), 1–12.

6. Howell and Prevenier, *From Reliable Sources*, 148.

7. For examples of alternate definitions to objective historical writing, see the below texts. Also note, in various cases, these texts refer to the important role scholar community and guidelines play in ensuring accountability. Joan Wallach Scott, "History in Crisis: The Others' Side of the Story," *American Historical Review* 94, no. 3 (June 1989): 690; Howell and Prevenier, *Reliable Sources*, 148–50, 29–30; Gaddis, *Landscape*, 125–27; Spitzer, *Historical Truth*, 4–5; Wolfgang Natter, Theodore Schatzki, and John Paul Jones, eds., *Objectivity and Its Other* (New York: Guilford Press, 1995); Sabina Lovibond, "The End of Morality?," in *Knowing the Difference: Perspectives in Epistemology*, ed. Kathleen Lennon and Margaret Whitford (New York: Routledge, 1994), 65; Ismay Barwell, "Towards a Defense of Objectivity," in Lennon and Whitford, *Knowing the Difference*, 89. Ismay does not reject objectivity but rather reframes it as simply a critical stance or point of view. Liz Stanley, "The Knowing Because Experiencing Subject: Narratives, Lives, and Autobiography," in Lennon and Whitford, *Knowing the Difference*, 146; Kathleen Lennon and Margaret Whitford, "Introduction," in Lennon and Whitford, *Knowing the Difference*, 5–7. Marnia Lazreg, "Women's Experience and Feminist Epistemology: A Critical Neo-Nationalist Approach," in Lennon and Whitford, *Knowing the Difference*, 59; Howard Zinn, *Politics of History*, xviii.

8. The QR code is located on the endsheets of the book. The code is dynamic and will locate the website regardless of any changes in the url, thereby providing archival access despite future changes.

9. For example texts that address the history and structure of the profession and its effect on women's history, see Hilda Smith, "Women Historians and Women's History: A Conflation of Absence," *Journal of Women's History* 4, no. 1 (Spring 1992): 133–42; Lovibond, "The End of Morality"; Barwell, "Towards a Defense of Objectivity"; Stanley, "The Knowing Because Experiencing Subject"; Lennon and Whitford, "Introduction"; Lazreg, "Women's Experience"; Novick, *That Noble Dream*, 491–511; Linda Gordon "Comments on *That Noble Dream*," *American Historical Review* 96 (June 1991): 683–87; Sara Alpern, Joyce Antler et al., *The Challenge of Feminist Biography: Writing the Lives of Modern American Women* (Chicago: University of Illinois Press, 1992); Bonnie Smith, "Gender, Objectivity, and the Rise of Scientific History," in *Objectivity and Its Other*, ed. Wolfgang Natter, Theodore Schatzki, and John Paul Jones (New York: Guilford Press, 1995), 51–66.

10. Alpern, Antler et al., *The Challenge of Feminist Biography*, 11; Bonnie Smith, *The Gender of History: Men, Women, and Historical Practice* (Cambridge, MA: Harvard University Press, 2000); Joan Scott, *Gender and the Politics of History* (New York: Columbia University Press, 1999), 178–98; Merry Weisner-Hanks, *Gender in History: Global Perspectives* (Malden, MA: Wiley-Blackwell, 2010), 224–27.

11. Valerie Yow, "'Do I Like Them Too Much?': Effects of the Oral History Interview on the Interviewer and Vice-Versa," in Perks and Thomson, *The Oral History Reader*, 56, 61–62; Dee Garrison, "Two Roads Taken: Writing the Biography of Mary Heaton

Vorse," in Alpern, Antler et al., *The Challenge of Feminist Biography,* 68; Elisabeth Perry, "Critical Journey: From Belle Moskowitz to Women's History," in Alpern, Antler et al., *The Challenge of Feminist Biography*, 79–96; Jacquelyn Dowd Hall, "Lives through Time: Second Thoughts on Jessie Daniel Ames," in Alpern, Antler et al., *The Challenge of Feminist Biography*, 146, 155; Elisabeth Perry, *Belle Moskowitz: Feminine Politics and the Exercise of Power in the Age of Alfred E. Smith* (Boston: Oxford University Press, 1987), xii–xv. Elizabeth Perry, biographer of her grandmother Belle Moskowitz, acknowledged in this same edited volume her familial relationship but never expounded on how she compensated for questions of scholarly distance. Instead, the introduction began with the announcement of her grandmother's death and public reaction. Moskowitz's demise before Perry was born provided some cover, and thus there appeared no conflict.

12. Notable exceptions came from the first generation of labor historians, who generally occupied a dual position as academic and activist. Arthur Schlesinger, "The Historian as Participant," *Daedalus* 100, no. 2 (Spring 1971): 339–58; Howard Zinn, *Politics of History*, 2, 12; Staughtan Lynd, "Guerilla History in Gary," in *Doing History from the Bottom Up: On S. P. Thompson, Howard Zinn, and Rebuilding the Labor Movement from Below*, ed. Lynd Staughton (Chicago: Haymarket Books, 2014), 47–54. I would note that these scholar-activists were particular to the period. I am not sure that I believe current academics, particularly freedom scholars, have the same license. See also Matthew Countryman, *Up South: Civil Rights and Black Power in Philadelphia* (Philadelphia: University of Pennsylvania Press, 2006), 1–12; Beryl Satter, *Family Properties: Race, Real Estate, and the Exploitation of Black Urban America* (New York: Metropolitan Books, 2009), 1–16.

13. See Jacquelyn Dowd Hall, "The Long Civil Rights Movement and the Political Uses of the Past," *Journal of American History* 91 (2005): 1233–63. For other examples, see Jeanne F. Theoharis and Komozi Woodard, eds., *Groundwork: Local Black Freedom Movements in America* (New York: New York University Press, 2005); Jeanne Theoharis and Komozi Woodard, eds., *Freedom North: Black Freedom Struggles Outside the South, 1940–1980* (New York: Palgrave Macmillan, 2003); Komozi Woodard, *A Nation within a Nation: Amiri Baraka (LeRoi Jones) and Black Power Politics* (Chapel Hill: University of North Carolina Press, 1999); William L. Van Deburg, *New Day in Babylon: The Black Power Movement and American Culture, 1965–1975* (Chicago: University of Chicago Press, 1992); Timothy Tyson, *Radio Free Dixie: Robert F. Williams and the Roots of Black Power* (Chapel Hill: University of North Carolina Press, 2001), 262–86. For additional commentary on Mae Mallory, see Martha Biondi, *To Stand and Fight: The Struggle for Civil Rights in Postwar New York City* (Cambridge, MA: Harvard University Press, 2006); Jeanne Theoharis, "Black Freedom Studies: Re-Imagining and Redefining the Fundamentals," *History Compass* 4, no. 2 (2006): 348–67; Peniel Joseph, ed., *The Black Power Movement: Rethinking the Civil Rights–Black Power Era* (New York: Routledge, 2006); Peniel Joseph, "Rethinking the Black Power Era," *Journal of Southern History* 75, no. 3 (August 2009): 707–16; Jeffrey O. G. Ogbar, *Black Power: Radical Politics and African American Identity* (Baltimore: Johns Hopkins University Press, 2004).

14. Jennifer Denetdale, Reclaiming Diné History: *The Legacies of Navajo Chief Manuelito and Juanita* (Tucson: University of Arizona Press, 2007), 5.

15. Collins, Black Feminist Thought, 252.

16. Michel-Rolph Trouillot, *Silencing the Past: Power and the Production of History* (Boston: Beacon Press, 1997), 26. According to Trouillot, silences entered the historical process in four areas: fact creation (making of sources), fact assembly (archives), narrative creation, and determination of significance.

17. One of the few exceptions was the Wisconsin Historical Society, which seized the opportunity to collect these materials much earlier than other archival institutions. As a result, WHS oddly has papers from across the United States related to 1960s activism, including a small group of papers by Cleveland CORE member Bonnie Holden. Such decisions are made by far-thinking archivists in tandem with the institutional effort of outreach.

18. Meier and Rudwick, *CORE*, 155, 472 n. 22; NAC Minutes, December 3, 1965–January 2, 1966, Series 3.1.2, Folder 6964, McKissick Papers, SHC.

19. Meier and Rudwick, *CORE*, 155, 472 n. 22; James Farmer, October 14–15, 1970, interview by Meier and Rudwick, Box 56, Folder 6, August Meier Papers, Schomburg Research Center, New York; Marvin Rich, May 21, 1969, interview notes, by Meier, Box 56, Folder 6, August Meier Papers, Schomburg Center for Research in Black Culture; Ruth Turner and Tony Perot, April 17, 1972, Box 57, Folder 1, interview by August Meier and Elliot Rudwick, August Meier Papers, Schomburg Center for Research in Black Culture.

20. Mack Henry Jones and Alex Willingham, founders of the National Conference of Black Political Scientists, voiced a similar critique in the *Social Science Quarterly* in 1970. The two political scientists particularly focused on subtexts in Meier and Rudwick's essay "Organizational Structure and Goal Succession." Jones and Willingham specifically referred to conceptualization, wording, and connotation in Meier and Rudwick's analysis about black nationalism (and black power). Jones and Willingham highlighted the appearance of negative undertones about black separatism, the erroneous presumption that organizational structure mitigated black nationalist proclivities, and a failure to recognize black nationalist ideology as an ever-present optional strategy within the black community. Their argument culminated in the belief that Meier and Rudwick's positionality as white liberal integrationists skewed the article in such a way as to grant greater value to integration over black separatism hidden behind a theoretical discussion about organizational structure and difference. Meier and Rudwick's response to the Jones and Willingham critique centers on their belief that Jones and Willingham's comments emanate from their focus on Meier and Rudwick's whiteness versus the argument, and that Jones and Willingham missed the point. See August Meier and Elliot Rudwick, "Organizational Structure and Goal Succession: A Comparative Analysis of the NAACP and CORE, 1964–1968," *Social Science Quarterly* 51, no. 1 (June 1970): 9–24; Mack H. Jones and Alex Willingham, "The White Custodians of the Black Experience: A Reply to Rudwick and Meier," *Social Science Quarterly* 51, no. 1 (June 1970): 31–36; and August Meier and Elliot Rudwick, "NAACP and CORE: Some Additional Theoretical Considerations," *Social Science Quarterly* 51, no. 1 (June 1970): 37–41.

21. Scholar Allesandro Portelli famously identified this distinction in his piece, "What Makes Oral History Different." Oral history can be doubly useful in its ability to provide

information and *meaning*. Alessandro Portelli, "What Makes Oral History Different," Perks and Thomson, *The Oral History Reader*, 36.

22. For additional information on aurality and its important role, see Sherna Gluck, "Women's Oral History: Is it So Special?" in *Handbook of Oral History*, ed. Thomas Charlton, Lois Myers, and Rebecca Sharpless (Lanham, MD: Alta Mira Press, 2006), 362; Walter Ong, *Orality and Literacy: The Technologizing of the Word* (New York: Methuen, 1982), 357–83; Siobhan McHugh, "The Affective Power of Sound: Oral History on Radio," in *Oral History Review* 39, no. 2 (Summer/Fall 2012): 187–206; Kathryn Anderson and Dana Jack, "Learning to Listen: Interviewing Techniques and Analysis," in Perks and Thomson, *The Oral History Reader*; Hugo Slim and Paul Thompson et. al, "Ways of Listening," in Perks and Thomson, *The Oral History Reader*.

23. The testimonio concept originated from Latin American literature and oral historians. It has since found use among various activist groups as a tool to express communal epistemology. Wise Todd, "Native American Testimonio: The Shared Vision of Black Elk and Rigoberta Menchú," *Christianity and Literature* 45, no. 1 (August 1995): 111–27; Kalina Brabeck, "Testimonio: A Strategy for Collective Resistance, Cultural Survival and Building Solidarity," *Feminism & Psychology* 13, no. 2 (May 2003): 252–58; Roberto Avant-Mier and Marouf Hasian, "Communicating 'Truth': Testimonio, Vernacular Voices, and the Rigoberta Menchú Controversy," *Communication Review* 11, no. 4 (2008): 323–45; John Beverly, "The Margin at the Center: On Testimonio," in *De/colonizing the Subject. The Politics of Gender in Women's Autobiography*, ed. Sidonie Smitha and Julia Watson (Minneapolis: University of Minneapolis Press, 1992), 91–114; Kathryn Blackmer Reyes and Julia Curry Rodriguez, "'Testimonio': Origins, Terms, and Resources," *Equity & Excellence in Education* 45, no. 3 (2012): 525–38; Avant-Mier and Hasian, "Communicating 'Truth,'" 323–45; John Beverley, *Testimonio: On the Politics of Truth* (Minneapolis: University of Minnesota Press, 2004), x–xi. According to Beverley, testimonio is political in nature, serves to interpret the world and change it, has a storytelling element, and generally is linked with national liberation movements. On collective memory and the black experience, see Kenneth J. Bindas, "Re-Remembering a Segregated Past: Race in American Memory," *History & Memory* 22, no. 1 (Spring/Summer 2010): 116–20; Gwendolyn Etter-Lewis, "Black Women's Life Stories: Reclaiming Self in Narrative Texts," in *Women's Words: The Feminist Practice of Oral History*, ed. Sherna Berger Gluck and Daphne Patai (New York: Routledge, 1991), 53–55; Linda Shopes, "Commentary: Sharing Authority," *Oral History Review* 30, no. 1 (January 1, 2003): 103–10.

24. Shared authority is a collaborative process that suggests that the interview is a co-authored product—created by the questions submitted and the answers given. Additionally, some scholars take the added step of allowing interviewees to review and "talk back" to the text (transcript or interpretive narrative). The process can delay the public presentation of information and can sometimes lead to conflicts regarding interpretation. A. Glenn Crothers and Tracy E. K'Meyer, "'If I See Some of This in Writing, I'm Going to Shoot You': Reluctant Narrators, Taboo Topics, and the Ethical Dilemmas of the Oral Historian," *Oral History Review* 34, no. 1 (Winter–Spring 2007): 77. Michael Frisch, *A Shared Authority: Essays on the Craft and Meaning of Oral and Public History* (Albany: State

University of New York Press, 1990), xxi–xxii; Michael Frisch, "Sharing Authority: Oral History and the Collaborative Process," *Oral History Review* 30, no. 1 (Winter/Spring 2003): 111–13.

25. Various articles reflect on the differences between interpretation and interviewee narrative. See Crothers and K'Meyer, "If I See Some of This in Writing," 90; Katherine Borland, "'That's Not What I Said': Interpretive Conflict in Oral Narrative Research," in Perks and Thomson, *The Oral History Reader*, 314–18; Kathleen Blee, "Evidence, Empathy, and Ethics: Lessons from Oral Histories of the Klan," in Perks and Thomson, *The Oral History Reader*, 323–27.

## Introduction: The CORE Spirit Lives

1. John Frazier was an activist in Mississippi. See Michael Vinson Williams, *Medgar Evers: Mississippi Martyr* (Fayetteville: University of Arkansas Press, 2011); Anthony Lewis, *Portrait of a Decade: The Second American Revolution* (New York: Random House, 1964); Manning Marable and Myrlie Evers-Williams, *The Autobiography of Medgar Evers: A Hero's Life and Legacy Revealed through His Writings, Letters, and Speeches* (New York: Basic Civitas Books, 2005); Clarice Campbell, *Civil Rights Chronicle: Letters from the South* (Jackson: University Press of Mississippi, 1997). For Frazier's relationship to the Unitarian church and his activities in Cleveland, Ohio, view Victor Carpenter, *Unitarian Universalism and the Quest for Racial Justice 1967–1982* (Boston: Unitarian Universalist Association, 1993); Mark Morrison-Reed, *Darkening the Doorways: Black Trailblazers and Missed Opportunities in Unitarian Universalism* (Boston: Skinner House, 2011). For materials on the Black Unitarian Fellowship and its relationship to Cleveland refer to the Humanist Fellowship of Liberation Records, 1965–1972, Western Reserve Historical Society (WRHS), Library and Archives Division, Cleveland, OH, Manuscript Series Number 3592 and John Frazier Papers, 1965–1972, WRHS, Manuscript Series Number 3593.

2. For information on Soul City, see Devin Fergus, *Liberalism, Black Power, and the Making of American Politics, 1965–1980* (Athens: University of Georgia Press, 2009); Devin Fergus, "Black Power, Soft Power: Floyd McKissick, Soul City, and the Death of Moderate Black Republicanism," *Journal of Policy History* 22, no. 2 (April 2010): 148–92; Timothy Minchin, "'A Brand New Shining City': Floyd B. McKissick, Sr., and the Struggle to Build Soul City, North Carolina," *North Carolina Historical Review* 82, no. 2 (April 2005): 125–55; Roger Biles, "The Rise and Fall of Soul City: Planning, Politics, and Race in Recent America," *Journal of Planning History* 4 (February 2005): 52–72; and Christopher Strain, "Soul City, North Carolina: Black Power, Utopia, and the African American Dream," *Journal of African American History* 89, no. 1 (Winter 2004): 57–74.

3. Ms. D. L. Waller to Pauline Frazier, March 26, 1975, Series 3.1.1, Folder 6783 General Correspondence, Floyd McKissick Papers.

4. Relatively little work has been done on CDCs or the historical circumstances of most modern community development corporations. Some current works trace organizational development or examine current trends in CDC structure. This is an area ripe for study. For examples of historical analysis of CDCs in the 1980s and 1990s, see Robert

Fisher, "Community Organizing in the Conservative 80s and Beyond," *Social Policy* 25, no. 1 (Fall 1994): 11–21; Jean-Marc Fontan, Pierre Hamel et al., "The Institutionalization of Montreal's CDECS: From Grassroots Organizations to State Apparatus?," *Canadian Journal of Urban Research* 12, no. 1 (Summer 2003): 58–76; Jamal Watson, "Black Churches Develop Congregations, Corporations," *Amsterdam News* 94, no. 30 (July 24, 2003): 1–2; Jordan Yin, "The Community Development Industry System: A Case Study of Politics and Institutions in Cleveland," *Journal of Urban Affairs* 20, no. 2 (Summer 1998): 137–57.

5. Linda Brown Douglas, "A Grass Roots Effort of the 60s Helps Businesses Today," *Business Weekly*, November 23, 1992, 1. Most information on SRCDC can be found in various online reports or best practices case studies. For information on Southeast Raleigh CDC, see Steve Waddell, "Outcomes of Social Capital Strategies," 4–6, 8–10, 12–13, 15, 21; "Three North Carolina Case Studies: Models of Community Lending," Enterprise Resources, www.practitionerresources.org/cache/documents/19314.pdft *(accessed July 12, 2011)*; Tim Gray, "Banks Plan Minority Loans," *News & Observer*, December 23, 1994, C9; No author, "Raleigh Civil Rights Activist Pauline Frazier Dies, 56," *News & Observer*, August 24, 1996, Obit B6; Alicia Williams, "Southeast Raleigh Community Resource Struggling," *News & Observer*, August 27, 1998, B1; Alicia Williams and Matthew Eisley, "Group's Problems Piled Up," *News & Observer*, August 29, 1998, B1.

6. Journal searches for scholarly articles with CORE in its title demonstrate the paltry number of available readings. Among the few but recent articles are Simon Wendt, "'Urge the People Not to Carry Guns': Armed Self-Defense in the Louisiana Civil Rights Movement and the Radicalization of the Congress of Racial Equality," *Louisiana History* 45, no. 3 (July 2004): 261–86; Roger Hansen, "Pioneers in Nonviolent Action: The Congress of Racial Equality in Cincinnati, 1946–1955," *Queen City Heritage* 52, no. 3 (1994): 23–35; Craig Turnbull, "'Please Make No Demonstrations Tomorrow': The Brooklyn Congress of Racial Equality and Symbolic Protest at the 1964–1965 World's Fair," *Australasian Journal of American Studies* 17, no. 1 (1998): 22–42; Karen Ferguson, "Organizing the Ghetto': The Ford Foundation, CORE, and White Power in the Black Power Era, 1967–1969," *Journal of Urban History* 34, no. 1 (2007): 67–100; Merl Reed, "The FBI, MOWM, and CORE, 1941–1946," *Journal of Black Studies* 21, no. 4 (June 1991): 465–79. Most pieces are yet to be published and appear in conference presentations. Others range from undergraduate senior thesis to local history magazines. Jeremy M. Shenk, "Julius Hobson's Dismissal from Washington DC CORE in 1964 as a Case Study of the Militant vs. Moderate Debate within the Civil Rights Movement of the 1960s" (BA thesis, Goshen College, 2001); Brian Purnell, "New CORE Studies: Rethinking CORE's Significance to the Civil Rights–Black Power Era," Paper presented at annual meeting for the Association for Afro-American Life and History, no date; Brian Purnell, "'We Struggled in Vain?': Brooklyn CORE and the Downstate Medical Center Protest during the Summer of 1963," Paper presented at the annual meeting for the Association for the Study of Afro-American Life and History, Atlanta, Georgia, September 26–October 1, 2006, Annual Meeting; Kristin Anderson-Bricker, "We Are Soldiers in the Army: Detroit CORE Forms in Support of the Southern Civil Rights Movement, 1960–1961," Paper presented at

the annual meeting for the Association for the Study of Afro-American Life and History, Atlanta, Georgia, September 26–October 1, 2006, Annual Meeting.

7. August Meier and Elliot Rudwick, *CORE: A Study in the Civil Rights Movement, 1942–1968* (New York: Oxford University Press, 1973). Particular attention has been given to challenging the notion of black power as the end of the civil rights movement or the cause of its demise. For only a few examples of older and newer historiography on this subject, see Woodard, *A Nation within a Nation*; William L. Van Deburg, *New Day in Babylon: The Black Power Movement and American Culture, 1965–1975* (Chicago: University of Chicago Press, 1992); Tyson, *Radio Free Dixie*; Jeanne Theoharis, "Black Freedom Studies: Re-Imagining and Redefining the Fundamentals," *History Compass* 4, no. 2 (2006): 348–67; Rhonda Y. Williams, *The Politics of Public Housing: Black Women's Struggles against Urban Inequality* (New York: Oxford University Press, 2004); Joseph, ed., *The Black Power Movement*; Peniel Joseph, "Rethinking the Black Power Era," *Journal of Southern History* 75, no. 3 (August 2009): 707–16; Jeffrey O. G. Ogbar, *Black Power: Radical Politics and African American Identity* (Baltimore: Johns Hopkins University Press, 2004); Susan Youngblood Ashmore, *Carry It On: The War on Poverty and the Civil Rights Movement in Alabama, 1964–1972* (Athens: University of Georgia Press, 2008); Jakobi Williams, *From the Bullet to the Ballot: The Illinois Chapter of the Black Panther Party and Racial Coalition Politics in Chicago* (Chapel Hill: University of North Carolina Press, 2013); Rhonda Y. Williams, *Concrete Demands: The Search for Black Power in the Twentieth Century* (New York: Routledge, 2015); Laura Hill and Julia Rabig, *The Business of Black Power: Community Development, Capitalism, and Corporate Responsibility in Postwar America* (Rochester: University of Rochester Press, 2012).

8. August Meier and Elliott M. Rudwick, *CORE: A Study in the Civil Rights Movement, 1942–1968* (New York: Oxford University Press, 1973). Elliot Rudwick, "CORE: The Road from Interracialism to Black Power," *Nonprofit and Voluntary Sector Quarterly* 1 (1972): 12–19. Meier and Rudwick's book ends in 1968, and thus cuts out pivotal experiences of CORE in the black power era, including CORE's major target city programs. Rudwick's essay, "The Road from Interracialism to Black Power," varied little from the book's premise and can be evaluated along the same lines.

9. The indoctrination of CORE as nearly tied solely to the Freedom Rides begins with children's books like Ann Bausum, *Freedom Riders: John Lewis and Jim Zwerg on the Front Lines of the Civil Rights Movement* (Washington, DC: National Geographic Children's Books, 2005); Deborah Kent, *The Freedom Riders* (Chicago: Children's Press, 1993). It continues with histories and autobiographical accounts such as Derek Catsam, *Freedom's Main Line: The Journey of Reconciliation and the Freedom Rides* (Lexington: University Press of Kentucky, 2009); Raymond Arsenault, *Freedom Riders: 1961 and the Struggle for Justice* (New York: Oxford University Press, 2006); Eric Etheridge, Roger Wilkins, and Diane McWhorter, *Breach of Peace: Portraits of the 1961 Mississippi Freedom Riders* (New York: Atlas & Co., 2008); James Peck, *Freedom Ride* (New York: Simon and Schuster, 1962); Mary Hamilton, Louise Inghram, and Others, *Freedom Riders Speak for Themselves* (Detroit: News & Letters, 1961); Thomas Armstrong and Natalie Bell, *Autobiography of a Freedom Rider: My Life as a Foot Soldier for Civil Rights* (Deerfield, FL: Health Communications,

2011); Phil Noble, *Beyond the Burning Bus: The Civil Rights Revolution in a Southern Town* (Montgomery, AL: New South Books, 2003); *Freedom Riders*, written by Stanley Nelson (United States: PBS Distribution, 2011), dvd. The documentary's focus moves from CORE to the Nashville student movement's "rescue" of the Freedom Rides. However, it excises the important fact that New Orleans CORE chapter played a leading role in Farmer's decision to restart the project.

10. George Houser, *Erasing the Color Line* (New York: Fellowship Publications, 1945), 7, 12–13; Jim Peck, *Cracking the Color Line: Non-Violent Direct Action Methods of Eliminating Racial Discrimination* (New York: Congress of Racial Equality, 1960). Another variant of the CORE philosophy can be found in Anna Holden, *A First Step Toward School Integration* (New York: Congress of Racial Equality, 1958).

11. James Farmer, *Freedom, When?* (New York: Random House, 1965).

12. No author, "Roy Innis, Al Sharpton Brawl on TV Talk Show," *Jet Magazine* (August 29, 1988), 22; no author, "Roy Innis: From Left-Wing Radical to Right-Wing Extremist," *Journal of Blacks in Higher Education* 39 (Spring 2003): 69–70.

13. The two most prominent books on CORE focus heavily on nonviolent philosophy. Inge Powell Bell, *CORE and the Strategy of Nonviolence* (New York: Random House, 1968); August Meier and Elliott Rudwick, *CORE, a Study in the Civil Rights Movement, 1942–1968* (Urbana: University of Illinois Press, 1975). Other texts have a tendency to wrap up CORE's history before or about 1968. Mary Kimbrough, *Victory without Violence: The First Ten Years of the St. Louis Committee of Racial Equality, 1947–1957* (Columbia: University of Missouri Press, 2000); Brian Purnell, "A Movement Grows in Brooklyn: The Brooklyn Chapter of the Congress of Racial Equality (CORE) and the Northern Civil Rights Movement during the Early 1960s" (PhD diss., New York University, 2006); Joan Singler, Jean Durning, and Bettylou Valentine, *Seattle in Black and White: The Congress of Racial Equality and the Right for Equal Opportunity* (Seattle: University of Washington Press, 2011); Kristin Anderson-Bricker, "Making a Movement: The Meaning of Community in the Congress of Racial Equality, 1958–1968" (PhD diss., Syracuse University, 1997); Brian Purnell, "'Drive Awhile for Freedom': Brooklyn CORE's 1964 Stall-In and Public Discourses on Protest Violence," in *Local Black Freedom Movements in America*, ed. Komozi Woodard and Jeanne Theoharris (New York: New York University Press, 2005), 45–76; Bobbie Knable, November 23, 1999, interview by Sheila Michaels in Columba University Oral History Archives; Thomas Sugrue's monumental synthesis on civil rights in the North published in 2008 testifies to the endurance of this linear history of CORE. Thomas Sugrue, *Sweet Land of Liberty: The Forgotten Struggle for Civil Rights in the North* (New York: Random House, 2008), 137, 495.

14. Ibid. Relatively few studies delve into CORE's post-1968 or its black power activism, and fewer still view it as having a positive impact on CORE or the communities in which it operated. Mike Flug and Congress of Racial Equality, *The Maryland Freedom Union: Workers Doings and Thinking* (Detroit: News & Letters, 1970); Thomas Tucker, "An Historical Study of the Involvement of the Congress of Racial Equality in Public School Desegregation Actions from 1954 through 1973" (PhD diss., Ohio State University, 1974); Louis C. Goldberg, "CORE in Trouble: A Social History of the Organizational Dilemmas

of the Congress of Racial Equality Target City Project in Baltimore (1965–1967)"
(PhD diss., Johns Hopkins University, 1970); Anna Beatrice Griebling, "Attitudinal and
Behavioral Deviation of White Civil Rights Supporters: A Study of the Columbus, Ohio
Chapter of the Congress of Racial Equality" (PhD diss., Ohio State University, 1966);
Ferguson, "Organizing the Ghetto"; Joe E. Leonard, "'We Are Catchin' Hell Down Here':
The Struggle for Public Accommodations and Voter Franchisement by the Congress of
Racial Equality in Louisiana, 1960–1965" (PhD thesis, Howard University, 2004).

15. There are a number of manuscripts that feature CORE prominently in local/
regional stories. Recent and well-known samplings of local studies that incorporate CORE
span across regions and include Adam Fairclough, *Race and Democracy: The Civil Rights
Struggle in Louisiana, 1915–1972* (Athens: University of Georgia Press, 1999); Komozi
Woodard, *A Nation within a Nation: Amiri Baraka (LeRoi Jones) and Black Power Politics*
(Chapel Hill: University of North Carolina Press, 1999); Clarence Lang, *Grassroots at
the Gateway: Class Politics and Black Freedom Struggle in St. Louis, 1936–75* (Ann Arbor:
University of Michigan Press, 2009); Robert O. Self, *American Babylon: Race and the
Struggle for Postwar Oakland* (Princeton, NJ: Princeton University Press, 2003); Charles
Payne, *I've Got the Light of Freedom: The Organizing Tradition and the Mississippi Freedom
Struggle* (Berkeley: University of California Press, 1995); Raymond A. Mohl, *South of the
South: Jewish Activists and the Civil Rights Movement in Miami, 1945–1960* (Gainesville:
University Press of Florida, 2004); Greta De Jong, *A Different Day: African American
Struggles for Justice in Rural Louisiana, 1900–1970* (Chapel Hill: University of North
Carolina Press, 2002); Patrick Jones, *The Selma of the North: Civil Rights Insurgency in
Milwaukee* (Cambridge, MA: Harvard University Press, 2009); Sugrue, *Sweet Land of
Liberty*; Bobbi Brown Knable interview.

16. There are a number of new histories that attempt to change or complicate how
we understand CORE. Leading that movement is Brian Purnell, *Fighting Jim Crow in the
County of Kings: The Congress of Racial Equality in Brooklyn* (Lexington: University Press of
Kentucky, 2013). Purnell does an excellent job of capturing the goodwill spirit of CORE in
a northern movement, particularly the personal relationships that make the movement both
a political/public and personal/intimate space. Purnell's work, however, falls within CORE's
classic historiography—ending Brooklyn's story in 1964. Brooklyn had a strong historical period of black power, particularly given Sonny Carson's role locally and nationally.
However, the book does chart the internal dynamics that eventually lead Brooklyn to black
power, particularly the rising militancy within the chapter. Most importantly, he points to
this evolution as a symbiotic smooth transition of power sharing. There are other historians
who've recently (within the last twenty years) written essays and dissertations on CORE.
Turnbull, "'Please Make No Demonstrations Tomorrow'"; Anderson-Bricker, "Making
a Movement"; Leonard, "We Are Catchin' Hell Down Here"; and Michael Washington,
"The Stirrings of the Modern Civil Rights Movement in Cincinnati," in Woodard and
Theoharris, *Groundwork*, 215–34.

17. James Farmer to Gene Preuss, February 18, 1991, Box 2J, Folder 3, James Farmer
Papers.

18. Ibid.

19. James Farmer, *Freedom, When?*, 57, 62, 77. James Farmer, *Lay Bare the Heart* (New York: Arbor House, 1985), 104. Leilah Danielson, "'Two-ness of the Movement': James Farmer, Non-violence, and Black Nationalism," *Peace & Change* 29, no. 3–4 (July 2004), 434, 442. Meier and Rudwick, *CORE*, 25, 426. Meier and Rudwick also mention the duality within CORE among members, though they give less credit to its position as part of the hybrid that created CORE.

20. Farmer, *Freedom, When?*, 77–80. Farmer, *Lay Bare*, 94.

21. Farmer, *Lay Bare*, 104.

22. Meier and Rudwick, *CORE*, 24–25.

23. Qtd. in Meier and Rudwick, *CORE*, 25.

24. Manning Marable, Race, Reform, and Rebellion: The Second Construction and Beyond in Black America, 1945–2006 (Jackson: University Press of Mississippi, 2007), 93; John D'Emilio, Lost Prophet, 456–57; Jervis Anderson, Bayard Rustin: Trouble I've Seen: A Biography (New York: HarperCollins, 1997), 313–18; Daniel Levine, Bayard Rustin and the Civil Rights Movement (New Brunswick, NJ: Rutgers University Press, 2000), 208–15.

25. Scholars view CORE interchangeably as reformist, pluralist, bourgeois, and separatist. For examples, see William L. Van Deburg, *Modern Black Nationalism: From Marcus Garvey to Louis Farrakhan* (New York: New York University Press, 1997), 175–81; Van Deburg, *New Day in Babylon*, 132–40; Dean E. Robinson, *Black Nationalism in American Politics and Thought* (New York: Cambridge University Press, 2001), 100–102; Meier and Rudwick, *CORE*, 335; Raymond Hall, *Black Separatism in the United States* (Hanover, NH: University of New England Press, 1978), 181–83, 207–9; "Introduction," in August Meier and Elliot Rudwick, eds., *Black Protest in the Sixties* (Chicago: Quadrangle Books, 1970), 20–21; Harold Cruse, *Crisis of the Negro Intellectual* (New York: William Morrow and Company, 1967), 546–52; John H. Bracey, August Meier, and Elliott M. Rudwick, *Black Nationalism in America* (Indianapolis: Bobbs-Merrill, 1970), li. Bracey and Meier's anthology introduction frames CORE's black nationalist economic program as bourgeois reformist. McKissick Enterprises, a corporation that was actually unassociated with CORE but created by national director Floyd McKissick, supposedly modeled this approach. It is important to note here that Floyd McKissick never personally initiated a black economic program while in CORE. Scholarship on black economic nationalism and CORE often fail to note that much of McKissick's activities in this arena fell under the aegis of the Cleveland Target City Project, which was not black capitalism but economic development. Though few study CORE's relationship to black economic power, more than a few represent black capitalism as a bourgeois reformist thrust by CORE. See Robert L. Allen, *Black Awakening in Capitalist America: An Analytic History* (Garden City, NY: Doubleday, 1969), 70; Manning Marable, *How Capitalism Underdeveloped Black America: Problems in Race, Political Economy, and Society* (Boston, MA: South End Press, 1983); Marable, *Race, Reform, Rebellion*, 139, 95–96; Van Deburg, *Modern Black Nationalism*, 175–81; Hall, *Black Separatism*, 117–22; Robinson, *Black Nationalism*, 93–94; Earl Ofari, *The Myth of Black Capitalism* (New York: Monthly Review Press, 1970), 71–72; James Jennings, *The Politics of Black Empowerment: The Transformation of Black Activism in Urban America* (Detroit: Wayne State University Press, 1992), 94–95; Joan Roelofs, *Foundations and Public*

*Policy: The Mask of Pluralism* (Albany: State University of New York Press, 2003), 95; Karin L. Stanford, *Black Political Organizations in the Post–Civil Rights Era* (New Brunswick, NJ: Rutgers University Press, 2002), 89; Marc Pilisuk and Phyllis Pilisuk, *How We Lost the War on Poverty* (New Brunswick, NJ: Transaction Books, 1976), 244; Dean Kotlowski, "Black Power Nixon Style: The Nixon Administration and Minority Business Enterprise," *Business History Review* 72, no. 3 (Autumn 1998): 417, 94–95; Allen, *Black Awakening*, 76, 183–87; Robert Weems Jr. and Lewis A. Randolph, *Business in Black and White: American Presidents and Black Entrepreneurs in the Twentieth Century* (New York: New York University Press, 2009), 115–18; Joshua Farrington, "'Build, Baby, Build': Conservative Black Nationalists, Free Enterprise, and the Nixon Administration," in *The Right Side of the Sixties: Reexamining Conservatism's Decade of Transformation*, ed. Laura Gifford and Daniel Williams (New York: Palgrave Macmillan, 2012), 61–80; Robert Weems and Lewis Randolph, "The National Response to Richard M. Nixon's Black Capitalism Initiative: The Success of Domestic Détente," *Journal of Black Studies* 32, no. 1 (September 2001): 66–84; Robert Weems and Lewis Randolph, "The Ideological Origins of Richard M. Nixon's 'Black Capitalism' Initiative," *Review of Black Political Economy* 29, no. 1 (Summer 2001): 49–53.

26. Although all listed do not agree, most scholars situate black power as an outgrowth of the larger philosophical tradition of black nationalism. There are several books that discuss the nature of black nationalism and its historical underpinnings in black intellectual and political thought. According to various scholars, classification within black power tended toward three (sometimes four) descriptors: pluralist, separatist, revolutionary, and cultural. The cultural component is less relevant within CORE and had less utility as an action plan for social, political, and economic black empowerment. For further summary of these varied approaches, see Marable, *Race, Reform, and Rebellion,* 94–97. Van Deburg, *Modern Black Nationalism,* 13–14; Bracey, Meier, and Rudwick, *Black Nationalism,* l–li; Jennings, *The Politics of Black Empowerment,* 88–103; Van Deburg, *New Day in Babylon,* 112–91; Meier and Rudwick, *Black Protest in the Sixties,* 19–23; John McCartney, *Black Power Ideologies: An Essay in African American Political Thought* (Philadelphia: Temple University Press, 1992), 111–27. Manning Marable and Leith Mullings, *Let Nobody Turn Us Around: Voices of Resistance, Reform, and Renewal: An African American Anthology* (Lanham, MD: Rowman & Littlefield, 2000), xxi–xxvi; Jennings, *The Politics of Black Empowerment,* 99–100; Robinson, *Black Nationalism,* 73; Jeffrey Ogbar, *Black Power: Radical Politics and African American Identity* (Baltimore: Johns Hopkins University Press, 2005), 123–58; Meier and Rudwick, *Black Protest,* 19–23; James Taylor, *Black Nationalism in the United States: From Malcolm X to Barack Obama* (Boulder, CO: Lynne Rienner Publishers, 2010), 238. McCartney posits another term for revolutionary black power that he calls counter-communalists.

27. Historically, there were many evolutions of populist thought in American history. Notable similarities include free education at all levels, limits on individual wealth, income equality, and suppressing exploitation within the capitalist system. I will explore this in greater detail in chapter 8.

28. Arguably, the act of self-defense in many ways cannot be categorized as an "integrationist" or "nationalist" philosophy within the black community. However, I categorize

self-defense as a contradiction of early CORE's initial mandate of nonviolent direct action. I also utilize it as an oppositional issue with ties to nationalism, in that the rhetoric of black power advocates of the 1960s situated self-defense as a tactic contrary to integrationist arguments for nonviolent direct action. As such, I use this dialectic to discuss armed resistance as a nationalist propensity of the black power era that appears in tensions among 1940s CORE members. I will discuss this again in chapter 2.

## 1. How CORE Began

1. In his autobiography, Farmer's reminiscences conflate the resignation of A. Philip Randolph with the first conference meeting of the Southern Negro Youth Conference (SNYC), which took place in 1937 in Richmond, Virginia, while he was still at Wiley College. SNYC was the youth arm of the National Negro Congress (NNC), a communist-backed black organization initially led by A. Philip Randolph. Randolph actually resigned from NNC in 1940, two years into Farmer's attendance at Howard University. Farmer's recollections are accurate but are out of place and time. The Methodist Youth Conference dates and sites are also incorrect, though he did attend such an event. Farmer was a resource person on the spiritual and activist relevance of fellowship cells at the 1942 National Conference of Methodist Youth at Miami University. Farmer's recollection of attending the conference during his Wiley College years are confirmed by his memories of previous attendance by other black Methodists Juanita Jackson and Karl E. Downs, as well as a talk given by Harold Fey. He likely attended the National Methodist Youth Conference in 1936 at Berea College, not more than three hours from Miami University. Farmer, *Lay Bare*, 127–29; Farmer to Jo Ann Robinson, February 28, 1978, Box 2, Folder: Correspondence and notes of Jo Ann Robinson, A. J. Muste Papers: Later Accessions in the Swathmore College Peace Collection (hereafter SCPC) at Swathmore College, PA; Agenda for National Assembly of Student Christian Associations, Box 1, Folder "Student Christian Associations" in Conferences, Conventions, Symposia, 1937–73 Records at Miami University Archives, Miami University, Oxford, Ohio (hereafter MUOhio); More Agenda for the National Assembly of Student Christian Associations, Box 1, Folder "Student Christian Associations" in Conferences, Conventions, Symposia, 1937–73 Records at MUOhio; Report of the First National Convocation of the Methodist Youth Fellowship, 1942, Box 23, Folder "Methodist Youth Fellowship National Convocation" in President Alfred H. Upham, Office Files, 1941–42, and Box 25, Folder "Methodist Youth Fellowship National Convocation," in Alfred H. Upham, Office Files, 1942–43, at MUOhio; Glenda Gilmore, *Defying Dixie: The Radical Roots of Civil Rights, 1919–1950* (New York: W. W. Norton, 2008), 356; Arsenault, *Freedom Riders*, 26; Andrew Kersten, *A. Philip Randolph: A Life in the Vanguard* (Lanham, MD: Rowman & Littlefield, 2007), 50; Cornelius Bynum, *A. Philip Randolph and the Struggle for Civil Rights* (Champaign: University of Illinois Press, 2010), 141–42; Jervis Anderson, *A. Philip Randolph: A Biographical Portrait* (Berkeley: University of California Press, 1986), 234–39; Cynthia Taylor, *A. Philip Randolph: The Religious Journey of an African American Labor Leader* (New York: New York University Press, 2006), 126; Paula Pfeffer, *A. Philip Randolph, Pioneer of the Civil Rights*

*Movement* (Baton Rouge: Louisiana State University Press, 1990), 39–40. For information on the Southern Youth Negro Conference, see *Arrangements Committee, Official Proceedings: Second All Southern Negro Youth Conference, On to Richmond! for the Southern Negro Youth Conference* (Washington, DC: SYNC, 1937); For information on Juanita Jackson, see Thomas Bynum, "'We Must March Forward!': Juanita Jackson and the Origins of the NAACP Youth Movement," *Journal of African American History* 94, no. 4 (Fall 2009): 487–508. For information on some black Methodists, see the work of Karl E. Downs, *Meet the Negro* (Los Angeles: Southern California-Arizona Annual Conference, 1943).

2. Mahadev Desai, "Non-violence and the American Negro," in *The Gandhi Reader: A Source Book of His Life and Writings*, ed. Homer Alexander Jack (Bloomington: Indiana University Press, 1956), 310. For more on Mays and Gandhi, see also Benjamin Mays, *Born to Rebel: An Autobiography* (Athens: University of Georgia Press, 1971), 155–57; Randall Jelk has an excellent discussion on the role of Howard University and Mays in the propagation of Gandhian philosophy. He also has an extensive discussion of Mays's influence on black internationalism and the intensive debates held at Howard University on Gandhian civil disobedience and social protest among other people of color. This atmosphere is essential to Farmer's intellectual development around these issues. Randall Jelk, *Benjamin Elijah Mays, Schoolmaster of the Movement: A Biography* (Chapel Hill: University of North Carolina Press, 2012), 121–29.

3. Farmer, *Lay Bare*, 135.

4. Ibid.; Rayford Logan, *Howard University: The First Hundred Years, 1867–1967* (New York: New York University Press, 1969), 323–406.

5. Rajmohan Gandhi, *Gandhi: The Man, His People, and the Empire* (Berkeley: University of California Press, 2007), 403; Farmer, *Lay Bare*, 135–36.

6. Farmer, *Lay Bare*, 9, 142.

7. Ibid., 135–36, 142. For more on Thurman's propagation of nonviolent philosophy, see Quinton Dixie and Peter Eisenstadt, *Visions of a Better World: Howard Thurman's Pilgrimage to India and the Origins of African American Nonviolence* (Boston: Beacon Press, 2011), 117–50. Dixie and Eisenstadt argue that Thurman's influence also stretched to other Howard University students and associates like Bill Sutherland, Pauli Murray, and Prentice Thomas. Farmer also gave credit to V. F. Calverton aka George Goetz. Goetz was a Marxist writer and editor of the *Modern Monthly*.

8. Jo Ann Robinson, *Abraham Went Out: A Biography of A. J. Muste* (Philadelphia: Temple University Press, 1981), 110. For additional information on Muste and nonviolence, see Leilah Danielson, "Christianity, Dissent, and the Cold War: A. J. Muste's Challenge to Realism and U.S. Empire," *Diplomatic History* (September 2006): 645–69.

9. John D'Emilio, *Lost Prophet: The Life and Times of Bayard Rustin* (New York: Free Press, 2003), 61; Jerald Podair, *Bayard Rustin, American Dreamer* (Lanham, MD: Rowman & Littlefield, 2009), 19; Daniel Levine, *Bayard Rustin and the Civil Rights Movement* (New Brunswick, NJ: Rutgers University Press, 1999), 23–24, 38. For a history of A. Philip Randolph and the March on Washington Movement (MOWM), see Anderson, *A. Philip Randolph: A Biographical*, 249–67; Kersten, *A. Philip Randolph*, 57–67, 137–47; Taylor, *A. Philip Randolph*; Pfeiffer, *A. Philip Randolph, Pioneer*, 128–76; Herbert Garfinkel, *When*

*Negroes March: The March on Washington Movement in the Organizational Politics for FEPC* (New York: Atheneum, 1959); Beth Thompkins Bates, *Pullman Porters and the Rise of Protest Politics in Black America, 1925–1945* (Chapel Hill: University of North Carolina Press, 2001), 162.

10. D'Emilio, *Lost Prophet*, 58; Robinson, *Abraham*, 111.

11. Elliot Rudwick and August Meier, "Origins of Nonviolent Direct Action in Afro-American Protest: Note on Historical Discontinuities," *Along the Color Line*, 307–405; Aldon Morris, *The Origins of the Civil Rights Movement* (New York: Free Press, 1984); Tyson, *Radio Free Dixie*, 27–28.

12. For information on Murray and nonviolent civil disobedience, see Gilmore, *Defying Dixie*, 386–93; Pauli Murray, *Song in a Weary Throat: An American Pilgrimage* (New York: Harper & Row Publishers, 1987), 201.

13. Taylor, *A. Philip Randolph: The Religious*, 160; Pauli Murray, *Song*, 138, 201; Gilmore, *Defying Dixie*, 386. Gilmore also points out that Pauli Murray, James Farmer, and Bayard Rustin all lived in the Harlem Ashram during the 1940s, interracial living space created by H. Holmes Smith, which also served as a site of cross pollination.

14. Juanita Morrow Nelson, interview by author, tape recording, Cleveland, Ohio, January 19, 2004; Pauli Murray, *Song*, 202.

15. Meier and Rudwick, *CORE*, 10–12; Joseph Kip Kosek, *"Richard Gregg, Mohandas Gandhi, and the Strategy of Nonviolence," Journal of American History* 91, no. 4 (March 2005); George Houser, interview by Katherine Shannon, transcript, September 11, 1967, Civil Rights Documentation Project, Moorland Spingarn Library, Howard University, 19; D'Emilio, *Lost Prophet*, 52–53; James Farmer, *Lay Bare*, 98–99, 109–12; Morris, *Origins*, 310; Joseph Kip Kosek, *Acts of Conscience: Christian Nonviolence and Modern American Democracy* (New York: Columbia University Press, 2009), 181. It bares noting that Farmer's personal philosophy was initially more aligned with Gregg; however, for a broader mass movement and CORE's organization, he inclined toward Shridharani.

16. Qtd. in Kosek, *Acts of Conscience*, 181. The general idea of this perspective can be found in Farmer, *Lay Bare*, 111.

17. Other members also read or followed the ideals of Shridharani. These include CORE founders Bernice Fisher, James Robinson, and George Houser, and FOR member Bayard Rustin. D'Emilio, *Lost Prophet*, 53; Murray, *Song*, 138; Farmer, *Lay Bare*, 93; James Robinson, interview by Elliot Rudwick, September 1967, Box 57, Folder 4, August Meier Papers (hereafter Meier Papers), Schomburg Library in New York, New York; Meier and Rudwick, *CORE*, 6; George Houser, *CORE: A Brief History* (New York: Congress of Racial Equality, 1949), 1–2.

18. Farmer, *Lay Bare*, 70–76; Marvin Rich, "The Congress of Racial Equality and Its Strategy," *Annals of the American Academy of Political and Social Science* 357 (January 1965): 113–14. James Farmer notes that he formulated the concepts that became the backbone of CORE during the early months of his time at FOR. Rich notes in his history that an incident in Farmer's hometown, before his arrival to Chicago, prompted the formation of the nonviolent proposal. There has been a great deal of discussion about who actually started CORE. However, given Farmer's early introduction to Gandhi at Howard University and

the nature of the memorandum—an actual step-by-step procedure to form a national non-violent organization, the date of the memorandum, and the activities that rise as a result of the proposal, his book accurately accounts the start of CORE with the memo. This is also confirmed in an unpublished autobiography Fisher wrote. She claims that Farmer crafted the memo in New York and sent it to Chicago. He arrived shortly thereafter and met with a group also experimenting with technique—though Fisher does not clarify actual group activity (likely it was a reference to the interracial Fellowship House that developed separate from the Brotherhood Memorandum). According to Fisher, six people met at Ida Noyes Cafeteria at the University of Chicago to think about applying Gandhian techniques. At the first meeting was George Houser, Jim Farmer, Joseph Guinn, Ken Cuthbertson, Hank Dyer, and Fisher. Bernice Fisher, "Confession of an Ex-Liberal," unpublished manuscript, no date, Box 2R648, Folder: Personal Materials: Correspondence of Lula and James Farmer, 1951–1976, Lula and James Farmer Papers. Additional information will follow in this chapter to further explain how Brotherhood started CORE. For the debate on the origin of CORE, see Robin Washington, "A Conversation with James Farmer," *Fellowship Magazine* 55, no. 4–5 (April/May 1992): 6–8, 17–18; George Houser and Homer Jack, "Getting to the CORE of Our History: Two Respond to Farmer," *Fellowship Magazine* 58, no. 7 (July–August, 1992): 3, 22; "Erasing the Color Line in the North," Conference, October 22, 1992, Bluffton University in Bluffton, Ohio. James Robinson stated that the main founders of CORE revolve on Jim Farmer, George Houser, and Bernice Fisher. A videotape of the conference is available from Bluffton University.

19. Farmer, *Lay Bare*, 358.

20. Muste to Farmer, January 19, 1942, Series A3, Box 2, Folder: Muste General Correspondence: Farmer, Fellowship of Reconciliation Papers (hereafter FOR Papers), SCPC.

21. A. J. Muste to Dear friend, no date, Papers of the Congress of Racial Equality Microfilm (hereafter CORE Papers), Reel 2, Series 1, Folder 33, Frames 1077–80. Enclosed in this letter is Farmer's memo from February 19, 1942, and March 9, 1942. Meier and Rudwick note that this concept only "bore striking resemblance to CORE as it later evolved." Meier and Rudwick, *CORE*, 7; Farmer to Muste, January 8, 1942; Muste to Farmer, January 19, 1942; Muste to Dear Friend, February 19, 1942; Series A3, Box 2, Folder: Muste General Correspondence: Farmer, FOR Papers, SCPC.

22. Houser, *CORE*, 1–2; George Houser interview, September 11, 1967, 11–12.

23. Houser, *CORE*, 1–2; Farmer, *Lay Bare*, 89; A. J. Muste to Dear Friend, February 19, 1942.

24. Farmer, *Lay Bare*, 90; Meier and Rudwick, *CORE*, 5; George Houser interview, September 11, 1967, 22; Fisher, "Confessions."

25. Farmer, *Lay Bare*, 90–91; Meier and Rudwick, *CORE*, 5.

26. Houser to Muste, July 13, 1942, Series A3, Box 2, Folder General Correspondence: Houser, FOR Papers, SCPC; Farmer, *Lay Bare*, 96–97; Houser, *CORE*, 3–8; Meier and Rudwick, *CORE*, 7; Robin Washington, "A Conversation"; George Houser and Homer Jack, "Getting to the CORE of Our History: Two Respond to Farmer"; Robinson interview, September 1967; George Houser interview, September 11, 1967. George

Houser, interview by John D'Emilio, September 17, 1992, Pomona, New York, transcript, Accession no. 06A-007, John D'Emilio Collection, SCPC, pp. 4–5; Houser to Morrow, July 7, 1948, Reel 8, Series III, Folder 12, No. 782, CORE Papers; Fisher, "Confessions." The formation of CORE was a bone of contention among the early members. Most historians simply do not enter the fray. Thomas Sugrue states that Houser and Farmer laid the groundwork for CORE, excluding Bernice Fisher. He also notes that according to Robinson, several members were labor oriented. Sugrue, *Sweet Land*, 145. Meier and Rudwick make this period appear as if the decision to form a group and initiate deseg-regation of White City Roller Rink in April operated separate from the Brotherhood Mobilization Plan. In part, this was a result of Houser's construction of history on CORE and an interview with James Robinson. Both Robinson and the history written by Houser excised key aspects of Farmer's presence. Houser later notes in an interview with Katherine Shannon that the cell and the proposal were two facets of CORE, but then later retracts this statement with author John D'Emilio. This oral history interview falls within a period of debate between Houser and Farmer in articles of the *Fellowship Magazine* regarding the origins of CORE and Farmer's disparaging remark that the Journey of Reconciliation was "unimportant." In this case, he suggested that the plan was only theoretical but that the race cell was interested in action (up until this point, that is not actually the case except for the interracial housing cooperative—which was not direct action and similar to the Harlem Ashram mission). Thus, according to Houser, CORE action was unrelated to Brotherhood. Although Meier and Rudwick reinsert some of Farmer's activities back into CORE's history, they depend on Robinson and Houser's argument that CORE would have existed *without* the Brotherhood plan. Resultantly, the memorandum was couched inaccurately as parallel but unrelated to CORE. In actuality, several aspects paint another picture, including the date of the memorandum, continued meetings of the Chicago study group simultaneous with CORE, focus on mass action and organization over discussion, tactical style, and particularly the key presence of Bernice Fisher, who incited further action. Thus, the proposal generated CORE. It would be more accurate to say then that the Brotherhood Mobilization Plan was CORE's start, but that the race cell gave it legs as Farmer intended.

27. Farmer, *Lay Bare*, 96–97; Houser, *CORE*, 3–4; Meier and Rudwick, *CORE*, 7. Although White City Roller Rink fell flat in terms of direct action, the initiators transi-tioned to a legal challenge of discrimination until the rink was confronted again by direct action in 1946.

28. Farmer, *Lay Bare*, 101–3.

29. James Farmer, "Race Logic of Pacifism," *Fellowship Magazine* 13 (February 1942): 24–25.

30. Minutes of National Council Committee Meeting, April 11, 1942, Series A2, Box 3, Folder Minutes of National FOR Council, FOR Papers, SCPC; Robinson inter-view, September 1967; Houser, *CORE*, 1–3; Meier and Rudwick, *CORE*, 8–9. Meier uses Houser's general charter meeting of 1942 as the foundational moment for CORE. I appropriate the FOR approval as the impetus for CORE. It is highly arguable that such a meeting took place because CORE received FOR backing and as follow up to the White City Roller Rink protest, an event precipitated by the Brotherhood plan. Additionally,

Houser's history lists no specific reason for the charter's meeting beyond general interest in a nonviolent interracial group after the White City protest. Finally, the April 11 go-ahead chronologically appeared before the charter meeting in late April. FOR sponsorship (however stilted) temporarily allowed Houser and other FOR members like Rustin and Farmer to devote the majority of their time to CORE.

31. Minutes of National Council Committee Meeting, April 11, 1942. "Technically," CORE's founding site is Columbus, Ohio, which author Glenda Rabby notes in her book, though without explanation. Glenda Alice Rabby, *The Pain and the Promise: The Struggle for Civil Rights in Tallahassee, Florida* (Athens: University of Georgia Press, 1999), 81.

32. Farmer, *Lay Bare*, 104–5; Kimbrough and Dagen, *Victory without Violence,"* 13–14; Meier and Rudwick, *CORE*, 5, 8; Houser to Morrow, July 7, 1948. Meier and Rudwick did not include Bob Chino and Hugo Victoreen in the original founders, but Farmer notes they appeared in the original meeting. Chino is responsible for the organization's original acronym name, CORE. Houser notes in a letter to Juanita Morrow that the group name came out of an executive meeting in June after the first large charter gathering. He includes Ken Cuthbertson, an American Friends Service Committee member, as an original founder but excludes Chino, Guinn, and Victoreen. Hugo Victoreen does not seem to continue his relationship to CORE, but there appears to be a strong possibility, presuming there was only one Hugo Victoreen associated with the University of Chicago, that he redirected his activities toward his career as a scientist analyzing cosmic rays. See David Roberts, *The Last of His Kind: The Life and Adventures of Bradford Washburn, America's Boldest Mountaineer* (New York: Harper, 2009), 228, 230; Barbara Washburn and Lew Freedman, *The Accidental Adventurer: Memoirs of the First Woman to Climb Mount McKinley* (Kenmore, WA: Epicenter Press, 2001), 85, 89, 115. Meier and Rudwick also list a charter meeting of CORE attended by approximately fifty people in late April. It is not clear as to whether the charter's subcommittee is Farmer's founder's list or if the two are separate. I included Farmer's list because he specifically attributed CORE's name to Chino, an important piece of information missing from Houser's history. Kimbrough and Dagen, *Victory without Violence*, 13. *Victory* also notes the same list from *Lay Bare the Heart* though there is no footnote confirming from where they received the information. As previously noted, Fisher also lists CORE founders. She does not include Chino or Victoreen, but she does add Ken Cuthbertson. Because he is on two founders lists, I include him. Fisher, "Confessions."

33. Farmer, *Lay Bare*, 90–93. For Robinson's letter and report regarding the Jack Spratt Coffee House Case, see CORE interview sheet, May 30, 1942, CORE Papers, microfilm, Reel 8, Series 2, Folder 12, Frame 705; James Robinson to Jack Spratt night manager, May 14, 1942, Reel 8, Series 2, Folder 12, Frames 698–99; no author, "Break Down Race Bars at 47th Street Café," *Chicago Defender*, May 15, 1943, 8; Meier and Rudwick, *CORE*, 13; James Robinson interview, September 1967. I triangulated the date of May 3 and 5, 1942, as the dates of the incident and the first miniature sit-in. This sit-in ended with the manager throwing their money at them. Farmer notes that this event took place before the twenty-plus group that sat in at Jack Spratt in May 1942, which ended in the full desegregation of Jack Spratt. Meier notes that this event ended in victory after a call to the police by the manager failed to garner the hoped-for response. Robinson's interview confirms the

small group sit-in, which occurred before the group of twenty or more, but gives no date. Farmer claims the event occurred before he sent his second memo to A. J. Muste for the Brotherhood Mobilization Plan. This would place the first small sit-in between February 19 and March 9, 1942. But, according to correspondence, it was in May.

34. Farmer, *Lay Bare*, 93.

35. Ibid.; Hamilton Bims, "CORE: Wild Child of Civil Rights," *Ebony Magazine* (October 1965), 37.

36. Farmer, *Lay Bare*, 91–92; James Robinson interview, September 1967.

37. No author, "Break Down Race Bars at 47th Street Café."

38. Farmer, *Lay Bare*, 94.

39. Report of the Chicago Youth Secretary, George Houser, September 12, 1942; Report of the Field Secretary, James Farmer, September 12, 1942; Series A2, Box 3, Folder Minutes FOR National Council, FOR Papers, SCPC.

40. Minutes of Executive Committee Meeting, September 29, 1942, Series A2, Box 3, Folder Minutes of National FOR Council, FOR Papers, SCPC; Minutes of Nonviolent Action Committee Meeting, October 26, 1942, Series A1, Box 3, Folder FOR Committee Program, FOR Papers, SCPC. October 26, 1942 Minutes also found in Box 2R596, Folder: General File: FOR, 1944–1968, Farmer Papers.

41. Minutes of Nonviolent Action Committee Meeting, October 26, 1942.

42. Minutes of Executive Committee Meeting, September 29, 1942; Minutes of Nonviolent Action Committee Meeting, October 26, 1942; Minutes of Nonviolent Action Committee Meeting, November 23, 1942, December 21, 1942, March 24, 1945, Series A2, Box 3, Folder FOR Committee Program, FOR Papers, SCPC; Meier and Rudwick, *CORE*, 16. Meier and Rudwick suggested that Muste accepted the separation of CORE and FOR. This "acceptance" actually hinged on the belief that CORE remained under FOR control as long as its staff created and ran it. However, when it became clear that FOR could not maintain power, tensions increased.

43. Minutes of Nonviolent Action Committee Meeting, November 23, 1942.

44. George Houser interview, September 11, 1967, 23.

45. CORE negotiated, protested, and worked mainly on restaurants and public accommodation. For a listing of CORE interview sheets that cover restaurants of concern in the Chicago Loop, see Reel 49, Series 6, Folder 13, n 281, CORE Papers; Houser, *CORE*, 4; Reel 8, Series 2, Folder 12, 699, 702–11, 721.

46. Meier and Rudwick, *CORE*, 17, 24–25.

47. Farmer, *Lay Bare*, 94.

48. Ibid., 403. For more on Gandhi and African Americans, see Sudarshan Kapur, *Raising Up a Prophet: African American Relationship to India* (Boston, MA: Beacon Press, 1992). See also Vijay Prashad, "Waiting for the Black Gandhi: Satyagraha and Black Internationalism," in *From Toussaint to Tupac: The Black International since the Age of Revolution*, ed. Michael O. West, William G. Martin, and Fanon Che Wilkins (Chapel Hill: University of North Carolina Press, 2009), 179–96; Mary King, *Mahatma Gandhi and Martin Luther King, Jr.: The Power of Nonviolent Action* (Paris: UNESCO, 1999); Christopher Waldrep, *African Americans Confront Lynching: Strategies of Resistance from the*

*Civil War to the Civil Rights Era* (Lanham, MD: Rowman & Littlefield, 2009), 98–99; Sean Chabot, *Transnational Roots of the Civil Rights Movement: African American Exploration of the Gandhian Repertoire* (Plymouth, United Kingdom: Lexington Books, 2012); David Hardiman, *Gandhi in His Time and Ours: The Global Legacy of His Ideas* (New York: Columbia University Press, 2003), 255–77; Nico Slate, *Colored Cosmopolitanism: The Shared Struggle for Freedom in the United States and India* (Cambridge, MA: Harvard University Press, 2012); Gerald Horne, *The End of Empires: African Americans and India* (Philadelphia: Temple University Press, 2008); Marc Gallicchio, *The African American Encounter with Japan and China: Black Internationalism in Asia, 1895–1945* (Chapel Hill: University of North Carolina Press, 2000), 148–49; Horace Cayton, "Fighting for White Folks," *Nation* 155, no. 13 (September 26, 1942): 267–70; Mahatma Gandhi, *The Essential Gandhi: An Anthology of His Writings in His Life, Work, and Ideas* (New York: Vintage Books, 2002).

49. Howard Thurman, *With Head and Heart: The Autobiography of Howard Thurman* (New York: Harcourt, Brace, Jovanovich, 1979), 105, 132–35.

50. Ibid., 132; Gandhi, *The Essential*, 280. This was quoted differently in other texts as "it may be through the Negroes that the unadulterated message of nonviolence will be delivered to the world."

51. Gilmore, *Defying Dixie*, 386–87.

52. Clayton, "Fighting for White Folks," 268.

53. Qtd. in Horne, *The End of Empires*, 118.

54. Farmer, *Lay Bare*, 112; Hardiman, *Gandhi in His Time*, 256–57; Kosek, *Acts of Conscience*, 180–81.

55. For discussion on Calverton and radicalism, refer to Haim Genizi, "V. F. Calverton, a Radical Magazinist for Black Intellectuals, 1920–1940," *Journal of Negro History* 57, no 3 (July 1972): 241–53; Leonard Wilcox, *V. F. Calverton: Radical in the American Grain* (Philadelphia: Temple University Press, 1992); Philip Abbott, *Leftward Ho!: V. F. Calverton and American Radicalism* (Westport, CT: Greenwood Press, 1993).

56. Farmer, *Lay Bare*, 137–44.

57. Meier and Rudwick, *CORE*, 15–16, 21; James Robinson interview, September 1967. James Robinson interview, December 1967, Box 57, Folder 4, Meier Papers.

58. James Robinson interview, September 1967; Meier and Rudwick, *CORE*, 22–23; Farmer, *Lay Bare*, 355–60; A. J. Muste to Friend, February 19, 1942. Robinson recalls that mass action was a construction of Farmer's Brotherhood Mobilization Plan. However, early Chicago CORE did not support it and instead preferred small group action. If the group grew, then the core cadre of nonviolent activists would serve as a model. There was, of course, dissention over this matter and Robinson represented only one side of it.

59. Farmer, *Lay Bare*, 111–12.

60. Farmer's reference to hiding his pacifism first publicly appears in his book *Lay Bare the Heart*; however, it was repeated sometime earlier in a 1978 letter exchange with author Jo Ann Robinson, writer of *Abraham Went Out: A Biography of A. J. Muste*. None of Farmer's comments appear in the book. James Farmer to Jo Ann Robinson, February 28, 1978.

61. Farmer to Jo Ann Robinson, February 28, 1978.

62. Muste to Houser and Farmer, June 4, 1943, Series A3, Box 2, Folder General Correspondence: Farmer, FOR Papers, SCPC.

63. Ibid.

64. Ibid.

65. Swomley to Muste, July 7, 1943, Series A2, Box 5, Folder Muste General Correspondence: Swomley, FOR Papers, SCPC.

66. Ibid.

67. James Farmer to George Houser, February 5, 1943, Reel 11, Series III, Folder 47, Frames 905–6, CORE Papers.

68. Garfinkel, When Negroes March, 144; D'Emilio, Lost Prophet, 60–61; Scott Bennett, Radical Pacifism: The War Resisters League and Gandhian Nonviolence in America, 1915–1963 (Syracuse, NY: Syracuse University Press, 2003), 95–96.

69. Letter from Swomley to Muste, July 7, 1943, and July 11, 1943; Series A3, Box 5, Folder General Correspondence: Swomley, FOR Papers, SCPC. Letter from Muste to Swomley, July 13, 1943; Series A3, Box 2, General Correspondence: Farmer, FOR Papers, SCPC; Farmer, *Lay Bare*, 155 56. Farmer was accused of being jealous of MOWM. This may or may not be true, though it can surely be said that Farmer distrusted MOWM's true intentions. Likely, Farmer was more dismissive of MOWM given Randolph's propensity to utilize various tools for specific political ends, thus not becoming the movement Farmer envisioned.

70. Farmer to Houser, February 5, 1943, Reel 11, Series III, Folder 47, No. 905–6, CORE Papers.

71. Swomley to Muste, July 11, 1943, Series A2, Box 5, Folder Muste General Correspondence: Swomley, FOR Papers, SCPC.

72. Ibid.; John Swomley, November 18, 1993, interview by John D'Emilio, Accession no. 06A-007, John D'Emilio Collection, SCPC; Meier and Rudwick, *CORE*, 16. Swomley claimed he was not antagonistic toward CORE, but that's questionable given this letter.

73. Muste to Swomley, July 13, 1943, Series A2, Box 5, Folder Muste General Correspondence: Swomley, FOR Papers, SCPC.

74. Farmer, *Lay Bare*, 111.

75. Ibid.

76. Ibid., 116.

77. Ibid., 116. Farmer to Jo Ann Robinson, February 28, 1978.

78. Houser to Muste, June 8, 1943, and Houser to Swomley, July 1, 1943; FOR Papers, Series A, Box 2, Folder Muste General Correspondence: Houser, FOR Papers, SCPC; Meier and Rudwick, *CORE*, 20, 22–23.

79. Swomley to Houser, July 6, 1943; Series A3, Box 2, Folder General Correspondence: Houser, FOR Papers, SCPC; Muste to Swomley, July 13, 1943.

80. Houser to Muste, December 28, 1943; Series A3, Box 2, Folder General Correspondence: Houser, FOR Papers, SCPC.

81. For examples references on Muste and nonviolence, see A. J. Muste, *Non-violence in an Aggressive World* (New York: Harper, 1972); Ira Chernus, *American Nonviolence:*

*The History of an Idea* (Maryknoll, NY: Orbis Books, 2004), 127–44; Leilah Danielson, *American Gandhi: A. J. Muste and the History of Radicalism in the Twentieth Century* (Philadelphia: University of Pennsylvania Press, 2014), 202–29; A. J. Muste, *The Essays of A. J. Muste* (Indianapolis: Bobbs-Merrill Company, 1967). Most of these essays refer directly or indirectly to nonviolence. For specific discussion on nonviolence, refer to A. J. Muste, "Sit Downs and Lie Downs," in Muste, *The Essays*, 203–6; A. J. Muste, "A Holy Disobedience," in Muste, *The Essays*, 355–77; Muste, "The World Task of Pacifism," in Muste, *The Essays*, 215–30; Muste, A. J. Muste, "What the Bible Teaches about Freedom," in Muste, *The Essays*, 279–95.

82. Muste to Houser, January 11, 1944; Series A3, Box 2, FOR Papers, General Correspondence: Houser, FOR Papers, SCPC.

83. Houser to Muste, February 23, 1944, Muste to Houser, February 25, 1944, Series A3, Box 2, Folder General Correspondence: Houser, FOR Papers, SCPC.

84. Minutes of Executive Committee Meeting, February 24, 1944, and March 28, 1944, FOR Papers, Series A-2, Box 3, Folder Minutes of National FOR Council, SCPC.

85. Muste to Swomley, December 3, 1945, Box 13, Folder Houser: National Staff Correspondence (1944–1945), Swomley Papers, SCPC.

86. Meier and Rudwick, *CORE*, 20–21.

87. Ibid.; Houser, *CORE*.

88. Bernice Fisher to George Houser, January 27, 1949, Reel 15, Series III, Folder 82, Frame 528, CORE Papers; Meier and Rudwick, *CORE*, 16; James Robinson interview, September 1967. Robinson also expressed concern about Houser running CORE, though Robinson claimed that Houser deliberately kept the organization small in order to make it more manageable for himself as national director of CORE.

89. Fisher, "Confessions."

90. Bernice Fisher to George Houser, June 6, 1944, Reel 11, Series III, Folder 47, 917–18, CORE Papers.

91. Bernice Fisher to "Slug," October 1, 1945, Reel 10, Series III, Folder 38, Frame 468, CORE Papers.

92. Ibid.

93. Fisher to Houser, July 12, 1944, Reel 11, Series III, Folder 47, Frame 921, CORE Papers.

94. Meier and Rudwick, *CORE*, 25.

95. Fisher to Houser, July 12, 1944.

96. Houser to Muste, April 28, 1944, Series A3, Box 2, Folder General Correspondence Houser Collection, FOR Papers, SCPC.

97. Houser to Swomley, July 12, 1944, Series C, Box 13, Folder National FOR Staff Correspondence: Houser (1944–1949), Swomley Papers, SCPC.

98. Farmer, *Lay Bare*, 155–57; D'Emilio, *Lost Prophet*, 61; Anderson, *Bayard Rustin*, 86.

99. Farmer, "Race Logic," 25.

100. August Meier and Elliot Rudwick, "The Origins of Nonviolent Direct Action," 349. For more ties to MOWM and CORE, see Jonathan Rosenberg, *How Far the Promised*

*Land?: World Affairs and the American Civil Rights Movement from the First War to Vietnam* (Princeton, NJ: Princeton University Press, 2006), 147–48.

101. Jay Holmes Smith to A. J. Muste, July 8, 1943, Series A3, Box 15, Folder FOR Muste Subject File: MOWM, FOR Papers, SCPC.

102. Bates, *Pullman Porters*, 167–76; Pamphlet, March on Washington Movement Policy Conference, *March on Washington Movement: Proceedings of Conference Held in Detroit, September 26–27, 1942* (Detroit: MOWM, 1942), Series A3, Box 15, Folder FOR Muste Subject File: MOWM, FOR Papers, SCPC. It is worth noting that there is a special section in the MOWM pamphlet on India.

103. March on Washington, Proceedings of Conference Held in Detroit, September 26–27, 1942, Series A3, Box 15, Folder FOR Muste Subject File: MOWM, FOR Papers, SCPC.

104. Meier and Rudwick, *CORE*, 23–25.

105. Bernice claimed Robinson's actions in Chicago had become detrimental to CORE. It was not clear what precipitated the break, but Robinson remained in Chicago. Fisher to Houser, July 12, 1944, Reel 11, Series III, Folder 47, Frame 922, CORE Papers.

106. Muste to Swomley, February 1, 1945; Muste to Swomley et al., May 7, 1945, Series A3, Box 2, Folder General Correspondence: Farmer, FOR Papers, SCPC. Houser on Farmer's dismissal is not clear on his reference to "organizational man," though one could argue for either interpretation—i.e., Farmer's refusal to tow the FOR line, or the belief that Farmer lacked organizational skills. George Houser to Irene Osborne, August 12, 1946, Reel 11, Series III, Folder 47, Frames 1255–56, CORE Papers.

## 2. Negroes Will Not Be Pacifists

1. Juanita Morrow Nelson, interview with author, Cleveland, Ohio, January 19, 2004. Cleveland CORE membership, April 28, 1949, Reel 9, Series III, Folder 16, Frame 85, CORE Papers; Notes on various chapters, no date, Box 3, Folder 4, Meier Rudwick Papers, Wisconsin Historical Society (hereafter WHS). The membership numbers possibly dropped tremendously after 1949. The record indicated that by spring 1949, the chapter had not—as yet—received any dues. This would be in line with some of the changes occurring within the chapter during this period, particularly with the loss of Juanita Morrow. Membership numbers from 1944 to 1945 could not be located, but it can be assumed to be smaller as the chapter's most active period appeared in 1946. Cleveland CORE was one of three chapters, Vanguard League of Columbus, Ohio, and the Kansas City, Kansas, with a measurable black membership. Rudwick and Meier, *CORE*, 24.

2. Cleveland CORE membership, April 28, 1949.

3. Russell H. Davis, *Black Americans in Cleveland from George Peake to Carl B. Stokes, 1796–1969* (Washington, DC: Associated Publishers, 1972), 231–32; Kenneth Kusmer, *A Ghetto Takes Shape: Black Cleveland, 1870–1930* (Urbana: University of Illinois Press, 1976), 241.

4. "Statement of the Cleveland Committee Organization on the Racial Policy of the YMCA," 1944, Reel 16, Series III, Folder 92, Frame 290, CORE Papers.

5. For more on Don't Buy campaigns, see Cheryl Lynn Greenberg, *"Or does it explode?": Black Harlem in the Great Depression* (New York: Oxford University Press, 1991), 116–21; Meier and Rudwick, "The Origins of Nonviolent Direct Action"; Drake St. Clair and Horace Cayton, *Black Metropolis: A Study of Negro Life in a Northern City* (Chicago: University of Chicago Press, 1993), 84-86, 295, 463; Ralph Crowther, "Don't Buy Where You Can't Work: An Investigation of the Political Forces and Social Conflict within the Harlem Boycott of 1934," *Afro-Americans in New York Life and History* 15, no. 2 (July 1990): 7–44; Michelle Pacifico, "Don't Buy Where You Cant Work: The New Negro Alliance of Washington," *Washington History* 6, no. 1 (1994): 66–88.

6. Kimberley L. Phillips, AlabamaNorth: African-American Migrants, Community, and Working-Class Activism in Cleveland, 1915–45 (Urbana: University of Illinois Press, 1999), 4, 190; Charles Harold Leob, The Future Is Yours: The History of the Future Outlook League, 1935–1946 (Cleveland: Future Outlook League, 1947); Kenneth M. Zinz, The Future Outlook League of Cleveland: A Negro Protest Organization (MA thesis, Kent State University, 1973).

7. Phillips, *AlabamaNorth*, 4, 208–10; Leob, *Future Is Yours*, 32, 53–57.

8. Phillips, *AlabamaNorth*, 240.

9. Ibid., 225, 240, 249; Zinz, *The Future Outlook*, 131–32.

10. George Houser, September 11, 1967.

11. Davis, *Black Americans*, 58, 127–29; Bessie House-Soremekun, *Confronting the Odds: African American Entrepreneurship in Cleveland, Ohio* (Kent, OH: Kent State University Press, 2002), 13–17, 32; Sharyn Kane and Richard Keeton, *In Those Days: African-American Life near the Savannah River* (Atlanta: National Park Service-Southeast Region, 1994), 20–23; Kusmer, *A Ghetto Takes Shape*, 10; Laura Tuennerman-Kaplan, *Helping Others, Helping Ourselves: Power, Giving, and Community Identity in Cleveland, Ohio, 1880–1930* (Kent, OH: Kent State University Press, 2001), 84–85; Barney and Brian Holly Warf, "The Rise and Fall and Rise of Cleveland," *Annals of the American Academy of Political and Social Science* 551 (May 1997): 209–10; Christopher G. Wye, "Midwest Ghetto: Patterns of Negro Life and Thought in Cleveland, Ohio, 1929–1945" (PhD diss., Kent State University, 1973), 4.

12. Davis, *Black Americans*, 309. For more information on population increases and expansion of the ghetto, see Kenneth Kusmer's *Ghetto Takes Shape* (previously cited); Raymond J. Jirran, "Cleveland and the Negro Following World War II" (PhD diss., Kent State University, 1972); William Franklin Moore, *"Status of the Negro in Cleveland"* (PhD diss., Ohio State University, 1953); Alonzo Gaskell Grace, "The Effect of Negro Migration on the Cleveland Public School System" (PhD diss., Western Reserve University, 1932); Robert L. Hodgart, "The Process of Expansion of the Negro Ghetto in Cities of the Northern United States: A Case Study of Cleveland, Ohio University Park, Pennsylvania" (Master's thesis, Pennsylvania State University, 1968); David E. Weber, "Negro Voting Behavior in Cleveland: 1928–1945" (Master's thesis, Kent State University, 1971).

13. Jirran, "Cleveland and the Negro," 272; Davis, *Black Americans*, 272–73, 329; Weber, "Negro Voting," 2.

14. Phillips, *AlabamaNorth*, 195, 197; Charles Harold Leob, *The Future Is Yours*, 19.

15. Davis, *Black Americans*, 271; Weber, "Negro Voting," 64.

16. Davis, *Black Americans*, 271, 330, 352.

17. Ibid., 271, 330, 352, 308.

18. Phillips, *AlabamaNorth*, 216.

19. Davis, *Black Americans*, 232, 332–33; Wye, *Midwest Ghetto*, 80.

20. Davis, *Black Americans*, 319; Kusmer, *A Ghetto Takes Shape*, 229; Judith Stein, *The World of Marcus Garvey: Race and Class in Modern Society* (Baton Rouge: Louisiana State University Press, 1986), 238–42; Stein, *The World of Marcus Garvey*, 238–41; Leonard Moore, *Carl B. Stokes and the Rise of Black Political Power* (Urbana: University of Illinois Press, 2002), 24–25; Andrew Fearnley, "Your Work Is the Most Important, But Without Branches There Can Be No National Work: Cleveland Branch of the NAACP, 1929–1968," in Kevern Verney and Lee Sartain, *Long Is the Way Hard: One Hundred Years of the National Association of the Advancement of Colored People (NAACP)* (Fayetteville: University of Arkansas Press, 2009), 205, 210–11; Davis, *Black Americans*, 307, 318–19; Wye, *Midwest Ghetto*, 440. W. O. Walker was a leading activist in the NAACP and greatly responsible for its support of more assertive organizations like the Future Outlook League. The organization also built a relationship with the labor organization, CIO. Additionally, the NAACP encouraged workers to participate in unions, helped the FOL during negotiations, and used CIO leaders in their protest activities.

21. Vanessa Northington Gamble, *Making a Place for Ourselves: The Black Hospital Movement, 1920–1945* (New York: Oxford University Press, 1995), 152–60, 177, 180, 268; Davis, *Black Americans*, 247–51; Kusmer, *A Ghetto Takes Shape*, 266; William Giffin, "The Mercy Hospital Controversy among Cleveland's Afro-American Civic Leaders, 1927," *Journal of Negro History* 61, no. 4 (October 1976). 333.

22. Phillips, *AlabamaNorth*, 213–14; Davis, *Black Americans*, 319.

23. "Jim Crow Absent in Restaurants," *Call and Post* article, Reel 9, Series III, Folder 16, Frame 131, CORE Papers.

24. No author, "Interracial Party Supplies Funds to Fight Jim Crow," *Call and Post*, June 2, 1945, 5b, c5.

25. No author, "CORE Hears Attorney on World Citizenship," *Call and Post*, October 19, 1946, 5A, c4; "Housing Is Topic of Gordon Simpson at CORE Meeting Thursday," *Call and Post*, September 15, 1945, 7A, c7.

26. No author, "Interracial Church Meets Thru-out June," *Call and Post*, May 25, 1946, 11a, c1.

27. No author, "Interracial Church Members Cause Stir at Zion Hill," *Call and Post*, September, 7, 1946, 12A, c3; "Interracial Church to Be Planned Sun. at Euclid Ave. Baptist," *Call and Post*, May 11, 1946, 13A, c1; "Plan for Meeting on Interracial Church, *Call and Post*, May 11, 1946, 13B, c8; "Interracial Church Forum Sparks Heated Discussion," *Call and Post*, May 4, 194, cover, c1.

28. Juanita Nelson, August 1967, Box 56, Folder 12, Meier interview, August Meier Papers; Sugrue, *Sweet Land*, 135. Morrow interview, 2004; Press Release on Action projects during CORE convention, May 27, 1946, Reel 16, Series III, Folder 27, Frame 726, CORE Papers. Abigail F. Brownwell, *Child Care Facilities for Dependent and Neglected*

*Negro Children in Three Cities: New York, Philadelphia, Cleveland* (New York: Child Welfare League of America, 1945), 165–68; Hortense Davis to George Houser, February 13, 1950, CORE Papers, Reel 9, Series III, Folder 16, Frame 97; Juanita Morrow to George Houser, October 7, 1946, Reel 9, Series III, Folder 16, Frame 57, CORE Papers. CORE had committees on dependent children, employment, and housing. The organization posed no major challenge to discriminatory practices in the latter two areas, but had some success with investigations into mistreatment of black children under social services. Juanita Morrow (Nelson), CORE's second black chairperson, noted that though members considered employment and residential inequality important, they failed to openly engage these issues. Ostensibly this was due to the belief that direct action campaigns against housing or the lack thereof would be an unwieldy and difficult campaign. The degree to which direct action could be characterized as not applicable depended more on what CORE members were willing to do versus if the tactic applied. The Future Outlook League, for example, launched a forceful direct action campaign on behalf of housing discrimination. They organized tenant groups in each building, threatened rent strikes, and forced the city and some of Cleveland's notorious slum landlords to deal with tenants' rights.

29. Meier and Rudwick, *CORE*, 21.

30. Gamble, *Making a Place*, 177, 180.

31. "CORE Hear Lucas on Hospital Situation," *Call and Post* article, Reel 9, Series III, Folder 16, Frame 127, CORE Papers.

32. "Statement of the Cleveland Committee Organization on the Racial Policy of the YMCA," Reel 16, Series III, Folder 92, Frame 290, CORE Papers; "Attorney Hits 'Y' Discrimination," *Cleveland Call and Post*, May 12, 1945, 10A.

33. Ibid.

34. "Progress Report on Efforts Toward Changing Racial Policy of the Cleveland YMCA, June 1945," Reel 16, Series III, Folder 92, Frame 321, CORE Papers. Report of the CORE Meeting with the Race Policy Committee with the Board of Trustees of Cleveland YMCA," Reel 16, Series III, Folder 92, Frames 300–301, CORE Papers.

35. George Houser to Editor of the *Call and Post*, June 12, 1945, Reel 16, Series III, Folder 92, Frame 302, CORE Papers.

36. Ibid.

37. No author, "*Call and Post* Newspaper Forum Presents: Should Negroes Support Cedar YMCA," *Call and Post*, June 9, 1945, 8A.

38. For more information on YMCAs and segregation, see Susan Kerr Chandler, "Almost a Partnership: African Americans, Segregation, and the Young Men's Christian Association," *Journal of Sociology & Social Welfare* 27 (1994): 97–111; Nina Mjagkij, *Light in the Darkness: African Americans and the YMCA, 1852–1946* (Lexington: University Press of Kentucky, 1994). Mjagkij examines the movement from cooperation and gradualism to desegregation. She also explains that the period following World War II generated an environment that pushed the YMCA to examine its position.

39. "Cleveland YMCA Branches Open Doors," *Call and Post* article, CORE Papers, Reel 16, Series III, Frame 340, Folder 92. "Cleveland Y Adopts Full Integration," *Call and Post* article, Reel 16, Series III, Folder 92, Frame 340, CORE Papers.

40. Moore, *Carl B. Stokes*, 23–24; Cora Lewis, "The McKinney Story: One Man's War against Sin," *Call and Post*, January 12, 1963, 9b.

41. No author, "CORE Hears Dr. Sharpe June 7: Public Is Invited to Public Meet, Dance of 4th Annual Confab," *Call and Post*, June 1, 1946; Norman S. Minor, Frank C. Lyons et al., "*Call and Post* Newspaper Forum Presents: Should Negroes Support Cedar YMCA," *Call and Post*, June 9, 1945, 8A; No author, "Community Leaders Back Cedar Branch Membership Drive," *Call and Post*, April 6, 1946, 5A.

42. Morrow interview, 2004; Morrow interview, 1967, Meier Papers.

43. Morrow interview, 2004; Rosalie G. Riegle, *Crossing the Line: Nonviolent Resisters Speak Out for Peace* (Eugene, OR: Cascade Books, 2013), 327. Morrow recalls that Howard University CORE emerged from this incident. The NAACP took credit for the event as a youth protest by their chapter. Actually, the group may have been influenced by both organizations but initially went under the name Howard University Civil Rights Committee. For more on Nelson's biography, see Marian Mollin, "The Limits of Egalitarianism: Radical Pacifism, Civil Rights, and the Journey of Reconciliation," *Radical History Review* 88, no. 1 (January 1, 2004): 126.

44. Morrow interview, 2004.

45. No author, "CORE Says Farewell to Former Chairman," *Call and Post*, August 17, 1946, 5A; Davis, *Black Americans*, 274; Raymond Jirran, "Cleveland and the Negro," 38–40. Jirran's manuscript is one of only a couple of sources to address CORE's role at Euclid Beach.

46. "Report of the Activities of the Cleveland Branch," 1946, Box 35, Folder 2, NAACP Cleveland Chapter Papers (hereafter NAACP Papers), Western Reserve Historical Society (hereafter WRHS)

47. Charles Leob, "Ejected from Euclid Beach Mixed Party: Park Management Admits Negro Patrons Barred from Swimming, Dancing, Skating," *Call and Post*, July 27, 1946, cover page, c1.

48. "Euclid Beach Authorities Openly Flout Civil Rights Laws; Members of Core to Sue after Manhandling," *Call and Post*, Reel 9, Series III, Folder 16, Frame 126, CORE Papers; Davis, *Black Americans*, 274; "Ejected from Euclid Beach Mixed Party," *Call and Post*, September 21, 1946, cover page, c1. "Burrell Asks $500 from Euclid Beach for Bias," *Call and Post* article, Reel 9, Series III, Folder 16, Frame 131, CORE Papers.

49. "Beach Guard Goes on Trial Sept. 30th," *Call and Post*, September 28, 1946, article, Reel 9, Series III, Folder 16, Frame 126, CORE Papers; "Beach Policeman to Face Jury on Sept. 30th," *Call and Post*, September 14, 1946, cover page, c5; "Clevelander Beaten, Evicted, by Private Police at Euclid," *Call and Post*, August 31, 1946, article, Box 41, Folder 2, Urban League Papers, WRHS. "'All-Woman Jury' Finds Vago Guilty of Beach Assault," *Call and Post*, cover, c1, November 16, 1946.

50. "Clevelander Beaten, Evicted, by Private Police at Euclid," *Call and Post*, August 31, 1946, Box 41, Folder 2, Urban League Papers, WRHS.

51. "These organizations Have Registered Their Support for Ordinance 2230-46 as of January 15, 1947," Box 41, Folder 2, Urban League Papers, WRHS; "Beach Policeman to Face Jury on Sept. 30th," *Call and Post*, September 14, 1946, cover page, c5; Future

Outlook League, "Minutes of FOL August 28, 1946," "Minutes of the FOL September 4, 1946," "Minutes of the FOL September 11, 1946," "Minutes of the FOL September 25, 1946," and "Minutes of the FOL October 2, 1946," Box 1, Folder 5, Future Outlook League Papers, WRHS. Established by Cleveland mayor Burke, the Amity Board was a response to the 1943 outbreak of violence and racial tension in Detroit. Early on, the Amity Board gained a surprising amount of power given its fledgling status. For more information, see Cleveland Community Relations Board, *Accepting the Challenge: A Commemorative History of the Cleveland Community Relations Board, 1845–1955* (Cleveland, OH: City of Cleveland, 1955).

52. "Outlook League Joins in Fight to Aid Victim," *Call and Post*, September 14, 1946. 4A, c8; "Report of the Activities of the Cleveland Branch, 1946," Box 2, Folder 1, NAACP Papers, WRHS.

53. "Core Members Protest Brutality of Euclid Beach Policemen," *Call and Post*, September 28, 1946, article, Reel 9, Series III, Folder 16, Frame 136, CORE Papers.

54. "Gestapo Methods at Euclid Beach," *Call and Post*, August 31, 1946, Page 4B, c1; Juanita Morrow, "Eyewitness Story of Beach Bigotry," *Call and Post*, September 28, 1946, Reel 9, Series III, Folder 16, Frame 131, CORE Papers; Bob Williams, "Guards Assault, Shoot Policemen," *Call and Post*, September 28, 1946, Reel 9, Series III, Folder 16, Frame 135, CORE Papers.

55. Ibid.

56. Ibid.

57. Ibid.

58. Letter from Tad Tekla to George Houser, September 30, 1946, Reel 9, Series III, Folder 16, Frame 51, CORE Papers; Juanita Morrow to George Houser, October 7, 1946, Reel 9, Series III, Folder 16, Frame 57, CORE Papers; "Wheels of Justice Move Very Slowly in Beach Assaults," *Call and Post*, Reel 9, Series III, Folder 16, Frame 129, CORE Papers; "Beach Opens April 24, No Rule on Dance Hall," 1947, *Call and Post*, Reel 9, Series III, Folder 16, Frame 130, CORE Papers.

59. Juanita Morrow to George Houser, September 1946, Reel 9, Series III, Folder 16, Frame 41–44, CORE Papers.

60. FBI Report to Assistant Attorney General Theron Candle, July 19, 1946, FBI Papers, author's possession; "Fourth Annual Convention," June 1946 minutes, Reel 9, Series III: Folder 25, Frame 737, CORE Papers.

61. Letter from George Houser to Juanita Morrow, October 2, 1946, Reel 9, Series III, Folder 16, Frame 53, CORE Papers.

62. Letter from Morrow to Houser, October 7, 1946," Reel 9, Series III, Folder 16, Frame 57, CORE Papers.

63. Morrow interview, 2004.

64. Lynn Coleman, Raymond Jirran, interview notes, Raymond Jirran Papers, unprocessed collection (hereafter Jirran Papers), WRHS.

65. Ibid.

66. George Houser to Juanita Morrow, October 2, 1946, Reel 9, Series III, Folder 16, Frame 53, CORE Papers.

67. Tad Tekla to *Cleveland News* Newspaper Editor, September 22, 1946, Reel 9, Series III, Folder 16, Frame 45, CORE Papers.

68. George Houser to Lynn Coleman, October 7, 1946, Reel 9, Series III, Folder 16, Frame 60, CORE Papers.

69. Lynn Coleman to George Houser, October 16, 1946, Reel 9, Series III, Folder 16, Frame 61, CORE Papers.

70. "'All-Woman Jury' Finds Vago Guilty of Beach Assault," *Call and Post*, November 16, 1946, cover, c1; "Victims Given Official Run Around in Euclid Beach Assault Complaints," *Call and Post*, October 5, 1946, cover, c1.

71. "Beach Opens April 24, No Rule on Dance Hall," *Call and Post* article, Reel 9, Series III, Folder 16, Frame 130, CORE Papers.

72. "Frame Up" and "Coleman's Injury Not Permanent," *Call and Post* article, Reel 9, Series III, Folder 16, Frame 127, CORE Papers; Juanita Morrow to George Houser, September 1946, Reel 9, Series III, Folder 16, Frames 41–44, CORE Papers; Juanita Morrow to George Houser, October 7, 1946, Reel 9, Series III, Folder 16, Frame 57, CORE Papers.

73. Memo Swomley to Muste, Houser, Rustin, July 25, 1946; dg226, Box 14, Folder Houser: National Staff Correspondence (1946–1949), FOR Papers.

74. Muste to Swomley and Sayre, August 13, 1946; dg226, Box 14, Folder Houser: National Staff Correspondence (1946–1949), FOR Papers.

75. Muste to Swomley, September 26, 1945, Series A-2, Box 5, Folder Muste General Correspondence. Swomley, FOR Papers—dg13, SCPC.

76. Worthy, Bill Sutherland, Ella Baker, Pauli Murray, and William Worthy participated in the original planning committee, according to historian John D'Emilio. See D'Emilio, *Lost Prophet*, 133. For more information on the Journey of Reconciliation, see Mollin, "The Limits"; Catsum, *Freedom's Main Line*; Raymond Arsenault, "You Don't Have to Ride Jim Crow: CORE and the 1947 Journey of Reconciliation," in *Before* Brown: *Civil Rights and White Backlash in the Modern South*, ed. Glenn Feldman (Tuscaloosa: University of Alabama Press, 2004). This same piece also appears in Arsenault's full-length monograph on the Freedom Rides. Ray Arsenault, *Freedom Riders: 1961 and the Struggle for Racial Justice* (New York: Oxford University Press, 2006), 11–55; Bayard Rustin and George Houser, *We Challenged Jim Crow: A Report on the Journey of Reconciliation, April 9–23, 1947* (New York: Fellowship of Reconciliation, 1947).

77. Juanita Morrow interview, 2004; Mollin, "The Limits," 118–19, 125–29. Mollin's essay provides the most extensive discussion of the exclusion of women from JOR and the gender conflicts within the pacifist movement; Katie Raymond to Lois Drushell, June 24, 1947, Reel 9, Series III, Folder 16, Frame 74, CORE Papers.

78. Meier and Rudwick, *CORE*, 20, 32; James Robinson interview, September 1967; James Robinson interview, December 1967; Lula Farmer, February 27, 1967, interview by Meier and Rudwick, Box 56, Folder 6, August Meier Papers, Schomburg Research Center, New York. Houser's title changes when he leaves Cleveland. Additionally, the authors claim that FOR jointly sponsored CORE projects. Actually, the situation was reversed. FOR projects incorporated CORE, a move that kept Muste from accusing Houser of divided

246 Notes to Pages 43–46

loyalties. JOR was one such example. JOR was generated within and for job obligations associated with the Racial Industrial Department in FOR. However, it was CORE inspired and led. Some CORE members, particularly expressed by James Robinson and the New York CORE chapter, considered JOR a "Houser Project," in part stemming from its direct association with FOR. As Meier and Rudwick noted, even JOR's name came out of FOR.

79. Rustin and Houser, *We Challenged Jim Crow*.

80. Ibid., 13–14; Meier and Rudwick, *CORE*, 35–39; Catsum, *Freedom's Main Line*, 44–45; Arsenault, *Freedom Riders*, 52–53; Mollin, "The Limits," 122.

81. George Houser interview, September 11, 1967, 48; Rustin and Houser, *We Challenged Jim Crow*, 2; Jim Peck, December 14, 1970, Box 57, Folder 1, interview by August Meier and Elliot Rudwick, Meier Papers.

82. For more information on Conrad Lynn and his many radical associations, see Herbert Shapiro, *White Violence and Black Response: From Reconstruction to Montgomery* (Boston: University of Massachusetts Press, 1988), 458; Samuel Walker, *In Defense of American Liberties: A History of the ACLU* (New York: Oxford University Press, 1990), 165; Paul Buhle, *Hide in Plain Sight: The Hollywood Blacklistees in Film and Television, 1950–2002* (New York: Palgrave Macmillan, 2003), 254; Catsum, *Freedom's Main Line*, 25, 32, 40, 47, 58; Tyson, *Radio Free Dixie*, 112–35.

83. For general discussion of the Journey in Chapel Hill, see Catsum, *Freedom's Main Line*, 28–40. For details regarding violence after the Journey, see Mark Pryor, *Faith, Grace, and Heresy: The Biography of Reverend Charles M. Jones* (Lincoln, NE: I-Universe, 2002), 119–36; Conrad Lynn, *There Is a Fountain: The Autobiography of Conrad Lynn* (Chicago: Lawrence Hill Books, 1993), 112–13; Reverend Charles Jones, interview by John Egerton, July 21, 1990. Interview A-0335 in Southern Oral History Program Collection (#4007); Igal Roodenko, interview by Jerry Wingate and Jacquelyn Hall, April 11, 1974, Interview B-0010 in Southern Oral History Program Collection (#4007).

84. Arnold Richard Hirsch, *Making the Second Ghetto: Race and Housing in Chicago, 1940–1960* (New York: Cambridge University Press, 1983), 53–55.

85. Ibid.; Robert J. Norrell, *The House I Live In: Race in the American Century* (New York: Oxford University Press, 2006), 166; Carl H. Nightingale, *Segregation: A Global History of Divided Cities* (Chicago: University of Chicago Press, 2012), 351–52.

86. Homer Jack, "Chicago Has One More Chance," *Nation*, no. 1, September 13, 1947, 251.

87. To Sir from Gerald Bullock and attached proposal "Can We Avert the Approaching Chicago Disaster?," August 1949, Reel 8, Series III, Folder 12, Frames 852–54, CORE Papers. The Fort Dearborn Massacre is a reference to an attack against US troops by the Potawatomi Nation during the War of 1812 after the federal government reneged on its agreement. The fort was burned down and prisoners taken.

88. Hirsch contends that there were seven major racial disturbances related to housing. CORE member Gerald Bullock's proposal for an emergency council for racial disturbances includes a reference to another incident that took place in Woodlawn. Hirsch argues that the Chicago news agencies and Housing Authority collaborated to hide information about these incidents, which accounts for the little available information

on these disturbances. Hirsch, *Making the Second Ghetto*, 75, 51–55; To Sir from Gerald Bullock, August 1949, letter and proposal, Reel 8, Series III, Folder 12, Frames 853–54, CORE Papers.

89. Meier and Rudwick, *CORE*, 32; Robert Gemmet to George Houser, December 15, 1946, Reel 8, Series III, Folder 12, Frame 727, CORE Papers; Barry Bessler, "Defend Negro Homes," *Chi-CORE News*, September 15, 1946, Reel 12, Series III, Folder 48, Frame 40, CORE Papers. Founder James Robinson believed that Bullock's refusal to oust SWP members stemmed from his overly sensitive need to any segregation or exclusion which replicated the black experience. James Robinson interview, December 1967.

90. Gemmet to Houser, December 15, 1946.

91. Randall Jelks, *African Americans in the Furniture City: The Struggle for Civil Rights in Grand Rapids* (Champaign: University of Illinois Press, 2006), 98, 123–24, 132–38; Merl E. Reed, "The FBI, MOWM, and CORE, 1941–1946," *Journal of Black Studies* 21, no. 4 (June 1991): 474–75.

92. Reed, "The FBI, MOWM, and CORE," 475–76.

93. Meier and Rudwick, *CORE*, 32. Meier and Rudwick focus on the inability of the national office to wield influence over local chapters. However, this issue is minor compared to the larger question of a membership that does not reflect the CORE created by FOR and Houser.

94. Lynn Coleman to George Houser, April 14, 1948," Reel 9, Series III, Folder 27, Frame 861, CORE Papers. The departure of major leaders would be a recurring problem with local COREs and eventually in the national office. Inability to replace departing members with equally charismatic figures often forced chapters into decline. This issue was also explained in the recently published history on Seattle CORE. Joan Singler et al., *Seattle in Black and White*, 199.

95. Juanita Morrow interview, 2004.

96. Ibid.; see also Michael Washington, "The Stirrings of the Modern Civil Rights Movement in Cincinnati."

97. Lynn Coleman to George Houser, April 17, 1948, Reel 9, Series III, Folder 16, Frame 861, CORE Papers.

98. Hortense Davis to George Houser, February 13, 1950, Reel 9, Series III, Folder 16, Frame 97, CORE Papers.

99. Tad Tekla to George Houser, November 15, 1951, Reel 9, Series III, Folder 16, Frame 104, CORE Papers.

100. Caroline Urie to George Houser, July ?, 1952, Reel 9, Series III, Folder 16, Frame 112, CORE Papers.

101. Summary of Skateland Project by Erosanna Robinson, Reel 9, Series III, Folder 16, Frames 112–16, 130, CORE Papers. The proprietor again sold his ownership in Skateland, but retained a minority percentage.

102. Ibid.

103. Ibid.

104. George Houser to Erosanna Robinson, August 6, 1952, Reel 9, Series III, Folder 16, Frames 117–18, CORE Papers. In fact, CORE under Houser in the spring of 1944

also attempted to break Skateland, but failed. Houser recalled that it was a difficult project and required a well-thought-out plan and considerable support to force a policy change.

105. No author, "Tests Democracy at Skateland, Girl Winds Up with Broken Arm," *Call and Post* article, Reel 9, Series III, Folder 16, Frame 130, CORE Papers.

106. Caroline Urie to George Houser, July ?, 1952, Reel 9, Series III, Folder 16, Frame 112, CORE Papers.

107. Erosanna Robinson to Jim Peck, May 21, 1952, Reel 9, Series III, Folder 16, Frames 110–11, CORE Papers.

108. National Convention Minutes, June 1952, Box 2, Folder 1, Meier Rudwick Papers, Wisconsin Historical Society.

109. Erosanna Robinson to Katie Raymond, December 8, 1952, Reel 9, Series III, Folder 16, Frame 119, CORE Papers.

110. Meier and Rudwick, *CORE*, 47, 62–65, 75. Meier and Rudwick do not give as much credit to staff exodus in the decline of CORE as I, except when it comes to black power. However, the loss of charismatic leadership appears again and again during the periods of interracial, nonviolent CORE and black power CORE.

111. Meier and Rudwick, *CORE*, 52–53. Project Report Rosedale Playground Campaign, September 1951–October 1952, June 5, 1953, Reel 16, Series III, Folder 89, Frames 118–22, CORE Papers. Meier and Rudwick exclude Mindlin in their major actors, but utilize his report. According to his report, Perry, Pelenius, and he were the only Washington CORE contacts working with Rosedale.

112. Ibid.

113. The previous quotes and discussion on these events all come from the Rosedale Project Report. Mindlin, "Project Report Rosedale."

114. Lula Farmer interview, February 27, 1967, August Meier Collection; Meier and Rudwick, *CORE*, 61; Jim Peck interview; James Robinson interview, December 1967. Farmer's mocking comments aside, she was not far from the truth. The Nelsons eventually went off the grid and continued to live sustenance-based lives until their deaths.

115. Ibid.; Meier and Rudwick, *CORE*, 58–59, 65–71.

116. Minutes of National Council Meeting, May 14–16, 1953, Series A2, Box 4, Folder: Minutes of National Council Meeting, 1953, FOR Papers, DG# 13, SCPC.

117. Minutes of FOR Executive Meeting, April 5, 1954 Series A2, Box 4, Folder: Minutes of FOR Executive Meeting, FOR Papers, DG# 13, SCPC.

118. John Swomley to Jo Ann Robinson, April 10, 1978, Series Two, Correspondence Folder, Jo Ann Robinson/Muste papers at SCPC.

## 3. An Eager Band

1. Ames to Houser, Peck, Robinson, March 29, 1955, Box 2R566: Records and Professional Activities, Folder CORE internal correspondence, 1955, Farmer Papers.

2. Kimbrough and Dagen, *Victory without Violence*, 36, 90; Meier and Rudwick, *CORE*, 70, 72, qtd. 75; James Robinson to Billie Ames, November 22, 1954, Box 2R566: Records and Professional Activities, Folder: CORE internal correspondence, July–December 1954.

3. Ames to James Robinson and George Houser, November 5, 1954, Box 2R566: Records and Professional Activities, Folder: CORE internal correspondence, July–December 1954.

4. Houser to Ames, February 8, 1955, Box 2R566: Records of Professional Activities, Folder: CORE internal correspondence, 1955, Farmer Papers; James Robinson to Ames, October 4, 1954, Box Records of Professional Activities, Folder: CORE internal correspondence, July–December 1954, Farmer Papers; Robinson to Ames, January 9, 1955, Records of Professional Activities, Folder: CORE internal correspondence, 1955, Farmer Papers; CORE Council Minutes, February 26–27, 1955, Box 2R566, Folder General Files: 1940s–1950s Civil Rights Miscellany, Farmer Papers; Meier and Rudwick, *CORE*, 72–73. Meier and Rudwick suggest that the Nelsons were so disaffected from CORE that they retreated to the sidelines. This was somewhat true, but the Nelsons were also heavily involved in the Peace Keepers. The two reemerged in the 1960s as the impetus for the Highway 40 protests. Plus, Ames's departure left the New York–St. Louis faction in charge. For more on the Nelsons in the 1960s, see Mary Stanton, *Freedom Walk Mississippi or Bust* (Jackson: University Press of Mississippi, 2003); Jo Ann Robinson, "Congress of Racial Equality," in *Organizing Black America: An Encyclopedia of African American Associations*, ed. Nina Mjagkij (New York: Garland, 2001).

5. Lula Farmer, February 27, 1967, interview by Meier and Rudwick, Box 56, Folder 6, August Meier Papers, Schomburg Research Center, New York. James Peck interview.

6. Morris, *Origins*, 130.

7. Ibid., 136. Meier and Rudwick, *CORE*, 41, 75–76. Morris posits that the Montgomery Bus Boycott was an essential component to CORE's stabilization. Meier and Rudwick mention the Montgomery boycott but give it little attention, comparatively.

8. Kimbrough and Dagen, *Victory*, 13.

9. Ibid., 52, qtd. 56, 58, 74, 91, 93–94, 98; Meier and Rudwick, *CORE*, 200; Singler et al., *Seattle in Black and White*, 77. A number of CORE historical essays both older and recently refer to the "patient" nature of goodwill action. Such term use operates in a vacuum in that it fails to articulate why "patience," especially by the 1960s, was not a virtue but a problem that in many ways reflected a privilege not afforded to black people given the yoke of segregation, violent resistance, and state recalcitrance. Eventually, patience in the name of good will took on a different meaning in the period of Freedom Now. This was especially expressed in *Seattle in Black and White*, where activists picked up the pace and expanded demonstrations after frustrations emerged over the slow progress in halting employment discrimination. Instead, a dialectical framework emerges in *Victory*, *CORE*, and *Seattle* in which patience becomes virtue and black power frustration and hostility. As the authors of *Victory* state it, "the new members, young black activists, began to differentiate between integration and equality, and to choose the latter as their goal." Though one could debate the notion that integration represented equality versus a conduit to it, underlining the notion was that black power did not rank equally or at all as a pathway to freedom.

10. Kimbrough and Dagen, *Victory*, 24–25; Lang, *Grassroots at the Gateway*, 114–18.

11. Morris, *Origins*, 132–34.

12. Qtd. in Meier and Rudwick, *CORE*, 83–84, 87.

13. Billie Ames to James Farmer, October 25, 1954, Box 2R566, Records and Professional Activities, Folder: CORE internal correspondence, July–December 1954, Farmer Papers.

14. Morris, *Origins*, 132, 137.

15. Meier and Rudwick, *CORE*, 87–90; qtd. Morris, *Origins*, 132.

16. Rabby, *The Pain and the Promise*, 121–22; Meier and Rudwick, *CORE*, 152.

17. Ironically, Anne Braden formed Louisville CORE, though CORE still distanced itself from the Bradens' association with SCEF. For more on SCEF, CORE, communism, and the Bradens, see Morris, *Origins*, 157; Rabby, *The Pain and the Promise*, 100–101. For more on Carl and Anne Braden and issues of communist affiliation and civil rights, see Catherine Fosl, *Subversive Southerner: Anne Braden and the Struggle for Racial Justice in the Cold War South* (Louisville: University Press of Kentucky, 2006), 290–91; Tracy K'Meyer, *Civil Rights in the Gateway to the South: Louisville, Kentucky, 1945–1980* (Louisville: University Press of Kentucky, 2009), 19–20.

18. Rabby, *The Pain and the Promise*, 106, 116–17, qtd. 117.

19. Ibid., 104–6. For more on the role of the Stephens sisters and Tallahassee CORE's influence on other chapters, see Jeffrey A. Turner, *Sitting In and Speaking Out: Student Movements in the American South 1960–1970* (Athens: University of Georgia Press, 2010), 96; Maxine D. Jones, "Black Women in the Florida Civil Rights Movement," in *Southern Black Women in the Modern Civil Rights Movement*, ed. Merline Pitre and Bruce A. Glasrud (College Station: Texas A&M University Press, 2013), 71–72; Tananarive Due and Patricia Stephens Due, *Freedom in the Family: A Mother-Daughter Memoir of the Fight for Civil Rights* (New York: Ballantine Books, 2003).

20. Rabby, The Pain and the Promise, 119–20.

21. Ray Arsenault, "Five Days in May: Freedom Riding in the Carolinas," in *Toward the Meeting of the Waters: Currents in the Civil Rights Movement in South Carolina during the Twentieth Century*, ed. Winifred B. Moor Jr. and Orville Burton (Columbia: University of South Carolina Press, 2008); Morris, *Origins*, 200, 214; Rabby, *The Pain and the Promise*, 87, 205.

22. Gordon Carey interview, May 14, 1972, Box 56, Folder 3, interview by August Meier and Elliot Rudwick, August Meier Papers, Schomburg Research Center, New York; James Robinson interview, April 28, 1971, Box 57, Folder 4, Meier interview, Meier Papers, Schomburg Research Center, New York. Robinson noted that the *CORE-lator's* showcase of nonviolent protest greatly enabled CORE's fundraising, even though its actual protest activity was far and few between.

23. Meier and Rudwick, *CORE*, 125, 128–29.

24. Ibid., 128–31; Farmer, *Lay Bare*, 193; Gordon Carey, interview by author, October 20, 2012.

25. For more information on Freedom Rides, see Carson, *SNCC*, 31–37; Shannon Lee Frystak, *Our Minds on Freedom: Women and the Struggle for Black Equality in Louisiana* (Baton Rouge: Louisiana State University Press, 2009), 132–37; Meier and Rudwick, *CORE*, 135–39; Gordon Carey interview, October 20, 2012; Taylor Branch, *Parting the Waters: America in the King Years 1954–63* (New York: Simon & Schuster, 1988), 412–50;

David Niven, *The Politics of Injustice: The Kennedys, the Freedom Rides, and the Electoral Consequences of a Moral Compromise* (Knoxville: University of Tennessee Press, 2003), 39–126; Peck, *Freedom Ride*; Catsum, *Freedom's Main Line*; Arsenault, "Five Days in May." The most extensive discussion on the Freedom Rides is Ray Arsenault, *Freedom Riders: 1961 and the Struggle for Racial Justice*.

26. Arsenault, "Five Days in May," 205.

27. Meier and Rudwick, *CORE*, 116, 152. Many older texts failed to give New Orleans credit, including Carson, *SNCC*, 35; Branch, *Parting the Waters*, 466–67; Frystak's book on civil rights in Louisiana recently corrected this oversight. See Frystak, *Our Minds on Freedom*, 117, 131–32, 134.

28. Meier and Rudwick, *CORE*, 170; Rabby, *The Pain and the Promise*, 140; Catsum, *Freedom's Main Line*, 310–11; Michael Ezra, *Civil Rights Movement: People and Perspectives* (Santa Barbara, CA: ABC-CLIO, 2009), 93; Sugrue, *Sweet Land of Liberty*, 370; Arsenault, *Freedom Riders*, 294.

29. Meier and Rudwick, *CORE*, 150, 226. Meier and Rudwick wrote that some chapters over- or underestimated their numbers. Partially this depended upon how chapter leaders determined numbers. Some based member numbers on active protest participants (not necessarily dues-paying members) and some considered active members only those who paid. In Cleveland's case, they counted active protest members. Additionally, as the chapter developed, they began to consider poor Clevelanders active members based on affiliation level not fees in order to solidify relationships and expand its work in the community.

30. Davis, *Black Americans*, 135, 221, 308, 329, 354, 415.

31. Urban League of Cleveland, *The Negro in Cleveland, 1950–1963: An Analysis of the Social and Economic Characteristics of the Negro Population; the Change between 1950 and 1963* (Cleveland: Cleveland Urban League, 1964), 1–2.

32. Urban League, *The Negro*, 4, 15.

33. Ibid., 16, 19; Davis, *Black Americans*, 330.

34. Urban League, *The Negro*, 19–20; Davis, *Black Americans*, 330.

35. Davis, *Black Americans*, 336–37; Urban League, *The Negro*, 12, 22, 31, 35.

36. Bob Modic, "More Alabamans on Relief Here Than There," article, Box 3, Folder 5, Paul Younger Papers, WRHS.

37. Urban League, *The Negro*, 8.

38. Davis, *Black Americans*, 343.

39. James McCain to James Robinson, August 19, 1959, Reel 42, Series 5, File 398, Frame 343, CORE Papers; Gregory Allen to James Robinson, December 12, 195, Reel 42, Series 5, File 398, Frames 351–52, CORE Papers.

40. Eula Morrow to Gordon Carey, December 4, 1959, Reel 42, Series 5, File 398, Frames 348–49, CORE Papers. Eula Morrow actually suggested that Cleveland's problems of racial inequality were not as pressing as they once were, but that she would lend her support anyway.

41. Brent expressed interest in starting a chapter, but national CORE asked that he wait for another interested party—graduate student Myrna Balk—to organize a local CORE. She never acted due to the constraints of her graduate work. Fredericka Teer to Myrna Balk,

October 7, 1961, Reel 42, Series 5, File 398, Frame 361, CORE Papers; Fredericka Teer to Al Brent, November 9, 1961, Reel 42, Series 5, File 398, Frame 366, CORE Papers; Fredericka Teer to Al Brent. March 5, 1962, Reel 42, Series 5, File 398, Frame 372, CORE Papers; "Core Names Brent Director," *Call and Post* article, Reel 42, Series 5, File 398, Frame 389, CORE Papers. The Africa Room was a designated meeting space in a building owned by the *Call and Post*. Fredericka Teer to Al Brent, April 16, 1962, Reel 42, Series 5, File 398, Frame 388, CORE Papers; Fredericka Teer to Richard Haley, April 16, 1962, Reel 42, Series 5, File 398, Frame 387, CORE Papers; Richard Haley Resume of Cleveland Trip, April 1962, Reel 42, Series 5, File 398, Frame 393, CORE Papers.

42. Al Brent to Fredericka Teer, March 30, 1962, Reel 42, Series 5, File 398, Frame 378, CORE Papers; "Cloud Heads CORE: Group May Split," *Call and Post*, Reel 42, Series 5, File 398; Frame 392, CORE Papers. Brent to Teer, April 25, 1962, Reel 42, Series 5, File 398, Frame 398, CORE Papers. Richard Haley to Al Brent, April 30, 1962, Reel 42, Series 5, File 398, Frame 398, CORE Papers. Fredericka Teer to Al Brent, May 1, 1962, Reel 42, Series 5, File 398, Frame 396, CORE Papers; Nate Smith and Donald Bean, interview by author, Cleveland, Ohio, June 21, 2004.

43. Lewis Robinson et al., Targets for 1962, Reel 42, Series 5, File 398, Frames 383–86, CORE Papers.

44. Ibid. Al Brent to Fredericka Teer, March 30, 1962, Reel 42, Series 5, File 398, Frame 378, CORE Papers.

45. Richard Haley Resume of Cleveland Trip, April 1962, Reel 42, Series 5, File 398, Frame 393, CORE Papers.

46. Ibid.

47. Smith/Bean interview.

48. Ibid.; Mary Hamilton to James McCain, May 3, 1962, memorandum, Reel 42, Series 5, File 398, Frames 400–401, CORE Papers; Mary Hamilton to James McCain, May 16, 1962, memorandum, Reel 42, Series 5, File 398, Frame 405, CORE Papers. Mary Hamilton to James McCain, May 19, 1962, memorandum, Reel 42, Series 5, File 398, Frame 408, CORE Papers.

49. Mary Hamilton to James McCain, May 19, 1962, memorandum, Reel 42, Series 5, File 398, Frame 408, CORE Papers. John Cloud to James Farmer and Richard Haley, August 22, 1962, Reel 42, Series 5, File 398, Frame 395, CORE Papers; "A Mother's Day Protest," 1962, article, Reel 42, Series 5, File 398, Frame 406, CORE Papers.

50. Ibid. Hamilton was not particularly happy with Brooklyn CORE either, according to historian Brian Purnell. Purnell, *Fighting Jim Crow*, 102–3. More discussion about CAMD appears in chapter 5.

51. Smith/Bean interview; Mary Hamilton to James McCain, May 3, 1962, memorandum, Reel 42, Series 5, File 398, Frames 400–401, CORE Papers; Mary Hamilton to James McCain, May 16, 1962, memorandum, Reel 42, Series 5, File 398, Frame 405, CORE Papers. Mary Hamilton to James McCain, May 19, 1962, memorandum, Reel 42, Series 5, File 398, Frame 408, CORE Papers; Mary Hamilton to John Cloud, June 11, 1962, Reel 42, Series 5, File 398, Frames 398–99, CORE Papers. Icabod Flewellen was a major collector of African American ephemera and objects. In 1953, Mr. Flewellen started

the Afro-American Cultural and Historical Society in his home on Harkness Avenue. When it was shown at the Cleveland "Parade of Progress" exhibition in 1964, it was considered one the largest Negro History Exhibits in the country. Don Bean recalled that Mr. Flewellen was a strong CORE member and active demonstrator. Chavers was president of the Negro American Labor Council Cleveland chapter. Mason Hargrove national president of UNIA after UNIA national headquarters moved to Cleveland in the 1940s.

52. Mary Hamilton to James McCain, May 19, 1962, memorandum, Reel 42, Series 5, File 398, Frame 408, CORE Papers.

53. Meier and Rudwick, *CORE*, 111.

54. Farmer, *Lay Bare*, 197.

55. Meier and Rudwick, *CORE*, 97.

56. Ibid.

57. Ibid., 209.

58. Outline of Civil Rights Organizations, Box 43, Folder 4, NAACP Papers, WRHS; also found in Box 1, Folder 3, Bonnie Gordon Papers, WHS. For more information on Mandel's important role in building the freedom school curriculum, see Brian Kelley, "Introduction," in reprint Bernard Mandel, *Labor, Free and Slave: Workingmen and the Anti-Slavery Movement in the United States* (Chicago: University of Illinois Press, 2002), xiv. Bernard Mandel taught at Rawlings Junior High School during the day and was a part-time instructor at Fenn College. Fenn College eventually merges with other institutions to become Cleveland State University. Also, all of the Weathers family was in CORE, but the brothers (Alex and Malcolm) were most active. Don Freeman, head of the Afro-American Institute, was not as active. However, the members of the Afro-American Cultural Institute formed the backbone for black nationalism in Cleveland extending their influence into a variety of organizations in the mid-1960s, including CORE. In addition, Donald Freeman later became the ideological father for the radical black power group RAM, Revolutionary Action Movement. The Afro-American Institute was founded in 1962. Its relationships were mostly related to black nationalist organizations. Police brutality was one of the major issues within the institute. Thus, Cleveland CORE has an exceedingly early introduction to the persons who shape black power locally in Cleveland and nationally.

59. Arthur Evans, interview by author, Columbus, Ohio, April 15, 2004.

60. Ibid.

61. Evans interview, 2004.

62. Farmer, *Lay Bare*, 320.

63. Althea Jones, Virginia Eubanks, with Barbara Smith, *Ain't Gonna Let Nobody Turn Me Around: Forty Years of Movement Building with Barbara Smith* (Albany: State University of New York Press, 2014), 24; Barbara Smith, May 7–8, 2003, interview by Loretta Ross, Voices of Feminism Oral History Project, Sophia Smith Collection, Smith College. Barbara Smith is famously known for co-organization of the Combahee River Collective and her coauthorship of the similarly named manifesto. From the 1970s through the 1980s, the organization played an important role in developing coalition politics and black feminism.

64. Smith/Bean interview; Ruth Turner, interview published in Robert Penn Warren, *Who Speaks for the Negro?* (New York: Random House, 1965), 380.

65. Tony Perot, interview by author, Washington, DC, March 19, 2004.

66. Perot interview, 2004.

67. Ibid.

68. Ibid.

69. Although both Bean and Smith refer to Cohen as a socialist, they note that this was mostly conjecture.

70. Bonnie Gordon, interview by author, Cleveland, Ohio, April 12, 2004. "Tussey, Richard," in *Encyclopedia of Cleveland History*, ed. John Grabowski and David Van Tassel (Bloomington: Indiana University Press, 1996). Richard Tussey became a member of the Socialist Labor Party in 1938. In 1941 he married Viola Bencsis, with whom he had two daughters, Bonnie L. and Romaine. The two divorced, and he married Jean Tussey. In his youth he worked for the Industrial Workers of the World (IWW). He later joined the Mechanics Educational Society of America and the Meat Cutters Union, which eventually merged to form the United Food and Commercial Workers Union. In 1960 he traveled to Cuba with the Fair Play for Cuba committee, a visit that later saw him hauled before the US Senate's Internal Security Committee.

71. Smith/Bean interview.

72. Ibid.

73. Ibid. Gordon interview. Gordon recalled CORE had no communists, but socialists were present.

74. Evans interview, 2004.

75. Ibid.

76. Antoine Perot, interview by author, Washington, DC, August 25, 2007.

77. Ibid.

78. Richard Haley to James McCain, March 17, 1963, Reel 42, Series 5, File 398, Frame 439, CORE Papers.

79. Smith/Bean interview.

80. Meier and Rudwick, *CORE*, 298, Joanne Klunder Hardy, interview by author, Lisbon, Maine, October 2006. Bruce Melville, interview by author, (date) Cleveland, Ohio. The standard of loyalty depended on the degree to which white participants believed in supporting black leadership. The Klunders and Bruce Melville, for example, believed that the movement was fundamentally an issue that affected the black community. As such, white membership could serve in support roles, but not usurp leadership.

81. Smith/Bean interview. "Wohl, Max," in Grabowski and Van Tassel, *Encyclopedia of Cleveland History*. Max Wohl was a socialist, former chair of the American Civil Liberties Union of Cleveland, and vice president of finance for Tremco Manufacturing Co. He retired early in 1969. Wohl left Tremco to volunteer full time with the American Civil Liberties Union of Cleveland. He boosted the membership and managed the local office without pay for fifteen years. Wohl ran for political offices as a Socialist Party candidate, including Ohio secretary of state.

82. Bruce and Lynn Warsaw, August 1971, interview by Meier and Rudwick, Box 57, Folder 7, Meier Papers.

83. Ibid.

84. I can not list every Cleveland CORE member. However, some members had leading roles particularly: Walter and Margie Grevatt, Nancy Thomas, Betty Gant, Chuck Burton, Thompson Gaines, Don Shanks, Ronald Tinsley, Edmond Pace, Joel Grossman, Bruce Warshall, Connie Jackson, Betty Renter, Dave Mack, Bruce Melville, Bruce and Lynn Warsaw, Roger Young, Grady Robinson, Linda Freeman, Booker T. Eddy, Ronald Tinsley (who would later work on Soul City), and Baxter Hill.

85. Ruth Turner and Tony Perot, April 17, 1972, Box 57, Folder 1, interview by August Meier and Elliot Rudwick; "CORE membership list," Box 1, Folder 3, Bonnie Gordon Papers, WHS; Bruce Klunder to James McCain, December 18, 1963, Reel 42, Series 5, File 398, Frame 464, CORE Papers.

86. Richard Haley report, April 19, 1962, Reel 42, Series 5, File 398, Frame 393, CORE Papers; Smith/Bean interview; Meier and Rudwick, *CORE*, 199, 305. Generally associate members were not full dues-paying members, but occasionally demonstrated. Their figures varied within Cleveland CORE over the years based on the chapter's level of activism and key protest activities. The first group of CORE's working and poor members came from its school desegregation and rent-strike campaign. The early associates numbered around two hundred—more or less—according to CORE leaders Ruth and Antoine Perot. This number grew to over two hundred with major events like the school desegregation movement. Perot interview, 2004. Ruth Turner, interview by author, Washington, DC, March 19, 2004.

87. Smith/Bean interview; Perot interview, 2007; Smith/Bean interview; Moore, *Carl B. Stokes*, 139.

88. Smith/Bean interview.

89. Ibid.; Gordon interview; CORE Constitution, Box 1, Folder 3, Bonnie Gordon Papers, WHS.

90. Agenda, November 26, 1963, Box 1, Folder 3, Bonnie Gordon Papers, WHS; Smith interview. Joanne Klunder, interview by John Britton, November 16, 1967, Ralph J. Bunche Oral History Collection (hereafter Bunche Papers), RJB #556, Moorland-Spingarn Research Center, Howard University.

91. Gordon interview.

92. Richard Haley to Ruth Turner, February 27, 1963, Reel 42:436, Series V: 398, CORE Papers. William Worthy is a well-known activist and journalist of the 1960s. Worthy is most known for his call for a black political party and his arrests and conviction by the US government for travel to banned countries like Cuba and China.

93. John Cloud to James McCain, August 22, 1962, Reel 42, Series 5, File 398, Frame 417, CORE Papers. Operation Window Shop was hardly confined to Cleveland CORE. Other groups also launched housing window shop protests. See Singler, et al., *Seattle in Black and White*, 109–12.

94. Richard Haley to James McCain, March 17, 1963, memorandum, Reel 42, Series 5, File 398, Frame 439, CORE Papers.

95. Ibid. The Federation of Ordinary People was a small group that apparently never got off the ground.

96. Bruce Warsaw to Gentlemen on December 24, 1962, Reel 42, Series 5, File 398,

Frame 422, CORE Papers. Commission for Civil Rights Legislation asked CORE to assist its push for fair housing in the legislature.

97. Cleveland CORE was not the only chapter moving away from CORE's earlier rules of action or focus from middle-class needs of housing to housing for the poor. Brooklyn CORE began in 1962 to address poor black residents' concerns around slum-lords and inadequate garbage collection and enforcement of health and sanitary codes. Brooklyn CORE also gained notoriety as one of the first chapters to become aggressive in its tactics. Cleveland CORE's aggression actually began in the spring of 1963 with its joint demonstration with Central Cadillac. This is discussed later in the chapter. See Meier and Rudwick, *CORE*, 183–87 and 200–203. For short commentary on Columbus CORE chaining themselves to gallery seats, see Joanne Klunder interview, November 16, 1967; Meier and Rudwick, *CORE*, 242.

98. Agenda, December 17, 1963, Box 1, Folder 3, Bonnie Gordon Papers, WHS.

99. The emergence of rent strikes varied from chapter to chapter. Chicago, New York, Brooklyn, and other East coast chapters, for example, started early. Cleveland fell relatively in the middle in terms of its focus on housing and rent strikes on behalf of poor black residents. Turner and Perot felt the rent strikes were good for CORE since it had too much of a middle-class bent. Warsaw categorized it as not a political sensibility but an issue of middle-class guilt by the more educated and economically stable black members of CORE, like Turner. See Ruth Turner and Tony Perot, 1972; Warsaw interview; Meier and Rudwick, *CORE*, 245–46, for other chapters; "Anatomy of a Rent Strike, Changes for Cleveland Negro," December 20, 1963, *Ohio Forum* article, Reel 42, Series 5, File 398, Frames 469–70, CORE Papers.

100. Fight Back Against Rats, Roaches, December 1963, flyer, Box 1, Folder 3, Bonnie Gordon Papers, WHS.

101. Ibid.

102. Ibid.

103. Agenda, December 26, 1963, Box 1, Folder 3, Bonnie Gordon Papers, WHS; no title, February 13, 1964, Box 1, Folder 3, Bonnie Gordon Papers, WHS; Ruth Turner, no title, notes on dissertation rough draft, 2008, in author's possession; no title, article on 8305 Hough rent strike, Reel 42, Series 5, File 398, Frame 451–52, CORE Papers.

104. Flyer no title, December 14, 1963, Bonnie Gordon Papers; Win Rent Strike, Start Two More press release, no date, Reel 19, Series 2, F:II:140, Frame 949, CORE Papers.

105. CORE Action Letter, April 1964. Reel 19, Series 2, File, F:II:140, Frame 901–2, CORE Papers; Agenda, December 26, 1963, Box 1, Folder 3, Bonnie Gordon Papers, WHS; no title, February 13, 1964, Box 1, Folder 3, Bonnie Gordon Papers, WHS; Ruth Turner, no title, notes on dissertation rough draft, 2008, in author's possession.

106. Meier and Rudwick, *CORE*, 245.

107. Perot interview, 2004; Meier and Rudwick, *CORE*, 198. The organization actually met in the Church of the Covenant in University Circle, situated adjacent to Hough, before moving to Hough. During most of the chapter's existence, however, it operated out of an office at the Luxor Building at 1740 Crawford Road in Hough.

108. Ibid.

109. Ibid.

## 4. Lonely Are the Brave

1. Racial incidents at Collinwood High School were hardly limited to individual intimidation. From 1969 to 1974, hordes of white students repeatedly attacked black students including one episode in 1970 where close to four hundred white high schoolers forced a group of black students to barricade and arm themselves with desk legs for protection. Rollin J. Watson and Robert S. Watson, *The School as a Safe Haven* (Westport, CT: Bergin and Garvey, 2003), 93–94; Lemberg Center for the Study of Violence, *U.S. Race-related Civil Disorders* (Watham, MA: The Clearinghouse, 1969), 113; no author, "Northern Race Violence—The Season Opens," *U.S. News & World Report* 58 (June 28, 1965), 6; George Condon and Robert McGruder, "Hatred Boils in Collinwood," *Cleveland Plain Dealer*, February 9, 1975, AA; "Cleveland School Is Closed for a Day by Racial Violence," *New York Times*, March 19, 1965, 19; OBU Minutes, December 13, 1969, Box 3, Folder 5, Humanist Fellowship Papers, WRHS.

2. Testimony of Bridgett Gilliam, December 5, 1963, Box 4, Folder 67, Council on Human Relations Papers (hereafter CHR Papers), WRHS.

3. Leonard Moore makes a similar argument for why black power emerges in Cleveland's freedom movement holistically. See Leonard Moore, "The School Desegregation Crisis of Cleveland, Ohio—Catalyst for Black Power in a Northern Town," *Journal of Urban History* 28, no. 2 (January 2002): 155.

4. Meier and Rudwick, *CORE*, 194.

5. "The Pilgrimage of Prayer for Public Schools," (February 1959) *CORE-lator* 75, Reel 13, E:III:76, Frames 451–52, Papers of the Congress of Racial Equality. Addendum, 1944–1968 (hereafter CORE Addendum), microfilm and originals at Martin Luther King, Jr. Library and Archives at the Martin Luther King, Jr. Center for Nonviolent Social Change; Jim Peck, ed., "Union to Promote School Integration," January 1951, Reel 13, Frame 397. *CORE-lator*, "CORE Active in School Situation" (October–November 1954), *CORE-lator* 63, Reel 13, Frame 423; "CORE Active in Nashville School Crisis," *CORE-lator* 71 (Fall 1957), Reel 13: 441; "Mobilize Community Support for Complete School Desegregation," *CORE-lator* 73 (Spring 1958), Reel 13, Frame 446, in E:III:76, CORE Addendum.

6. Meier and Rudwick, *CORE*, 193; Tucker, "An Historical Study," 26–27.

7. Ibid., 247–48; Jakobi Williams, The Bullet or the Ballet: The Illinois Chapter of the Black Panther Party and Racial Coalition Politics in Chicago (Chapel Hill: University of North Carolina Press, 2013), 66; Dionne Danns, Something Better for Our Children: Black Organizing in Chicago Public Schools, 1963–1971 (New York: Routledge, 2003), 29–55; Adam Cohen and Elizabeth Taylor, American Pharaoh: Mayor Richard J. Daley, His Battle for Chicago and the Nation (New York: Little, Brown, & Company, 2000), 282, 304; "School Board Picketed by Parents," CORE-lator, Reel 13, E:IV:21, Frames 432–33, "Desegregate Chicago Public Schools," CORE-lator, Reel 13: in E:IV:21, Frames 441–42, CORE Addendum.

8. Michael Stolee, "The Milwaukee Desegregation Case," in *Seeds of Crisis: Public Schooling in Milwaukee since 1920,* ed. John Rury and Frank A. Cassell (Madison: University of Wisconsin Press, 1993), 234, 239–45; Jack Dougherty, *More Than One*

*Struggle: The Evolution of Black School Reform in Milwaukee* (Chapel Hill: University of North Carolina Press, 2004), 107–15. Milwaukee CORE went to Chicago CORE for help in instituting the boycott and workshops to help persuade parents to join the boycott. Eventually, Brown left and became part of the Federation for Independent Schools as president of Harambee School Board.

9. Clarence Taylor, *Knocking at Our Own Door: Milton A. Galamison and the Struggle to Integrate New York City Schools* (New York: Columbia University Press, 1997), 120–21; Jeremy Larner, "The New York School Crisis," *The Urban School Crisis* (New York: League for Industrial Democracy/United Federation of Teachers, AFL-CIO, 1966), 8–23.

10. Taylor, *Knocking at Our Own Door,* 131–32; Jerald E. Podair, *The Strike That Changed New York: Blacks, Whites, and the Ocean Hill-Brownsville Crisis* (New Haven, CT: Yale University Press, 2002), 71–72, 145–47; Larner, "The New York School Crisis," 178–79. For more on the Ocean Hill-Brownsville conflict, see also Gen Harris, *The Ocean Hill-Brownsville Conflict: Intellectual Struggles between Black and Jews at Mid Century* (Lanham, MD: Lexington Books, 2012), and Charles Isaacs, *Inside Ocean Hill-Brownsville: A Teacher's Education, 1968–1969* (Albany, NY: Excelsior Editions, 2014).

11. Doris H. Pieroth, "With All Deliberate Caution: School Integration in Seattle, 1954–1968," *Pacific Northwest Quarterly* 73, no. 2 (April 1982): 50–61.

12. Meier and Rudwick, *CORE,* 247–48; "Testimony Given to the Philadelphia Board of Education," *CORE-lator* (October 17, 1962), Reel 13, E:IV:38, Frame 926; "San Francisco School Sit-in," *CORE-lator* 98 (November 1962), Reel 13, E:III:76, Frame 492, CORE Addendum.

13. Lewis G. Robinson, *The Making of a Man: An Autobiography* (Cleveland: Green, 1970), 64.

14. Ibid., 65; Willard Richan, Racial Isolation in the Cleveland Public Schools: A Report of a Study Sponsored by the United States Commission on Civil Rights (Cleveland: Case Western Reserve University, 1967), 54–55.

15. Ibid.

16. UFM to UFM Cooperating Organizations, no date, Box 36, Folder 5, Urban League Papers (hereafter UL Papers); Donna McIntyre Whyte, "African-American Community Politics and Racial Equality in Cleveland Public Schools: 1933–1973" (PhD diss., Case Western Reserve University, 2003), 168–69; Smith/Bean interview; Meier and Rudwick, *CORE,* 227. Ruth Turner and Nate Smith to Dear Friend, July 29, 1963, Box 16, Folder 305, United Food and Commercial Workers Papers (hereafter UFCW Papers), WRHS.

17. Isaiah Pogue to UFM steering committee, May, 19, 1964, Box 36, Folder 5, UL Papers, WRHS. Ruth Turner served the ironic position of "secretary" in Cleveland, for the National Action Council, and the national office. A recurring theme, the title little reflected her influence in all three secretarial positions.

18. For additional information on the United Freedom Movement and Employment protests, see Box 3, Folder 2, Paul Younger Papers, WRHS.

19. For discussion on African American School Segregation in the pre-WWII period, see Carolyn Jefferson, "An Historical Analysis of the Relationship between the

Great Migration and the Administrative Policies and Practices of Racial Isolation in the Cleveland Public Schools, 1920–1940" (PhD diss., Cleveland State University, 1991); Regennia Williams, "Equity and Efficiency: African American Leadership and Education Reform in Cleveland, Ohio 1915–1940" (PhD diss., Case Western Reserve University, 2001); Regennia Williams, "Reading, Writing and Racial Uplift: Education and Reform in Cleveland, Ohio," in *Education and the Great Depression,* ed. E. Thomas Ewing and David Hicks (New York: Peter Lang Publishing, 2006), 107–29; Whyte, *African American Community,* 31, 55; Richan, *Racial Isolation,* 33–34.

20. Juanita Morrow, "Is Cleveland School System Headed toward Segregation?," *Call and Post,* November 4, 1944, 8A, c1.

21. Whyte, African American Community, 52, 64–65; Richan, Racial Isolation, 35.

22. Whyte, African American Community, 55–56; Richan, Racial Isolation, 38.

23. Moore, "The School Desegregation Crisis," 135–36; Whyte, *African American Community,* 86–88; Richan, *Racial Isolation,* 39.

24. Whyte, *African American Community,* 77–81; New Comer's Committee minutes, April 22, 1957, Box 7, Folder 3, NAACP Papers, WRHS.

25. Whyte, African American Community, 104.

26. Report, no date, Box 2, Folder 6, Paul Younger Papers (hereafter Younger Papers), WRHS.

27. Students for Civil Rights at Western Reserve, "Cleveland Education Chronology," *The Informer,* Box 1, Folder 1, Bruce Klunder Papers (hereafter Klunder Papers), WRHS; also in Box 29, Folder 2, NAACP Papers; Whyte, *African American Community,* 16, 135, 105–6; Richan, *Racial Isolation,* 40, 44–45.

28. Report of Executive Secretary, January 9 February 6, 1962, Box 1, Folder 5, NAACP Papers, WRHS.

29. Richan, *Racial Isolation,* 47; Moore, "School Desegregation," 136; Whyte, *African American Community,* 171. Hazeldell Parent Association came from students, teachers, and parents associated with Hazeldell Elementary School, which had the largest group of transported students at eight hundred. "Cleveland Education Chronology"; Moore, "School Desegregation," 140.

30. Joanne Klunder to Raymond Jirran, July 4, 1971, Jirran Papers, WRHS; Ann Skinner, "Pickets Are Expected at 2 Schools Today," Ardelia Dixon scrapbook, unprocessed collection, WRHS. Ardelia Dixon unprocessed collection at WRHS is a scrapbook of newspaper articles on school desegregation protest and other civil rights activities in Cleveland. For a chronology of the school desegregation movement from 1962 to 1964, see "An Interpretation Paper of the United Freedom Movement: A Short History of the Cleveland Board of Education versus United Freedom Movement," April 1964, Box 36, Folder 5, UL Papers, WRHS, and Sidney Vincent to CRC and some others, February 10, 1964, confidential memo, Box 36, Folder 835, Jewish Community Federation Papers. Although much of the materials are redundant, archival materials related to school desegregation but not often cited in this manuscript can also be found in the Ralph Locher Papers, Betty Younger Papers, and the Rabbi Lelyveld Papers.

31. Moore, "School Desegregation," 137; Whyte, *African American Community,* 174.

32. "Campaigners for School Issues Plan to Work Until Polls Close," no date, article, Box 3, Folder 5, Younger Papers, WRHS.

33. "An Interpretation Paper," April 1964; Sidney Vincent to CRC and some others, February 10, 1964.

34. "Cleveland Education Chronology"; Whyte, *African American Community*, 3–4, 172–73, 178. Donna Whyte argues that while historians and scholars focused more intensively on integration as the main aspect of the civil rights freedom movement, black opinion on race and education was more complex and diverse. In the case of Cleveland, the actual concerns and goals of black parents in Cleveland was desegregation not integration. I would argue that integration sometimes seeped into the dialogue of UFM due to the organizational inclinations of its members—particularly the NAACP, but also CORE.

35. Smith/Bean interview; Perot interview, 2004; Turner interview, 2004; Meier and Rudwick, *CORE*, 229.

36. Ibid., 248–49. For additional sources on the Cleveland school protests in Cleveland, see Raymond Jirran's "Cleveland and the Negro"; Williams, "Equity and Efficiency." For articles on SBE sit-ins, police brutality of protestors, economic boycott, and other related school desegregation article excerpts from various newspapers, see Box 5, Folders 3–4 and Box 59, Folder 1, NAACP Papers.

37. Whyte, African American Community, 179.

38. UFM, "Position Paper on Educational Needs," March 2, 1964, Box 36, Folder 5, UL Papers, WRHS.

39. "An Interpretation Paper of the UFM," April 1964; Richan, *Racial Isolation*, 55–56.

40. Whyte, *African American Community*, 180; "An Interpretation paper of UFM," April 1964; "Cleveland Education Chronology"; Richan, *Racial Isolation*, 57.

41. Whyte, African American Community, 181; Richan, Racial Isolation, 57.

42. Moore, "School Desegregation," 141; Whyte, *African American Community*, 183; "Cleveland Education Chronology"; Richan, *Racial Isolation*, 57.

43. Untitled report, September 27, 1963, United Freedom Movement Files, Federal Bureau of Investigation Papers (hereafter FBI Papers), author's possession; "An Interpretation paper of UFM," April 1964; "Cleveland Education Chronology"; Whyte, *African American Community*, 184.

44. Meier and Rudwick, *CORE*, 232–33. Meier talks about CORE's decision to focus on hires based on historical exploitation, obstruction, and unequal access to work. Any "deficiencies" in the hired employee would be corrected with training by the employer as part of an overall rebalance in racial ratio. UFM applies this notion to increase educational access.

45. Whyte, *African American Community*, 184–85; "An Interpretation paper of UFM," April 1964; "Cleveland Education Chronology"; Sidney Vincent to CRC and some others, February 10, 1964; "Hazeldell Principal Soothes Hot Parents on Cold Morning," *Call and Post* article, January 18, 1964, Box 3, Folder 5, Younger Papers.

46. No title, no date, portion missing, manuscript begins with "of the class day, or roughly 10% integration," Box 28, Folder 5, NAACP Papers. Whyte argues that black parents—unlike the civil rights organizations—were not opposed to the neighborhood policy per se—even if it meant that all the black students were in one school. Their issue had

to do with allocation of resources, mistreatment of their children, and the SBE's aggressive maintenance of segregation over all else.

47. "An Interpretation paper of UFM," April 1964; Whyte, *African American Community*, 186.

48. "United Freedom Movement," January 29, 1964, United Freedom Movement file, FBI Papers, author's possession; Richan, *Racial Isolation*, 61; "Fight Erupt at 2 Schools," January 27, 1964, *Cleveland Press* article, Box 5, Folder 3, NAACP Papers; "Cleveland Education Chronology."

49. Turner interview, 2004. Perot interview, 2004; Richan, *Racial Isolation*, 61–62; George Barmann, "Insults, Fists, Threats, Traded by Angry Crowd," "Just Like in South Says Victim of Mob," and William Barnard, "Urgent Pleas Kept Negroes from Walking into Mob," Tony Natale and Norman Malchak, "Mob Hurls Eggs, Smashes 4 Autos in Wild Melee," and "Violence Shatters Long Peace" in Ardelia Dixon Scrapbook, unprocessed collection, WRHS.

50. Turner interview, 2004; Perot interview, 2004.

51. Ibid.

52. William Barnard, "Urgent Pleas Kept Negroes from Walking into Mob," Ardelia Dixon Scrapbook, WRHS.

53. Ruth Turner interview, 2004; Tony Natale and Norman Malchak, "Two Negroes Beaten by Crowd in Murray Hill School Fighting," *Cleveland Press* article, January 30, 1964, Box 3, Folder 5, Younger Papers, WRHS.

54. Tony Natale and Norman Malchak, "Two Negroes Beaten," January 30, 1964; William Barnard, "Urgent Pleas Kept Negroes from Walking into Mob," Ardelia Dixon Scrapbook, WRHS.

55. "15 Stay, Other Sit-Ins Leave to Plan Big Rally," Ardelia Dixon scrapbook, WRHS; Don Robertson and William C. Barnard, "41 Stage All-Night Sit-In at School Board Building," and "175 Demonstrators Sit in Halls, Picket School Administration Bldg.," Box 3, Folder 5, Younger Papers.

56. No title, February 2, 1964, notes of UFM Meeting at Antioch Baptist Church, Bonnie Gordon Papers, author's possession.

57. Ibid.

58. Sidney Vincent to CRC's and Some Others, February 10, 1964; Cleveland to Director, February 4, 1964, United Freedom Movement file, FBI Papers, author's possession; "United Freedom Movement Report," February 4, 1964, United Freedom Movement Papers, FBI Papers, author's possession; Richan, *Racial Isolation*, 63.

59. "Cleveland Education Chronology."

60. Moore, "School Desegregation," 147–48; Whyte, *African American Community*, 189; Norman Malchack and Dick Feagler, "School Sit-Ins End up Fight as 22 Go to Jail," no date, Ardelia Dixon scrapbook, WRHS.

61. Sidney Vincent to CRC's and Some Others, February 10, 1964.

62. Ibid.

63. "United Freedom Movement Report," February 4, 1964, United Freedom Movement Papers, FBI Papers, author's possession; Richan, *Racial Isolation*, 64–65; Report

of Executive Secretary, January 14–February 13, 1964, Box 1, Folder 6, NAACP Papers, WRHS.

64. Don Robertson, "Mixed Classes Now, Is Board Promise," February 5, 1964, *Cleveland Plain Dealer* article, Box 3, Folder 5, Younger Papers.

65. "An Interpretation paper of UFM," April 1964; UFM, "Position Paper on Educational Needs," March 2, 1964, Box 36, Folder 5, UL Papers, WRHS.

66. Moore, "School Desegregation," 148–49.

67. Ibid., 150; Minutes of CCHR, March 24, 1964, Box 24, Folder 5, NAACP Papers, WRHS; "Why Not in the City of Cleveland?: The Educational Park—a new idea for integrated quality education," no date, Box 24, Folder 5, NAACP Papers, WRHS; "Cleveland Education Chronology"; "Education Park," Reel 5, A:II: 36, Frames 1150–51, CORE Addendum; educational complex, Reel 14, E:IV:16, Frame 358, CORE Addendum; "The Educational Complex," Reel 5, A:II:36, Frame 1153, CORE Addendum. CCHR entertained ideas for creating integration through large educational parks. Education Parks collapsed several schools into one large facility similar to a college campus. The multigrade buildings shared facilities like libraries, auditoriums, health centers, etc., while centralizing school sources into one space. Other school districts like Orange County District for New Jersey, Fort Lauderdale, FL, and Brooklyn, NY, also considered educational parks. The idea of the education park came from sociologist Max Wolff. Wolff published some of his work in *Toward Integration of Northern Schools*, a series of articles on school desegregation published in 1963. His essay focused on a discussion of school desegregation in Plainfield, New Jersey, and Gary, Indiana, and featured essays from Kenneth Clark, Dan W. Dodson, Carl F. Hansen, and June Scahaloff. These infrastructures would include a strong curriculum and house elementary, middle, and junior and senior high school students. The park's innovative curriculum, teaching staff, and pedagogical methods aimed to garner a broad range of students across racial backgrounds. The modern form of the educational park is the smaller magnet school phenomena. Cleveland CORE began to strongly support the educational park as an alternative for volunteer integration of schools. In 1963, the *Journal of Educational Sociology* launched a special issue on the subject. Max Wolff, "Toward Integration of the Northern Schools," *Journal of Educational Sociology* 36, no. 6 (February 1963).

68. Minutes of CCHR, February 15, 1964, Box 24, Folder 5, NAACP Papers, WRHS; Minutes of CCHR, February 20, 1964, Box 24, Folder 5, NAACP Papers, WRHS; Minutes of CCHR, February 20, 1964, Box 24, Folder 5, NAACP Papers, WRHS; Civil Rights Report, no date, Box 1, Folder 5, Albert Pennybacker Papers, WRHS.

69. Whyte, *African American Community*, 194–95; "An Interpretation paper of the UFM," Resignation of superintendent. Bruce Klunder Papers-mss 4220, Box 1, f1 article "Cleveland Education Chronology."

70. CORE on School Crisis: *Plain Dealer* ad taken out by CORE: "CORE Speaks Out on the School Desegregation Crisis," no date, *Plain Dealer* article, Bonnie Gordon Papers, author's possession.

71. Turner interview, 2004, 2004; Evans interview, 2004; Perot interview, 2004. None of the interviewed participants recalled exactly how they got either Malcolm X or

Louis Lomax to speak, but Turner believes that they utilized James Farmer as a contact. Ostensibly he made the request on their behalf.

72. Turner to author, email, April 19, 2007.

73. Malcolm X, "Ballot or the Bullet," *Malcolm X Speaks,* ed. George Breitmann (New York: Grove Weidenfeld, 1990), 30.

74. Raymond Jirran, "Cleveland and the Negro," 216; no author, "This Week in Focus: A Time to Weep," *Cleveland Press,* Saturday, April 11, 1964, 9.

75. "Cleveland Education Chronology"; Joanne Klunder to Raymond Jirran, July 4, 1971, Raymond Jirran Papers, unprocessed collection, WRHS; no author, "Violence Resumed at School: Wire Fence to Be Erected," *Cleveland Press,* 4a.

76. "Cleveland Education Chronology."

77. Joanne Klunder to Raymond Jirran, June 8, 1969, Raymond Jirran Papers, unprocessed collection, WRHS; Klunder interview, 1967.

78. Klunder interview, 2006.

79. Joanne Klunder to Raymond Jirran, June 26, 1969, Raymond Jirran Papers, unprocessed collection, WRHS. Klunder interview, 1967.

80. Klunder interview, 1967.

81. White was cleared of any wrongdoing, although many still believe he reversed the machine deliberately. Others considered it a horrible accident. White maintained that he did not know Klunder was behind him. Antoine Perot, Ruth Turner interview, 2004. Louis Cifford, "The Impossible Happens in Cleveland," *New York World-Telegram and Sun,* April 9, 1964, 8; no author, "Minister Is Killed in School Violence: Picket Run Over by Bulldozer," *Cleveland Press,* Tuesday, April 7, 1964. Richan, *Racial Isolation,* 67–68.

82. UPI, "Bulldozer Kills Rights Picket," *New York World Telegram,* Tuesday, April 7, 1964; no author, "Fear, Hatred Reign in Wake of Rioting," *Cleveland Press,* 4A; George Barman, "City's Worst Rights Riots Follow Minister's Death," *Cleveland Plain Dealer,* April 8, 1964, 9; no author, "10 Policemen Hurt in Riot," *Cleveland Plain Dealer,* April 8, 1964, 11. There are various figures for police injuries between eight and twelve.

83. No author, "Fighting Follows Minister's Death," *Cleveland Press,* Wednesday, April 8, 1964, 7A.

84. Ruth Turner interview, 2004; "New Cleveland Crisis," no date, article, Box 19, Folder 9, Ralph Locher Papers, WRHS.

85. Activities of the Community Relations Board for 1964, Ellsworth Harpole to Ralph Locher, February 11, 1965, Community Relations Board, unprocessed collection, WRHS; no author, "Fear, Hatred," cover page and 4a; George Barmann, "Gas Is Used to Halt Mobs," *Cleveland Plain Dealer,* cover page, April 8, 1964.

86. "What Four Brave Women Told Their Children," magazine article, Box 1, Folder 1, Klunder Papers, WRHS.

87. Klunder interview, 2006; no author, "'He Died Loving-Hoping,' Says Widow of Rev. Klunder," *Cleveland Press,* Wednesday, April 8, 1964, 4.

88. "We Are Dedicated," *Time Magazine* 83, no. 16 (April 17, 1964), 42; "The Backlash," *Time Magazine* 83, no. 17 (April 24, 1964), 41.

89. Whyte, *African American Community*, 199; Richan, *Racial Isolation*, 67; Malcolm X, *By Any Means Necessary* (New York: Pathfinder, 1992), 25. SAC, Cleveland to FBI Director, memorandum regarding Malcolm X Appearance at CORE Sponsored Event, April 17, 1964, *Section 1*. March–April 1964, FBI File on Muslim Mosque, Inc., Federal Bureau of Investigation Library, *Archives Unbound*. The file can be found in Gale's database: Federal Surveillance of African Americans 1920–1984. Often this exchange is described as Malcolm X's dismissal of Klunder's sacrifice. Actually, he noted in a previous radio interview that Klunder's death represented a serious recognition by whites of the sacrifices required to end inequality. His exchange with participants at the Militant Labor Forum rather reflects his challenge to audience members who seized the situation as a circumstance to lay claim to white activists' important role in the movement while they ignored the black community's long history of sacrifices and deaths.

90. Don Robertson, "Rev. Bruce Klunder Eulogized as 'Man Who Died for Friends,'" *Cleveland Plain Dealer*, April 10, 1964, front page, 4. Below "1500 Hear Rev. Klunder Eulogized."

91. No author, editorial, "Use of Force Is Intolerable," *Cleveland Plain Dealer*, 10.

92. No author, "Farmer, CORE's Chief, Pledges Good Faith by Chapter Here," *Cleveland Plain Dealer*, April 10, 1964, 8. The same day, on the next page over, an article announced the formation by Lewis Robinson of the Medgar Evers Gun Club. No author, "Rifle Club Organizer Suspended by City," *Cleveland Plain Dealer*, April 10, 1964, 11; No author, "Cleveland Pays Sad Farewell to Rev. Bruce Klunder," April 10, 1964, *Cleveland Press* article, Box 3, Folder 5, Younger Papers, WRHS. Not much was mentioned in the *CORE-lator*. The next issue focused on the Harlem and Rochester riots. Additionally, CORE Freedom Summer volunteers James Chaney, Michael Schwerner, and Andrew Goodman went missing. Finally, a small article appeared, entitled, "Widow of CORE Victim Pickets," July–August 1964, *CORE-Lator*, issue 107, Reel 13, E:III:76, Frames 514–17, CORE Addendum. This relatively small feature might have fed later beliefs that the *CORE-lator* no longer reflected the movement's direction.

93. Ruth Turner interview, 2004; Clifford, "The Impossible."

94. "Cleveland Education Chronology"; "An Interpretation paper of UFM," April 1964; "School Board Amends Building Truce," April 10, 1964, *Cleveland Press* article, Box 3, Folder 5, Younger Papers, WRHS.

95. "An Interpretation paper of UFM," April 1964; "School Board Amends," April 10, 1964; "Cleveland Education Chronology."

96. Ibid.

97. Marjorie Schuster, "Rights Group Will Attend Boycott Rally," January 8, 1964, article, Box 3, Folder 5, Younger Papers, WRHS; Taylor, *Knocking at Our Own Door*, 129–30.

98. "School Boycotts in Four Cities," *CORE-lator* 105 (March/April 1964), Reel 13, E:III:76, Frame 511. In New York, Cincinnati, Chicago, and Boston—in New York 44 percent of total enrollment stayed out of school February 11 later followed with Cincinnati where 26,400 stayed out of the 83,500 students, and Chicago, February 25, 172,350 out of 470,000 even with six black aldermen against the boycott. February 26, Boston, 20,571 out of 92,844.

99. Marjorie Schuster, "Rights Aids Here Back School 'Freedom Days,'" January 20, 1964, article, Box 3, Folder 5, Younger Papers, WRHS; Ann Skinner, "School Boycott, Mass Picketing Considered by Hazeldell Parents," no date, article, Box 3, Folder 5, Younger Papers, WRHS; "School Boycott, Mass Picketing," no date; "Bus Class Picketing to Begin Tomorrow," January 27, 1964, *Cleveland Press* article, Box 5, Folder 3, NAACP Papers, WRHS.

100. "Cleveland Education Chronology"; Richan, *Racial Isolation*, 68–69; "Freedom School Coordinating Committee: Excuse for Absence," no date, Bonnie Gordon Papers, author's possession.

101. Whyte, *African American Community*, 203; "Cleveland Education Chronology."

102. Meier and Rudwick, *CORE*, 249; Whyte, *African American Community*, 204; Ruth Turner interview, 2004; Tony Perot interview, 2004. This number has changed from source to source, most persons interviewed put the number at about 98 percent, Whyte at 85–95 percent, and Meier and Rudwick at 92 percent.

103. For more information on Mandel's important role in building the freedom school curriculum, see Kelley, "Introduction," xv–xxiii.

104. "CRM Teacher's guide," no date, Box 1, Folder 1, United Freedom Papers, WRHS; "Freedom School Personnel," no date; no title, various papers on Freedom School, including supervisor's sheet, teacher's guide, list of freedom schools, Bonnie Gordon papers, author's possession; "Glenville Area Attend Freedom Schools," no date, flyer, Box 2, Folder 6, Younger Papers, WRHS.

105. Ibid.

106. Ibid.

107. Whyte, *African American Community*, 205; Joanne Klunder to Raymond Jirran, July 4, 1971.

108. Report of Executive Secretary, April 8–May 5, 1962, Box, Folder 6, NAACP Papers, WRHS.

109. Report of Executive Secretary, June 3–July 7, 1964, Box, Folder 6, NAACP Papers, WRHS.

110. Report of Executive Secretary, July/August 1964, Box, Folder 6, NAACP Papers, WRHS; no author, "Rights Units Plan Mall Rally Monday: Leaders Rule Out School Picketing," Saturday, April 11, 1964, cover page; "Complaint for Injunction and Declatory Judgment for Charles Craggett, et al.," Box 25, Folder 2, NAACP Papers, Box 25, Folder 2; "Motion for Preliminary Injunction," Box 26, Folder 2, NAACP Papers, WRHS; Whyte, *African American Community*, 206. Children included Alvonia Brown, Marco Brown, Charles Craggett, George Craggett, Suandra Craggett, Charles Hamilton, Ida Hamilton, Mark Hamilton, Pamela Hamilton, Deborah Jean Jackson, Robert Jackson, Rochelle Jackson, Dwayne Jenkins, Keith Jenkins, Kevin Johnson, Lamont Johnson, Byron Lewis, Gretta Mattox, Belinda C. Newkirk, Benjamin F. Newkirk, and Michael Stradford.

111. Whyte, *African American Community*, 206; Civil Rights Report, no date, Box 1, Folder 5, Albert Pennybacker, WRHS; Minutes of the Urban League, April 21, 1964, Box 5, Folder 2, UL Papers, WRHS. The Urban League divided over whether to support the levy arguing that not to do so would mean that the schools would still have no funding.

112. Emergency Clergy Committee for Civil Rights, "Cleveland Civil Rights Report," September 15, 1964, Box 2, Folder 35, Karl Bruch Jr. Papers, WRHS.

113. Ibid.

114. Ibid.

115. Ibid.

116. Report of Executive Secretary, September 1–October 6, 1964, Box 1, Folder 6, NAACP Papers, WRHS.

117. Ibid.; Whyte, *African American Community*, 208; Emergency Clergy Committee for Civil Rights, "Cleveland Civil Rights Report."

118. "Boycott of Howe School Appears Ended," no date, article, Box 59, Folder 1, NAACP Papers, WRHS; "UFM Supports Howe Boycott," no date, article, Box 59, Folder 1, NAACP Papers, WRHS.

119. Richan, *Racial Isolation*, 73–75. I would argue that some black parents found a way to protest and go around the SBE without direct action. Catholic private schools experienced an increase in black children in attendance from the first wave of migration through the 1960s and 1970s at their schools, much of which was subsidized by programs of the church. There was such an increase that it became a requirement for all non-Catholics attending school to convert to Catholicism as a deterrent from overcrowding. Many of the Hazeldell parents were working families who were upwardly mobile though most only had a high school education. Private school subsidies would allow them to send their children to Catholic private school and escape the Cleveland public schools. For information on black Catholics in Cleveland, see Dorothy Blatnica, *At the Alter of Their God: African American Catholics in Cleveland* (New York: Garland Publishing, 1994); Emergency Clergy Committee for Civil Rights, "Cleveland Civil Rights Report," October 27, 1964, Box 2, Folder 35, Karl Bruch Jr. Papers, WRHS; Whyte, *African American Community*, 210; "Boycott of Howe School," no date; Klunder to Jirran, July 4, 1971.

120. Richan, *Racial Isolation*, 69; Press Release on School Segregation in Cleveland, no date, Box 43, Folder 4, NAACP Papers, WRHS; no title, January 7, 1965, Box 29, Folder 1, NAACP Papers, WRHS; Leonard B. Stevens, *More Than a Bus Ride: The Desegregation of the Cleveland Public Schools* (Cleveland, OH: Office on School Monitoring & Community Relations, 1985).

121. Cleveland Chapter CORE Action Letter, June 1965, Bonnie Gordon Papers, author's possession.

## 5. New Directions to Black Power

1. Robinson, *The Making of a Man*, 28.

2. Ibid.

3. For discussion about Robert Williams and references to Mae Mallory, see Tyson, *Radio Free Dixie*, 262–86; Robert Williams, *Negroes with Guns* (Chicago: Third World Press, 1973), 104; Arsenault, *Freedom Riders*, 407–18; CAMD CORE FILE is in Reel 2, Folder 19, Frames 231–75; Monroe File, Box 17, Folder 322, UFCW Papers.

4. Mae Mallory, interview by Malaika Lumumba, February 27, 1970, Bunche Papers, RJB#523, Moorland-Spingarn Research Center, Howard University; Robin D. G. Kelley,

*Freedom Dreams: The Black Radical Imagination* (Boston: Beacon Press, 2002), 74; James Forman, *The Making of Black Revolutionaries* (New York: MacMillan Company, 1972), 207; Sugrue, *Sweet Land of Liberty*, 318; Williams, *Negroes with Guns*, 69; Emily Crosby, "It Wasn't the Wild West: Keeping Local Studies in Self Defense Historiography," in *Civil Rights from the Ground Up: Local Struggles, A National Movement*, ed. Emilye Crosby (Athens: University of Georgia Press, 2011), 196–97, 215; Arsenault, *Freedom Riders*, 411–12.

5. Memorandum from James Farmer to Core groups, April 12, 1962, Reel 2, Series, File 19, Frame 255, CORE Papers.

6. Berta Green to James Farmer, March 21, 1962, Reel 2, Series 1, File 19, Frame 250, CORE Papers; James Farmer to Berta Green, March 29, 1962, Reel 2, Series 1, File 19, Frame 251, CORE Papers; Berta Green to James Farmer, May 14, 1962, Reel 2, Series 1, File 19, Frame 264, CORE Papers; Meier and Rudwick, *CORE*, 202; Peniel Joseph, *Waiting 'Til the Midnight Hour: A Narrative History of Black Power in America* (New York: Henry Holt & Company, 2006), 312; Arsenault, *Freedom Rides*, 417. There were two groups organized around support of the Monroe defendants. The first group mentioned here is the Committee to Aid the Monroe Defendants. Most activists believed the group was heavily influenced by the Communist Party. The second organization, Monroe Defense Committee also viewed CAMD as a front by radicals making Monroe an instrument for its own political agenda. According to Meier and Rudwick, the Monroe Defense Committee consisted mostly of black members while the Committee to Aid the Monroe Defendants mainly had a Trotskyite leaning. CORE had less problems associating with MDC than CAMD, but if CORE could avoid both groups altogether while maintaining a supportive stance toward the Monroe defendants that was preferable.

7. Berta Green to James Farmer, May 14, 1962.

8. See all of Monroe file, Box 17, File 322, UFCW Papers, WRHS; Meier and Rudwick, *CORE*, 202; Monroe Defense Committee to Dear Brothers and Sisters, February 5, 1962, Box 17, F322, UFCW Papers, WRHS.

9. Evans interview, 2004; Ruth Turner and Tony Perot interview; Sugrue, *Sweet Land of Liberty*, 318; CAMD Supporters List, no date, Reel 2, Series 1, File 19, Frame 270, CORE Papers. Supposedly, the idea to back Mallory came from Max Stanford; however, Evans membership in the Afro-American Institute (intellectual parent to RAM), the very early association of John Cloud with CAMD, and the broad community support likely meant that a number of influences directed CORE toward the Mallory case.

10. Agenda, November 26 and December 3, 1963, Box 1, Folder 3, Bonnie Gordon Papers, WHS.

11. Minutes of NAC Steering, January 24, 1964, Box 2R570, Folder CORE Minutes and Reports, James and Lula Farmer Papers, Center for American History, University of Texas at Austin; Meier and Rudwick, *CORE*, 202–3.

12. Richard Haley to W. S. McIntosh, December 6, 1963, Reel 23, Series V, File 89, Frame 973, CORE Papers.

13. Richard Haley to W. S. McIntosh, December 6, 1963, Reel 23, Series V, File 89, Frame 973, CORE Papers. John E. Maddox to Dayton CORE executive board, December 10, 1963, Reel 23, Series V, File 89, Frames 980–83, CORE Papers; John E. Maddox to

Dayton CORE executive board, December 10, 1963, Reel 23, Series V, File 89, Frames 980–83, CORE Papers. As executive secretary for Dayton CORE, W. S. McIntosh became embroiled in a nasty internal fight with Dayton chairman, John Maddox, over his accused mismanagement of CORE and compromising alliances with the governor's office. According to Maddox, McIntosh admitted that he hindered Dayton CORE's participation in the Mallory march because of his promise to Jack Coles, an aide of Ohio governor Rhodes, not to embarrass the governor. In exchange for his cooperation, his son, Jay McIntosh, would retain his state job without any interference from the governor or his office. Eventually, Maddox and McIntosh's in-fighting spilled over into the newspapers, and Dayton CORE's membership drives and protest activities ground to a screeching halt. Maddox resigned from his position as chairman of Dayton CORE shortly thereafter.

14. "Communism in Cleveland CORE," March 13, 1964, Reel 20, F:III:39, Frames 1249–50, CORE Addendum.

15. "Setback in Mallory Extradition Fight: Carolina Court Agrees to Send Commissioner to Cuba to Take Testimony of Robert F. Williams and Family," press release, March 6, 1962, Reel 2, Series 1, File 19, Frame 246, CORE Papers; Mae Mallory interview; David Cohen interview, October 12, 1971, Meier and Rudwick interviewer notes, Box 56, Folder 3, August Meier Papers, Schomburg.

16. Warren, *Who Speaks for the Negro*, 377; Meier and Rudwick, *CORE*, 206–7.

17. Malcolm X, "Message to the Grass Roots," *Malcolm X Speaks: Selected Speeches and Statements* (New York: Gove Weidenfeld, 1990), 8.

18. Farmer, *Lay Bare*, 222–25.

19. David Dennis interview, June 30, 1972, Box 56, Folder 5, August Meier Papers. Ronnie Moore had the opposite stance in Fairclough, *Race & Democracy*, 342; Wesley Hogan, *Many Minds, One Heart: SNCC's Dream for a New America* (Chapel Hill: University of North Carolina Press, 2007), 158–59, 162.

20. Floyd McKissick, *Three Fifths a Man* (London: Macmillan Co., 1969), 137–38; NAC discussion—NAC Steering Committee Minutes, July 30–July 2, 1964?, Box 2R571, Folder: NAC Steering Committee, James and Lula Farmer Papers. There are various references to CORE and its stance on self-defense. On violence in Mississippi and Louisiana, seeCharles Cobb, *This Non-Violent Stuff Gone Get You Killed: How Guns Made the Civil Rights Movement Possible* (New York: Basic Books, 2014); Crosby, "It Wasn't the Wild West," 194–255; Simon Wendt, *Spirit and the Shotgun: Armed Resistance and the Struggle for Civil Rights* (Gainesville: University Press of Florida, 2007), 95–99, 181–82; Akinyele Umoja, [AU: Umoja or Uomoja, as below?] *We Will Shoot Back: Armed Resistance in the Mississippi Freedom Movement* (New York: New York University Press, 2013), 94–98; Akinyele Uomoja, "The Ballot and the Bullet: A Comparative Analysis of Armed Resistance in the Civil Rights Movement," *Journal of Black Studies* 29, no. 4 (March 1999): 558–78, and 562–63, 566. Uomoja particularly challenges Meier and Rudwick's regional thesis of self-defense as a northern phenomenon. Lance Hill, *Deacons for Defense: Armed Resistance and the Civil Rights Movement* (Chapel Hill: University of North Carolina Press, 2004); Farmer, *Lay Bare*, 246–51; Fairclough, *Race & Democracy*, 193–94, 341–43; Leonard, "'We Catchin' Hell Down Here," 107–8, 131 ,166–79. On

Violence in Florida, see Stewart Weschler, July 23, 2013, interview by Nishani Frazier, in author's possession.

21. On Louisiana CORE and violence, see DeJong, *A Different Day*, 193–94, 175–76; Frystak, *Our Minds on Freedom*, 189, 192–93; Farmer, *Lay Bare*, 246–51; Fairclough, *Race & Democracy*, 341–69; Leonard, "We Are Catchin Hell," 174–77.

22. For more information on the Deacons for Defense, see Simon Wendt, "Roots of Black Power: Armed Resistance and the Radicalization of the Civil Rights Movement," in *The Black Power Movement: Rethinking the Civil Rights–Black Power Era*, ed. Peniel Joseph (New York: Routledge, 2006), 147–50; Hill, *Deacons for Defense*; Fairclough, *Race & Democracy*, 341–69.

23. SAC Detroit to Director FBI, January 19, 1965, Medgar Evers Gun Club, Bureau File 157-1624-23. This is a NARA digitized FBI document on RAM and MERC; Ruth Turner and Perot interview, 2007; David Swiderski, *Approaches to Black Power: African American Grassroots Political Struggle in Cleveland, Ohio* (Amherst: University of Massachusetts Press, 2013), 148; Wendt, *Spirit and the Shotgun*, 161–66; "Rifle Club Leader Expects Violence," April 6, 1964, Box 59, Folder 1, NAACP Papers. Despite Cleveland CORE's attitude toward the Medgar Evers Gun Club, Arthur Evans noted that after the Murray Hill incident it became clear Cleveland CORE championed self-defense.

24. Robinson, *Making of a Man*, 58–59; Gordon interview.

25. Robinson, *Making of a Man*, 60.

26. James Russell to Albert Cleage, May 3, 1963, Bonnie Gordon Papers, CORE Accessioned Records, WRHS.

27. Robinson, *Making of a Man*, 61.

28. Ibid., 62.

29. Floyd McKissick later had a similar take. McKissick, *Three Fifths*, 134; Richard Haley report, April 19, 1962, Reel 42, Series V, File 398, Frame 393, CORE Papers; Mary Hamilton to James McCain, May 3, 1962, Reel 42, Series V, File 398, Frames 400–401, CORE Papers. Mary Hamilton, in fact, complained about and attempted to bypass John Cloud during Cleveland CORE's earlier stage. She spoke with the Freedom Fighters about becoming a CORE chapter, but they refused to be nonviolent.

30. Ibid.

31. Robinson, *Making of a Man*, 57–58, 62; Evans interview, 2004.

32. Robinson, *Making of a Man*, 63–64.

33. Outline of Civil Rights Organizations, Box 43, Folder 4, NAACP Papers. The Job Seekers were an offshoot of the Freedom Fighters, mostly centered on the leadership of Ancusto Butler. Formed in 1962, the organization eventually died in the late 1960s. Supposedly it was a one-member organization.

34. Evans interview, 2004; Gordon interview, Perot interview, 2004.

35. "Welcome to the picket line," no date, Box 1, Folder 3, Bonnie Gordon Papers, WHS.

36. Robinson, *Making of a Man*, 66. It is unclear exactly which members were doing what on the picket line. The picket line demonstrations were antithetical to CORE rules of action, however there is no point of comparison for how CORE members' actions differed or compared to the Freedom Fighters.

37. Ibid.

38. Ibid., 66.

39. "Resolution Passed at the Northern Negro Grass Roots Leadership Conference," Detroit, Michigan, November 9–10, 1963, Bonnie Gordon Papers, CORE Accessioned Records, WRHS. Historian David Swiderski corrects my earlier dissertation argument that the conference did not follow through on the proposal. Apparently, they did so in a later plenary session. Swiderski, *Approaches to Black Power*, 135; Grace Lee Boggs, *Living for Change: An Autobiography* (Minneapolis: University of Minnesota Press, 1998), 128.

40. Perot interview, 2004; Robinson, *Making of a Man*, 66; Perot interview, 2007. Lewis recalled that CORE left in October, but CORE members attended the Grassroots conference along with the Freedom Fighters in November to gather support for Central Cadillac. More likely, CORE left the Central Cadillac protest shortly after that.

41. James Russell to Albert Cleage, June 3, 1963, Bonnie Gordon Papers, CORE Accessioned Records, WRHS; Speech by Reverend Albert Cleage, no date, Bonnie Gordon Papers, CORE Accessioned Records, WRHS; Albert Cleage, speech excerpt, no date, Bonnie Gordon Papers, CORE Accessioned Records, WRHS. For further background on Albert Cleage, see Angela Dillard, "Religion and Radicalism: The Reverend Albert D. Cleage, Jr. and the Rise of Black Christian Nationalism in Detroit," in *Freedom North: Black Struggles Outside the South, 1940–1980*, ed. Komozi Woodard and Jeanne Theoharis (New York: Palgrave Macmillan, 2003), 153–75; Van Deburg, *New Day in Babylon*, 237–40; Timothy Murphy, "The Influence of Socialism in Black and Womanist Theologies: Capitalism's Relationship as Source, Sin, and Salvation," in *Black Theology: An International Journal* 10, no. 1 (April 1, 2012): 28–48.

42. Evans interview, 2004.

43. Ibid.

44. Clarence Lang also notes the multiple membership of CORE members in St. Louis. Lang, *Grassroots at the Gateway*, 114–18.

45. For information on the Afro-American Institute and RAM, examine Max Stanford, *Black Nationalism and Revolutionary Action Movement: The Papers of Muhammad Ahmad*, Gale Digital Collection; The Black Power Movement, Part 3, Revolutionary Action Movement Papers, 1962–1996, Muhammad Ahmed, Ernie Allen, John Bracey, Randalph Boehm (Bethesda, MD: UPA Collections, 2002); Robin Kelly, *Freedom Dreams*, 72–76; Report By the Committee of Un-American Activities, House of Representatives, "Guerilla Warfare Advocates in the United States," May 6, 1968, House Report number 1351 (Washington, DC: US Government Printing Office, 1968), 21; Swiderski, *Approaches to Black Power*, 108, 124–30, 235–36; Robin Kelly and Betsy Esch, "Black Like Mao: Red China and Black Revolution," in *Afro Asia: Revolution, Politics, and Cultural Connections*, ed. Fred Ho and Bill Multen (Durham, NC: Duke University Press, 2008), 107–22; Sanford, "Revolutionary Action Movement," 2; Van Deburg, *New Day*, 165, 168; Sugrue, *Sweet Land*, 316–21, 335–38.

46. Stanford, *Black Nationalism;* Kelly, *Freedom Dreams*; Swiderski, *Approaches to Black Power*; Ho and Multen, *Afro Asia*; Sanford, "Revolutionary Action Movement"; Van Deburg, *New Day*; Sugrue, *Sweet Land*.

47. Max Stanford, "Revolutionary Action Movement: A Caste Study of an Urban Revolutionary Movement in Western Capitalist Society" (Master's thesis, Atlanta University, 1986), 112.

48. House of Representatives, Guerilla Warfare Advocates, 33; John Bracey interview, July 22, 1971, Box 56, Folder 2, August Meier Papers; David Cohen, July 25, 1971, Box 56, Folder 3, August Meier Papers; and Arthur Evans, interview by Meier and Rudwick, March 13, 1971, Box 56, Folder 5, August Meier Papers; Sugrue, *Sweet Land*, 316–21, 335–38.

49. Turner to Dear Friend in Freedom, March 8, 1965, Box 16, Folder 305, UFCW Papers, WRHS.

50. Mac Warren, ed., Independent Black Political Action: The Struggle to Break with the Democratic and Republican Parties (New York: Pathfinder, 1982), 17–27; Omar Ali, In the Balance of Power: Independent Black Politics and Third Party Movements in the United States (Athens: Ohio University Press, 2008), 141–42; Sugrue, Sweet Land, 308–9; Joseph, Waiting 'Til, 84–94.

51. Antoine Perot et al. to Dear Friend, December 10, 1963, Box 1, Folder 4, Bonnie Gordon Papers, WHS; Charles Snorton et al. to Dear Friend, December 2, 1963, Box 1, Folder 4, Bonnie Gordon Papers, WHS. Representatives also included the Freedom Fighters, Negro American Labor Council, NAACP, Defenders of Rights, Job Seekers, Afro-American Institute, and various black labor, church, and community groups.

52. Minutes of Committee, December 9, 1963, Box 1, Folder 4, Bonnie Gordon Papers, WHS.

53. Ibid.

54. Ibid.

55. Ibid.

56. Platform and Program—Independent Black Political Action, n.d., Box 1, Folder 4, Bonnie Gordon Papers, WHS.

57. Charles Snorton et al. to Dear Friend, December 2, 1963, Box 1, Folder 4, Bonnie Gordon Papers, WHS; "Get the Party Bosses Off Your Back!!," no date, Box 1, Folder 4, Bonnie Gordon Papers, WHS.

58. For examples of the changing nature of the southern black freedom movement, see Hasan Jeffries, *Bloody Lowndes: Civil Rights and Black Power in Alabama's Black Belt* (New York: New York University Press, 2009); Susan Youngblood Ashmore, *Carry It On: War on Poverty and the Civil Rights Movement in Alabama, 1964–1972* (Athens: University of Georgia Press, 2008); Alton Hornsby, *Black Power in Dixie: A Political History of African Americans in Atlanta* (Gainesville: University Press of Florida, 2009); Fergus, *Liberalism, Black Power*; and Tracy E. K. Meyer, *Civil Rights in the Gateway to the South: Louisville, Kentucky, 1945–1980* (Lexington: University Press of Kentucky, 2009), 145–77.

59. Of the various foundations, Ford was particularly known for its grants to community organizations involved in the black freedom movement. It also figures prominently in the history of CORE. See Allen, *Black Awakening*, 121–32; Jerry Gershenhorn, "'Not an Academic Affair': African American Scholars and the Development of African Studies in the United States, 1942–1960," *Journal of African American History* 94, no. 1 (2009):

44–68; Ferguson, "Organizing the Ghetto"; Noliwe M. Rooks, *White Money/Black Power: The Surprising History of African American Studies* (Boston: Beacon Press, 2006), 26–30, 85–89; Lang, *Grassroots at the Gateway*, 232, 236–37; ; Kenneth Jolly, *Black Liberation in the Midwest: The Struggle in the St. Louis, Missouri, 1964–1970* (New York: Routledge, 2006), 134–36; Fabio Rojas, *From Black Power to Black Studies: How a Radical Social Movement Became an Academic Discipline* (Baltimore: Johns Hopkins University Press, 2007), 130–66; Noel A. Cazenave, *Impossible Democracy: The Unlikely Success of the War on Poverty Community Action Programs* (Albany: State University of New York Press, 2007), 31–48; Karen Ferguson, *Top Down: The Ford Foundation, Black Power, and the Reinvention of Racial Liberalism* (Philadelphia: University of Pennsylvania Press, 2013), 70–73.

60. Of particular import to this discussion are the texts, which incorporate the history of civil rights with the War on Poverty programs. See Ashmore, *Carry It On*; Robert Bauman, *Race and the War on Poverty: From Watts to East L. A.* (Norman: University of Oklahoma Press, 2008); Robert Bauman, "The Black Power and Chicano Movements in the Poverty Wars in Los Angeles," *Journal of Urban History* 33, no. 2 (2007): 277–95; Lias Gayle Hazirjian, "Combating Need: Urban Conflict and the Transformation of War on Poverty and the African American Freedom Struggle in Rocky Mount, NC," *Journal of Urban History* 34, no. 4 (2008): 639–64; William S. Clayton, *Freedom Is Not Enough: The War on Poverty and the Civil Rights Movement in Texas* (Austin: University of Texas Press, 2010), 65–83.

61. National Director Report, July 1964 Reel 9, C:II:80, Frame 785, CORE Addendum; Meeting with NAC and Staff, June 29, 1965, Series 3.1.2, Folder 6833, McKissick Papers, SHC and in Reel 9, C:I:107, Frame 989, CORE Addendum.

62. Meier and Rudwick, *CORE*, 232; David Cohen, December 19, 1970, interview by Meier and Rudwick, Box 56, Folder 3, Meier Papers. Norman Hill's influence on the Cleveland chapter is a subject of debate. Meier and Rudwick argue that Turner and Perot were particularly influenced by Hill, which helped to explain their underlying inclinations toward black power. The authors gleaned their information from interviews they conducted, though they do not say which interviews. After reviewing Turner, Perot, and Cohen interviews and a conversation with the Hills, the genealogy of influence is in question especially given the local influences independently driving Cleveland chapter in that direction. David Cohen notes that Cleveland CORE and Hill were not the same in their thinking on community organization, but that they ran parallel. More importantly, the two factions come to community organizing in different ways, particularly Hill's insistence that community organizing was not synonymous or a step toward black power.

63. Doris Innis, Roy Innis, Carl Rachlin, and Val Coleman were among the many members who believed Hill wished to replace Farmer. Although it did not stand that the Hills intended to replace him with Rustin, since many CORE members wanted to replace Farmer with any number of alternatives for various reason. Doris Innis interview, October 1971, Box 56, Folder 9; Roy Innis, October 4, 1971, Box 56, Folder 9; Carl Rachlin, December 14, 1970, Box 57, Folder 2, all interviews by Meier and Rudwick, August Meier Papers. Val Coleman interview, January 6, 1999, Sheila Michael Oral History Project, Columbia University Oral History Center.

64. Peter Drucker, Shachtman and His Left: A Socialists Odyssey through an American Century (New York: Humanity Books, 1993), 268–72; Anderson, Bayard Rustin, 211, 231, 271–73; Bayard Rustin, I Must Resist: Bayard Rustin's Life in Letters (San Francisco: City Lights Publishers, 2012), 254–57; William P. Jones, The March on Washington: Jobs, Freedom, and the Forgotten History of Civil Rights (New York: W. W. Norton, 2012), 161, 170.

65. Drucker, Shachtman and His Left; Anderson, Bayard Rustin; Rustin, I Must Resist; Jones, The March on Washington.

66. Drucker, *Max Shachtman*, 295–96; NAC Steering Committee Minutes, August 8–9, 1964, Reel 9, C:II:89, Frames 841–42, CORE Addendum; Forman, *Making of a Revolutionary*, 389; David Halberstam, "CORE Aide Resigns in Campaign Split: Hill Would Curb Rallies and Seek Political Unity," *New York Times* (September 4, 1964), 10.

67. David Cohen interview, December 19, 1970. Cohen noted that issues like these made Cleveland CORE's community organization strategy different from Hill.

68. Meier and Rudwick, *CORE*, 330.

69. Goldberg, *CORE in Trouble*, 15. Minutes of the 23rd Annual Convention, July 1–5, 1965, McKissick Papers.

70. Annual Report to the National CORE Convention, July 1, 1965, Reel 9, C:I:98, Frame 910–15, CORE Addendum.

71. Steering Committee Minutes, September 26, 1964, Reel 9, C:I:90, Frames 848–49, CORE Addendum.

72. James Farmer, National Director's Staff Report, July 1962, Reel 9, C:I:56, Frame 522, CORE Addendum.

73. Meier and Rudwick, *CORE*, 331.

74. Ibid., 209.

75. Meeting with NAC and Staff, June 29, 1965, Series 3.1.2, Folder 6833, McKissick Papers, SHC and in Reel 9, C:II:103, Frame 989, CORE Addendum; Turner on "exposing" in NAC Meeting, December 31, 1965–January 2, 1966, Series 3.1.2, Folder 6964, McKissick Papers, SHC; Meier and Rudwick, *CORE*, 410.

76. NAC Meeting, December 31, 1965–January 2, 1966; Meier and Rudwick, *CORE*, 410.

77. Meeting with NAC and Staff, June 29, 1965, Series 3.1.2, Folder 6833, McKissick Papers, SHC; Meier and Rudwick, *CORE*, 127; Alan Gartner, interview notes, by August Meier, no date, Box 56, Folder 6, August Meier Papers, Schomburg Center for Research in Black Culture.

78. Evans to Dear Friend, March 24, 1964, Box 16, Folder 305, UFCW Papers, WRHS; Ellsworth Harpole to Ralph Locher, *Report on the Activities of the Community Relations Board for 1964*, February 11, 1965, Cleveland Community Relations Board, unprocessed collection, WRHS; Arthur Evans, Ruth Turner, and Juanita Powers to Dear Friend, July 23, 1964, Box 16, Folder 305, UFCW, WRHS; Evans to Dear Friends, August 17, 1964, Box 16, Folder 305, UFCW Papers, WRHS; Why Ohio Delegates Should Support the Seating of the Mississippi Freedom Democratic Party Delegation, August 20, 1964, Box 16, Folder 305, UFCW Papers, WRHS.

79. Nationally, most chapters rarely addressed this issue until after 1962. By 1964, it was one of the leading problems among the local chapters and for the national office. Many chapters and the national office believed that the issue of police brutality could also serve as a rallying point for interest in CORE among poor black residents. Meier and Rudwick, *CORE*, 194, 250; "CORE's Plans for Eliminating Police Brutality in Cleveland," July 6, 1964, Box 16, Folder 305, UFCW Papers, WRHS; Woodard, *A Nation within a Nation*, 78–80, 101; Leonard Moore, *Black Rage in New Orleans: Police Brutality and African American Activism* (Baton Rouge: Louisiana State University Press, 2010), 54–59; Max Herman, *Fighting in the Streets: Ethnic Succession and Urban Unrest in the Twentieth Century* (New York: Peter Lang, 2005), 78; Jolly, *Black Liberation in the Midwest*, 55–58; Marilynn Johnson, *Street Justice: A History of Police Violence in New York City* (Boston: Beacon Press, 2003), 229–37; Countryman, *Up South*, 226–27.

80. Booker T. Eddy Testimony, Reverend Vincent Haas Testimony, Ruth Turner Testimony, United States Commission on Civil Rights Ohio, Hearing held in Cleveland, Ohio, April 1–7, 1966 (Washington, DC: Supt. of Docs.), 559–68, 624.

81. James Naughton, Michael Roberts, and William Barnard, "Making of a Mayor," *Plain Dealer Sunday Magazine* (December 10, 1967), 8; James Haskins, *A Piece of the Power: Four Black Mayors* (New York: Dial Press, 1972), 14.

82. Ibid.; Report of Executive Secretary, June 1–July 6, 1965, Box 1, Folder 6, NAACP Papers, WRHS.

83. Cleveland CORE News, no date, Series 3.1.2, Folders 6870–71, Floyd B. McKissick Papers (hereafter the McKissick Papers), Southern Historical Collection (hereafter SHC), University of North Carolina at Chapel Hill (hereafter UNC).

84. Evans interview, 1971.

85. Ibid.; David Cohen, December 19, 1970.

86. Gordon interview.

87. Meier and Rudwick, *CORE*, 390; Evans interview, 1971; Ruth Turner to Floyd McKissick, January 30, 1965, Series 3.1.2, Folders 6870-71, McKissick Papers, SHC.

88. Perot interview, 2004; CORE Organization, Staff, and Departments National Officers List, Series 3.1.2., Folder 7029, McKissick Papers, SHC; Minutes of the 23rd Annual Convention, July 1–5, 1965, Durham, NC, Series 3.1.2, Folder 6840, McKissick Papers, SHC.

89. Ruth Turner, "A New Direction," *Cleveland CORE Action Letter*, no date, Box 16, Folder 305, UFCW Papers, WRHS.

90. Ibid.

91. CORE newsletter, November 16, 1965, Box 16, Folder 305, UFCW Papers, WRHS.

92. Turner to Dear Friend, October 5, 1965, Box 16, Folder 305, UFCW Papers, WRHS.

93. Alan (no last name) to James Farmer, October 6, 196?, Box 2R566, Folder 8, James and Lula Farmer Papers, University of Texas at Austin.

94. First Annual Workshop of UFM, December 12, 1964, Box 43, Folder 4, NAACP Papers, WRHS.

95. Report of Executive Secretary, November 3–December 1, 1964, Box 1, Folder 6, NAACP Papers, WRHS.

96. United Freedom Movement Steering Committee Meeting, August 19, 1965, Box 43, Folder 4, NAACP Papers, WRHS.

97. Ibid., no date; Carolyn Jean Bowers, *Civil Rights in Cleveland: The Movement for School Desegregation 1963–1964* (Master's thesis, Case Western Reserve University, 1989), 62. Bowers argues that the UFM lost legitimacy and membership when the NAACP left, which was partially true. However, its activities already had waned. UFM also fell because CORE began to lose its own organizational footing in 1965, and could not maintain itself and UFM.

98. Ruth Turner interview, 2004.

99. Cleveland CORE News.

100. CORE newsletter, November 16, 1965, Box 16, Folder 305, UFCW Papers, WRHS; "Ford Funds Save Local CORE in Nick of Time," July 15, 1967, CORE clipping file, *Cleveland Press* Collection (hereafter CPC), Cleveland State University Archives (hereafter CSU Archives).

101. Turner to Dear Friend, October 5, 1965; Ruth Turner to Ronnie Moore, October 6, 1965, Reel 19, F:II:140, Frames 929–30, CORE Addendum.

102. Meier and Rudwick, *CORE*, 235–39; Arthur Evans interview, 1971; Arthur Evans to Employment Committee of United Freedom Movement, July 19, 1963, Box 43, Folders 3–4, NAACP Papers, WRHS; CORE newsletter, February 1966, Reel 19, F:II:140, Frames 932–33, CORE Addendum; CORE employment work in St. Louis, see Lang, *Grassroots at the Gateway*, 114–18.

103. Ibid. This number corresponds to the black population percentage in Cleveland; Statement About CORE, no date, Box 7, Folder 152, Inner City Protestant Parish Papers, WRHS. Operation Breadbasket was an SCLC program based in Chicago. The program spread nationally under its director, Jesse Jackson. It does not appear to be a national mandate or that other CORE chapters helped the Breadbasket boycott. Cleveland's association likely stemmed from Jackson's frequent visits and the city's close location to Chicago. House-Soremekun, *Confronting the Odds*, ix; Michael Eric Dyson, *I May Not Get There With You: The True Martin Luther King, Jr.* (New York: Free Press, 200), 81.

104. CORE newsletter, February 1966, Reel 19, Series F:II:140, Frame 934, CORE Addendum.

105. Herb Callender to Employment Chairman, April 19, 1966, Reel 19, Series F:II:140, Frame 936, CORE Addendum; Judith Nussbaum to Baxter Hill, April 19, 1966, Reel 19, Series F:II:140, Frame 936, CORE Addendum.

106. Students for a Democratic Society and Congress of Racial Equality, *Proposal for Creating a Movement of Unemployed in Cleveland* (New York: Students for a Democratic Society, 1964). For ERAP in Cleveland, Wesley Hogan, "How Democracy Travels: SNCC, Swarthmore Students, and the Growth of the Student Movement in the North, 1961–1964," *Pennsylvania Magazine of History and Biography* 126, no. 3 (July 2002): 437–70; Jennifer Frost, *An International Movement of the Poor: Community Organizing and the New Left in the 1960s* (New York: New York University Press, 2001), 50–90, 139–43.

107. RAC Meeting, December 4, 1965, Reel 8, B:II:23, Frames 1087–89, CORE Addendum.

108. Ibid.

109. Ibid.

110. Ruth Turner to All NAC Members, "Regarding Suggested Policy Statement on CORE's Approach to the War on Poverty," Series 3.1.2, Folder 6950, McKissick Papers, SHC.

111. This appeared to be a recurring theme for a couple of chapters. See Jolly, *Black Liberation in the Midwest*, 130; Matteo Suarez interview, Sheila Michaels Oral History Collection, Columbia University Oral History Center; Oretha Castle, May 26, 1970, interview by James Mosby, Moorland Spingarn, Howard University; Meier and Rudwick, *CORE*, 361–64; Kent Germany, *New Orleans after the Promises: Poverty, Citizenship, and the Search for the Great Society* (Athens: University of Georgia Press, 2007), 101.

112. Lisle Carter and Edward Sylvester, "Cleveland CORE—Target City: An Assessment of the Foundation's Grants to the Special Purposes Fund of CORE," August 1969, Reel 1864, Grant Number 67-446, Section 5, Ford Foundation Papers, 4.

113. Convention Minutes of CORE, July 1–July 4, 1966, Box 2, Folder 1, Meier and Rudwick Papers, WHS.

114. Ibid. Ruth Turner initially became NAC secretary in 1964 at Kansas, Missouri, CORE Convention until she moved to the national office in 1966. "Ruth Turner Is National CORE Official" (July 25, 1964), 3A.

115. Robert Curvin interview notes, January 1969, August Meier interviewer, Box 56, Folder 4, August Meier Papers, Schomburg Center for Research in Black Culture.

116. News release, July 7, 1966, Series 3.1.2, Folder 6775a, McKissick Papers, SHC; McKissick, *Three Fifths*, 140.

## 6. Breaking the Noose

1. *Witness, Civil Rights USA*. Interview with Stokely Carmichael. London: BBC, 2012.

2. CORE Convention Minutes, June 27–30, 1963, Reel 9, C:II:66, Frame 554, CORE Addendum; City of East Cleveland, *East Cleveland: Response to Urban Change* (Washington, DC: Communication Service Corporation, 1969), 271; Meier and Rudwick, *CORE*, 96–97; 153–55.

3. Meier and Rudwick, *CORE*, 203–7.

4. Stokely Carmichael, *Ready for Revolution: The Life and Struggles of Stokely Carmichael* (New York: Scribner, 2005), 161–62; Roy Innis interview; Convention Minutes, June 27, 30, 1963, Box 2R570, Folder CORE Minutes and Reports, James and Lula Farmer Papers; Anne Valk, *Radical Sisters: Second Wave Feminism and Black Liberation in Washington, DC* (Champaign-Urbana: University of Illinois Press, 2010), 20–23. Harlem CORE also backed Hobson. Julius Hobson ruled Washington CORE with a strong hand undermining Roena Rand (black CORE activist). In some cases, members characterized Hobson as also patriarchal. Women do take stronger chapter positions after he leaves.

5. NAC Minutes, November 8–10, 1963, Box 2R570, Folder: CORE Minutes and Reports, James and Lula Farmer Papers. Cedric Johnson, *Revolutionaries to Race Leaders: Black Power and the Making of African American Politics* (Minneapolis: University of Minnesota Press, 2007), xxxvi, 65–66, 155–56.

6. Farmer, *Lay Bare*, 255.

7. Other leaders were also considered, including Rudy Lombard and Lolis Elie. Gordon Carey interview, May 14, 1972.

8. Ibid.; Jim Peck to James Farmer, November 11, 1965, Box 4, Folder 4, Meier/ Rudwick Papers, WHS; Farmer, *Lay Bare*, 255–56.

9. Germany, *New Orleans after the Promises*, 224–45; Fairclough, *Race & Democracy*, 382; David Dennis interview, Meier Papers.

10. NAC Minutes, September 26, 1964, Reel 9, C:II:90, Frame 848, CORE Addendum; Ruth Turner and Tony Perot interview, 2007. For more on Milwaukee CORE and MUSIC, see Oral History Interview with Cecil Brown Jr. and Loretta Brown, August 9, 1995, Part II and Part III in UW Milwaukee: The March on Milwaukee Civil Rights History Project, accessed on June 18, 2013. Dougherty, *More Than One Struggle*, 98.

11. James Peck interview.

12. Oretha Castle interview.

13. Matteo Suarez interview, August, 11, 1969, Robert Wright, interviewer New Orleans, Civil Rights Documentation Project, Moorland Spingarn; Oretha Castle interview.

14. On this episode within CORE, see Meier and Rudwick, *CORE*, 169. Oretha Castle interview; Matteo Suarez interview, 1969; Adam Fairclough, *Race & Democracy*, 295. For a different perspective of its meaning to chapter vitality and black power, see Flystak, *Our Minds on Freedom*, 189–90.

15. Farmer, *Lay Bare*, 265.

16. George Wiley, April 25, 1972, interview by August Meier, Box 57, Folder 7, interview notes, August Meier Papers, Schomburg Center for Research in Black.

17. Meier and Rudwick, *CORE*, 407. George Wiley interview; Val Coleman, July 29, 1972, interview by Meier and Rudwick, Box 56, Folder, 3, August Meier Papers. Val Coleman believed Farmer contacted Turner to see how the votes lined up.

18. Belinda Robnett, "Formal Titles and Bridge Leaders: Reply to Keys," *American Journal of Sociology* 102 (May 1997): 1698–1701. In my interview with Turner, she noted that the black power platform was a conglomeration of different ideas among CORE members. Alan Gartner interview; James Farmer, interview by Meier and Rudwick, Box 56, Folder 6; Marvin Rich, May 21, 1969, interview notes, by Meier, Box 56, folder 6, August Meier Papers, Schomburg Center for Research in Black Culture; Will Ussery, by Robert Martin, July 17 (no year), Civil Rights Document Project at Moorland Spingarn, Howard University; George Wiley, interview by Meier, April 25, 1972, Box 56, Folder 6, interview notes, August Meier Papers, Schomburg Center for Research in Black Culture; Doris Innis, interview, interview by Meier, October 1971, August Meier Papers, Schomburg Center for Research in Black Culture.

19. Farmer, *Lay Bare*, 267; Jim Peck, December 14, 1970; NAC Meeting with Staff, June 29, 1965, Reel 11, E: I:48, Frame 260, CORE Addendum; Gartner to NAC, August 12, 1965, Reel 11, E:I:48, Frames 275–76, CORE Addendum.

20. Marvin Rich interview, December 21, 1970, August Meier Papers.

21. Dave Dennis interview, June 30, 1972, interview by Meier and Rudwick, Box 56, Folder 5; Richard Haley, August 12, 1969, interview by Meier and Rudwick, Box 56, Folder 7; Ruth Turner and Tony Perot interview, 1972; Anna Holden interview, September 1971, Box 56, Folder 8, interview by Meier and Rudwick; Alan Gartner interview; Carl Rachlin interview; David Cohen interview, December 19, 1970; Norman Hill, May 24, 1969, interview by Meier and Rudwick, Box 56, Folder 8; Jim Peck interview. All in Meier Papers. Jimmy McDonald, November 5, 1969, interview by James Mosby, Moorland Spingarn, Howard University.

22. Farmer, *Lay Bare*, 265. Ruth Turner, handwritten notes on dissertation rough draft, 2008, in author's possession.

23. Morris, *Origins*, 131–32.

24. Richard Haley, August 12, 1969, August Meier Papers; Anna Holden interview, September 1971.

25. Ruth Turner and Tony Perot interview, 1972.

26. Carl Rachlin, Report of General Council, Reel 9, C:II:101, Frames 926–27, CORE Addendum; Rich SEDF Director press release March 30, 1965 Reel 11, E:II:64, Frame 566; Minutes of CORE National Convention, June 20–July 1, 1962, Reel 9, C:I:55, Frame 501, CORE Addendum; Ruth Turner and Tony Perot interview, 1972. Turner claims that Rich also usurped union contacts and redirected that funding as well.

27. NAC Minutes, December 31, 1965–January 2, 1966, Series 3.1.2, Folder 6964, McKissick Papers, SHC, UNC; Farmer, *Lay Bare*, 264–65.

28. Ibid.

29. Jimmy McDonald interview; Bob Curvin interview, January 1969; Importantly, many factors impacted CORE's financial standing.

30. Norman Hill interview. Val Coleman also confirmed this. Val Coleman, January 6, 1999, interview by Sheila Michaels, Columbia University Oral History Center.

31. "4 Negroes Denounce City Hall, Black Power," September 17, 1966, *Plain Dealer* article, Box 29, Folder 3, UL Papers, WRHS; Franklin Anderson, interview by author, Chapel Hill, North Carolina, January 3, 2004; Cecil Brown, Black Power Position Paper, August 14, 1966, Box 2R572, Folder CORE Professional Activities: Misc., James and Lula Farmer Papers; Robert Curvin, July 31, 1966, interview by August Meier, Box 56, Folder 4, Meier Papers.

32. Roy Innis interview; Ruth Turner and Tony Perot interview, 1972. Relevant to note, Turner and Perot defined black nationalism as a current formulation at time of interview. They considered themselves black nationalist as defined in the 1970s. However, they did not consider themselves black nationalist when they supported black leadership. This distinction hinged on the idea that they still believed in integration, but through black-led organizations.

33. Ruth Turner, "Black Power," 467; Doris Innis interview.

34. Ruth Turner and Tony Perot Interview, 2007.

35. Doris Innis interview; Michael Flug, "Organized Labor and the Civil Rights Movement of the 1960s: The Case of the Maryland Freedom Union," *Labor History* 31, no. 3 (1990): 345. Flug has no specific reference here. This may come from his personal recollections. Velma Hill was particularly helpful in raising the gender question in CORE and its assertion into this text. For other references on gender issues, see Anna Holden interview, September 1971, Box 56, Folder 8, interview by Meier and Rudwick.

36. Qtd. in Allen, *Black Awakening*, 55.

37. Floyd McKissick, *Constructive Militancy: A Philosophy and a Program* (New York: Congress of Racial Equality, 1966), 2.

38. Ruth Turner, e-mail message to author, April 8, 2015; McKissick, *Constructive Militancy*.

39. "The following resolutions were adopted at the 23rd Annual National Convention of the Congress of Racial Equality held in July 1966 at Baltimore, Maryland," Series 3.1.2, Folder 6842, McKissick Papers, SHC.

40. News release, July 7, 1966, Series 3.1.1, Folder, 6775a, Floyd McKissick Papers, SCH.

41. Ruth Turner, "Black Power," 468; Ruth Turner and Tony Perot interview, 1972. Her reputation lead to a high degree of animosity among white and black integration ist leaders because she insisted that black leadership with white committed members as supporters lead CORE. It was not a position meant to belittle the contribution of whites to CORE, after all the death of white member Bruce Klunder greatly affected Turner. More accurately, her attitude stemmed from the belief that the black community had to be the directors of their own movement. For information on Ruth Turner and black power, see Belinda Robnett, *How Long, How Long: African American Women in the Struggle for Civil Rights* (New York: Oxford University Press, 1997), 168; Robnett, "Formal Titles and Bridge Leaders," 1698–1701; David Keys, "Historical Sociology and CORE Data: Comment on Robnett," *American Journal of Sociology* 102 (May 1997): 1693–98. For information on Turner and white reaction, see Alan Gartner interview; Robert Curvin, January 1969. Marvin Rich, May 21, 1969, interview notes by Meier, Box 56, Folder 6, Meier Papers; Will Ussery interview; George Wiley, April 25, 1972, Box 56, Folder 6, interview notes by Meier, August Meier Papers, Schomburg Center for Research in Black Culture; Doris Innis interview; Norman Hill interview.

42. Warren, Who Speaks for the Negro?, 381.

43. Arthur Evans interview, 1971; Cecil Brown, Black Power Position Paper, August 14, 1966, Box 2R572, Folder CORE Professional Activities: Misc.

44. Bracey et al., *Black Nationalism*, 470.

45. NAC Minutes, December 31, 1965, closed session, Box 4, Folder 4, Meier/ Rudwick Papers, WHS.

46. Ibid.

47. Meier and Rudwick, *CORE*, 149, 225, 335–36, 411.

48. NAC Minutes, October 23, 1965, Series 3.1.2, Folder 6964, McKissick Papers, SHC, UNC; NAC Minutes, June 1965; Meier and Rudwick, *CORE*, 336, 411. Meier

and Rudwick note that donations decreased possibly due to CORE's stance at the Atlantic Convention and on Vietnam, while other news catching events like urban rebellions turned attention away from the organization's activities. The authors also noted that the anti-Semitic insults of a Mount Vernon CORE member impacted its Jewish donations, which were a large proportion of CORE's mailing list monies. Undoubtedly all of these played a role in CORE's reduced income. However, Meier and Rudwick skip over the obvious issue of competitive mailings from SEDF, which provided the alternate and conventional appeal of civil rights as a southern problem that needing solving.

49. James L. Farmer, April 25, 1979, recorded interview by Sheldon Stern #2, 25–26, John F. Kennedy Library Oral History Program.

50. NAC Minutes, December 31, 1965–January 2, 1966, McKissick Papers.

51. Ibid.; James Farmer, "Suggested Guide Lines for Future Organizational Expansion," April 3, 1965, Series 3.1.2, Folders 6870–71, McKissick Papers, SHC, UNC.

52. James Farmer to Task Force Members, March 27, 1964, Reel 11, E:I:40, Frame 49, CORE Addendum; James Farmer to Field Staff, May 5, 1964, Reel 11, E:I:40, Frame 51, CORE Addendum; NAC Meeting with Staff, June 29, 1965.

53. Rich to McKissick, April 13, 1966, Reel 11, E:I:64, Frame 633, CORE Addendum; Meier and Rudwick, *CORE*, 411.

54. Special Steering Committee, January 15, 1965, Reel 9, C:I:91, Frame 853, CORE Addendum; Minutes of the 23rd Annual Convention, Durham, NC, July 1–5, 1965, Series 3.1.2, Folder 6840, McKissick Papers, SHC, UNC; NAC Minutes, December 31, 1965–January 2, 1966, Series 3.1.2, Folder 6964, McKissick Papers, SHC, UNC.

55. National Director's Report, July 1, 1965, Frame Reel 9, C:I:98, Frame 912, CORE Addendum.

56. "Northern Summer Task Force Project, Chicago, IL," 1964, Box 2R572, Folder: CORE Professional Activities: Misc, James and Lula Farmer Papers; NAC Minutes, September 6, 1964, Reel 9, C:I:90, Frame 849, CORE Addendum.

57. Goldberg, "CORE in Trouble," 18–19; NAC Minutes, March 18–20, 1966, Box 2R571, Folder CORE Minutes and Reports, James and Lula Farmer Papers.

58. Flug, "Organizing Labor," 324–30; ibid., 19–21.

59. Ibid., "Rose Named to Top CORE Post," *Baltimore Afro-American*, May 1, 1973. It appears work with labor unions in Baltimore solidified ties with local activists and continued to have reverberations. William E. Rose was a member of Bethlehem Steel and Shipyard Workers for Equality and went on to become Baltimore CORE chairman. Also for CORE's relationship to Bethlehem workers, see news article, Len Shindel, "They Acted Like Men and Were Treated Like Men," February 17, 1992, *Baltimore Sun*, 11A; Rhonda Williams, "The Pursuit of Audacious Power: Rebel Reformers and Neighborhood Politics in Baltimore, 1966–1968," in *Neighborhood Rebels: Black Power at the Local Level*, ed. Peniel Joseph (New York: Palgrave Macmillan, 2010), 225–26.

60. CORE and black power, see Meier and Rudwick, *CORE*, 402–10, 420. For CORE and Baltimore TCP, see Goldberg, "CORE in Trouble"; Memo from George Wiley to NAC, Regarding Proposals for Northern Thrust, no date, Series 3.1.1, 6775a, McKissick Papers, Southern Historical Collection of the University of North Carolina at Chapel Hill

(SHC); Ruth Turner and Tony Perot challenge much of Goldberg's account of events at the Baltimore TCP. Ruth Turner and Tony Perot, handwritten notes on dissertation rough draft, 2008, in author's possession; Williams, "The Pursuit of Audacious Power," 219–27.

61. Kenneth Durr, Behind the Backlash: White Working-Class Politics in Baltimore, 1940–1980 (Chapel Hill: University of North Carolina Press, 2003), 130–32; Judith Stein, Running Steel, Running America: Race, Economic Policy, and the Decline of Liberalism (Chapel Hill: University of North Carolina Press, 1998), 137–40; Rhonda Williams, "Black Women, Urban Politics, and Engendering Black Power," in Peniel, The Black Power Movement, 84–86; Goldberg, "CORE in Trouble," 116–23, 184, 339; "CORE Deficit May Close Office," CORE clipping file. Cleveland Press Collection (CPC), Cleveland State University Archives (CSU), Cleveland.

62. No author, "Ku Klux Klan Finds Things Have Changed in Baltimore," *Muhammad Speaks*, June 24, 1966, 27.

63. Goldberg, "CORE in Trouble," 116–23.

64. "CORE Deficit May Close Office," CORE clipping file. CPC, CSU Archives.

65. NAC Minutes, August 27, 1967, Reel 10, C:I:122, Frame 15, CORE Addendum.

66. Goldberg, "CORE in Trouble," 131–35.

67. Ibid., 184, 339.

68. Flug, "Organizing Labor," 342–44; Advisory Committee Minutes, January 26, 1967, Reel 9, C:I:114, Frame 1041, CORE Addendum.

69. Ruth Turner and Tony Perot, handwritten notes on dissertation rough draft, 2008, in author's possession; Ruth Turner and Tony Perot interview, 1972.

70. Minutes of NAC meeting, December 17, 1966, Series 3.1.2, Folder 6965 McKissick Papers, SHC, UNC.

71. Ibid.

72. NAC Minutes, January 22–23, 1966, Box 2R571, Folder CORE Minutes and Reports.

73. Robert Allen noted in *Black Awakening* that Cleveland became a site of movement interest based on a secret meeting of civil rights leaders. However, internal dynamics within these organizations, particularly CORE, determined this decision. Selection of the city was divided over how Chicago, Newark, and Cleveland might engender various outcomes. In addition, the decision was made over the objections of NAC, which wanted more cities from which to choose. Allen, *Black Awakening*, 123; NAC Minutes, April 22–April 23, 1967, Box 2, Folder 5, Meier/Rudwick Papers, Wisconsin Historical Society, Madison.

74. Gene Roberts, "Cleveland CORE Gets New Life; Staff Weighs Use of Ford Aid," no date, CORE clipping file, CPC, CSU Archives.

75. Bob Curvin interview, July 31, 1966.

76. Davis, *Black Americans*, 404; "The Pattern Emerges: An Unfinished Calendar of Terror," July 23, 1966, *Cleveland Plain Dealer* article, Ardelia Dixon Scrapbook, WRHS; Kenneth Huszar, "Driver of Bullet-Torn Car Charged," no date, *Cleveland Plain Dealer* article, Ardelia Dixon scrapbook, WRHS.

77. Davis, *Black Americans*, 404; "The Pattern Emerges," July 23, 1966; "Driver of Bullet-Torn Car Charged," no date; Todd Michney, "Race, Violence, and Urban

Territoriality: Cleveland's Little Italy and the 1966 Hough Uprising," *Journal of Urban History* 32, no.3 (2006): 404–28.

78. NAC Minutes, April 22–April 23, 1967.

79. "Description of Ford Foundation Grant to the Special Purpose Fund of CORE for a Community Action Project in Cleveland," Report 012579, Ford Foundation Papers.

80. Most newspapers, and subsequently historians, assumed that the Cleveland chapter received the Ford grant. However, it was actually an attempt by national CORE to regain fiscal footing. Meier and Rudwick, *CORE*, 420.

81. "New 'Black Program' Is Aim of $175,000 CORE Study," no date, CORE clipping file, CPC, CSU archives; CORE Target City Cleveland Project to McGeorge Bundy, 1968, Series 3.1.2, Folders 6870–71, McKissick Papers, SHC; Joseph Goulden, *The Money Givers* (New York: Random House, 1971), 265–66.

82. Meier and Rudwick, *CORE*, 420; Allen, *Black Awakening*, 123. For more on Ford and CORE, see Ferguson, "Organizing the Ghetto"; Rooks, *White Money/Black Power*; Kai Bird, *The Color of Truth: McGeorge Bundy and William Bundy: Brothers in Arms* (New York: Simon and Schuster, 1998); Ferguson, *Top Down*, 70–73.

83. Kai, *The Color of Truth*, 20; Goulden, *The Money Givers*; Bird, *The Color of Truth*, 381–88; Homer Wadsworth, "Private Foundations and the Tax Reform Act of 1969," *Law and Contemporary Problems* 39, no. 4 (Autumn 1975): 255. The tax reform's effect drastically changed management style, encouraged professionalization, and initiated revised grant structures within private foundations. See *Private Foundations and the Tax Reform Act of 1969*. Duke University School of Law, 1975; William H. Smith and Carolyn P. Chiechi, *Private Foundations before and after the Tax Reform Act of 1969* (Washington, DC: American Enterprise Institute for Public Policy Research, 1974); United States Congress Senate Committee on Finance, and Subcommittee on Foundations, *Private Foundations: Hearings before the Subcommittee on Foundations of the Committee on Finance on the Role of Private Foundations in Today's Society and a Review of the Impact of Charitable Provisions of the Tax Reform Act of 1969 on the Support and Operation of Private Foundations* (Washington, DC: United States Congress, 1974); Jordan D. Luttrell, "The Effect of the Private Foundation Provisions of the Tax Reform Act of 1969 on Community Development Corporations," *Law and Contemporary Problems* (Spring 1971): 238–76; John R. Labovitz, "The Impact of the Private Foundation Provisions of the Tax Reform Act of 1969: Early Empirical Measurements," *Journal of Legal Studies* 3, no. 1 (January 1974): 63–105; Peter Frumkin, "The Long Recoil from Regulation: Private Philanthropic Foundations and the Tax Reform Act of 1969," *American Review of Public Administration* 28, no. 3 (1998): 266–86; K. Martin Worthy, "The Tax Reform Act of 1969: Consequences for Private Foundations," *Law and Contemporary Problems* 39, no. 4 (January 1975): 232–54; Isabelle Fisher, "The Tax Reform Act: 'Private Foundations' and 'Publicly Supported' Organizations Defined," *Dance Magazine* (January 1971): 83; Edward G. Thomson, "The Tax Reform Act: Some Considerations about Private Operating Foundations," *Dance Magazine* (March 1971): 98.

84. Bird, The Color of Truth, 393.

85. "Rumpus in Hotel Mars Last Session of CORE Parley," July 6, 1968, CORE clipping file, CPC, CSU Archives.

86. Kenneth Marshall, "Log: National Convention in Oakland, California," Box 2, Folder 2, WHS. It was unclear whether Marshall actually authored these notes or had them in his possession; Goldberg, "CORE in Trouble," 205–6.

87. Sonny Carson, *The Education of Sonny Carson* (New York: Norton, 1972), 170–71.

88. Ibid.

89. Marshall, "Log: National Convention in Oakland, California."

90. Ibid.

91. Ibid.

92. For discussion regarding CORE and foundations, see Minutes of National Convention, June 20–July 1, 1962, Reel 9, C:I:55, Frame 503, CORE Addendum; Rooks, *White Money/Black Power,* 26–30, 85–89; Rojas, *From Black Power to Black Studies,* 130–67; Hill, *Deacons,* fn 31, 289–90; Allen, *Black Awakening,* 121–32; Ferguson, "Organizing the Ghetto"; Lang, *Grassroots at the Gateway,* 232, 236–37; Jolly, *Black Liberation in the Midwest,* 134–36. Morris, *The Origins,* 281–82, discusses some of the undo weight given to northern elites in sustaining movement. I'd extend that discussion to say that some undo weight has been given to how northern elites (foundations) dictated or manipulated the movement. For discussion regarding SNCC and foundations, see Howard Zinn, *SNCC: The New Abolitionists* (Boston: Beacon Press, 1965), 58–59; 41–42, 70, 92.

93. Floyd McKissick interview, October 16, 1968, interview by Robert Wright, Moorland Spingarn Research Center, Howard University; Carter and Sylvester, "Cleveland CORE," 35.

94. Marshall, "Log: National Convention in Oakland, California."

95. "We Want Control, Says CORE Director," December 9, 1967, *Cleveland Plain Dealer* article, Box 29, Folder 5, UL Papers, WRHS.

96. "Ford Grant Aided Stokes, New Book Says," March 16, 1971, CORE clipping file, CPC, CSU Archives. It's more likely that this percentage was much higher given later condemnation that CORE registered only or close to only black Clevelanders. Goulden, *The Money Givers,* 263; Haskins, *A Piece of the Power,* 19.

97. "The Real Black Power," *Time Magazine* 90, no. 20 (November 17, 1967), 47, 48, 49; Stanley Tolliver, May 14, 2008, interview by author, in author's possession.

98. "The Real Black Power," 41. For more information on Carl Stokes, see Moore, *Carl B. Stokes;* "The Making of a Mayor," *Sunday Plain Dealer* Magazine (December 10, 1967).

99. "The Real Black Power"; Haskins, *A Piece of the Power,* 3–20; Moore, *Carl B. Stokes,* 15.

100. Haskins, *A Piece of the Power,* 3–20; Moore, *Carl B. Stokes,* 15.

101. Haskins, *A Piece of the Power,* 3–20; Moore, *Carl B. Stokes,* 15. "Ford Grant Aided Stokes, New Book Says," March 16, 1971, CORE clipping file, CPC, CSU; Goulden, *The Money Givers,* 263; "CORE Sets Registration Campaign," September 13, 1968, CORE clipping file, CPC, CSU; "CORE Completes Its Voter Drive with 10,000 total," October 3, 1968, CORE clipping file, CPC, CSU; Lisle Carter and Edward Sylvester, "Cleveland CORE—Target City: An Assessment of the Foundation's Grants to the Special Purposes Fund of CORE," August 1969, Reel 1864, Grant Number 67-446, Section 5,

Ford Foundation Papers, 13–14. CORE argued that the Cleveland Target Project's first year was a great success, pointing to its position as a key player in the selection of not only Carl Stokes but also his brother Louis Stokes, cofounder of the Congressional Black Caucus, when Cleveland TCP added more registered voters to the rolls the following year. Additionally, Ford Foundation's report evaluated CORE's role in the formation of the Twenty-First Congressional District and suggested that its leadership among the community groups became central to its creation, and thus the subsequent election of Louis Stokes to Congress. As a result Milwaukee Urban League requested and received technical support for its voter registration drive in February 1968.

## 7. Harambee City

1. "We Want Control, Says CORE Director," December 9, 1967, *Cleveland Plain Dealer* article, Box 29, Folder 5, UL Papers, WRHS.

2. Moore, *Carl B. Stokes*, 10, 37, 40–43.

3. Qtd. in Meier and Rudwick, *CORE*, 423; Allen, *Black Awakening*, 126, 131–12. For discussion of CORE black power and elitism, see Allen, *Black Awakening*, 70, 121–32, 144; Marable, *Race, Reform, and Rebellion,* 139; Ferguson, "Organizing the Ghetto"; Bracey et al., *Black Nationalism*, li. Roy Innis presented a report on Harlem CORE's activities around small business investment corporations and black control of schools at the 1967 CORE convention. Robert Allen, and many scholars, suggested that these ideas determined the character of CORE. Accordingly, they insisted that CORE constituted a bourgeoisie elite that replaced a white face with a black one, using "white money" to do it. By doing so, CORE opened the door to corporate control of black communities and turned its members into elite middlemen. By extension, it was a flawed decision that purportedly precipitated the group's betrayal of black power.

4. Resolution of the Workshop on Black Economic Building Power, July 1967 CORE convention, Reel 10, C:I:117, Frame 1090, CORE Addendum.

5. Ibid., Frame 1086.

6. For more information on CDCs and the black community, see Stewart Perry, "Federal Support for CDCs: Some of the History and Issues of Community Control," *Review of Black Political Economy* 3, no. 3 (1972): 17–42; William Tabb, "Perspectives on Black Economic Development," *Journal of Economic Issues* 4, no. 4 (1970): 68–81; Frederick Sturdivant, "Community Development Corporations: The Problem of Mixed Objectives," *Law and Contemporary Problems* 36, no. 1 (1971): 35–50; Luttrell, "The Effect of the Private Foundation," 238–76; Laura Hill and Julia Rabig, ed., *Business of Black Power: Community Development, Capitalism, and Corporate Responsibility in Postwar America* (Rochester, NY: University of Rochester Press, 2012).

7. "We Want Control, Says CORE Director," December 9, 1967, *Cleveland Plain Dealer* article, Box 29, Folder 5, UL Papers, WRHS; "CORE Names Evans New Head of Target Cleveland Project," June 22, 1968, CORE clipping file, CPC, CSU Archives; "Civil Rights and Human Rights Conference: Workshops," Series 3.1.2, Folders 6870–71, McKissick Papers, SHC, UNC; "Biographical sketches of Speakers," Series 3.1.2, Folders

6870–71, McKissick Papers, SHC, UNC; "A Nation within a Nation: Core's Proposal for Economic Development and Control of Black Areas," Series 3.1.2, Folder 6970, McKissick Papers; "CORE Names Evans," June 22, 1968. See also more detailed documents in Series 3.1.2, Folders 6870–71, McKissick Papers; Carter and Sylvester, "Cleveland CORE," 27. Will Ussery was Target Cty's acting director for three months until a formal hire.

8. Jerry M. Flint, "CORE Bids Business Set Up Plants for Negroes," April 5, 1968, *New York Times*, Box 30, Folder 545, Carl Stokes Papers (hereafter Stokes Papers), WRHS.

9. CORENCO Fact Sheet, no date, Box 30, Folder 545, Stokes Papers, WRHS; Carter and Sylvester, "Cleveland CORE," 31. CORE initially considered developing cooperatives. The idea was pursued "in some depth" including conferences with the Cooperative League of America. However, it went with the CDC structure. Likely, this was due to Ussery's influence.

10. "Open Application for Funding Grants to CORE Development Corporation," April 4, 1968, Box 30, Folder 545, Stokes Papers, WRHS.

11. "CORE Unveils $10-Million Plan to Help City Negroes," April 5, 1968, CORE clipping file, CPC, CSU Archives.

12. Robert H. A. Ashford, "The Binary Economics of Louis Kelso: A Democratic Private Property System for Growth and Justice," in *Curing World Poverty: The New Role of Property*, ed. Rev. John H. Miller (St. Louis, MO: Social Justice Review, 1994), 100; Louis O. Kelso and Mortimer J. Adler, *Capitalist Manifesto* (New York: Random House, 1958), 57, Louis O. Kelso and Patricia Hetter, *Two-Factor Theory: The Economics of Reality—How to Turn Eighty Million Workers into Capitalists on Borrowed Money and Other Proposals* (New York: Vintage Books, 196), 31.

13. Ashford, "The Binary Economics," 100; Kelso and Adler, *Capitalist Manifesto* (New York: Random House, 1958), 6; Kelso and Hetter, *Two-Factor Theory*, xv–xxi; 3–8.

14. Kelso and Adler, *Capitalist Manifesto*, 54; see also Kelso and Hetter, *Two-Factor Theory*, 14–17.

15. Kelso and Adler, *Capitalist*, 67–69.

16. Ibid., 85–86.

17. Kelso and Hetter, *Two-Factor Theory*, 57.

18. Though the CORENCO proposal is written by Wilfred Ussery, CORE's national chairman, the structure and wording directly copies from Kelso's language in *Capitalist Manifesto* and *Two-Factor Theory* as well it might given that Kelso directly served as a consultant for this proposal.

19. "Community Role Aired by CORE," no date, CORE clipping file, CPC, CSU Archives.

20. Floyd McKissick, "CORE's Program: Building a 'Second Economy,'" *New Generation* (Spring 1968): 15–18; NAC Minutes, October 13–15, 1967, Reel 10, C:I:123, Frame 22, CORE Addendum.

21. "CORE Bids Business," April 5, 1968.

22. CORENCO Fact Sheet, no date; "Open Application for Funding Grants," April 4, 1968, 31–33.

23. Ibid.

24. CORENCO Fact Sheet, 35; "Businessmen Urged to Aid Black Capitalism in Ghetto," October 30, 1968, CORENCO clipping file, CPC, CSU Archives.

25. Ibid., 34–35.

26. Minutes of Cleveland Target City Project Review Board Friday, March 22, 1968, Series 3.1.2, Folders 6870–71, McKissick Papers, SHC, UNC.

27. Ibid.

28. Ussery to Dear Sir, October 18, 1968, Box 30, Folder 545, Stokes Papers, WRHS.

29. "Businessmen Urged to Aid," October 30, 1968.

30. Ibid.; "Open Application for Funding Grants," no date.

31. Kotlowski, "Black Power—Nixon Style," 423.

32. Ibid., 420–25; Weems and Randolph, "The National Response," 67.

33. Bird, *Color of Truth*, qtd. 381–82, 409; Many argue that the plan was the basis for Nixon's illegal break-in into the Watergate Hotel. For more information on the Huston plan, see Joan Hoff, *Nixon Reconsidered* (New York: Basic Books, 1994), 288–94.

34. Wadsworth, "Private Foundations," 255; Bird, *Color of Truth*, 381–82.

35. *Private Foundation: Hearings Before the Subcommittee.* Several private and corporate foundations provide testimony to end the 4 percent tax. Counter testimony focused on foundation power and media control. Additionally, opposition forces tended to focus on later grants to civil rights group, which reflected from their perspective the foundations' continual tendency to act with impunity.

36. Ford Foundation, "National Affairs: Ford Foundation Annual Report 1978" (New York: Ford Foundation, 1978), 9.

37. CORE Target City Cleveland Project to McGeorge Bundy, no date, Reel 1864, Grant # 67-446.

38. Ernest Howard and Kermit Scott, "Organization, Goals, and Objectives, and Policies of CORE Target City Program," August 20, 1967, Series 3.1.2, Folders 6870–71, McKissick Papers, SHC, UNC.

39. Howard and Scott, "Organization, Goals, and Objectives and Policies of CORE," August 20, 1967.

40. Ibid.; Minutes of Cleveland Target City Project Review Board, Friday, March 22, 1968, Series 3.1.2, Folders 6870–71, McKissick Papers, SHC, UNC. This board eventually consisted of Roy Innis, associate national director; Tony Perot, program director for CORE Special Purpose Fund; Phil Carter, director of TCP; Wilfred Ussery, national chairman; Marlene Wilson, national secretary; Elijah Turner, national treasurer; Robert Lucas, regional chairman, North-Central Region; Nate Smith, treasurer; Franklin Anderson, chairman of CORE; Aubrey Kelly, 2nd vice chairman of Cleveland CORE; and Louise Sanders, Cleveland CORE.

41. Minutes of Cleveland Target City Project Review Board, Friday, March 22, 1968.

42. Ibid.

43. Ibid.

44. Phillip Carter to no addressee, no date, Series 3.1.2, Folders 6870–71, McKissick Papers, SHC, UNC; "CORE Names Evans New Head," June 22, 1968. Newspapers actually noted that the national office "promoted" him to run their national programming. In reality, he seemed to have resigned under duress.

45. Ibid.

46. "CORE Names Evans New Head," June 22, 1968.

47. "CORE Plans Boycott of GE Products, Calls Job Practices Unfair," July 9, 1968, *Wall Street Journal* article, Box 30, Folder 545, Stokes Papers, WRHS; "Rumpus in Hotel," July 8, 1968.

48. "CORE Plans Boycott of GE," July 9, 1968; R. V. Corning to Mayor Carl Stokes, July 11, 1968, Box 30, Folder 545, Stokes Papers, WRHS; R. V. Corning to Carl Stokes, June 27, 1968, Box 30, Folder 545, Stokes Papers, WRHS.

49. "CORE Boycott of GE Products On in Cleveland," July 10, 1968, *Home Furnishing Daily* article, Box 30, Folder 545, Stokes Papers, WRHS.

50. Franklin Anderson to Dear Friend, June 21, 1968, Box 30, Folder 545, Stokes Papers, WRHS.

51. Donald Bean to Carl Stokes, January 13, 1969, Box 30, Folder 545, Stokes Papers, WRHS.

52. "Donald Bean Takes CORE Job," no date, Donald Bean clipping, CPC, CSU Archives; biographical card file, no date, Donald Bean clipping, CPC, CSU Archives; "Ex-CORE Aid Gets City Post," May 2, 1969, *Cleveland Plain Dealer* article, Donald Bean clipping file, CPC, CSU Archives.

53. Ibid.; "CORE Charters Cleveland Chapter," December 9, 1972, CORE clipping file, CPC, CSU Archives; "CORE Speakers Urge 'Separation,'" Saturday, May 25, 1968, CORE clipping file, CPC, CSU Archives; To Whom It May Concern, September 11, 1968, Box 30, Folder 545, Stokes Papers, WRHS; "Cook Succeeding Bean as Interim CORE Chief," December 31, 1968, Charles Cook clipping file, CPC, CSU Archives; "Time Lag Dims Second CORE Voter Sign-up Victory," April 7, 1969, CORE clipping file, CPC, CSU Archives.

54. "Form Separate City Innis Tells Negroes," January 9, 1969, CORE clipping file, CPC, CSU Archives; "Community Role Aired by CORE," March 8, 1969, CORE clipping file, CPC, CSU Archives; "Cook Succeeding Bean"; "CORE Aim: Money Power," September 22, 1969. CORE clipping file, CPC, CSU Archives.

55. "CORE Aim: Money Power"; "Bank Aid Is Sought by CORE Here," no date, CORE clipping file, CPC, CSU Archives.

56. Ibid.

57. "CORE Aid Shot 3 Times in 'Accident,'" no date, Charles Cook clipping file, CPC, CSU Archives.

58. "Operation Black Unity," December 3, 1969, Operation Black Unity Files, FBI Papers, author's possession.

59. Letterhead, no date, Box 1, Folder 1, Operation Black Unity Papers (hereafter OBU Papers), WRHS; Walter Johnson, "The Summer of Unity," http://www.nhlink.net/ClevelandNeighborhoods/hough/SummerOfUnity.htm (accessed May 6, 2004); Edward A. Bood to OBU, July 28, 1969, Box 33, Folder 608, Stokes Papers, WRHS. Additional members included Afro-American Society of Case Western Reserve University, Avery A.M.E. Church, Black Information Service, Bruce Klunder Freedom House, Cleveland Association of Afro-American Educators, Community Fighters, East 63rd Black Nationalists, Judo and Karate Academy, Northern Christian Leadership Conference (aka SCLC), and Poor People's Partnership.

60. "Operation Black Unity," December 3, 1969.

61. OBU Minutes, December 13, 1969, Box 3, Folder 5, Humanist Fellowship Papers, WRHS.

62. Johnson, "The Summer of Unity"; Chronology McDonald's, no date, Box 32, Folder 583, Stokes Papers, WRHS. For extended conversation on OBU and HADC, see Nishani Frazier, "A McDonald's That Reflects the Soul of a People: Hough Area Development Corporation and Community Development in Cleveland," in Hill and Rabig, *Business of Black Power*, 68–94.

63. Moore, *Carl B. Stokes*, 123.

64. "Chronology McDonald's"; "Bullet Ended Man's Dream to Be City's First Black Owner of a McDonald's," July 22, 1969, *Cleveland Press*, article in Box 1, Folder 3, OBU Papers; Moore, *Carl B. Stokes*, 122.

65. Edward Bood to Wendell Erwin, Charles Cook, W. O. Walker, Revs. Donald Jacobs, Emanuel Branch, E. Randal T. Osborne, Jonathan Ealy, and Bishop David Hill, July 3, 1969, Box 32, Folder 583, Stokes Papers, WRHS; Edward Bood to Operation Black Unity, July 31, 1969, Box 33, Folder 608, Box 32, Folder 583, Stokes Papers, WRHS; Moore, *Carl B. Stokes*, 124; Ronald Jones, *Standing Up and Standing Out: How I Teamed with a Few Black Men, Changed the Face of McDonald's, and Shook Up Corporate America* (Nashville, TN: World Solutions, 2006), 123, 160–61, 174–75. Roland Jones, an early black executive at McDonald's corporation, discusses this issue in great detail. Purchase prices for stores with strong sales could be more expensive. Banks were loath to lend money for "ghetto" enterprises. Eventually, a number of franchises went out of business due to a variety of factors, much of which hinged on high purchase costs and unequal loan practices.

66. "Chronology McDonald's."

67. Moore, *Carl B. Stokes*, 125; Position Paper of Operation Black Unity, July 24, 1969, Box 33, Folder 608, Stokes Papers, WRHS.

68. "Chronology McDonald's"; Edward Bood to Operation Black Unity, July 31, 1969.

69. Johnson, "The Summer of Unity."

70. Moore, *Carl B. Stokes*, 128–29; "News Press Release by McDonald's Corporation, Inc.," January 22, 1970, Box 32, Folder 583, Stokes Papers, WRHS; Edward Bood to OBU, no date, Box 33, Folder 608, Stokes Papers, WRHS; James Davis to Stanley Tolliver, December 4, 1969, HADC Collection, Box 23, Folder 441, WRHS.

71. "McDonald's Says It Asked Hough Corp. to Buy In," April 7, 1970, *Cleveland Press* article, Box 1, Folder 4, OBU Papers, WRHS; "McDonald Sit-Down Unit May Be Run by Blacks," no date, article, Box 1, Folder 4, OBU Papers, WRHS.

72. Jonathan Ealy, W. O. Walker, and Donald Jacobs to James C. Davis, Esq., December 23, 1969, Box 32, Folder 583, Stokes Papers, WRHS. and Operation Black Unity to James C. Davis, January 12, 1970; James C. Davis to W. O. Walker, Donald Jacobs, and Jonathan Ealy, March 9, 1970, Box 32, Folder 583, Stokes Papers, WRHS.

73. Ibid.

74. OBU minutes, December 13, 1969, and OBU minutes, December 20, 1969, Box 3, Folder 5, Humanist Fellowship Papers, WRHS; OBU collection, January 31, 1970, Box 1, Folder 1, OBU Papers, WRHS.

75. Register of Hough Area Development Corporation Records, March 30, 1988, WRHS, in collection guide files; Harvard Law Review Association, "Community Development Corporations: Operations and Financing," *Harvard Law Review* 83, no. 7 (May 1970): 1571–73; Summary of HADC activities, no date, HADC Records, WRHS, Box 4, Folder 74.

76. Harvard Law Review Association, "Community Development," 1573.

77. Summary of HADC activities, no date, HADC Records, WRHS, Box 4, Folder 74.

78. Qtd. in Moore, *Carl B. Stokes*, 126.

79. Article "CORE chief Raps Absent Leaders," August 27, 1969, Box 3, Folder 36, *Cleveland Plain Dealer*, UL Papers, WRHS.

80. OBU Minutes of January 24, January 31, 1970, Box 1, Folder 1, OBU Papers, WRHS.

81. "Fire Probers Deny Charges of Lateness," October 28, 1969, CORE clipping file, CPC, CSU Archives; OBU Minutes, November 22, 1969, Box 1, Folder, OBU Papers, WRHS; OBU Minutes, November 22, 1969, Box 1, Folder 1, OBU Papers, WRHS.

82. Dick Peery interview, May 14, 2008, in author's possession; Tolliver interview. Although both interviewees confirm rumors circulated about CORE's attempted independent dealings with McDonald's, neither would reveal on tape their knowledge about those persons purportedly involved.

83. "Fire Probers Deny Charges of Lateness," October 28, 1969.

84. OBU Negotiating Committee Report, November 15, 1969, Box 1, Folder 1, OBU Papers.

85. FBI Cleveland to Director re: Operation Black Unity, October 3, 1969, Operation Black Unity Files, FBI Papers, author's possession.

86. "Lawyers Try, Try Again to Return Rabbi Hill," no date, *Call and Post* article, Box 48, Folder 2, UL Papers, WRHS.

87. Press release, October 1969, Box 1, Folder 4, OBU Papers, WRHS.

88. OBU Minutes, March 14, 1970, Box 1, Folder 1, OBU Papers, WRHS; OBU Minutes, February 28, 1970, Box 1, Folder 1, OBU Papers, WRHS; OBU Minutes, May 16, 1979, Box 1, Folder 1, OBU Papers, WRHS; Moore, *Carl B. Stokes*, 130. Nishani Frazier, "The 'Other' Jim Jones: Rabbi David Hill, House of Israel, and Black American Religion in the Age of Peoples Temple," *Jonestown Report* 14 (October 2012), sec. 21; Silvia Vidal and Neil Whitehead, "Dark Shamans and the Shamanic State: Sorcery and Witchcraft as Political Process in Guyana and the Venezuelan Amazon," in *In Darkness and Secrecy: The Anthropology of Assault Sorcery and Witchcraft in Amazonia* (Durham, NC: Duke University Press, 2004), 74–75. For additional information on Hill in Guyana, see Perry Mars, *Ideology and Change: The Transformation of the Caribbean Left* (Detroit: Wayne State University Press, 1998), 100. Supposedly, the House of Israel had a membership of 8,000. People's National Congress was believed to be a cult, but also a military arm of the political party.

89. Smith/Bean interview; Jones, *Standing Up*, 155; No title, October 10, 1969, excerpt from Urban Enterprise article, Box 1, Folder 4, OBU Papers, WRHS.

90. Carter and Sylvester, "Cleveland CORE—Target City," 54–57.

91. Ibid.
92. Ibid.
93. Ibid., 32, 37, 41–42.
94. Ibid., 20.

## 8. A Nation under Our Feet

1. For additional information on Cleveland during this period, see Richard Straddling, *Where the River Burned: Carl Stokes and the Struggle to Save Cleveland* (Ithaca, NY: Cornell University Press, 2015).

2. Alex Poinsett, "The Economics of Liberation," *Ebony Magazine* (August 1969), 151; Alex Poinsett, "Roy Innis: Nation Builder," *Ebony Magazine* (October 1969), 176; Roy Innis, "Separatist Economics: A New Social Contract," in Haddad and Pugh, *Black Economic Development*, 52.

3. Stokely Carmichael, "What We Want," *New York Review of Books* 7 (September 22, 1966), 5–6, 8; Carmichael and Hamilton, *Black Power*, 172–73.

4. William Safire, *Safire's Political Dictionary* (New York: Random House, 1978), 58. The idea came from the New York Stock Exchange positive assertion of capitalism as "people's capitalism." Nixon had a choice among black entrepreneurship, black enterprise, and black capitalism. Also, John McClaughry, "Promoting Civil Society Among the Heathen: A Memoir," unpublished. John McClaughry Papers, in author's possession; Gar Alperovitz and John McClaughry interview, May 22, 2014, Interview by author, in author's possession. On Richard Nixon and black capitalism, see Robert Weems Jr., and Lewis A. Randoph, *Business in Black and White: American Presidents and Black Entrepreneurs in the Twentieth Century* (New York: New York University Press, 2009); Joshua Farrington, "'Build, Baby, Build,': Conservative Black Nationalists, Free Enterprise, and the Nixon Administration," in Gifford and Williams, *The Right Side of the Sixties*, 61–80; Kotlowski, "Black Power—Nixon Style," 409–45; Dean Kotlowski, *Nixon's Civil Rights: Politics, Principle, and Policy* (Cambridge, MA: Harvard University Press, 2002), 125–51; Fergus, *Liberalism, Black Power*, 196–231; "Disappointing Start," *Time Magazine* 94, no. 7 (August 15, 1969), 81; "Birth Pangs of Black Capitalism," *Time Magazine* 92, no. 16 (October 18, 1968), 124–27; Weems and Randolph, "The National Response"; Robert Weems and Lewis Randolph, "The Ideological Origins of Richard M. Nixon's 'Black Capitalism' Initiative," *Review of Black Political Economy* 29, no. 1 (Summer 2001): 49–53; Ibram Rogers, "Acquiring a 'Piece of the Action': The Rise and Fall of the Black Capitalism Movement," in *The Economic Civil Rights Movement: African Americans and the Struggle for Economic Power,* ed. Michael Ezra (New York: Routledge, 2013); Theodore Cross, *Black Capitalism: Strategy for Business in the Ghetto* (New York: Atheneum, 1974).

5. Most critics tended to lump all efforts of black capitalism as a reflection of Nixon's agenda, excising or ignoring black agency, business history, strategy, and differing intentions. For discussion on this subject, see Laura Hill and Julia Rabig, "Toward a History of the Business of Black Power," in *Business of Black Power: Community Development, Capitalism, and Corporate Responsibility in Postwar America*, ed. Laura Hill and Julia Rabig

(Rochester, NY: University of Rochester Press, 2012), 29; Michael O. West, "Who's Black Power," in Hill and Rabig, *Business of Black Power*, 294–95. For examples, see Forman, *Making of Black Revolutionaries*, 459; Weems and Randolph, "The National Response"; Earl Ofari Hutchinson, *The Myth of Black Capitalism* (New York: Monthly Review Press, 1970); Andrew Brimmer, "Profit v Pride: The Trouble with Black Capitalism," *Nation's Business* (May 1969), 73–79; Allen, *Black Awakening*; E. Franklin Frazier, "Negro Business: A Social Myth," in *Black Bourgeoisie* (c. 1957; rpt., New York: Free Press, 1997), 153–73; F. D. Sturdivant, "The Limits of Black Capitalism," in *Black Business Enterprise: Historical and Contemporary Perspectives*, ed. Ronald Bailey (New York: Basic Books, 1971), 114–23; Manning Marable, *How Capitalism Underdeveloped Black America: Problems in Race, Political Economy, and Society* (Boston, MA: South End Press, 1983); Huey Newton, "An Interview with Huey Newton," in Bracey et al., eds., *Black Nationalism*, 542–43.

6. Black National Economic Conference, "Black Manifesto," *New York Review of Books* 13, no. 1 (July 10, 1969); Forman, *Making of Black Revolutionaries*, 543–51; West, "Who's Black Power," 283; Rogers, "Acquiring," 177–78; Dan Georgakas and Marvin Surkin, *Detroit, I Do Mind Dying: A Study in Urban Revolution* (New York: St. Martin's Press, 1975), 78–81.

7. James Boggs, "Myth and Irrationality of Black Capitalism," in *Pages from a Black Radical's Notebook: A James Boggs Reader*, ed. Stephen M. Ward and Project Muse (Detroit: Wayne State University Press, 2011), 185–94.

8. "The Economics of Liberation," 154; Boggs, "Myth and Irrationality," 189–91; Forman, *Making of Black Revolutionaries*, 543–51. As an aside, the manifesto and CORENCO's shared objectives also included independent media (TV and newspaper) outlets, and research and training centers.

9. Steven Hahn, A Nation under Our Feet: Black Political Struggles in the Rural South from Slavery to the Great Migration (Cambridge, MA: Harvard University Press, 2003), 31.

10. Ibid., 26.

11. Ibid., 27.

12. Jessica Gordon Nembhard, *Collective Courage: A History of African American Cooperative Economic Thought and Practice* (University Park: Pennsylvania State University Press, 2014), 3–4, 28–30, 33–47. Nembhard begins the collective tradition with communes or communal living. She also helpfully outlines the importance of collectives beginning in the nineteenth century.

13. Ibid., 63–65, 73; W. E. B. DuBois, Economic Co-operation among Negro Americans: Report of a Social Study made by Atlanta University, under the Patronage of the Carnegie Institute of Washington, D. C., together with the Proceedings of the 12th Conference for the Study of the Negro Problems, held at Atlanta University, on Tuesday, May the 28th, 1907 (Atlanta: Atlanta University Press, 1907), 152–54.

14. C. H. Fearn, "A Negro Cooperative Foundry," in The Negro in Business: A Report of a Social Study Made Under the Direction of Atlanta University; Together With the Proceedings of the Fourth Conference for the Study of Negro Problems Held at Atlanta University May 30–31, 1899, ed. W. E. B. DuBois (Atlanta: Atlanta University Press, 1899), 67.

15. Lawrence Goodwyn, *Democratic Promise: The Populist Moment in America* (New York: Oxford University Press, 1976), xiii, qtd., xiv.

16. Ibid., xii, xv; Lawrence Goodwyn, *The Populist Moment: Short History of the Agrarian Revolt in America* (New York: Oxford University Press, 1978), viii, xxiv.

17. Nembhard, *Collective Courage*, 66–71, 81, 159–60; George M. Frederickson, *Black Liberation: A Comparative History of Black Ideologies in the United States* (New York: Oxford University Press, 1995), 159; W. E. B. DuBois, "Forum, Fact and Opinion: Our Economic History," *Pittsburgh Courier*, July 3, 1937, 11; W. E. B. DuBois, "Forum Act and Opinion: Other Effects of Co-Operation," *Pittsburgh Courier*, July 10, 1937, 11.

18. Goodwyn argues that 1890s populism fundamentally changed capitalism itself. This is also inferred in the work of UNIA and black populists. But, it bears noting that these two movements act along or against capitalism in different ways. Goodwyn, *Democratic Promise*, xiii, xiv; Frederickson, *Black Liberation*, 173; Omar Ali, *In the Lion's Mouth: Black Populism in the New South, 1886–1900* (Jackson: University Press of Mississippi, 2010), xiv–v; Alan Brinkley, *Voices of Protest: Huey Long, Father Coughlin, and the Great Depression* (New York: First Vintage Books, 1993), 165–68.

19. Hill and Rubig, *Business of Black Power*, 19. They also discuss the Nation of Islam, though the two religious groups reflected two different collective approaches—one that included an internal economy with free market principles, and the other collective capitalism in Father Divine and Daddy Grace, where all members shared in the bounty—relatively all considering that Grace and Divine positioned themselves for greater access to the group wealth. Rogers also refers to Garvey and the Nation of Islam as early progenitors of "black capitalism." For summaries of black capitalism's history, see Ibram Rogers, "Acquiring," 172–74; Van Deburg, *New Day*, 117–223.

20. Dallam, *Daddy Grace*, 131, 163–69; "Daddy Grace," *LIFE*, October 1, 1945, 51–61; Benjamin Sevitch, "When Black Gods Preached on Earth: The Heavenly Appeals of Prophet Cherry, Daddy Grace, and Father Divine," *Journal of Communication and Religion* 19, no. 1 (March 1, 1996): 229–30; John O. Hodges, "Charles Manuel 'Sweet Daddy' Grace,'" in *African American Religious Thought*, ed. Cornel West and Eddie Glaude Jr. (Louisville: Westminster John Knox Press, 20003), 609–11, 613. After the numerous suits, taxes, legal fees, and estate division between church and Grace assets, the church's worth was still at $7 million.

21. Fredrickson, *Black Liberation*, 139.

22. Minutes of CORE National Convention, June 20–July 1, 1962, Reel 9, C:I:55, Frame 501, CORE Addendum.

23. National Director's Staff Report, July 1962, Reel 9, C:I:56, Frame 525, CORE Addendum.

24. Innis interview, 1971; Ollie Leeds interview, April 28, 1971, August Meier and Elliot Rudwick interviewers, Box 56, Folder 10, August Meier Papers, Schomburg Research Center; M. G. Lord, *Forever Barbie: The Unauthorized Biography of a Real Doll* (New York: William Morrow & Co., 1994), 167–70; "Black Dolls Are Now Big Business," *Ebony Magazine* (December 1969), 90–91.

25. West, "Whose Black Power," 289–91; David Goldberg, "From Landless to Landlords: Black Power, Black Capitalism, and the Co-optation of Detroit's Tenants' Rights

Movement, 1964–1969," in Hill and Rabig, *Business of Black Power*, 170; Marable, "How Capitalism," 292 n60; Weems and Randolph, *Business in Black and White*, 115–18; Allen, *Black Awakening*, 147.

26. Marable, Race, Reform, Rebellion, 96; Marable, How Capitalism Underdeveloped, 139.

27. James Jennings, The Politics of Black Empowerment: The Transformation of Black Activism in Urban America (Detroit: Wayne State University Press, 1992), 20.

28. Ibid., 23, 59.

29. Will Ussery interview.

30. Floyd McKissick, "CORE's Program: Building a Second Economy," WHCF: SMOF: Leonard Garment: Alpha-Subject Files, Box 120, Folder: 1968 Campaign Name Files: Louis Kelso; Floyd McKissick, "Nation within a Nation: CORE's Proposal for Economic Development," Reel 5:648–50, A:II:32 "Finances Expected," *Sarasota Herald-Tribune*, February 13, 1969, 10; Zachery Gillan, "Black Is Beautiful, But So Is Green: Capitalism, Black Power, and Politics in Floyd McKissick's Soul City," in *The New Black History: Revisiting the Second Reconstruction*, ed. Elizabeth Kai Hinton and Manning Marable (New York: Palgrave Macmillan, 2011), 277–78; Christopher Strain, "Soul City, North Carolina and the Business of Black Power," in *The Economic Civil Rights Movement: African Americans and the Struggle for Economic Power*, ed. Michael Ezra (New York: Routledge, 2013), 196; Citizen's Crusade Against Poverty to National Board, April 10, 1968, Reel 5, A:II:29, Frame 616, CORE Addendum. CORE was not the only institution to embrace Two-Factor Economy. The Citizen's Crusade Against Poverty provided complimentary copies of the book for consideration. CCAP's National Advisory Board included a who's who of activists and labor proponents including Dorothy Height, Dolores Huerta, Whitney Young, Martin Luther King, Walter Reuther, Roy Wilkins, and A. Philip Randolph.

31. Innis, "Separatist Economics," 52–55. See also Frank Davis, *The Economics of Black Community Development* (New York: Markham Publishing Co., 1972), 116–75. Davis suggests a similar structure of economic "separateness." However, he includes within this system a "national ghetto development corporation," investment banks, business enterprises, credit corporations, etc. all of which act together to create a monopoly, raise labor value (more pay for the work you do), increase enterprise, etc. Part of the distinction I make here has less to do with how production and profit is created through a separate "ghetto" economy model, and more to do with how that model operates as a system, that is, within this separatist model who and how many people gain profit/wealth/employment and to what degree wide distribution of wealth stabilizes financial decline as a whole.

32. This assumption reverberated even among historians who charged that Nixon co-opted Innis and McKissick. Weems and Randolph, *Business in Black and White*, 115–18; Allen, *Black Awakening*, 147; Farrington, "'Build, Baby, Build,'" 61, 64–66, 68; Floyd B. McKissick Sr., interview, August 9, 1982, Eugene E. Pfaff interviewer, Greensboro Voices Collection at University of North Carolina at Greensboro; Alperovitz and McClaughry interview; McClaughry, "Black Ownership and National Politics," in Haddad and Pugh, *Black Economic Development*; Fergus, *Liberalism, Black Power*, 226; John McClaughry to John Conyers, October 29, 1968, McClaughry Personal Papers, in author's possession.

According to McClaughry and Alperovitz—both of whom were present at the meeting—conversation did not include a secret deal. Nixon used the meeting to complain that the black community was "in the pocket" of the Democratic Party and that he hoped to convince McKissick to switch parties. He awkwardly appealed to the CORE leader on the basis of their "shared time" at Duke University (Nixon graduated from Duke Law School). Nixon failed to realize that McKissick attended North Carolina Central Law School and that his time at Duke University had been spent organizing workers. More likely, as historian Devin Fergus argued, McKissick switched party allegiances based on other pragmatic realities. In the author's interview, McClaughry and Alperovitz noted that Innis did not attend the meeting with Nixon but McKissick came with two other aides. However, in McClaughry's letter to John Conyers and his summary of the meeting in "Black Ownership" he mentions Innis's presence at the meeting. Perot notes that he attended this meeting, but I can not corroborate his memory. These conflicting recollections may stem from multiple meetings.

33. Carson, *The Education*, 186.

34. NAC Minutes, September 10–11, 1966, Reel 9, C:II:112, Frame 1026, CORE Papers Addendum; Turner's support of MFU was a good example of black power, see NAC Minutes, December 17, 1966, Reel 9, C:I:114, Frame 1032, CORE Addendum; CORE National Advisory Committee, January 29, 1967, Reel 9, C:1:14, Frame 1041.

35. Floyd McKissick to Elijah Muhammad, March 3, 1967, Reel 6, A:II:66, Frame 528, CORE Addendum. NAC Minutes, April 22–23, 1967, Reel 9, C:I:115, Frame 1058, 1060, CORE Addendum.

36. Steering Committee Minutes, January 15, 1965, Reel 9, C:II:91, Frame 852, CORE Addendum; Statement of Income, May 31, 1965, Reel 9, C:II:102, Frames 931–32, CORE Addendum; NAC Minutes, June 4, 1966, Reel 9, C:I:109, Frame 1009, CORE Addendum; Steering Committee Minutes, August 16, 1966, Reel 9, C:II:111, Frames 1017–19, CORE Addendum; NAC Minutes, September 10–11, 1966, Reel 9, C:II:112, Frame 1021, CORE Addendum; NAC Minutes, December 17, 1966, Reel 9, C:II:113, Frame 1030, CORE Addendum: December 17, 1966, Reel 9, C:II:114, Frame 1032, CORE Addendum; CORE National Advisory Committee, January 29, 1967, Reel 9, C:I:14, Frame 1041, CORE Addendum.

37. Advisory Committee Minutes, January 26, 1967, Reel 9, C:I:114, Frame 1038, CORE Addendum; Turner, "Black Power," 465.

38. NAC Minutes, April 22–23, 1967, Reel 9, C:I:115, Frame 1055, and NAC Steering, April 8–9, 1967, Reel 9, C:I:115, Frames 1043–45, CORE Addendum. McKissick's reduction of debt did not garner him any support from NAC. In fact, condemnation from NAC turned ugly, and they especially blamed McKissick for avoiding CORE's problems.

39. For more on CSD and its subsequent edition, Community Corporate Act (CCA), see Gar Alperovitz et al., "Are Community Corporations the Answer?" in *Citizen Participation in Urban Development* 2, ed. Hans B. C. Spiegel (Washington, DC: N.T.L. Institute for Applied Behavioral Science, 1969); "Community Development Corporations—A New Model" (Cambridge, MA: Urban Ghetto Study Program of the

Laboratory for Environmental Studies, Massachusetts Institute of Technology, 1968); "Community Development Corporations: A New Approach to the Poverty Program," *Harvard Law Review* 82 (January 1969): 661–67; "Community Self-Determination: The Bill and the Debate," *New Generation Special Issue* (Fall 1968); "From Private Enterprise to Public Entity; The Role of the Community Development Corporation," *Georgetown Law Journal* 57, no. 5 (May 1969): 956–91; Sturdivant, "The Limits of Black Capitalism"; Martin Rein, *Social Policy: Issues of Choice and Change* (New York: Random House, 1970). Clarence Funnye, "We Don't All Have to Be in the Ghetto Just to Be Brothers," in *The Economics of Black America*, ed. Harold Vatter and Thomas Palm (New York: Harcourt, Brace, Jovanovich, 1972), 244–64; Sar A. Levitan, *"Community Self-Determination* and Entrepreneurship: Their Promises and Limitations," *Poverty and Human Resources Abstracts* 4, no. 1 (January–February 1969): 16–24; Eugene Harrington and Harry Specht, "Community Self-Determination Act as a Vehicle for Community Organizing," *Texas Southern Intramural Law Review* 1, no. 2 (1970): 124–39; Kenneth H. Miller, "Community Capitalism and the Community Self-Determination Act," *Harvard Journal on Legislation* 6, no. 4 (May 1969): 413–61; Tony Perot interview, 2004; John McClaughry, "Black Ownership," 41; John McClaughry and Gar Alperovitz interview, May 22, 2014. Some confusion exists over the extent of Innis's contribution. Alperovitz and McClaughry do not recall much about Innis's role in crafting the bill, but McClaughry notes in his essay that it started from a brain-storming session at Harvard's John F. Kennedy School of Government. Perot notes that CORE sent Roy Innis to Harvard to obtain aid in writing the legislation.

40. McClaughry, "Black Ownership," 43–46.

41. Levitan, "Community Self-Determination"; Miller, "Community Capitalism"; Harrington and Specht, "Community Self-Determination," 413–15, 126–31.

42. McClaughry, "Black Ownership," 40–41; Alperovitz and McClaughry interview. Tony Perot interview, 2004; Weems and Randolph, *Business in Black*, 117; McClaughry to John Conyers, October 29, 1968, McClaughry personal papers, author's possession. This same letter can also be found in the Nixon Presidential Papers and in the Floyd McKissick Papers.

43. Robert F. Kennedy on McKissick and Black Power: Thomas F. Jackson, *From Civil Rights to Human Rights: Martin Luther King, Jr., and the Struggle* (Philadelphia: University of Pennsylvania Press, 2007), 296; Jack Newfield, *Robert Kennedy: A Memoir* (New York: New American Library, 1988), 74; Edward R. Schmitt, *President of the Other America: Robert Kennedy and the Politics of Poverty* (Amherst: University of Massachusetts Press, 2010), 171–73, 123; Jean Stein, *American Journey: The Times of Robert Kennedy* (New York: New American Library, 1972, 1970), 221; Matthew A. Crenson, *Downsizing Democracy: How America Sidelined Its Citizens and Privatized Its Public* (Baltimore: Johns Hopkins University Press, 2004), 73; CORE and RFK: James L. Farmer interview, April 25, 1979; John Christopher Walter, *The Harlem Fox: J. Raymond Jones and Tammany, 1920–1970* (Albany: State University of New York Press, 1989), 12, 206. Many Harlem black leaders castigated Farmer for his decision to support Robert Kennedy. However, Farmer had his own issues with some of Harlem's black politicians, especially Adam Clayton Powell, who

purportedly undermined his efforts to create a War on Poverty literacy program because he failed to "kiss the ring" as it were. In fact, Farmer left CORE under the presumption that the program was confirmed by the Johnson administration but last-minute maneuverings ended the project leaving Farmer to fend for another career after the directorship of CORE. Farmer later noted that other forces including President Johnson were also at work. On Farmer and Powell, see Farmer, *Lay Bare*, 301–5.

44. James L. Farmer interview, April 25, 1979, 25–26; Perot interview, 2004. According to Perot, James Farmer had a direct line to Bobby Kennedy, who purportedly claimed that he'd help end CORE's debt altogether once he became president. Kennedy certainly gave aid during his time as a senator.

45. Certainly others held this perspective. There were a number of African Americans who backed Richard Nixon in both 1968 and 1972. Many, like McKissick, simply viewed it as a politically astute and pragmatic stance—particularly after Nixon became president. Though defined as "conservative" such definitions failed to represent the complex and strategic decisions of black activists. McKissick eventually returned to the Democratic Party during the presidency of Ronald Reagan. Fergus, *Liberalism, Black Power*, 266; "McKissick Forms Group to Help Republican Party," *Jet Magazine* (November 2, 1972), 21.

46. John McClaughry, "Community Corporation Act of 1971"; White House Central Files: Staff Members and Office Files: Leonard Garment, Box 129, Folder Minority Business and Expanded Ownership in Richard Nixon Presidential Papers.

47. McClaughry, "Black Ownership," 42–43; Weems, *Business in Black*, 117.

48. McClaughry, "Black Ownership," 45–46.

49. Black Caucus, "President Nixon," in Vatter and Palm, *The Economics of Black America*, 187–97; Weems, *Business in Black*, 116.

50. McClaughry, "Black Ownership," 45–46.

51. A. Wright Elliot, "'Black Capitalism' and the Business Community," in Haddad and Pugh, *Black Economic Development*, 76; Peter McNeish, "Where Does the Money Come From," in Haddad and Pugh, *Black Economic Development*, 94; Hill, "FIGHTing for the Soul of Black Capitalism," 60–61; McClaughry and Alperovitz interview. Reverend Florence condemned the bill and Innis so strongly at a public presentation that white business leaders scooted toward the door to avoid what appeared to be a coming melee.

52. Funnye, "We Don't All Have to Be in the Ghetto," 244–64.

53. Roy Innis and Norman Hill, "Black Self Determination: A Debate," *New Generation* 51, no. 2 (Summer 1969): 18–26, 22.

54. McClaughry to Garment, July 22, 1970, WHCF: SMOF: Leonard Garment: Alpha-Subject Files, Box 130, Folder: Minority Business and Expanded Ownership; Rowland Evans and Robert Novak, *Nixon in the White House: The Frustration of Power* (New York: Vintage Books, 1972), 135–47; Anthony Summers, *The Arrogance of Power: The Secret World of Richard Nixon* (New York: Penguin Books, 2001), 354; Stephen E. Ambrose, *Nixon: Volume 2: The Triumph of a Politician, 1962–1972* (New York: Simon and Schuster, 1989), 18–188, 364–65; Evans and Novak, *Nixon in the White House*," 135–47; Tom Wicker, *One of Us: Richard Nixon and the American Dream* (New York: Random House, 1995), 488–89; Carl Lieberman, "Southern Strategies, and Desegregation of

Public Schools," *Richard M. Nixon: Politician, President, Administrator*, ed. **Leon** Friedman and William Levantrosser (New York: Greenwood Press, 1991), 144–45; Alvy L. King, "The Incoherence of the Civil Rights Policy in the **Nixon** Administration," in Friedman and Levantrosser, *Richard M. Nixon*, 161–65.

55. Arthur Blaustein, "Cities, Ghettos, and the Politics of the Absurd," *New Generation* 51, no. 2 (Summer 1969): 35.

56. Arthur I. Blaustein, ed., *The American Promise: Equal Justice and Economic Opportunity* (New Brunswick, NJ: National Advisory Council on Economic Opportunity, Transaction Books, 1982), back cover; Blaustein, "Cities, Ghettos, and the Politics of the Absurd," 32–36.

57. Andrew Brimmer, "The Negro in the National Economy," in *Race and Poverty: The Economics of Discrimination*, ed. John P. Kain (Englewood Cliffs, NJ: Prentice-Hall), 89–99.

58. Courtney Blackman, *Black Capitalism in Economic Perspective* (New York: Economic Research Dept., Irving Trust Co., 1973), 10; Brimmer, "The Negro."

59. Levitan, "Community Self Determination," 20–22.

60. Rein, Social Policy, 277.

61. Ibid., 276–78. For studies on corporate efforts to acquire black markets during this period, see Nishani Frazier, "A McDonald's That Reflects"; Hill, "FIGHTing for the Soul"; Lindsey Fetz, "Creating a Multicultural Soul: Avon, Corporate Responsibility and Race in the 1970s," in Hill and Rabig, *Business of Black Power*, 116–56.

62. Nishani Frazier, "Soul of a People," in Hill and Rabig, *Business of Black Power*; Michael O. West, "Whose Black Power," 291. HADC director Frank Anderson's ideological inclination stymied McDonald's move to create community ownership, but he was not responsible for the business's demise. The restaurant never fully gained a consistent profit thus prohibiting both the director and the HADC board from implementing policies based on ideological bents whatever they were.

63. Rein, *Social Policy*, 273–74.

64. "From Private Enterprise to Public Entity," 956–58.

65. Donald Rumsfeld to Russell Long, no date, White House Central Files: Staff Members and Office Files: Leonard Garment, Box 128, Folder Minority Business and Expanded Ownership in Richard Nixon Presidential Papers.

66. Rabig and Hill, *Business of Black Power*, 29; Kotlowski, "Black Power—Nixon Style," 409–45; McClaughry, "Black Ownership," 43–46.

67. John McClaughry to Len Garment, Bryce Harlow, John Mitchell, President-elect Richard Nixon, November 13, 1968, John McClaugry's personal papers, in author's possession; McClaughry, "Black Ownership," 48–49.

68. Kotlowski, *Nixon's Civil Rights*, 173.

69. David McKennedy to White House, memo re: CSD Act, Feb 17, 1969, WHCF: SMOF: Leonard Garment: Alpha-Subject Files, Box 132, Folder: Minority Business and Expanded Ownership.

70. Secretary of Commerce Maurice Stans to President re: CSD, February 18, 1969, WHCF: SMOF: Leonard Garment: Alpha-Subject Files, Box 132, Folder: Minority Business and Expanded Ownership.

71. No author, Comments on Outline Draft, parts II and III; White House Central Files: Staff Members and Office Files: Leonard Garment, Box 129, Folder Minority Business and Expanded Ownership in Richard Nixon Presidential Papers; to President and White House from Secretary HUD George Romney, no date, WHCF: SMOF: Leonard Garment: Alpha-Subject Files, Box 132, Folder: Minority Business and Expanded Ownership.

72. Leonard Garment to Charles Williams, memo, December 23, 1970, White House Central Files: Staff Members and Office Files: Edwin Harper, Box 45, Folder Environmental Financing.

73. Charles Williams to Len Garment, memo, December 23, 1970, WHCF: SMOF: Leonard Garment: Alpha-Subject Files, Box 131, Folder: Minority Business and Expanded Ownership.

74. McClaughry, "Community Corporation Act of 1971"; White House Central Files: Staff Members and Office Files: Leonard Garment, Box 129, Folder Minority Business and Expanded Ownership in Richard Nixon Presidential Papers; Len Garment to White House, December 25, 1970?, WHCF: SMOF: Leonard Garment: Alpha-Subject Files, Box 131, Folder: Minority Business and Expanded Ownership; Office of Debt Analysis to Weidenbaum, memo, March, 5, 1971, WHCF: SMOF: Leonard Garment: Alpha-Subject Files, Box 132, Folder: Minority Business and Expanded Ownership.

75. For examples of conflicted behavior by Nixon and his aides, see Herbert G. Klein, *Making It Perfectly Clear* (Garden City, NY: Doubleday, 1980), 316–18; Rowland Evans and Robert Novak, *Nixon in the White House: The Frustration of Power* (New York: Random House, 1971), 37–74; James Reichley, *Conservatives in an Age of Change: The Nixon and Ford Administrations* (Washington, DC: The Brookings Institution, 1981); Stephen Ambrose, *Nixon: Volume II, The Triumph of a Politician, 1962–1972* (New York: Simon and Schuster, 1989), 239–47, 363–65, 473–78; Rick Perlstein, *Nixonland: The Rise of a President and the Fracturing of America* (New York: Scribner, 2008), 359–61; John Ehrlichman, *Witness to Power: The Nixon Years* (New York: Simon and Schuster, 1982), 75–112.

76. Richard Nixon, The State of the Union Address, January 22, 1970.

77. John Oberdorfer to Garment, September 10, 1979 WHCF: SMOF: Leonard Garment: Alpha-Subject Files, Box 132, Folder: Minority Business and Expanded Ownership; K. N. Davis Jr. to Garment, memo on Foreign Government Devices to Broaden Business Opportunity, March 12, 1970, WHCF: SMOF: Leonard Garment: Alpha-Subject Files, Box 130, Folder: Minority Business and Expanded Ownership; Garment to Department of State, November 6, 1970, WHCF: SMOF: Leonard Garment: Alpha-Subject Files, Box 130, Folder: Minority Business and Expanded Ownership; Garment to Jim Allison, November 6, 1970 WHCF: SMOF: Leonard Garment: Alpha-Subject Files, Box 130, Folder: Minority Business and Expanded Ownership.

78. "Slum Groups Get Free Stock Offer," no date, WHCF: SMOF: Leonard Garment: Alpha-Subject Files, Box 130, Folder: Minority Business and Expanded Ownership; WHCF: SMOF: Leonard Garment: Alpha-Subject Files, Box 130, Folder: Minority Business and Expanded Ownership. Each of the above groups have a file or are incorporated in boxes of White House papers associated with Expanded Ownership.

79. Weems, *Business in Black*, 117–19; "McKissick Forms Group to Help Republican Party," *Jet Magazine* (November 2, 1972), 21.

80. Leonard Garment to Peter Flannigan, February 2, 1970, White House Central Files: Staff Members and Office Files: Darrell Trent, Box 8, Folder Reading Reference to Small Business Corp and Related Matters, DMT Personal File, in Richard Nixon Presidential Papers.

81. Ibid.

82. John McClaughry, "Promoting Civil Society Among the Heathen: A Memoir," unpublished, John McClaughry personal papers, in author's possession.

83. John McClaughry to Len Garment, September 8, 1969, WHCF: SMOF: Leonard Garment: Alpha-Subject Files, Box 130, Folder: Minority Business and Expanded Ownership.

84. McClaughry to Larry Jobe, November 6, 1970, and McClaughry to McBundy, September 16, 1970; WHCF: SMOF: Leonard Garment: Alpha-Subject Files, Box 130, Folder: Minority Business and Expanded Ownership; Len Garment to (author unclear), August 20, 1970, WHCF: SMOF: Leonard Garment: Alpha-Subject Files, Box 130, Folder: Minority Business and Expanded Ownership; John McClaughry, "Expanded Ownership: a Proposal to the Sabre Foundation," June 27, 1970, WHCF: SMOF: Leonard Garment: Alpha-Subject Files, Box 131, Folder: Minority Business and Expanded Ownership. At this point Mcclaughry begins representing himself as the PRINCIPLE drafter of the CSD bill.

85. For examples of this, see Jacquelline Dowd Hall, "The Long Civil Rights Movement: The Political Uses of the Past," *Journal of American History* 91, no. 4 (March 2005): 1233–63; "Expanded Capital Ownership: The Only Answer," no date, John McClaughry Personal Papers.

86. Ronald Reagan, "Expanded Capital Ownership: The Only Answer," John McClaughry Personal Papers. Gil Troy, *Morning in America: How Ronald Reagan Invented the 1980's* (Princeton, NJ: Princeton University Press, 2005), 92–93. Within pop culture both Nixon and Reagan gained images of nefarious, evil-like characters. These caricatures continue to proliferate on the Internet long after their presidencies. For Reagan as the devil, see also *Boondocks*, "The Garden Party," November 6, 2005, Rebel Base Production Companies; Edward M. Yager, *Ronald Reagan's Journey: Democrat to Republican* (Lanham, MD: Rowman & Littlefield, 2006), 79; Suicidal Tendencies, *I Shot the Devil*, Frontier album, 1983.

87. Levitan, "Community Self-Determination," 24.

## 9. Until . . .

1. Poinsett, "Roy Innis: Nation Builder," 173.

2. Floyd McKissick to Roy Innis, June 19, 1968, Correspondence, 1961–1982, Folder 6780, Series 3.1.1, McKissick Papers; Turner and Perot, interview by author, Washington, DC, August 25, 2007. Neither Turner nor Perot recall such a letter and insist they were not involved in such an effort. In Turner's case, this was likely true, given her earlier conflict with Innis and what she viewed as his misogynistic comments.

3. Tucker, "An Historical Study," 37.

4. Farmer, *Lay Bare*, 320; Project Evaluation, August 1969, Reel 1864, Grant number 67-446; Ruth Turner and Tony Perot, notes on dissertation, 2008, in author's possession.

5. Floyd McKissick to Tony Perot, June 17, 1968, 3.1.1, Folder 6780, Mckissick Papers, SCH, UNC.

6. Ruth Turner and Tony Perot, Dissertation notes, 2008, in author's possession; Will Ussery interview, January 10, 2008, in author's possession; Carter and Sylvester, "Cleveland CORE," 33–34.

7. "Rumpus in Hotel Mars Last Session of CORE Parley," July 6, 1968, CORE clipping file, CPC, CSU Archives.

8. "CORE Group Forms New Alliance," no date, CORE clipping file, CPC, CSU Archives; "Rebel CORE Group to form New Outfit," no date, CORE clipping file, CPC, CSU Archives; Poinsett, "Roy Innis: Nation Builder," 174.

9. Meier and Rudwick, *CORE*, 425.

10. Ibid., 419, 424. CORE actually started its transition to black separatism in the early months of Innis's leadership of CORE and the withdrawal of projects and programs propagated by the black power populists.

11. Johnson, Revolutionaries to Race Leaders, 110.

12. Hall, *Black Separatism,* 146–47.

13. Poinsett, "Roy Innis: Nation Builder," 176.

14. Tucker, "An Historical Study," 74–77.

15. Ibid., 74–77, 132.

16. Help free the Cleveland 3!, flyer, no date, Box 1, Folder 4, James Miller Papers, WRHS.

17. "CORE Seeks $16,000 for Reading Project," May 3, 1970, CORE clipping file, CPC, CSU Archives; "CORE Will Present Plan Here for Unitary Schools," March 19, 1970, CORE clipping file, CPC, CSU Archives; Ad from Women's Committee of CORE, October 23, 1970, CORE clipping file, CPC, CSU Archives.

18. "CORE Charters Cleveland Chapter," December 9, 1972, CORE clipping file, CPC, CSU Archives.

19. "CORE Urges Police Review Board," March 8, 1973, CORE clipping file, CPC, CSU Archives; "Police Review Call Joined by 6 Groups," March 9, 1973, CORE clipping file, CPC, CSU Archives; "Group Demands Changes in Police Hiring, Training," June 28, 1973, CORE clipping file, CPC, CSU Archives; "CORE Will Press for Police Review Board," August 21, 1973, CORE clipping file, CPC, CSU Archives; "Police Brutality Hearing Set," November 1, 1973, CORE clipping file, CPC, CSU Archives; "CORE Here Installs a Hotline for Reporting Police Brutality," November 3, 1973, CORE clipping file, CPC, CSU Archives.

20. "CORE Recruiting Blacks to Help Develop Uganda," May 6, 1973, CORE clipping file, CPC, CSU Archives.

21. No author, "CORE Plans Mideast Job Venture," *New York Times*, June 17, 1978, 8.

22. Thomas Johnson, "Innis Back from Africa, Asks Aid for Black Interests There," *New York Times*, August 22, 1971, 18; Gerald Fraser, "Innis Says CORE Is Pushing to

Build Black Links with Africa," *New York Times*, April 9, 1973, 4.

23. No author, "James Farmer Quits CORE in Angola Feud," *New York Times*, February 20, 1976, 48; Thomas Johnson, "Blacks Assail CORE on Angola Recruits: Farmer Protests Lack of Data Seen, 'Hysterical Envy Charged,'" *New York Times*, February 14, 1976: 3; Thomas Johnson, "CORE Chief Cancels a Speech on Coast after a Black Protest," *New York Times*, February 13, 1976, 2.

24. Jack Anderson, "Was Waverly Yates an Innis Target?" *The Hour*, October 25, 1978, 5; Steven Weisman, "Alleged Attackers of Innis' Son Taken from School and Beaten," *New York Times*, January 13, 1972, 1; no author, "3 CORE Members Put on Probation for Beating Youths," *New York Times*, April 29, 1972, 15.

25. "James Farmer Quits CORE in Angola Feud," February 20, 1976, *New York Times*, CORE vertical file, Michigan State University Special Archives (hereafter MSU); "Civil Rights: CORE War," August 28, 1978, *Newsweek* article, CORE vertical file, MSU.

26. No author, "CORE Calls Lawsuit 'Racist' and 'Cheap Political Trick,'" *Jet Magazine* (January 18, 1979), 13.

27. Woody Klein, "Reviving the Dream: A Westport View," *New York Times*, April 1, 1979, CN 115.

28. Greg Harris, "The Great Adventure of Roy Innis and CORE," *Amsterdam News*, May 9, 1981, 16; "Farmer vs Innis," *Afro-American*, August 5, 1978, no page number; Andrew Cooper, "Seek to Oust CORE's Innis," *Amsterdam News*, July 8, 1978, A1; Annette Samuels, "McKissick, Farmer Seek CORE's Roy Innis Ouster," *Amsterdam News*, August 12, 1978, A1.

29. Paul Delaney, "The Struggle to Rally Black Americans: The 1970s Have Been Hard Times for the Civil Rights Movement, and It's Up to Ben Hooks to Revive not Only the NAACP, but also the Hopes of 23 Million Blacks," *New York Times*, July 15, 1979, SM5.

# Index

Historically Black Colleges and Universities, 56
Hobson, Julius, 138–39, 276n4
Hodge, Henry, 55–56
Holden, Anna, 56, 143
Holden, Bonnie, 220n17
Holly, John O., 28, 29, 31, 64, 160
Holmes, Clarence, 81
Holt, Bonnie: *See* Gordon, Bonnie Holt
homeownership, 62
Home Ownership Foundation Act (1967), 205
hotel chains, 60
Hough: Cleveland CORE headquarters, 71, 72;
  community development projects, 199; hous-
  ing inadequacies, 30, 62; population shifts,
  29–30, 61; racial violence, 153, 155; relay
  classes, 82; rent strikes, 74; school construction levies, 83; school desegregation protests,
  81, 95; voter registration and education
  project, 130
Hough Area Citizens for Better Schools
  Committee, 82, 83
Hough Area Development Corporation
  (HADC): CORE economic development
  policies, 182; Expanded Ownership plans,
  204; functional role, xxvii, 186, 214; government-based funding, 162–63; McDonald's
  franchise, 176–79, 181, 200, 297n62
House of Israel, 174, 180–81
Houser, George: apartheid protest, 51–52;
  background, 8, 9; and Bernice Fisher, 22–23;
  and Billie Ames, 53, 54; Brotherhood
  Mobilization Plan, 9, 11; Cleveland
  CORE, 27–29, 32–34, 40–42, 47; CORE
  membership debate, 15; on CORE origins,
  xxviii, 232n18, 233n26; editorial letter, 33;
  Fellowship of Reconciliation (FOR), 16–23,
  42–43, 51–52; Journey of Reconciliation,
  43–44, 245n78; as Non-Violent Action
  Secretary, 20–25, 51–52; pacifism, 24;
  philosophical conflict, 51; relationship with
  A. J. Muste, 20–22, 42–43, 245n78; and the
  Socialist Worker Party (SWP), 46
housing discrimination, 246n88
housing inadequacies, 29–30, 132
Howard, Ernest, 169
Howard Johnson hotels, 60
Howard University, 3–4, 6, 14, 34, 138, 229n1
Howard University Civil Rights Committee, 34,
  243n43
Huerta, Dolores, 293n30
Human Relations Council, 84
Human Rights Defenders, 80, 132
Humphrey, Hubert H., 195
*Huston Plan*, 168
Huston, Tom, 168
hyper pacifism, 51

**I**

Ida Noyes Cafeteria, 232n18
Indian independence movement, 13–14
Industrial Workers of the World (IWW), 254n70
inequality, 109
inner city businesses, 181
Innis, Doris, 145, 272n63
Innis, Niger, xxix, 216
Innis, Roy: attempted removal as national director, xxix, 212; background, xxv, 207; black
  power activism, 145, 208–10, 215; as CORE
  associate director, 207; CORE leadership
  roles, xxv, xxvii; as CORE national
  director, 171, 172, 179, 182, 208–11;
  economic empowerment programs, 167,
  169, 185–86, 187, 190–93, 202, 210–11;
  gangster persona, 211; gender bias, 145–46;
  Harambee City Project, 170; as Harlem
  Commonwealth Council director, 204; philosophical conflict, 157, 158, 211–12; power
  struggles, 211–12, 272n63; as TCP board
  member, 286n40; travel to Africa, 210–11
Institute of Politics (Harvard University), 194,
  196
institutionalized racism, xxv, 31
integration: *See* school desegregation
Internal Revenue Service (IRS), 133, 193
International Typographical Union, 127
International Worker's Association (IWA), 46
interracial dancing, 38
interracial marriages, xxix, 140
interracial sexual intimacy, 140–41
Interstate Commerce Commission (ICC), 60
interstate travel, 43, 59, 60
*Irene Morgan v. Virginia* (1946), 43
Irrationality of Capitalism (Boggs), 187

**J**

Jack, Homer, 9, 43, 45
Jackson, Connie, 255n84
Jackson, Deborah Jean, 265n110
Jackson, Jesse, 275n103
Jackson, Juanita, 229n1
Jackson, Mississippi, 60
Jackson, Perry, 27, 33, 34
Jackson, Robert, 265n110
Jackson, Rochelle, 265n110
Jack Spratt Coffee House, 10, 234n33
Jacobs, Donald, 176–77
jail-ins, 58
Javits, Jacob, 196
J. E. and L. E. Mabee Foundation, 168
Jefferson, Missouri, 56
Jenkins, Dwayne, 265n110
Jenkins, Keith, 265n110

Maddox, John, 268n13
Malcolm X, 94, 98, 111, 112–13, 119, 264n89
Mallory, Mae, 65, 110–12, 119, 267n9
Mandel, Bernard, 67, 69, 71, 101–2, 128, 253n58
Marable, Manning, 191
March on Washington Movement (MOWM), xxxii, 5, 6, 16, 17–18, 23–24, 70, 120, 237n69
Marion, South Carolina, 56
Marshall University, 163
Marshall, Wanda, 119
Martin, Alexander, 33
Martin Luther King Jr. Center, xxvii
Martin Luther King Jr. Plaza, 177
Maryland, 60
Maryland Freedom Union (MFU), 150–52, 193
mass civil disobedience, 5–7, 15, 18
Mattox, Gretta, 265n110
Mau-Mauism, 89
Max S. Hayes Trade School, 85
Mays, Benjamin E., 3–4, 13, 14, 230n2
McAllister, Ralph, 85, 89, 93, 100, 101, 102, 103, 105
McCain, James: black power activism, 145; as CORE field secretary, 56, 57, 63; Mallory extradition case, 112; on Marvin Rich, 143; philosophical conflict, 57
McCall, David, 193
McCarthy, Eugene, 196
McClaughry, John, 194, 195–97, 201–2, 203, 204–5, 294n32
McComb, Mississippi, 59
McDonald, Jimmy, 145
McDonald's, 173–76, 178–81, 200, 288n65, 297n62
McGovern, George, 196
McIntosh, W. S., 111–12, 268n13
McKinney, Wade, 33, 34, 48
McKissick Enterprises, 191, 204, 208, 227n25
McKissick, Floyd: black power policy, xxvi; as CORE national director, 135, 137; CORE politics, 139–40, 142, 147; departure from CORE, 208; economic empowerment programs, 163, 166, 190–93; financial issues, 193–94; on Ford Foundation grants, 158–59; gender bias, 145–46; internal politics, 207–8; and Maryland Freedom Union (MFU), 152; philosophical conflict, 157; relationship with Richard Nixon, 294n32, 296n45; relationship with Robert F. Kennedy, 196; relationship with Roy Innis, xxix, 207, 212
McKnight, William, 100
McNeish, Peter, 197
means-oriented membership, xxx, 25, 66, 123, 139, 190

Meat Cutters Union, 254n70
Mechanics Educational Society of America, 254n70
Medgar Evers Gun Club, 99, 114
media outlets, 166–67
Meier, August, xxviii, xxix, xxx, 44, 71, 78, 142–43, 148, 209
Melville, Bruce, 69, 255n84
Memorial Elementary, 85, 87, 89
Mercantile Cooperative Company, 188
Mercy Hospital Association, 30–31, 32
Meredith March Against Fear, 137
Metzger, John, xxv
Miami, Florida, 56
Miami University, 194
militant activism: Congress of Racial Equality (CORE), 44, 50–51, 112–13, 138–40, 213; developmental evolution, 214–16; economic empowerment, 186–87; racially-motivated violence, 114; school desegregation protest, 87–89, 91–92. *See also* Freedom Fighters
Militant Labor Forum, 98
Mills, Wilbur, 168
Milwaukee CORE, 78–79, 126, 140, 147, 258n8
Milwaukee United School Integration Committee (MUSIC), 78–79
Mindlin, Albert, 50–51
Mississippi: Democratic Party convention delegates, 124–25; Freedom Rides, 59, 60, 148; voter registration and education project, 113–14
Mississippi Freedom Democratic Party (MFDP), 124–25, 215
Mississippi Freedom Labor Union, 150
Mississippi State Democratic Party, 125
Mississippi Summer Project, 113
Mitchell, John, 198, 201
Monroe Defendants, 65, 110–11
Monroe Defense Committee (MDC), 111–12, 119, 267n6
Monroe, North, 69
Monroe, North Carolina, 44, 65, 69, 110
Montgomery, Alabama, 53, 55, 56, 60
Montgomery Bus Boycott, 53, 55, 56, 249n7
Moore, David, 74
Moore, Ronnie, 59, 140–41, 149
Moorland–Spingarn Research Center (MSRC), 158
Morehouse College, 3, 14
Morgan, Irene, 43
Morris, Aldon, 55, 143
Morris, George, 33
Morrow, Eula, 27, 63, 251n40
Morrow, Juanita: *See* Nelson, Juanita Morrow
Moses, Bob, 113
Moskowitz, Belle, 219n11

New Orleans, Louisiana, 59–60, 80
Newtown, North Carolina, 110
New York, 60
New York City, 122, 185
New York Citywide Committee for Integrated
    Schools, 79
New York CORE, 51, 79, 100–101, 102
*New York Daily News*, 185
New York RAM, 119
*New York Times*, xxxii, 114
New York Urban Coalition, 208
nightriders, 114
Nixon, Richard, 167–68, 183, 186, 194, 195–
    98, 201–6, 214, 290n5, 294n32, 296n45
nonprofit organizations, 168–69, 192, 205. *See
    also* Ford Foundation
nonviolent civil disobedience: Action Discipline
    methodology, 12–13; black nationalism
    impacts, 121–23; Brotherhood Mobilization
    Plan, xxviii, 6–9, 11, 16; Cleveland, Ohio,
    63; CORE philosophy, 55–56, 113, 118–19;
    emerging literature, 3; Freedom Fighters,
    115–18; Gandhian philosophy, 4, 5–6,
    12–25, 54; interracial brotherhood philos-
    ophy, xxviii–xxxii; March on Washington
    Movement (MOWM), 17–18. *See also* sit-in
    demonstrations
Non-Violent Direct Action (NVDA)
    Committee, 11–12, 16, 20, 23
North Carolina, xxvi, 58, 59
North Carolina A&T University, 58
North Central Regional CORE, 135, 171
Northern Freedom Labor Union, 150
Northern Negro Grass Roots Leadership
    Conference, 117–18
Northern Summer Task Force Project, 150
Norton, Eleanor Holmes, 158

**O**

Oakland, California, 157, 181, 186
Oakland CORE, 71
Oberlin College, 67
Ocean Hill-Brownsville community, 79
Odham, Charles, 51, 139, 140
Offender Aid and Restoration (OAR), xxvi
Office of Child Development, 208
Office of Economic Opportunity (OEO), 122,
    153, 158, 162, 176, 192, 199, 201
Office of Minority Business Enterprise (OMBE),
    167, 186
Ohio Black Concern Committee, 174
Ohio Civil Rights Commission, 73, 127, 163
Ohio House Chambers, 73
Ohio State Civil Rights Law, 36, 37, 38
Ohio State House of Un-American Committee,
    70

Oldham, Charles, 54, 55–56, 59
Oldham, Marian, 54
Ong, Walter, xvii
Operation Black Unity (OBU), 162, 173–81
Operation Boot Strap, 186
Operation Breadbasket, 133, 191, 275n103
Operation Window Shop, 73, 255n93
Opportunities Industrialization Center (OIC),
    xxvi
Oregon State College, 95
organized labor, 280n59
Orsby, Hubert, 113
Outhwaite housing project, 30
Outhwaite School for Boys, 81
overcrowded housing, 62, 74–76
Owens, David, 74
Owens, Major, 125
Oxford, Ohio, 113

**P**

Pace, Edmond, 255n84
pacifism, xxix–xxxi, 3, 4–5, 7–9, 14, 19–24,
    54, 55, 213. *See also* Gandhian nonviolent
    ideology; goodwill nonviolent direct action;
    nonviolent civil disobedience
Palenius, Lillian, 50, 51
Parchman Farm Penitentiary, 60
Parks, Rosa, 53
Parrino, Thomas J., 112
paternalism, 109, 143
patriarchal structure, 145–46
patronage, 109
Payne, Lawrence O., 27, 33
Peacemakers, 51
Peck, James, xxviii, 43, 51, 53, 54–55, 140, 142,
    144
Penny, Wanda, 54
People's Board of Education, 79
People's Movement for the Liberation of Angola,
    211
Percy, Charles, 196
Perot, Antoine: as Action Committee chairman,
    67, 71; background, xxvi, 68; Baltimore
    Target City Project (TCP), 151–52; black
    power policy, 278n32; community-involved
    strategies, 128, 216; as CORE field secretary,
    150; as CORE program director, 135, 153;
    as CORE vice chairman, 70; departure from
    CORE, 208; economic empowerment,
    161–62, 169; and elite black leadership, 76;
    Ford Foundation negotiations, 156, 169;
    Freedom Now Party (FNP), 120; on funding
    issues, 144; internal politics, 170, 207; and
    Maryland Freedom Union (MFU), 193; as
    National Action Council (NAC) official,
    130; political activism, 131, 145; rent strikes,